THE FOOT

SPAIN

THE
Pocket
GUIDE

Spain

MARGARET GREENWOOD

Series Editor: Andrew Sanger

SIMON & SCHUSTER

LONDON SYDNEY NEW YORK TOKYO SINGAPORE TORONTO

THE footloose GUIDE

Spain

MARGARET GREENWOOD

Series Editor: Andrew Sanger

SIMON & SCHUSTER

LONDON·SYDNEY·NEW YORK·TOKYO·SINGAPORE·TORONTO

A CIP catalogue record for this book is
available from the British Library
ISBN 0–671–71023–0

Typeset in Sabon & Futura by
Falcon Typographic Art Ltd, Fife, Scotland
Printed and bound in Great Britain by
Harp erCollinsManufacturing, Glasgow

Illustrations by Julian Abela-Hyzler

The following sections of this guide were written by Matthew
Collins: Andalusia; Barcelona: bar and restaurant listings; Valencia:
bar and restaurant listings; Costa Dorada, Sitges and Tarragona;
Delta de L'Ebre Natural Park; Deltebre; Port Bou; Figuerres;
Andorra.

CONTENTS

v

I should like to thank the following for their help: Zarina Ahmad, Mateen Ahmad, Elena Iglesias, Jack Holland, Ruth Stoker, Maggie Keenan, Javier and Nanu in Estramadura, and David in Salamanca.

Place Names

In Spain it is not unusual to find the names of towns, regions, streets and museums written in Castilian in one situation and in the local language (Galician, Catalan or Euskada – the Basque language) in another. In this book place names and regions are generally given in English, with Castilian or regional names alongside where this information is helpful to the traveller. The names of museums, galleries and other sights are given in the language which you are most likely to see in the streets. A translation into English is given where the meaning is not immediately obvious from the subsequent description. Names of streets and squares are given according to local signposting.

INTRODUCTION

When the first planeloads of cheap package-deal holiday-makers arrived on the Mediterranean coast in the late 1950s, Spain didn't know what had hit it. The money, the bikinis and the liberal attitudes of northern Europeans set to swing into the sixties sent shock waves through the poor, agricultural communities of the south. These rural backwaters had changed little in over a hundred years. Isolated from the rest of the world and starved of interaction with other cultures, the young men working in the new hotels could not cope with the alien lifestyles that had landed on their doorsteps. A special psychiatric ward had to be set up in a Malaga hospital to deal with the number of local men suffering from shock: they even became known as "waiters' wards". Such was the gulf between Spain and the rest of Europe in the sixties. The church, the family and most of all the state were central to the moral life of the country, and Spain's cultural development was stultified by General Francisco Franco's fascist dictatorship until his death in 1978. Things have changed.

The high-rise hotels and the mass commercialism of those early years have continued to grow, but venture inland and the extent of real change is immediately apparent – most of all in the energy of the people. Romantic images of rural villages clustering round dusty old churches, peopled by a simple, uneducated peasantry, no longer hold. Spain has an embarrassment of ancient monuments in a charming state of decay and if you are in search of the historic and picturesque you will rarely be disappointed, but sleepy rural communities are, with a few notable exceptions, a thing of the past. In the northwest you will see people working the land in a way that it has been worked for centuries, using solid-wheeled carts pulled by cattle and scything small hay fields by hand, but for the most part the Spanish no longer live in the countryside. Movement to cities has brought with it a host of urban problems – poverty, poor housing and overcrowding – but it has also brought about a great deal of exciting social change. After the precarious early years in transition from dictatorship to democracy, a terrific energy and creativity have been unleashed, most evident in the behaviour of the young.

There is in Spain a whole generation who have no first-hand knowledge of fascism, and know only the stories within their families of the Franco years. Growing up free from the fear and oppression that dogged their parents' youth, young Spaniards appear determinedly modern. Go to any sizeable town in Spain and you will find discos and clubs heaving with people hellbent on enjoying themselves. It is a great place to head for if you want to holiday with people who know how to party. Some of this is undoubtedly due to unemployment (at around 20 per cent) – how else do they manage to stay up dancing *all* night? – but there is a confusing mix of forces at work. There seems to be an almost palpable sense of optimism, springing from an awareness that the country is changing fast. Fashion is extremely important, and the independent, self-assured, young women dress in a way that sets aside decades of family-based Catholic morality. Increased sexual freedom and assertive dress codes are also seeing off that ever-hopeful anachronism, the macho male, former beach-predator now demoted to minor irritant of the *costas*. It can only be good news for women abroad. Doubtless some of the excessive dance and fashion frenzy is fuelled too by uncertainty of what the future may bring, but whatever the implications, there is no denying the lively youth culture in towns all over Spain.

This energy is a symptom of other social and political changes. Membership of the European Community has had an important effect not only on the improved economy, but also on attitudes and expectations. Spaniards see membership of Europe as a sign of acceptance by the world outside, an affirmation that they have come through the change from fascism to democracy and are flowering as a people. Young people everywhere are eagerly learning foreign languages, particularly English, seeing the greater international community and the jobs that it may provide as their entrance into a future burning with the hope of prosperity.

With this newfound pride in being Spanish, the country remains one of the most regionally distinct nations in Europe. Catalans see themselves as Catalan first, Spanish second, and the same goes for inhabitants of other provinces, but for the Spanish strong regional identity does not necessarily conflict with nationalism. Nor is it divisive: on the whole, Spaniards will talk about visiting another part of the country with interest, not animosity. It is a diversity born of geography: Spain is a huge country with the scenic variety of a minor continent. The stark heat of Castile's scorched red *mesetas* seems a million miles from the life of the small, cultivated green fields of Galicia; the pine-clad inlets of the northwest coast, blurred by mists and clawed by storms, have nothing in common with the sandy, sun-mellowed coves of the Balearics. No wonder the peoples of these regions find little to bind them together.

History too has played a major part in forging these differences. When the Moorish (north African) invasions of the 8th century swept over the peninsula, the few Christian communities that survived were isolated from one another, largely in the mountains of the north and the east. There they developed different languages and customs, and when the Reconquest came it was made up of a mixture of peoples. It is from these early, deep roots that strong regional identities flourish today. There are six languages still spoken in Spain: Castilian, Galician, Basque, Aragonese, Catalan and Bable (found in tiny Asturian communities). The official language is Castilian, but around 25 per cent of the population speak one of the others. In recent times Franco's ruthless suppression of all but the official language, and of local customs, only fuelled the strength of regional feeling.

This breadth of cultural forces makes for richly rewarding exploration for the visitor. Not only are there many landscapes to enjoy, but there remain all manner of fascinating traditions too. Most enjoyable are the distinct food and fiestas of the regions. Strong culinary traditions are very much alive: people still know how to cook, and you can expect to eat well in the most modest of surroundings. Everybody has their favourites, but it is generally agreed that the Basque cuisine is the best in the country, arguably followed by that of Galicia. Multiple drinking traditions persist, too, from the cider houses of Asturias to the bodegas of Andalusia's sherry country.

The greatest celebrations of regionalism, though, are the fiestas. They form an important link with the past and yet, as Spain becomes increasingly modern, fiestas grow from strength to strength; the last seven years have seen a marked increase in the number held right across the country. They follow the seasons and cycles of the Christian church, but with a vigour and relish that are wholly irreverent. There is nothing unusual about Christianity taking over pagan festivals, but in Spain the pagan elements are very close to the surface. The dramas are expressed through fire, masks and dancing, and satirical figures goad religious and civic authorities. Not surprisingly, many fiestas were suppressed by Franco, as indeed they had been by the church in previous centuries. Raw and macabre, the celebrations today retain a medieval quality, staring good and evil squarely in the face,

dramatizing both the heavenly and the demonic. Puppets, bonfires, giants, dwarfs and carnival tricks are enlisted to celebrate the Christian stories and re-enact mock battles with the Moors. No energy is spared and fiestas are accompanied by much eating, drinking and dancing. These spectacles are modern Spain at its most vibrant; there could be no more exciting time to visit the country.

THE PRACTICAL SECTION

RENFE (National Railways)

Narrow Gauge Railways

km 0   100   200

miles 0   100

GETTING TO SPAIN

FROM THE UK

Air

Spain is a great destination for cheap flights – if you have the flexibility to book at the last minute. Discount charter flights to Mediterranean resorts are available in high-street travel agents all over the country: Málaga, Valencia, Alicante and Palma de Mallorca are frequent cheap options. Look out too for ads in the local press and in the Sunday papers for agencies offering special deals. Cut-price package deals are also widely available and can be worth buying for the flight even if you do not want to use the accommodation that goes with it.

For mainland destinations, Iberia airlines have scheduled flights to all major cities; if you intend to hire a car when you arrive, it is worth checking out fly-drive offers with either Iberia or British Airways before booking your flight.

Land and Sea

If you are heading for the north coast by car it is worth considering using Brittany Ferries, which operate between Plymouth and Santander two days a week. The crossing takes 24 hours, is fairly expensive and can be very rough – but it does at least avoid the long haul through France, with savings on time and petrol.

For those without transport, the options are train or coach. There are daily direct Eurolines coaches from London Victoria to Barcelona, taking around 25 hours; less frequent services run to Madrid, Alicante, Zaragoza, Santander and Santiago. It is not a great way to travel, but tickets can be left open for six months – which gives you great flexibility. In many ways the coach is preferable to the train journey (more expensive and with tickets valid for two months), since this involves crossing Paris between the Gare du Nord and Gare d'Austerlitz, for which you need French currency with you.

FROM THE USA

GETTING THERE FROM THE USA

Flights direct from the USA to Spain can be good value. Between them *Pan Am*, *TWA* and *American Airlines* provide a range of scheduled and charter flights direct to Madrid from Washington DC, Dallas-Fort Worth, San Diego, San Antonio, San Francisco, Miami, Los Angeles and New York. These last three, along with Chicago, are also served by the

Spanish airline *Iberia* – well worth considering if you want to book a connecting flight within Spain as part of your ticket. Prices vary considerably according to season, and it is also worth checking out flights via London (with *British Airways*), Frankfurt (with *Lufthansa*) or Amsterdam (with *KLM*).

TRAVEL WITHIN SPAIN

Trains

There is a huge range of train services in Spain operated by the RENFE company, with a variety of prices to match. *Electrotren*, *TER*, *Talgo* and *Pendular* are the swishest, the fastest and the most expensive of these. Regular services are described as *expresso* or *rápido*, while *semi-directos* and *tranvías* are usually slower. The *correo* (mail train) is unbelievably slow.

Prices and journey times are similar to those of buses; look out for "blue days" (*días azule*) for cheaper RENFE travel. If you want to avoid lengthy queuing at busy train stations – and this can be an especially good idea at stations in Madrid – you can reserve your seat in advance (up to two hours beforehand) at a travel agency. A travel agent is far more likely to have the time to explain to you the fares and speeds of different journeys than is a harassed RENFE employee. There is a nominal booking fee of around 200 pesetas.

If you are going to be doing a lot of train travel, it may be worth getting a RENFE rail pass – though it pays to think through how you are going to use it with the aid of a RENFE rail-line map (on the walls of all stations): rail lines fan out from Madrid like the spokes of a wheel and often connections have to be made via the capital – a time-consuming business. Taking a bus can often prove a far more sensible option. Bear in mind, too, that there are a couple of private routes for which RENFE passes are invalid. FEVE, a private company, operates services along the north coast between El Ferrol and Bilbao, and along the Mediterranean coast from Alicante to Denia.

Buses

Reliable bus services operate throughout the country, often providing the only direct public transport between provincial centres. They are often quicker, generally around the same price as standard train services, and on the whole equally comfortable. Remember that Sunday services are massively reduced.

TRAVEL BETWEEN THE BALEARICS

Ferries

Ferries connect Ibiza to Mallorca and Mallorca to Menorca at least once a week; ferries from Mallorca to Barcelona and Valencia operate six days a week; those between Menorca and Ibiza and the mainland less frequently. All this should tell you that manipulating the ferry timetables to travel within the Balearics and to the mainland can prove something of a headache. What's more, journeys are lengthy; for example, Ibiza to Mallorca takes four and a half hours, Ibiza to Barcelona takes 10 hours. All these services are run by Trasmediterránea, except the Ibiza–Denia route, which is operated by Flebasa; information numbers and booking offices are given in relevant chapters.

Air

Interisland flights run by Iberia and Aviaco are not much more expensive than ferries, take a fraction of the time, and offer far more frequent services: call into any travel agent for prices and timetables. Aside from the busy holiday and festival periods, seats can usually be booked the day before – sometimes even later. Peak season is quite a different story with seats booked up weeks ahead.

Spain is a big country and if you want to visit its extremes, taking an **internal flight** can save a day's hard travelling. Local airports connect with Madrid and with Mediterranean resorts during the summer. Services are operated by Aviaco and Iberia; local information numbers are given in the Guide.

Car and Moped Hire

Hiring a **car** in Spain can be surprisingly inexpensive. Atesa is a reliable Spanish company, and the big international firms all have booking offices at airports and in large cities. If you know you will want a car, **fly-drive** deals arranged in advance can be very reasonably priced.

Car thefts are common in large cities – hire cars are easily spotted and seen as a soft target, so don't leave anything in the vehicle, or, if you have to, lock it in the boot. Most cities operate cheap parking with "pay and display" machines along just about every central street. Keep a lookout too for the "no parking" signs, depicting a car being towed away. The traffic police are alarmingly efficient and getting your car back is a costly and time-consuming business.

On the whole, driving in Spain is straightforward and there are very few temperamental or bolshy road-users. Do be careful, though, out on empty main roads: drivers overtaking on sharp, blind bends and the brows of hills claim lives every holiday weekend.

Mopeds are a particularly popular option on the Balearics for getting to out-of-the-way places – like hospitals. Every year there are dozens of accidents as holiday-makers, swept along by the excitement of exotic surroundings, leap on to mopeds and head for the hills – barely pausing to remind themselves that this is Spain and if you are British or Irish all your reflexes tell you to drive on the left. It is easy to make a mistake. If you are going to hire a moped, it is worth giving some thought to the kind of distances you reasonably want to cover in the time you have. Check that the insurance you buy covers theft when you arrange your moped hire. You will probably be asked to leave your passport or driving licence as security.

WHERE TO STAY

GUEST HOUSES

Fondas are accommodation at rock bottom prices. They are indicated by a white "F" on a square blue sign. They are not listed in this guide, but are invariably easy to find near the cathedral or the Plaza Mayor in any old town. They usually offer a very plain room in someone's house, and can be pretty tatty: the main drawback with going to look at a room in a *fonda* is having politely to say no if it is too down-market to contemplate – lumpy beds can be a particularly off-putting feature. The upside is that the owners can be extremely friendly, especially in the less touristed areas of the north.

Pensiones and **Casa de Huéspedes** are indicated by a "P" and a "CH" respectively. They offer a similar set-up to *fondas*, though they are usually of better quality and a bit more expensive.

Hostales (Hs) and **bostal-residencias** (HsR) are yet a notch further up the scale.

In these, as in the preceding categories, it is usual to find that the owners live on the premises – a consideration for single women travellers.

HOTELS

Hoteles (H) are graded from one to five stars, though until you reach the four-star category there is a huge amount of overlap between the quality of what you get; often a good *hostal-residencia* can be far more pleasant than a two-star hotel.

Right at the top of the market are the *paradores* – state-run four-and five-star hotels housed in beautiful ancient monuments. Most travellers can't afford to stay in them, but if you can they may make your trip. If, for example, your journey to Santiago de Compostela is going to be a once-in-a-lifetime experience, then staying in the hospital of the Catholic Monarchs overlooking the Plaza del Obradoire might just be worth the expense.

PRICES

In this guide **cheap to moderate** includes doubles in high season for as little as 1,500 pesetas up to 7,200 pesetas (about £8.50–£41); they are listed in ascending order of price. **Smarter options** include prices above this figure.

If you are travelling alone you can expect a poor deal just about everywhere: the majority of rooms are let as doubles and in high season finding a single can be near impossible. You may well end up having to pay for a double, though it is always worth bargaining for a reduction in this situation, especially if you make it clear you want to stay for three or four days – a factor that can often swing things in your favour.

FOOD AND DRINK

All resort and tourist towns have restaurants that offer easy-to-read, easy-to-order tourist menus, a reliable enough way to ease yourself into eating in Spain, but rather dull. There is a great range of places and ways to eat that are wholly Spanish, and once you have explored them you will never settle for the menu in translation again.

FOOD

Tapas Bars

Tapas are tiny, tasty, high-protein portions of food usually taken with a small glass of wine or a small beer while standing at a bar. You will find them in *tascas*, bodegas, *cervecerías* and *tabernas*. Bar-hopping is a popular early-evening pastime, and you will often find that the *tapas* are so good and filling that you don't want to go and eat in a restaurant afterwards. If you do, many *tapas* bars have a *comedor* to the rear, where you can order a full meal.

The broad *tapas* spectrum ranges from the omnipresent tortilla – a lump of potato omelette on a piece of white bread – to all sorts of elaborately presented morsels, particularly delicious when they incorporate seafood, olives, peppers and mayonnaise. An abundance of fresh seafood ensures that north Atlantic coastal towns have particularly fine *tapas*, but Madrid too gets the best of the catch. *Jamón* – a mildly smoky ham, tough and thinly sliced off the beast's limb before you – is popular all over the country. The best is the *jamón extremeño* or *jamón serrano* produced in Extremadura from acorn-fed pigs. These are best enjoyed standing beneath a dense canopy of yellowing *jamónes* hanging from the rafters.

Substantially larger than *tapas* are **raciones**, again available in bars, comprising much the same food. A *racione* is in effect a very cheap light meal: try *pinchos morunos*, delicious kebabs, or order a *racione* of *boquerones*, crispy, fried whitebait (make sure they are *fritas* – whitebait are also served soused in vinegar); *morcilla*, a kind of peppery black pudding; or just ask for a *bocadillos*, a sandwich.

Budget Eating

If you are travelling on a budget, one of the cheapest ways to eat well is to order a *menú del día* around midday, or a *plato combinado*. Both are usually good value, if a little predictable. A *menú del día* will usually be three courses: soup or a salad – always crisp and fresh – followed by a plain piece of grilled fish or meat, accompanied by more salad, followed by either coffee, a pudding or some fruit. You can often get all this, with a glass of wine thrown in, for as little as 800 pesetas; in busy tourist places a *menú del día* will typically cost around 1,200–1,600 pesetas, but there is usually a cheaper option nearby in less picturesque surroundings where the food can be just as good. Socially these cheap alternatives are the equivalent of a café in England, but plain Spanish food is generally fresh and filling.

Platos combinados cost around the same as *menú del días*, though you get just the one course: typical combinations are *calamares* (squid – fried), *chuleta* (chops) or tortilla (omelette), all served with salad and chips. Anaemic colour photos advertising the food may put you off, but in fact you can expect it all to be freshly cooked and quite decent, if a little plain.

Mesóns and Restaurantes

The Spanish eat late. Restaurants usually open around 20.30 or 21.00 and serve until midnight; this varies and exceptions are indicated in the Guide. A *mesón* is a traditional eating house alongside a bar, usually a very convivial place to take your meal; *restaurantes* can be more formal. Both offer *menú del días*, but unless you are really short of cash it is much more fun exploring less predictable areas of the menu. Regional traditions in Spain are so strong that you really should make the most of local specialities.

In Castile *cordero* (lamb) is a great mainstay: try *caldereta de cordero*, lamb stew, or *lechazo asado*, roast suckling lamb, a particular speciality of Segovia. You can also expect to see plenty of game on the menu at affordable prices: *cordonices asadas*, roast quails, and *perdiz estofada*, partridge stew, are both popular in Extremadura and in Cuenca and Toledo. In Galicia and Asturias sensible, savoury stews keep out the cold – *fabada asturiana* is widely available, a hotpot of white beans, often quite lardy, with sausages in it.

Not surprisingly seafood plays an important part in all coastal regions. *Marisquerías* are devoted to serving nothing but fish and shellfish. The Basque country has Spain's most highly rated culinary tradition and here fish, often accompanied by quite sharp, acid sauces, is a crucial ingredient: try *marmitako*, a tuna-fish stew. In the northwest, *pulpo* (octopus) is a great favourite, making its way into briny *tapas* and delicious casseroles. You will see *empanadas* in bars throughout Galicia – a kind of pie filled with a mixture of fish, peppers and tomatoes. On the Mediterranean coast fish and shellfish are just as tempting; it has to be said, though, that you are more likely to get food poisoning here because of the heat. If you have had a stomach upset, it is a good idea to avoid not only seafood but also mayonnaise, since if not properly refrigerated it can go off quickly.

Gazpacho and paella, those twin favourites of the tourist menu, are also products of the south – the former a chilled cucumber, tomato and garlic soup made from a recipe so foolproof it is invariably delicious; the latter perhaps the least reliable dish you can order in Spain. Typically this famous rice dish contains a mixture of shellfish, but in fact just about anything can be added: chicken, rabbit, bits of ham, red peppers and peas. A good paella is based on moist, crisp saffron rice, the ingredients fresh and distinct. Sadly, mass tourism has meant the provision of paella-on-demand, death to the creative fluidity necessary for a truly fine paella, spawning dish after dish of soggy rice churned over with leftovers. If you want to eat paella, choose your restaurant carefully and if possible order it the day before.

Postres are quite literally "afters". Spain is not a great country for puddings, but it is worth making the most of things where anything beyond *belados* – ice cream – or plain fruit is on offer. *Flan caramelo* – caramel custard – can be delicious, invariably made on the premises. A particularly good version is *tocino de cielo*, which means "bacon from heaven". *Leche fritas* is an even more indulgent treatment of this simple, milky pudding: deep fried and sprinkled with cinnamon. In Mediterranean towns you might try *turrón de jijón*, a soft honey and nut nougat.

DRINK

Vino – **wine** – is served with the simplest of meals, and taken in bars with *tapas*. What you get will vary enormously from place to place, and Spanish red can be very rough, but it is so cheap it is always worth a shot, and you can be very pleasantly surprised. If you want red ask for *tinto*, white *blanco*; a rosé is called either a *rosada* or a *clarete*. Bodegas are traditional cellars where you can sample a great variety of wines and sherries. High on atmosphere, full of well-seasoned barrels and deep, throaty laughter, in out-of-the-way places they tend to be something of a male preserve. Wine buffs will know that the riojas from Logrono are Spain's most famous good-quality wines; if you can't afford these it is best to stick to whatever is produced locally. A light, refreshing alternative to make the connoisseurs cringe is *vino de verano*, a mixture of wine and soda or lemonade, served with ice. *Sangría* is very similar, but with added fresh fruit juice and brandy, popular in tourist resorts, a delicious drink for a balmy evening.

Cerveza – beer – in Spain is a kind of lager: San Miguel is the most famous export of this type. Order a *caña* for a small glass of draught (*caña doble* for a bigger one), otherwise expect to be given bottled beer, always a good deal dearer. Non-alcoholic drinks are available in all bars: *zumo de narania* is orange juice, *tónica* is as you might expect. *Horchata*, a milky drink made of almonds or tigernuts, is delicately flavoured and has a strangely granular texture; it is usually sold in the streets.

Café con leche – milky coffee made with freshly ground coffee beans – is excellent everywhere, full of flavour yet quite mild and without a trace of bitterness. If you want it black, ask for a *café solo*. Finally, tea is widely available in Spanish bars. If you order tea with milk you may well be given a lukewarm mix of milk and water with a teabag still in it: it is best to ask for the milk after you have been given the tea.

MONEY MATTERS

EXCHANGE

You can change cash, most types of traveller's cheques and Eurocheques at banks (*banco*) and at some building societies (*caja de ahorro*), though the latter sometimes charge a large amount in commission. Banks are open Monday to Friday 9.00–14.00; during the winter they are also open on Saturdays between 9.00 and 13.00. The department store El Corte Inglés in major cities is worth getting to know for its banking facilites, which are open during shop hours, as well as for just about anything you may have forgotten to bring with you. Most of the stores have an information desk managed by an English-speaking assistant: they can be amazingly helpful.

Credit cards are widely accepted in shops, some hotels, smart restaurants and petrol stations. Some can be used to withdraw money from hole-in-the-wall cash machines – though hefty interest is charged from the minute you receive the money: check with your credit-card company before you leave.

CURRENCY AND HOW TO BUDGET

Coins come in 1, 5, 10, 25, 100, 200 and 500 pesetas pieces, notes in units of 500, 1,000, 2,000, 5,000 and 10,000 pesetas.

Spain is no longer the great European holiday bargain it used to be: membership of the EC has made a big difference to the economy, so that visitors can expect to spend nearly as much as they would anywhere else in western Europe.

If you can share accommodation with a friend, and limit your eating and drinking to the cheapest of places, you can get by on as little as £110–£140 a week; on £220 a week you can holiday well.

PHONING HOME

International or local phone calls are easiest from *Telefónica* booths, the most common form of *locutorio*, found in all cities and many large towns. Calls are metered – you dial from a booth and pay the cashier afterwards and most accept credit cards. Internal calls are cheaper after 20.00, international calls after 22.00. For international calls dial 07, wait for the tone, and then dial the country code (44 for Britain, 1 for Canada and the USA), then the number minus its first 0.

WHAT TO PACK

Spain is a country of climatic extremes and what you take will depend on where and when you intend to travel. If you are heading for a Mediterranean resort – in fact anywhere south of Madrid – any time between May and September you can expect sunshine, at its strongest in June, July and August. Even in March and November the temperature averages somewhere around 18–21°C (65°–70°F). Cold spells and rain are not unheard of, so an additional item of warm clothing is usually a good idea. Generally, though, if you are travelling from Britain, imagining really strong heat presents the biggest obstacle to sensible packing. Sunblocks and sunscreens are essential, especially for the start of your holiday.

If you are heading for the north coast, waterproofs are advisable whatever time of the year you travel. Average temperatures in Santander from May to September range from 17° to 22°C (63°–72°F). Needless to say, anybody heading for the mountains of the Pyrenees or the Picos de Europa should go prepared as for any high peaks – with waterproofs, maps, compass and warm, light-weight clothing.

KEY DATES IN THE HISTORY OF SPAIN

BC

11th–5th centuries: Celts settle in the north; Phoenicians settle in the south.
3rd century: Carthaginians invade Andalusia; Punic Wars.
3rd century BC–1st century AD: Roman colonization of Spain; introduction of Latin language.

AD

1st century: Christianity arrives in Spain.
5th century: Arrival of the Visigoths, who become the predominant power in Spain for around 200 years.
711: Arab invasion of Andalusia; within seven years the Moorish conquest of Spain is complete.
718: Victory of small Christian army against the Moors at Covadonga, Asturias.
756: Cordoba becomes the capital of Moorish Spain.
11th century: Christian Reconquest gains strength.
1085: Christians take Toledo.
1469: Marriage of Isabella of Castile and Ferdinand of Aragon – Los Reyes Católicos, the Catholic Kings.
1478: Isabella creates the Inquisition to persecute Jews, Moors and later Protestants.
1479: Ferdinand becomes king of Aragon, so uniting Christian Spain under one crown.
1492: The Reconquest is finally completed with the Christian capture of Granada. The Catholic Monarchs order the expulsion of the Jews. Christopher Colombus arrives in the New World.
1516: Charles V succeeds to the throne and within five

years is elected Holy Roman Emperor. His territories thus include Spain, Germany, Austria, Franche-Comté, the Low Countries, Naples, Sicily and Sardinia.

1519: Spanish conquistadors arrive in Mexico.

1532: Spanish conquistadors arrive in Peru.

1556–98: Philip II rules, making Madrid the capital of Spain. By the time of his death his vast empire is weakened by massive debt.

1571: Battle of Lepanto: naval victory against the Turks, giving Spain and its Italian allies command of the Mediterranean.

1588: Sinking of the Armada.

1609: Expulsion of remaining Moors from Spain; Low Countries obtain their independence of Spain.

1618–48: Thirty Years' War, fought at great expense. Spain emerges weakened and no longer a major European power.

1700: Philip, Duke of Anjou, grandson of Louis XIV, becomes Philip IV of Spain.

1701–14: War of the Spanish Succession: Spain loses Gibraltar, Minorca, Luxembourg, Flanders and its Italian territories. Philip V, a Bourbon, becomes king of Spain; the country subsequently heavily influenced by affairs in France.

1759–88: Reign of Charles III engineers economic improvement.

1805: Spain aids Napoleonic France in war against England. Battle of Trafalgar: Spanish naval power destroyed by British.

1808: Napoleon puts his brother Joseph on the Spanish throne. The War of Independence (also called the Peninsular War) ensues. French eventually driven from Spain.

1813: Buenos Aires, Uruguay, Paraguay, Chile and Colombia declare their independence of Spain.

1814: Ferdinand VII regains throne and rules as an absolute monarch.

1833–76: Carlist Wars.

1873: Declaration of the First Spanish Republic.

1874: Restoration of the Bourbon monarchy in the person of Alfonso XII.

1898: Spanish–American War results in Spain losing Puerto Rico, the Philippines and Cuba.

1914–18: Spain remains neutral during World War I. Unemployment and inflation fuel domestic unrest; strikes in Catalonia are severely suppressed.

1923: General Miguel Primo de Rivera establishes a dictatorship with the support of Alfonso XIII.

1930: Oppressive regime so unpopular that General Primo de Rivera is forced into exile.

1931: Elections produce a socialist republican majority; political reform includes provincial autonomy for certain regions. Second Republic declared. King chooses to go into exile.

1933: José Antonio Primo de Rivera (son of the general) founds the right-wing Falange party.

1936 (February): Election won by left-wing Popular Front.

1936–39: Spanish Civil War: Franco's Nationalists take most of the southwest; the rest of the country continues to support the Republican government.

1939–75: Franco dictatorship.

1953: Franco accepts American aid in exchange for US nuclear bases in Spain.

1955: Spain becomes part of the United Nations.

1975: Death of Franco; Bourbon Juan Carlos crowned king; return to democracy.

1982: PSOE – Socialist Workers' Party – led by Felipe González, elected in landslide victory for the left.

1986: Spain becomes part of the European Community.

1992: This year promises to put Spain at the centre of Europe: Barcelona hosts the Olympics, Madrid is Cultural Capital of Europe, the Expo 92 fair is being held in Seville, and Spain celebrates the 500th anniversary of Columbus's arrival in the New World.

MADRID AND AROUND
Madrid and
Castilla-La Mancha

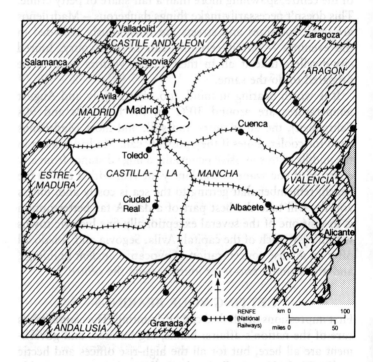

MADRID

Madrid is rarely picturesque. Broad, leafy avenues backed by
elegant parks flank it east and west; a handful of intriguing
narrow lanes sheltered between old convents and churches

graft on to a stately Plaza Mayor; the ornate Royal Palace is magnificently sited and the city's museums house an awesome wealth of art treasures. But even when all this is said, it is a place of very specific attractions, not at all to everybody's tastes. Big, bad and urban, Madrid is an uncompromisingly modern city, with all the excitement that goes with it. Its rich cultural life offers theatre, opera and great football, along with a night scene of bars, dance venues and restaurants second to none. But there is a downside too and you can expect to see prostitution and drug addiction in many parts of the centre, spawning more than a fair share of petty crime. This doesn't necessarily make things dangerous – Madrileños are great socialites and streets are boisterously crowded in the evenings – but it certainly can be unsavoury. Inured city-dwellers take it all in their stride; visitors have to be prepared to do the same.

It is worth bearing in mind, too, that in July and August temperatures are around 30°C (in the high 80s and 90s Fahrenheit), the air is dusty and still, and most Madrileños head for cooler climes if they possibly can. Madrid is bang in the middle of this massive peninsula, a huge distance from any coast, so if you want to combine your visit with a trip to the beach, remember that getting to the sea is costly and, unless you fly, will take the best part of a day. A far better option is to visit one of the several exceptionally fine historic towns within easy reach of the capital: Avila, Segovia and Toledo all offer an intense concentration of evocative ancient buildings, and are within a two-hour journey from the centre.

GETTING YOUR BEARINGS

First impressions of Madrid can be daunting. The capital takes care of the nation's affairs: banks, big business and government are all here, but for all the high-rise offices and hectic traffic, Madrid is actually much smaller and more manageable than it initially appears, and there is no need to feel swamped by the pace and modernity of it. The metro system is cheap, efficient and easy to master and taxis provide an inexpensive means of getting around the centre late at night. Our map is on a small scale; excellent detailed street maps can be picked up at any of the tourist offices, or bought at newsstands.

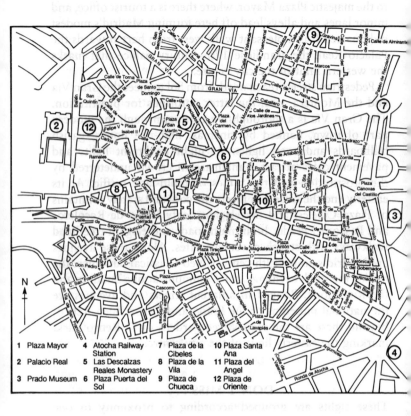

1	Plaza Mayor	4	Atocha Railway Station	7	Plaza de la Cibeles	10	Plaza Santa Ana
2	Palacio Real	5	Las Descalzas Reales Monastery	8	Plaza de la Vila	11	Plaza del Angel
3	Prado Museum	6	Plaza Puerta del Sol	9	Plaza de Chueca	12	Plaza de Oriente

Puerta del Sol is the best place to get your bearings; after all, the rest of Spain does. Philip II decreed that it should be the focal centre of the whole country from which all distances from Madrid should be measured; the precise spot chosen for this purpose is now just outside the Presidencia de la Comunidad de Madrid. However, don't expect any moving historic monuments: Puerta del Sol, a junction of several main roads, is noisy and congested with people hurrying through town, traders flogging cheap lighters, souvenirs and postcards, and harried street performers, all hustling for business amid the sweat and fumes of the city. None the less it remains a useful focal point. A short walk to the southwest brings you to the majestic Plaza Mayor, where there is a tourist office, and minor lanes and alleys lead off here forming Madrid's modest old quarter. It is a pleasant walk west from here towards the Palacio Real, the grandiose 17th-century palace that marks the western limit of the city centre.

Pedestrian streets reach north from Sol to meet the Gran Vía and the Montera area, the latter notorious for prostitution. The Gran Vía is a thoroughfare cutting through the modern part of town, flanked by cinemas, high-rise hotels, garish billboards and neon lights. At night its bright lights and pavement cafés attract a mainstream crowd undeterred by the prostitution and the fumes of multi-lane traffic. At its easterly end the Gran Vía meets the cool and stately fountains of Plaza Cibeles, and the elegant, leafy Paseo de Recoletos and Paseo del Prado, both main roads and elegant tree-lined walkways with stylish pavement cafés. Along these avenues are Madrid's grand 19th-century Neo-Classical buildings: the banks, the stock exchange, the Communications Building and the Ritz Hotel. Ranged in adjacent streets and avenues are the national museums of the Prado and Casón Buen Retiro; beyond these are the sequestered gardens of El Retiro Park, marking the easterly limit of the city centre.

DON'T MISS . . .

These sights are grouped according to proximity to one another, and the nearest metro station is indicated.

The Prado
Paseo del Prado, s/n, Tel: 420 28 36.
Metro: Atocha and Banco de España.
Entrance: 400 pesetas; No charge for EC citizens under 21.
Open Tuesday–Saturday 9.00–19.00, Sundays and holidays 9.00–14.00.

This is one of the world's great art galleries and picking highlights from such a collection becomes futile; the following is an indication of the breadth of work on show. Art lovers can expect to want to devote a couple of days to the place.

Largely the collection of consecutive Spanish monarchs,

the paintings and sculpture in the Prado reflect their pan-European tastes. The works of Mantegna, Fra Angelico, Raphael, Veronese, Tintoretto and Titian are all represented here, as are paintings from the Flemish schools: Hieronymus Bosch, Memling and Rogier van der Weyden. There is a collection of Greek and Roman sculpture, too, and of course a wealth of Spanish art. It is the perfect place to consider the weighty contribution of Spanish painters over the centuries, with magnificent collections of work by both Goya and Velázquez, along with paintings by El Greco, Murillo and Zurbarán.

Casón del Buen Retiro
(Alfonso XII, 28. Metro: Retiro and Banco de España. Open Tuesday–Saturday 9.00–19.00, Sunday and holidays 9.00–14.00.)

This museum houses Picasso's painting "Guernica", a huge abstract canvas expressing the artist's anguish and horror at the German bombing of the town of Guernica in 1937 during the Spanish Civil War (see p. 21).

The rest of this building is given over to 19th-century Spanish painting, for which entrance is via Calle Felipe IV, 28.

The Retiro Park nearby is also worth seeing; see below.

Thyssen-Bornemisza Collection in Palacio de Villahermosa
(Paseo del Prado, 8.)

One of the world's greatest private collections of paintings – second only to that of Queen Elizabeth II – is here on loan to the city of Madrid. Highlights include "St Catherine of Alexandria" by Caravaggio and a portrait of Henry VIII by Holbein.

National Archaeological Museum
(Serrano, 13, Tel: 403 66 07. Metro: Serrano and Colon. Open Tuesday–Sunday 9.15–13.45.)

A major national collection of archaeological finds from all over the country, tracing the early history of the peninsula: Punic, Roman, Visigothic, Muslim and Romanesque periods are all well represented and in the grounds are copies of the

Velázquez and Goya in the Prado

Diego Velázquez (1599–1660), Spain's first truly great painter, is amply represented in the Prado. He was court painter to Philip IV, and this collection includes some of his finest work. Velázquez produced paintings that combine technical brilliance with a rare detached integrity. He is really a painter's painter and appreciating the subtleties of his achievement takes time, but his subject matter is very accessible. His paintings of figures at court allow the insipid characters of his sitters to show through with arresting honesty. Look out for "Baltasar Carlos", a spirited equestrian portrait of a weak child, the heir to the Spanish throne. Consider along with it the portrait of "Francisco Lezcano", a sickly dwarf hired by the king as Baltasar Carlos's companion: the bare honesty of the portrayal confronts us with a devastating understanding of Lezcano's lot in life. Perhaps the most unusual of Velázquez's court paintings is "Les Meninas" (Maids of Honour), which, with its tricks with mirrors and opening doors, shows the ordinary comings and going of court life as if the artist glimpsed the scene just as he was passing by. Velázquez has included himself in the picture, pausing in front of a canvas as he paints the royal couple who stand where we stand viewing in the gallery – their reflection is shown in the mirror behind him.

Francisco de Goya (1746–1828) The Prado offers a taste of the prolific and varied output of Spain's greatest artistic genius – Francisco Goya. In enchanting and rumbustious scenes of country life, his tapestry cartoons, designed for the Madrid factory, show his total command of drawing and composition early on in his long career. "Parasol" and the mannequin tossed in the blanket in "El Pelele" are both sound examples from this period. The canvases "Maja Nude" and "Maja Clothed" demonstrate a more mature painterly brilliance, and look out too for the exquisite poise and technique in "Doña Tadea Arias de Enriquez". But it is in his paintings of royalty, his satires and his politically inspired pieces that Goya is at his greatest. "3 May, 1808" is a large, shocking canvas showing the shooting of Spanish hostages by French soldiers in the War of Independence; "The Disasters of War", a collection of etchings, records the horrors of war with an even greater bitter intensity. The famous "Colossus" is also here, a mysterious canvas showing a giant stalking through a war-savaged, terrified landscape, symbolizing chaos dispersing the rationality promised by the ideas of the Enlightenment which Goya had so passionately embraced.

> Goya's portraits of the Spanish royal family are astounding as much in the fact that he continued to be a court favourite as in his mastery of paint. With wholly unflattering honesty, and yet with humanity too, Goya portrayed the king and his family as sublime chumps; yet still he kept on getting the commissions. No visit to the Prado would be complete without viewing them, enjoyable for his apparently effortless command of the medium combined with sheer nerve.

cave paintings of Altamira. Also on show here is the famous "Dama de Elche" (Lady of Elche); see p. 333.

Plaza Mayor
(Metro: Sol.)

The Plaza Mayor is a magnificent, stately square, bound by the colonnading of grandiose 17th-century buildings on all sides. Designed by Juan de Herrera for Philip II, it was completed in 1617; the dark slate roofs are of Flemish inspiration. The central equestrian statue is the work of two Italians, Juan de Bolonia and Pietro Tacco. The sculptors certainly knew how to curry favour with the king: Philip III sits astride his horse proud and imperious for all posterity, without a hint of the weak and ineffectual ruler he actually was. The plaza was the centre of Spanish society in the 17th century: bullfights, royal processions and the terrifying auto-da-fés of the Inquisition were all held here. Today it is a haven of elegant civility, and it is hard to believe the hectic Puerta del Sol is just a stone's throw away. There are fine terrace cafés: sit with a drink and admire the scene.

The old quarter of town nearby is also worth seeing; see below.

Palacio Real
(Calle de Bailén, Tel 248 74 04. Metro: Opera. Entrance 400 pesetas; free on Wednesdays. Open: Tuesday–Saturday 9.30–17.45, Sunday and holidays 9.30–14.00.)

This grandiose royal palace was designed by Italian architects on the site of the old alcazar, which had been destroyed by fire. It was built between 1737 and 1764, and the setting must have been superb in those days: colonnaded arches flank the forecourt framing expansive views away from the city to the high, snow-capped sierras.

The guided tour (in English) takes you through state rooms decorated in the 18th and 19th centuries, with flourishes of gilt ornamentation, chandeliers and rich tapestries; parts of the palace are still used for state visits. Magnificent frescoes by Tiepolo adorn the throne room and walls are hung with the works of Goya, Rubens, Watteau and Velázquez. Look out in particular for the portraits of Charles IV and of Queen Maria Luisa by Goya in the ambassador's audience chamber. Art enthusiasts may feel disappointed; here first-rate canvases are swamped by the excessive splendour of the rooms and the guided tour is too swift for lengthy contemplation.

An 18th-century pharmacy displays tinted bottles and herbal cures in an adjacent wing, and across the forecourt is an exceptionally enjoyable armoury. It is a massive collection: lethal weapons stand alongside suits of armour worn by seven-year-old princes; there is even armour for a greyhound; but most impressive of all are the equestrian displays. Avenues of prancing, rearing, armoured horses fill the huge hall; walk down between them for a vivid sense of the fear and clamour of battle.

Convento de las Descalzas Reales

(Plaza de las Descalzas. Metro: Sol. Open Tuesday–Thursday and Saturday 10.30–12.30 and 16.00–17.30, Friday 10.30–12.30, Sunday and holidays 11.00–13.30.)

This small monastery is a treasure house of 16th- and 17th-century religious art, all displayed in the manner in which it was intended: shrine after shrine is extravagantly decorated with statuary, paintings and weirdly kitsch toy-doll Jesuses, each opening on to the upper courtyard like a glittering treasure chest. Access is via a sumptuously rich, frescoed staircase. Adjacent small galleries house outstanding paintings of the Spanish royal family. Works by Gerard David and Titian, a grand series of tapestries after designs by Rubens and a particularly fine "Adoration of the Magi" by Brueghel the Elder are just some of the highlights.

The convent was founded in 1559 by Joanna of Austria, daughter of Charles V, for the Poor Clares, occupying a former palace of the kings of Castile. It became a retreat for members of the nobility seeking periods of seclusion, and the collection is the accumulation of lavish, costly gifts that they bestowed upon the order.

ALSO WORTH SEEING . . .

El Retiro Parque
Escape from the unrelenting heat of the city to this stately park with its fountains, formal flower beds, mature trees, ornate glass-house and boating lake. Planned on a grand scale in the 17th century, it was the garden of a royal palace, the remaining part of which is now the Casón del Buen Retiro Museum. Today it is a public park offering peace and tranquillity; impromptu entertainment livens things up at weekends.

Convent of the Incarnation
(Plaza Encarnación. Metro: Opera. Open Tuesday–Saturday 10.30–13.00 and 16.00–18.00, Sunday and holidays 10.30–13.00.)
This convent, founded in 1611 by Margaret of Austria, wife and cousin of Philip III, contains a rich collection of reliquaries and 17th-century paintings.

Lázaro Galdiano
(Calle Serrano, 122. Tel: 261 49 79.
Open Tuesday–Saturday 10.00–14.00, closed August.)
A major museum with a superb collection of enamel work from the Byzantine to the medieval periods, exquisite jewellery, and paintings by Constable, Reynolds, Gainsborough, Tiepolo and Goya.

Museo Sorolla
(General Martínez Campos, 37. Tel: 410 15 84. Metro: Iglesia. Open Tuesday–Sunday 10.00–14.00, closed August and holidays.)
Small museum in the house of Joaquin Sorolla (1863–1923),

famous for accomplished paintings in a style clearly influenced by the French Impressionists. Typical works capture the qualities of light and water in Mediterranean settings.

A Walk Around the Old Quarter
For a wander round one of Madrid's oldest quarters, follow Calle Cuchilleros from the Plaza Mayor and make your way via Calle San Justo to the Plaza de la Vila. The small square harbours a quiet selection of medieval, Renaissance and Baroque architecture: the brick and granite Casa de la Villa, built 1695, has typical Madridian slate spires; the Casa de Cisneros is early 16th century, while the Torre de los Lujanes is older still and shows Mudéjar influences.

From here it is a short walk to Plaza de la Paja where the El Obispo Chapel and the church of San Pedro stand side by side. The chapel is late Gothic, and it is worth stepping inside to admire the tombs and the altarpiece. San Pedro's has a 14th-century Mudéjar tower.

Casa de Campo Park
(Metro: Batán.)
The chief attractions of this park are its boating lake, zoo, public swimming pool and the cable car that takes you there; catch it from Paseo del Pintor Rosales, near the Palacio Royal.

The Rastro
(Calle Ribera de Curtidores. Metro: Latina.)
This lively Sunday market is something of a Madridian institution. It is best to arrive early in the morning; by noon the place is thick with people and by 14.00 things are starting to be packed away.

The central spine of the market heaves with clothes, jewellery and souvenir stalls; explore its outer reaches to uncover old books, paintings, rusty gardening tools, dodgy electrical goods and a dusty array of intriguing junk stalls.

MADRID: FACTFILE

Tourist Offices Plaza Mayor, Tel: 266 54 77. Metro: Sol. Open Monday–Friday 10.00–14.00 and 16.00–20.00, Saturday 10.00–14.00.

Plaza de España, Torre de Madrid. Tel: 541 23 25. Metro: Plaza de España. Open Monday–Friday 9.00–19.00 Saturday 9.30–13.30.

Barajas Airport, International Arrivals. Tel: 205 86 56. Open Monday–Friday 8.00–20.00, Saturday 8.00–13.00.

Chamartín Station, Tel: 315 99 76. Metro: Chamartín. Open Monday–Friday 8.00–20.00, Saturdays 8.00–13.00.

Duque de Medinaceli, 2, Tel: 429 49 51. Metro: Gran Vía, Sevilla. Open Monday–Friday 9.00–19.00, Saturdays 9.00–13.00.

Airport Madrid-Barajas, Tel: 408 52 00. Bus to airport from Colon Square, Tel: 431 61 92.

Train Stations Chamartín Station, Avenida Pío XII. Metro: Charmartín.

Atocha Station, Glorieta de Emperador Carlos V. Metro: Atocha.

Príncipe Pío Station, Paseo de la Florida. Metro: Norte.

Railway information, Tel: 429 02 02.

Bus Stations Estacion Sur de Autobuses, Calle Canarias, 17. Tel: 468 42 00. Metro: Palos de la Frontera.

Auto-Res, Fernandez Shaw, 1. Metro: Conde Casal.

Continental Auto, Calle Alenza, 20. Metro: Rios Rosas.

Taxi Tel: 247 82 00 and 445 90 08.

Car Hire Atesa, Gran Vía, 59. Tel: 248 97 93.

Phone Booths Gran Vía, 30. Open round the clock. Metro: Gran Vía.

Virgen de los Peligros, 19. Metro: Sevilla.

Main post office, Plaza de Cibeles. Metro: Banco. Open 8.00–13.00.

Paseo de Recoletos, 41. Open round the clock. Metro: Colon.

Phone Code: 91

WHERE TO STAY
Cheap to Moderate

Mocelo HsR**, Calle del Prado, 10, 1. Tel: 429 49 63.

Sud-Americana, Paseo del Prado, 12. Tel: 429 25 64.

Santander HR*, Calle Echegaray, 1. Tel: 429 95 51.

Ingles H***, Calle Echegaray, 8. Tel: 429 65 51.

Filo HsR*, Plaza de Santa Ana, 15. Tel: 522 40 56.

Santa Bárbara HsR**, Plaza de Santa Barbara, 4. Tel: 445 73 34.

Alicante HsR**, Arenal, 16, 2nd floor. Tel: 531 51 78.

Moderno, Arenal, 2. Tel: 531 09 00.

Aresol HS***, Arenal, 6, 3rd floor. Tel: 532 24 27.

Londres HR**, Galdo, 2. Tel: 531 41 05.

Regente HR***, Mesoneros Romanos, 9. Tel: 521 29 41.

Opera HR***, Cuesta Santo Domingo, 2. Tel: 541 28 00.

Smarter Options

Regina HR***, Alcalá, 19. Tel: 521 47 25.
Carlos V HR***, Maestro Vitoria, 5. Tel: 531 41 00.
Tryp Reina Victoria H****, Plaza del Angel, 7. Tel: 531 45 00.
Hotel Tryp Rex HR***, Gran Vía, 43. Tel: 247 48 00.

WHERE TO EAT

The most enjoyable way to sample Madrid *and* eat at the same time is to indulge in the time-honoured practice of *tascas*-hopping – that is, moving from bar to bar sampling the *tapas* and taking a glass of wine or a beer as you go. Many of these bars have a *comedor* to the rear, where you can sit down to a full meal. Two areas are particularly good for this: Huertas and the old town to the southwest of the Plaza Mayor.

Sol, Plaza Mayor and Huertas

Museo del Jamón, Calle de San Jerónimo. Vast *jamón* emporium offering every conceivable cured ham you could wish for. Either stand at the bar beneath the *jamónes* swaying from the rafters, or sit in the restaurant upstairs.
El Anglano, Calle de la Paz, 4. Quiet, traditional, dusty, old tiled bar serving cheap *raciones*.
Taberna de Dolores, Calle de Jesus. Excellent traditional *tapas* bar.
Los Gatos, Calle de Jesus, 2. Good, traditional *tapas* bar.
Villa Rosa, Calle de Núñez de Arce, off Plaza Santa Ana. Fabulously tiled with scenes of Seville, Granada and Córdoba, this is a lively *tapas* bar – and there are plenty more along this street.
La Venecia, Calle Echegaray, 7. Raw old *tapas* bar, ancient atmosphere.
Café Cervantes, Calle de León. A popular, trendy place to eat between the Lichensteins and the tarnished mirrors: serves pizza, pasta and crepes.
La Bioteka, Amor y Dios, 3. Tel: 429 07 80. That Spanish rarity – a macrobiotic, vegetarian restaurant. Clean, wholesome and good.
Farfalla, Calle Santa María, 17. Tel: 467 89 24. Very cheap, very popular Argentinian restaurant.
Casa Ciriaco, Calle Mayor, 84. Tel: 248 06 20. Friendly, traditional Spanish restaurant. Cheap.
El Teatro, Calle Prim, 5. Tel: 531 17 97. Bistro and bar serving good Basque food.
La Quintana, Calle Bordadores, 7. Tel: 542 04 88. Near Convento de las Descalzas Reales. Good-quality seafood restaurant; fairly pricey.
Casa Gallega, Bordadores, 11. Tel: 541 90 55. Smart Galician restaurant offering very varied seafood menu.
Casa Mingo, Paseo de la Florida, 2. Tel: 247 50 31. This restaurant is

out in the west of the city. Take the metro to Estación del Norte (from Sol to Opera, then change): it is worth the trip.

Sideria with a great atmosphere serving fried chicken, *empanadas*, salads and *cabrales* – a delicious cheese. Open till 1.30 in the morning.

Chueca and Hortaleza

La Carreta, Barbieri, 10. Tel: 532 70 42. Cheap Argentinian restaurant serving plenty of beef to the sounds of live Argentinian music.

Taberna Carmencita, Calle Libertad, 16. Tel: 531 66 12. Traditional tiled *taberna* serving Basque dishes.

Casa Gades, Calle del Conde de Xiquena, 4. Tel: 232 30 51. Cheerful restaurant for steaks and pizzas.

Café Latino, Augusto Figueroa, 47. Old-fashioned café-bar serving good food.

Nabucco, Calle Hortaleza, 108, Tel: 410 06 11. Tastefully appointed Italian restaurant serving good pizzas. Surprisingly cheap.

Paseo del Prado

Machu-Pichu, Infantas, 10. Tel: 521 18 01. Good Peruvian and Salvadorean restaurant.

Café Espejo, Paseo Recoletos, 31. Very stylish up-market Basque restaurant.

Malasaña

This area is much more popular for bars and music than it is for eating. None the less there are a handful of cheap and decent places to eat.

La Gata Flora, Plaza Dos de Mayo, 1. Tel: 521 20 20. Good, inexpensive Italian restaurant.

Maravillas, Plaza Dos de Mayo, 9. Excellent pizza and wild gateaux in an atmosphere so friendly even the African grey parrot talks to you.

Calle Hartzenbusch and Calle Cisneros, just northeast of Glorieta de Bilbao, have a varity of hectic bars and cheap restaurants to choose from.

Hartzenbusch, Calle Hartzenbusch, 8. Tel: 445 16 67. Hearty German restaurant and bar offering a good range of beers, schnapps, Dutch *oulde jenever*, plus frankfurters and apple strudel.

NIGHTLIFE

Madrid's nightlife is unbeatable, with a huge range of bars, restaurants and dance venues to choose from. Live music is on offer any night of the week, along with theatre, opera and cabaret. Flamenco is not indigenous to the city, but of course you can find it here in the capital.

If you want to experience the place as the Madrileños do, head for one of the areas listed below and move from bar to bar, rather than staying in one place all night. At weekends most bars stay open till 3.00, and in any given area there are usually plenty that keep going far later. Discos sometimes have a cover charge, bars with dance floors never do and are just as popular. Madrid's *Guía del Ocio* is invaluable for comprehensive weekly What's On listings; available from newsstands.

Malasaña

Metros: Bilbao and Tribunal. Plaza Dos de Mayo is at the heart of this area; it can look quite rough, with the drug culture here pretty much in evidence. None the less it is a nice square to sit out in, and the surrounding streets harbour a great range of bars for music, dancing and talking. The area attracts a good mix of age groups, from 18 to late forties. Particularly lively streets include Calle de Velarde and Calle de Ruiz, both of which run off Plaza Dos de Mayo.

La Habana, San Vicente Ferrer, 23. Good spot for dancing to Latin and African rhythms till 5.00.

Nairobi, Calle San Vicente Ferrer, 37. A trendy hangout for arty rap fans.

Café El Foro, Calle de San Andrés. Trendy, popular bar done out as a series of kitsch antique shops. This is a great venue for live bands.

El Parnasillo, Calle de San Andrés. Upbeat Odilon Redon-inspired café-bar playing the best of Athens, Georgia, and attracting an animated crowd.

Café Comercial, Glorieta Bilbao. Old, faded and dilapidated traditional café-bar that is socially very much alive. This is something of a Madridian institution and an important meeting place throughout the day; less important in the evenings.

Café Ruiz, Calle de Ruiz, 11. Sit in the plush red drinking booths of this Edwardian-style bar for quiet drinking in a relaxed, vaguely intellectual atmosphere.

Café Ajenjo, Galeria de Robles, off Calle de Ruiz. Ancient bar-cum-pharmacy-cum-junk-shop with antique and intimate atmosphere.

Ragtime, Calle de Ruiz, 20. Smoky, battered jazz bar, unpretentious and homely, with lots of comfy seats to settle in for the evening.

King Creole, Calle Alte de San Pablo. A good place to dance to rock and roll and mainstream rock music.

Nueva Vision, Calle de Velarde. Young, fun, sweaty bar playing early eighties New Wave *à la* Cure, Depeche Mode, Soft Cell, etc.

La Via Lactea Calle de Velarde. Soft punk-rock bar.

El Mago, Calle de Velarde. Relaxed, mainstream rock bar with South American Indian trappings.

Magerit Bar, Calle de Divino Pastor (off Calle de Ruiz). New Age bohemian bar for quiet, laid-back drinking.

Café Isadora, Calle de Divino Pastor, 14. Named after Isadora Duncan, this is a laid-back, arty café-bar with a vaguely 1920s feel to it. Black and white tiled floor, bentwood chairs and walls covered in old mirrors and film posters.

Chueca and Hortaleza

Metro: Alonso Martínez and Chueca. This includes Calle de Hortaleza, which runs from the Gran Vía to Plaza Alonso Martínez. There are plenty of gay bars and, again, drugs are evident on the streets.

Comic Bar, Calle Hortaleza, 49. Very much a boys' club: there is a pool table, huge comic characters stalk the walls, and a fluorescent green Mini revs up behind the bar; a purely male, electro-funk, gay bar.

Metal, Calle Hortaleza. Big electro-funk dance floor for gay men.

Cruising, Calle Perez Galdos, 5. As you might imagine, this is a strictly male, gay bar.

Agapo, Calle Madera. Fun dance venue.

Duplex, Calle Hortaleza, 64. Mainstream American pop and dance imports, popular with gays but not exclusively; a good mixed atmosphere. Open till 3.00, at weekends till 5.00.

Café Vaiven, Travesa de San Mateo, 2. No-nonsense, straight, upwardly mobile dance-floor and pick-up place. Fun atmosphere and dear drinks.

Tunnel Bar, Plaza Santa Barbara. Raucous R & B and rock-and-roll bar packed with boisterous bopping.

Nearby: Calle de Barceló

Several discos along here attract hordes of teenagers.

Pacha, Calle de Barceló, 11. All-night brat-pack disco.

Barceló, Calle de Barceló. Trendy café serving cheap *raciones* and house music.

Huellas de Libertad, Calle de Libertad, 9. Tiny bar playing excellent Latin music.

Huertas

Metro: Antón Martín. This area includes Calle de las Huertas, the lanes that run from it and the area around Plaza Santa Ana. It is something of a favourite for the sheer variety of bars for drinking, dancing, talking and eating at all hours. In parts it merges with one or two fairly seedy streets which single women may find a little uncomfortable; target the main spots listed here and you should easily avoid these.

Plaza Santa Ana itself is a lovely leafy little square, a pleasant place to sit out early evening in the middle of the hectic city centre. **Cervecería Alemana** at No. 6 is a popular option for beers, or sit out on the pavement at **Cervecería Santa Ana** at No. 10.

Café Central, Plaza del Angel, 10. Tel: 369 41 43. Superb original Deco decor and fine relaxed atmosphere in this jazz café-bar, which has live music nightly 22.00–2.00 (till 3.00 at weekends); jazz tapes during the daytime and good *tapas*, too. Cover charge for some acts, around 500–600 pesetas.

Taberna de Dolores, Calle Jesus. Tall, narrow, traditional tiled *tapas* bar, extremely popular throughout the day.

Los Gatos, Calle Jesus, 2. Convivial, down-to-earth *tapas* bar packed with a lively, mixed crowd.

No Se Lo Digas a Nadie ("Don't tell anyone"), Calle Ventura de la Vega, 7. Feminist bar for dancing, performances, exhibitions, etc.; once purely for lesbians, now a mixed crowd, though predominantly women.

Café Nueva Banbleri, Travesia de la Primavera. Charmingly dilapidated, smoky jazz café with faded mirrors and potted palms, attracting an arty, wholly non-dressy crowd.

La Brocense, Calle Lope de Vegas, 30. Intimate, candle-lit bar with heavy lace drapes and huge wicker armchairs, serving cocktails and a wide range of Irish, Jamaican and other spirited coffees.

Almodo, Calle Lope de Vega, 7. Lively little bar playing great Latin music.

Casa Pueblo, Calle de León. One of the oldest café-bars in Madrid, Casa Pueblo retains a beautiful curved marble bar, brass rails and huge, ornate mirrors. A live pianist induces a laid-back atmosphere.

Café Jazz Populart, Calle Huertas, 22. Jazz café-bar decked with brass horns, banjos and photos of jazz greats. A good place to catch live performances.

El Ayunmiento, Calle Huertas/Plaza de Matute. Just let the beat hijack your feet: this is a lively Latin bar and one of the most popular dance venues in this part of town.

Café Ombu, Calle de Santa Polonia. Popular salsa bar for frenzied dancing.

Taberna Elioa, Calle Santa Maria, 42. Mixed crowd, excellent atmosphere, playing various boisterous forms of world folk music. This bar serves Guinness and Youngers Tartan Bitter – definitely the place to head for if you are pining for a drop of the amber nectar.

Café Concierto La Fidula, Calle Huertas, 57. Without a doubt the most restrained, tasteful café-bar around. Cocktails, spirits, liqueurs and coffees are all served to the strains of superb (sometimes live) classical music. Light, delicious munchies are also available – plum cake, biscuits, salads and cheeses.

Café La Fontaneria, Calle Huertas, 38. Pink bar with piped black metal innards churning out Latin dance sounds. Hot and popular.

Casa Patas, Calle Canizares, off Calle de Atocha. Tel: 228 50 70. A good place to catch flamenco performances Thursday, Friday and Saturday till 3.00.

Paseo Del Prado

Metros: Banco de España and Colón. Graced with grandiose Neo-Classical architecture, home to Madrid's banks and big businesses, this area is elegant, cosmopolitan and stylish. Sit out beneath the leafy avenues at the terraces of chic (and expensive) café-bars.

Café Espejo, Paseo Recoletos, 31. Fabulous, polished Art Nouveau

Bar Etiquette

Eating and drinking in Spain is initially baffling for the visitor. You can be refused beer in one place, whisky in another, and just when you think you have found a likely watering hole, you suddenly find yourself under huge social pressure to eat tough sausages with olives. For the weary traveller this can be a nightmare. Bars, pubs, *tabernas* and *mesóns* all have very specific functions and you choose where to go accordingly. To drink Coke or beer, head for a *bar* or a *cervecería*; to drink wine, try a *taberna* or *bodega*. For *raciones* (substantial snacks), try a *mesón*, where you will also often find a *comedor* to the rear for full meals. Finally, a Spanish *pub* is a place to hear music and drink beer or spirits, but not wine.

Traditional codes of behaviour are still very important in Spain. It is usual to pay for all your drinks at the end of the night and not before. An attempt to pay as you drink (or as you eat, if it is a *tapas* bar) may offend. You may find yourself corrected, or at least get the uncomfortable feeling that the bartender — and everyone else — considers you socially neurotic. After all, you are a guest at the bar; don't you think we trust you? However, it is a tradition that is inevitably changing because of the current growth in the size and style of bars, pubs and discos. It becomes impractical to operate the old, honourable ways when a place is packed to the gills with swaying, drunken hordes. Spend a couple of minutes observing what everybody else does while you are waiting to be served, and then follow suit.

café-bar with huge period mirrors and chandeliers. Very smart and expensive.

Café Recoletos, Paseo de Recoletos. Elegant terrace café for early-evening drinking beneath the palms and chestnut trees.

Café Gijón (pronounced He-hon), Paseo de Recoletos, 21. Famous old café-bar with grandiose gilt-framed mirrors and marble-topped tables; popular with writers and journalists.

The Old Quarter

The Plaza Mayor is a fine place for early-evening drinks on the terraces, and adjacent lanes conceal quiet, quaint bars. The area is perhaps best savoured in the cool and peace of the evening once the traffic has died down.

THEATRES

Sala Triangulo, Calle Buenvista, 23. Tel: 530 68 91. Metros: Antón Martín and Lavapiés. Small theatre producing much modern drama – Tennessee Williams, Ionesco, Havel etc.
Teatro Español, Plaza Santa Ana. Classical Spanish theatre productions.
Circulo de Bellas Artes, Marques de Casa Riera, 2. Metro: Banco de España. Modern theatre.
Centro Cultural de la Villa, Plaza de Colón. Modern theatre.

SEGOVIA

Segovia offers one of the very best day trips out from Madrid. It is situated 80 km north of the capital, beyond the mountains of the Sierra de Guadarrama. The air is clear, the views are expansive and the town preserves an exceptional concentration of historic sights. If you want to stop overnight – and, once here, it is a tempting option – remember that accommodation becomes scarce at weekends; arrange your hotel in advance if possible.

Segovia sits on a small, rocky hilltop, wrapped round by medieval city walls, its skyline a jumble of ancient monuments: the cathedral, the alcázar (Moorish fortress), Romanesque

---

Football

Madrid is a great city for football – check in the local papers for fixtures (generally early evening to avoid the heat).

Real Madrid play in the magnificent Estadio Santiago Bernabéu, as does the Spanish national team: take metro line 8 and exit at Lima.

Atlético Madrid play at Estadio Vicente Calderón: take metro line 5 and exit at Pirámides.

church towers, and a superb Roman aqueduct that neatly bisects the valley below like a curtain of stone. Perfectly regular, tall, slender stems, as disciplined as the engineers who built them, reach up to form two tiers of arches. Still operative (though the water now runs through pipes), it was built around AD 1, bringing water to the town from above the Puente Alta reservoir 16 km away. It remains one of the finest such structures in the world, dwarfing the little streets that fan out from beneath it.

GETTING TO SEGOVIA

Trains from Madrid's Atocha station; buses from Paseo de Florida, 11; metro Norte.

A WALK THROUGH SEGOVIA

Climb the steps up right beside the aqueduct to appreciate just how straight this monumental construction is and take in the views over the low surrounding hills dotted with cypress trees, warm yellow stone church belfries and the red-tiled roofs of houses; beyond these are high sierras, often snow-covered well into early summer.

The Old Town

Inside the town walls Segovia is a beguiling collection of little squares, alleyways, 16th-century town mansions and crumbling Romanesque churches; an immensely pleasurable place to walk around.

Enter the old city from the top of the aqueduct steps, walk down Calle Grabador Espinosa and turn right into Calle Juan Bravo. (There is a second, broader flight of steps from the Plaza Azoguejo beneath the aqueduct, which also feeds directly into this street, but it does not offer such outstanding views of the aqueduct.)

Calle Juan Bravo threads its way through the old mansion quarter of Segovia, and past the church of San Martín. Examine the building from all sides, and look out too for the exceptional carvings around the portal and in the apse. Romanesque churches are an integral part of the town's character: during the Middle Ages Segovia was the capital of Castile, and the wealth of 12th- and 13th-century churches here is a reminder that the province was a key source of strength during the Reconquest.

Lanes from the front of the church of San Martín lead to the Plaza de Franco (Plaza Mayor), Segovia's central square complete with café-bars, bandstand, and the east end of the bulky, blond stone cathedral nudging its way into view. The tourist office is here, too – a handy place to pick up a map or arrange accommodation.

The Cathedral

(Open summer 9.00–19.00 daily; winter Monday–Friday 9.00–13.00 and 15.00–18.00, Saturday and Sunday 9.00–18.00.)

Frenziedly decorative pinnacles trim the cathedral's flat walls and façades, as if decoration were some kind of afterthought. Above them rises a peculiar plain-knit ribbed dome, a second smaller dome and a square tower. The last Gothic church to be built in Spain, it dates from 1525. The interior of the cathedral is strangely cold and alienating, with only elaborate wrought-iron grilles relieving its bareness. The cloister (which houses a small ecclesiastical museum) dates from the 15th century and was moved here stone by stone from a spot one kilometre away after Segovia's earlier cathedral was destroyed during a civic revolt.

Follow Calle Marques del Arco from the front of the cathedral towards the west end of the city and the Alcázar.

The Alcázar

(Entrance 250 pesetas. Open summer 10.00–19.00; winter 10.00–18.00).

Pencil-thin towers sharpened to slate-black points form the picture-book fairy-tale roof line of the Alcázar. It stands at the far, precipitous northwest end of the plug of rock on which the whole town is founded, a superb location affording views out across open country. Two rivers cut below either side of the citadel here, and beyond them stretch barren rocky land and eerily wooded slopes. Such an excellent site has held a fort for centuries: the present alcázar dates from the 12th and 13th centuries, was considerably altered in the 15th and then largely rebuilt after a fire in 1862.

Intensely ornate Mudéjar decoration covers the ceilings inside: look out for the throne room with its red and blue interlocking patterning, and the masses of gold mouldings, tiled walls and tapestry-draped chambers. Climb the tower – if you have a head for heights – for stupendous views.

Look over the city walls to left of the Alcázar as you leave it: below you can make out a series of church buildings, including the polygonal church of La Vera Cruz.

Church of La Vera Cruz
(Open Tuesday–Sunday 10.30–13.30 and 15.30–19.00, closes 18.00 in winter.)
To reach this church, take the lane from in front of the Alcázar along the town wall to your left (with your back to the castle). Follow it as it swings back west down the hillside and through an old gateway in the city walls. Keep straight ahead, crossing the river, and find the church signposted off to the right.

The church of La Vera Cruz is perfectly constructed, beautiful in the simplicity of its design. It is a chunky polygonal building with simple Romanesque doorways set in plain walls. Consecrated around 1208, it was a church of the order of the Knights Templar and is hugely evocative of the solemnity of their rituals.

Inside, a small circular nave (used only by the knights of the order) is divided by arches into 12 sections, and at its centre is the inner temple, the heart of La Vera Cruz. Low arches at the four cardinal points give access to the inner temple, and a staircase leads to a second floor: the *Lignum Crucis* – the alleged piece of the True Cross, from which the temple gets its name – would have been placed on a small stone altar table here.

Take a look at the Gothic altarpiece depicting the Passion of Christ lodged in the small chapel adjacent to the church, and climb the tower for views over the countryside.

Outside the city walls on this side of Segovia is also the monastery of El Parral, which has a fine 16th-century altarpiece and richly carved doors.

Back into the Citadel
Re-enter the old city through the gateway you left by and follow the lane as if towards the aqueduct until you see a tall square Romanesque tower, with the clear sky visible through the arches of its six storeys. This is the church of San Esteban, one of the most charming from this period in Segovia. Wonderfully proportioned, its Romanesque arcaded gallery is supported by richly carved capitals, and the arches are covered in bold zigzag designs.

Back Beside the Aqueduct
Away from the old walled town there is one particularly fine Romanesque church worth looking out for. Follow Avenida Fernandez Ladreda from Plaza Azoguejo beneath the aqueduct towards the bus station. The little church of San Clemente is on the left along here; a little farther down on the right is the church of San Millán. It is an exceptional example of pure Romanesque, with a porticoed gallery, carved capitals and an 11th-century Mozarabic tower; inside are 12th-century murals.

El Escorial

(Trains from Atocha and Charmartín stations. El Escorial lies 50 km from Madrid.

Open summer Tuesday–Sunday 10.00–13.30 and 15.30–18.00; winter Tuesday–Sunday 10.00–13.30 and 15.00–18.00. Closed 10 August and 1 January.

Fascinating and extremely unlikeable, the monastery of San Lorenzo de El Escorial is a wholly fitting monument to the man who built it. Philip II was the most powerful man in Europe in his day: he ruled Spain, Sicily, Franche-Comté, Milan, the Low Countries, Mexico and Peru; he destroyed Turkish power at Lepanto and conquered the Philippines and Portugal. His religious fanaticism was as great as his political power: he expelled the Moriscos (Moors) from Spain, founded the Inquisition and bloodily suppressed the Protestants of the Netherlands.

El Escorial was built in thanksgiving for his victory over the French at St Quentin in Flanders, and the ambition of the design is as overwhelming as its execution: a combined monastery and palace in which the devout king would live, rule, pray and die. It is a chilling, foreboding place with massive grey granite walls, looming in the foothills of the bleak Sierra de Guadarrama. Despite the sheer size of the complex, it was all built between 1563 and 1584. The original design was by Juan de Toledo, but it was completed by Juan de Herrera and the frightening austerity of the place is an unmistakeable effect of his style.

Inside, Philip's spartan, gloomy rooms are powerfully evocative of his life as a despot and an ascetic monk: a door connects his private rooms with the massive, ponderous church, and in his old age he would gaze upon the Herrera high altar from his bed. The severe austerity of the building is matched, too, by the tortuous spirituality of the paintings by El Greco: look out for "Martyrdom of St Maurice and the Theban Legionary" and his "Vision of Philip II". The Royal Pantheon was begun in 1617, 19 years after Philip's death. Hideous marble sarcophagi contain the remains of Spanish monarchs; the Princes' Pantheon is a moving mausoleum of royal children.

At odds with the tone of the whole place, the royal apartments are sumptuously decorated and reflect the quite different tastes of subsequent monarchs. The chapterhouses and sacristy have paintings by Titian and Velázquez, and the library is well worth seeing for its lavishly painted, barrel-vaulted ceiling and its vast collection of precious manuscripts.

TOLEDO

Crammed on a rocky hilltop, Toledo's cathedral, alcázar, synagogues and churches vie for space, crammed tightly together between its ancient walls, bounded by the swiftly flowing river Tagus below. The city boasts a rich concentration of Arab, Jewish and Christian monuments, a unique celebration of the cultural forces that have forged Spain's identity; it remains one of the most dynamic historic cities in Europe. Narrow, twisting lanes cleave to the hillside, the dusty streets themselves evoking a vibrant history.

The skyline of towers and battlements, ragged against the empty, glaring *meseta* sky, is as famous as it is dramatic; the powerful landscape, which charged the paintings of El Greco, is as thrilling today as it was when he painted it in the 16th century. El Greco lived and worked in Toledo for 37 years, and some of his most celebrated works are kept within the churches and galleries of the city.

Whether you want to immerse yourself in great medieval architecture, absorb the intensities of one of the most powerful artists of Spain's Golden Age, or simply stroll through ancient streets, a day – at least – in Toledo is an absolute must for anyone travelling through central Spain. The city is easily accessible as a day trip from Madrid: by train from Madrid's Atocha station; by bus from Estación Sur de Autobuses, Calle Canarias, 17, metro Palos de la Frontera.

Toledo was long prized as a strategic fortified settlement. In Roman times it was sufficiently important to mint its own coins, and had a fine circus and an aqueduct. The Visigoths made it their capital between the 6th and 8th centuries; when the country fell to the Moors, Toledo became part of the Córdoba emirate, and in 1012 capital of an independent Moorish kingdom. Under the rule of Islam, Moors, Jews and Christians (Mozarabs) lived peacefully within the city.

Religious tolerance remained a feature of the city even after the Christian takeover of Toledo in 1085, a key victory in the wars of the Reconquest. It was an atmosphere in marked contrast to the Moorish–Christian campaigns bloodily raging further south. The peaceful coexistence of these cultures lasted for a remarkable length of time, and the city became a centre of religious, intellectual and artistic excellence, greatly patronized by royalty. This tolerance was at its most liberal under Christian rule during the 13th century, and the stability it engendered formed the bedrock of a cultural dynamism unsurpassed in Spain: the wealth of art and architectural treasures that remain today bear witness to the prosperity and creative output of the time. Only in the 14th century, with increasingly zealous Christian powers determined to homogenize the culture throughout Spain, did this enriching cosmopolitanism come to an end. In 1355 there was a pogrom in the city, and in 1391 Jews worshipping at the synagogue of Santa María la Blanca were massacred. Ruthless Ferdinand and Isabella, the Catholic Kings, created the Inquisition in 1480, with specific orders brutally to root out all Jews, and in 1492 they ordered the mass expulsion of Jews from Spain. It was the end of a great era for Toledo.

Throughout the 15th and early 16th century Spanish monarchs continued to lavish money on the city: Ferdinand and Isabella built the monastery of San Juan, and Emperor Charles V rebuilt the alcázar. In 1561 the city's fortunes were overshadowed by the creation of Madrid, some 70 km north, as the nation's capital. Toledo was left as the seat of the primacy of Spain, as it remains today.

GETTING YOUR BEARINGS

Just about everything you will want to see in Toledo is inside the city walls. Its ancient narrow streets are best explored on foot. If you have arrived by bus or train, a second bus from either station will take you up to Plaza Zocódover, a small square high on the east side of town, the best place from which to get your bearings. The tourist office in the plaza can help you with accommodation and maps.

The plaza is triangular: from one corner Cuesta del Alcázar; from another, Calle de la Cuesta de las Armas heads back down the hillside, eventually leading to the road north out of the city. The mosque of El Cristo de la Luz is the main monument of interest in this part of town, so it is a good idea to visit it as you leave. From Plaza de Zocódover's third corner, Calle del Comercio plunges between dusty, old buildings into the heart of the city, offering the best route for leisurely exploration of some of Toledo's great monuments.

Calle del Comercio leads, through various changes of name, to Toledo Cathedral. Across the cathedral square stands the Ayuntamiento: follow the lane that runs to the right of it, and bear right again at the rear of the building. This will bring you to Calle de Santo Tomé, off which both the Taller del Moro and the Church of Santo Tomé are signposted.

Calle de Santo Tomé becomes Calle del Angel and eventually leads to Calle de los Reyes Católicos, a road rather than a lane, which cuts round the edge of the hillside. Straight ahead, at the junction of the two, stands the monastery of San Juan de los Reyes. Turn left here to explore the old Jewish quarter, including the synagogues of Santa María la Blanca and El Tránsito, and the Casa del Greco.

DON'T MISS . . .

The Cathedral

(350 pesetas buys entrance into the Tesoro, Coro, Sala Capitular, Nuevas Salas, Sacristia. Open 10.30–13.00 and 15.30–19.00, till 18.00 in winter; Sunday 10.30–13.30 and 16.00–19.00, till 18.00 in winter.)

Squeezed askew between crooked streets, Toledo Cathedral appears a confused mixture of styles, impressive in its bulky decorative elaboration rather than any overall harmony of design. Building began in 1227 following a French Gothic plan, but this was gradually obscured by countless additions up to the late 15th century.

Inside, however, the building has a grandeur and breadth

of architectural and artistic interest that is wholly absorbing. Huge, massy pillars soar upwards, the black and white marble floor stretches across a vast space before you, and brilliant stained glass fills the nave with light. All parts of the cathedral are worthy of detailed exploration: one visit is not really enough to do it justice.

The choir, or *coro*, is split on two levels. The carving of the choir stalls is particularly interesting: the upper section dates from the 16th century, the work of Berruguetein (who also produced the sinous alabaster carving of the Transfiguration here), the lower shows a series of scenes depicting the conquest of Granada and dates from the late 15th century. Beneath the seats are everyday scenes of medieval life – the harvesting of grapes, feeding the pigs, – and lots of small animals sporting among foliage.

The sanctuary. Directly opposite the *coro*, the altarpiece is a mass of gold-painted, carved wooden panels. Walk around the ambulatory behind it to view the famous Transparente.

The Transparente. A marble sculpture of the Virgin and Child is lit dramatically by a single shaft of light piercing the gloom. It is the cathedral's most theatrical sculptural gimmick – a Baroque contrivance, the work of Narciso Tomé in 1732. Turn round to see the precisely located window that creates this effect, along with figures of saints and disciples ascending into the light, with all the realism of a band of vaudeville characters.

You may start to notice hats dangling from the ceiling in surrounding chapels: it is customary that when a cardinal dies his hat is hung from a thread above his tomb and left there until it rots.

The chapter house. The antechamber to the *Sala Capitular* (chapter house) has a gorgeously decorated gold Mudéjar ceiling and a doorway as intricate as tendrilled lace. Patterns reach an even greater intensity in the ceiling of the chapter house itself, which shines with gold. The walls are covered in 16th-century frescoes of the powerful bishops of the cathedral, and there are two later portraits by Goya. Other frescoed scenes include the life of Christ and the Day of Judgement.

The sacristy houses a small museum holding some major works of art including a series of paintings of apostles by El Greco, and his masterly "El Expolio" (Christ stripped of his robes). It is a typically energetic composition – someone hews the cross, a tumultuous band of captors have Christ bound – yet as the central figure he transmits a weighty calm that transcends the strife and turmoil of the scene. Also on display here are "Christ taken by Soldiers" by Goya and "Cardinal Borja" by Velázquez, along with work by Anthony Van Dyck, José de Ribera and Titian.

With so much good painting to look at, it is easy to miss out on the other treasures held here. Make sure you see the superb 13th-century Limoges reliquaries, a marvellous 12th-century statue of Santa María de Toledo with filigree gold and bejewelled crown, and a strangely graceful 13th-or 14th-century Virgin and Child.

Nuevas Salas: the New Galleries. Access via the sacristy. These rooms hold dozens of episcopal vestments, and a collection of paintings which include a particularly powerful "John the Baptist" by Caravaggio and pictures by El Greco and Bellini.

The treasury. A mass of gilt: the *tesoro* is the cathedral's jewellery box. Finely tooled chalices and sumptuous reliquaries along with a dazzling array of bejewelled archbishop's accessories all vie for attention beneath a heavy, gold-painted ceiling. The massive 16th-century monstrance on show here is still carried through the streets of Toledo at Corpus Christi celebrations.

The Alcázar

(Open 9.30–13.30 and 16.00–18.30, 17.30 in winter. Entrance to the rear of the building.)

A visit to the Alcázar is a must for anyone interested in the Spanish Civil War or military history; it also offers great views of Toledo. The massive fortress commands a powerful position overlooking surrounding hills. Rebuilt many times since the Middle Ages, the current building is the result of restoration work carried out after its near-total destruction in 1936.

Still in the hands of the army, the Alcázar houses a chilling military museum. Room after room displays a deadly array of swords, guns, cannon, rifles and revolvers. In the crypt below are all you might need to reconstruct a picture of the Civil War: radio equipment, Harley Davidsons, explosives and even

The Siege of the Alcázar

The siege of the Alcázar at Toledo was a remarkable episode in the story of the Spanish Civil War. In June 1936 a group of Nationalists under the leadership of Colonel Moscardó were beseiged inside the Alcázar by Republican forces; along with them were around 600 women and children. The fortress proved impenetrable to attack, and the siege lasted eight weeks. After many attempts to force a surrender, the Republicans spoke with Moscardó by telephone, informing him that they held his son Luis hostage, and would shoot him unless they submitted immediately. In the conversation that ensued, Moscardó refused to surrender and said to his son, "If it be true, commend your soul to God, shout *Viva España*, and die like a hero." The Republicans did not in fact carry out their threat, though Luis was killed some weeks later. Eventually Franco came and relieved Moscardó and his forces.

a bullet-riddled copy of the *Illustrated London News*. Down here, too, are the dungeon-like rooms that housed 600 women and children during the course of the eight-week siege in the summer of 1936, including a makeshift, dingy hospital where two babies were born.

Most evocative of all is Colonel Moscardó's operational command room, left just as it was after the siege. Bullet holes pock the walls, the ceiling is falling in as if a bomb exploded only yesterday, and the original battered furniture is coated in masonry and dust from heavy shelling. Here you can hear a recording of the telephone conversation between Colonel Muscardó, who was in this room at the time, and his son Luis, held captive by Republican forces. A transcript of the conversation is on the wall.

The whole Alcázar museum is a celebration of the Nationalists who held cover here; unsavoury but strangely fascinating in its crude manipulation of emotions.

Museo de Santa Cruz

(Find it by walking through the horseshoe-shaped arch off Plaza de Zocódover. Entrance 200 pesetas. Open Tuesday–Saturday 10.00–18.30, Sunday 10.00–14.00, Monday 10.00–14.00 and 16.30–18.30).

This was originally built as a hospital in the 15th century. The plateresque façade of the building is the work of Covarrubias. The rich art collection it houses today includes work by Berruguete, Ribera and El Greco – the best of which is his "Altarpiece of the Assumption". The museum has 30 16th-century Flemish tapestries; look out, too, for the especially arresting 15th-century zodiacal tapestry, designed to hang in Toledo Cathedral. A massive battle pennant, which was flown by Don Juan of Austria at the Battle of Lepanto, hangs between two floors here, giving a tremendous sense of the scale and drama of ships engaged in warfare.

San Juan de los Reyes
(Open 10.00–13.45 and 15.30–18.45; 15.30–17.45 in winter.)
Elaborately ornamented, this choice celebration of Isabelline Gothic was built by Ferdinand and Isabella in thanks for their victory over the Portugese at Toro in 1476. The monastery was intended to include their burial chapel: notice the emblems and monograms included in the decoration. The adjacent cloisters are an even more splendid combination of Gothic, Renaissance and Mudéjar styles. Climb to the second floor for a closer look at the gargoyles and the intricate interlocking patterning of the Mudéjar vaulting.

The chains that hang on the church façade were removed from Christian prisoners freed from the Moors at the reconquest of Granada.

Synagogue of Santa María la Blanca
(Entrance 100 pesetas. Open 10.00–14.00 and 15.30–19.00; to 18.00 in winter.)
Set in a dusty, walled garden, the run-down exterior of Santa María la Blanca conceals a real architectural treat: twenty-four pillars supporting horseshoe arches forest the nave, each topped by highly unusual capitals – worth coming to see in themselves. The carving is bold, heavy and regular, as if macramed stone; the designs are based on pine cones and foliage. Similarly beautiful are the slim strips of highly coloured ceramic floor tiling.

During the 12th century this was Toledo's most important

synagogue, the chief focus of worship for a population of around 12,000 Jews. But in 1391 the synagogue was the scene of a massacre, the beginnings of brutal anti-Semitism in the city, and the breakdown of Toledo's previously famous religious tolerance. The synagogue was taken over by Christians in the 14th century and converted into a church: remarkably, the Almohade-style art was left untouched. Christian additions include a 16th-century wooden altarpiece.

El Tránsito Synagogue

(Entrance free. Open Tuesday–Saturday 10.00–13.45 and 16.00–17.45, Sunday 10.00–13.45.)

Exquisite, lacelike Mudéjar stucco work decorates the upper walls of the synagogue's one long chamber, and concentric star-shaped tracery fills the windows. It is an interior of subtle beauty: climb to the upper gallery to inspect the stucco work more closely and appreciate the delicate colouring and fluidity of the foliage motif, quite a surprise after the strong sense of patterning and repetition that you get from down below. From here is a far clearer view of the carved cedarwood ceiling, too.

The synagogue was built in 1357 on the orders of Samuel Ha-Levi Abulafia, treasurer to Pedro the Cruel of Castile. After the expulsion of the Jews in 1492, the building was taken over by the order of Calatrava (as the synagogue of Santa María Lá Blanca had been), who converted it into a monastery. Today the monastery rooms hold a Sephardic museum of Jewish culture.

El Greco's House

(Entrance 200 pesetas. Tuesday–Saturday 10.00–19.00, 18.00 in winter, Sunday 10.00–14.00).

El Greco never actually lived in this house, but in part of one that once stood here. A delightful central courtyard sets a romantic scene with Mudéjar-inspired tiles and plasterwork, rough-hewn balconies and ivy dancing across the walls. Inside rooms are filled with contemporary furnishings. There is an extremely pretty garden. The whole place has a deftly managed charm and it is a great spot to allow the imagination to wander back into the 16th century.

A small gallery alongside houses a collection of paintings of apostles by El Greco and his famous "View of Toledo", which shows the city's skyline to have changed little since the days when he lived here.

Church of Santo Tomé

(Entrance 100 pesetas. Open 10.00–13.45 and 15.30–17.45, till 18.45 in summer.)

The church of Santo Tomé houses one of El Greco's most famous paintings, "The Burial of Count Orgaz" (1586). It is a huge work, originally commissioned for this building. The lower half of the painting shows St Stephen and St Augustine lowering the Count into his tomb, surrounded by a busy crowd of nobles and notables of the day, including, it is said, Cervantes, Velázquez and El Greco himself. The upper section shows the Count's soul being received into a tumultuous spiritual world seething with heavenly bodies.

El Greco

Doménikos Kyriakos Theotokopoulos (1548–1614), known as El Greco, was born in Crete. Early in his career he went to Venice and studied painting under Titian. In 1577 he moved to Toledo, where he lived and painted until his death.

He was perhaps the most starkly idiosyncratic European artist of his day. Painting almost exclusively religious scenes, he achieved a profound psychological intensity in his greatest work.

In some, like "The Burial of Count Orgaz", the brushstrokes have a volatile, flamelike quality which evokes a sense of spiritual ecstasy. Sour, uneasy colours typify his work: pewter greys and greens energize skies; inky blues and acid yellows charge the folding robes of saints and apostles. Violent, chaotic and disturbing compositions suggest conflict, agony and piety as tortuous forms struggle within the confines of the picture.

Make sure you see the best of his work in Toledo: "El Expolio" (in the cathedral), "The Burial of Count Orgaz" (in the church of Santo Tomé and "A View of Toledo" (in Casa del Greco).

ALSO WORTH SEEING . . .

Museo Taller D. Moro

(Entrance 100 pesetas. Open Tuesday–Saturday 10.00–14.00 and 16.00–18.30; Sunday 10.00–14.00.)

Just one long, rectangular room lit by grilled windows, this former palace now houses a modest collection of 13th–16th-century Islamic tiling. Intricate Mudéjar stucco work decorates the walls, and at either end of the room an Arabic horseshoe arch, decorated with fine interlocking patterns and edged with Islamic scripts, connects to a small square chamber.

Church of San Román

(Open Tuesday–Saturday 10.00–14.00 and 16.00–18.30; Sunday 10.00–14.00.)

The church houses a museum of Visigothic art, which includes some particularly sumptuous pieces of jewellery. The building itself is a fascinating mix with the aisles divided by Moorish horseshoe arches and Christian frescoes decorating the walls;

the 12th-century Mudéjar tower originally stood separate from the main body of the church.

El Cristo de la Luz

The mosque of El Cristo de la Luz dates from the 10th century, the only intact pre-Reconquest building in Toledo. In the 12th century it was converted into a Mudéjar church, though the overall appearance remained thoroughly Muslim: a series of domes rise above soaring columns in a design based on the great mosque at Córdoba.

Hospital of Tavera

(Open 10.30–13.30 and 15.30–18.00.)
This museum contains major works by El Greco, including "The Baptism of Christ", "The Holy Family" and a portrait of Cardinal Tavera (the original founder of the hospital). The collection also includes paintings by Ribera, Titian and Tintoretto.

FACTFILE

Tourist Office, Plaza Zocódover, Tel: 22 14 00. Open 10.00–18.00 daily. Puerta de Bisagra (just north of the city walls). Tel: 22 08 43. Open Monday Saturday 9.00–14.00 and 16.00–18.00
Train Station, Paseo de la Rosa. Tel: 22 12 72. *RENFE* office, Calle Sillería, 7. Tel: 22 12 72.
Bus Station, Ctra. de Circunvalación. Tel: 21 58 50 and 22 63 07.
Taxi, Cuesta del Alcázar. Tel: 21 23 96. Also at Vega Alta. Tel: 22 16 96.
Telephone code 925.

WHERE TO STAY

Cheap to Moderate

Madrid P**, Marqués de Mendigorría, 7. Tel: 22 11 14.
Labrador HsR**, Juan Labrador, 16. Tel: 22 26 20.
Los Guerreros HsR**, Avenida de la Reconquista, 8. Tel; 21 18 07.
Martín H**, Covachuelas, 12. Tel: 22 17 33.
Maravilla H**, Calle Barrio Rey, 7. Tel: 22 33 04.
Real H***, Calle Real del Arrabel, 4. Tel: 22 93 00.
Carlos V H***, Trastamara, 1. Tel: 22 21 00.

Smarter Options

Cardenal HR***, Paseo Recaredo, 24. Tel: 22 49 00.
Parador Conde de Orgaz H****, Paseo de los Cigarrales. Tel: 22 18 50.

WHERE TO EAT
Cheap to moderate

Santa Fé, 2. Find it through the horseshoe-shaped arch off Plaza de Zocódover. Cheap, pleasant and airy restaurant in the centre of town serving standard Spanish menu; they have a good-value *menú del día* around midday for those on a budget.

Ramon del Rio. Find it by taking the first lane to the right off Calle del Comercio as you leave Plaza Zocódover. Pleasant, typical Spanish restaurant with terrace seating on a quiet lane; central and cheap.

Bar Ludeña, Plaza Magdalena, 10. Great *tapas* available throughout the day, and a *comedor* offering a cheap *menú del día*: good value and very popular with locals.

Rincón del Bohemio, Calle de la Sierpe, 4. Tel: 21 37 32. A useful, though not particularly inspiring, cheap option if you need to eat while the Spanish siesta: tourist restaurant that stays open all day.

Restaurant Alex, Calle Amador de los Rios. Sitting on a cobbled, tree-filled square, this is one of the prettiest places to eat in Toledo. A very varied menu includes plenty of seafood and the local speciality – quail.

El Patio, Plaza San Vicente, 4. Standard Spanish menu in exceptionally charming setting: the courtyard of an old mansion, with elegant palms and burbling fountain.

Pastucci, Calle de la Synagoga. Cheap pizzas to take out or eat at the bar.

Plácido, Calle de Santo Tomé, 6. An extremely pretty place to eat out on a tree-shaded patio, right in the heart of tourist-land – where you can buy anything from a rabbit's foot to a full-length sword. The menu offers local game specialities such as quail and partridge; fairly expensive for standard Castilian fare.

Smarter Options

Hierbabuena, Calle Cristo de la Luz, 9. An intimate, refined restaurant offering superior Spanish menu. It lies tucked away near the mosque of El Cristo de la Luz.

Adolfo, Calle Granada, 6. Tel: 22 73 21. Good-quality traditional menu; expensive.

NIGHTLIFE

Venues here are described in the order in which you will come to them if you walk from Plaza de Zocódover.

Paseo del Miradero

Located just below Plaza Zocódover: take Cuesta de las Armas and the *paseo* is a small hillside park off to your right. Sit drinking coffee or beer on the terrace here and enjoy expansive views over the surrounding countryside. **El Cairo** is an open-air bar with a disco; once things get going the place is lively till 3.00 or 4.00.

Plaza Magdalena

Found just off Plaza Zocódover via Calle Barrio Rey. A large, ancient stone doorway on the plaza conceals a couple of lively *tapas* bars: this little square is popular with a late-teens, early-twenties crowd. **Bar Ludeña** is a popular local *tapas* bar; by night the jukebox acts as a magnet for young Toledans.

Calle de la Sillería and Calle de los Alfileritos

Calle Sillería runs off Plaza Zocódover, and soon becomes Calle de los Alfileritos, eventually leading to the church of San Vicente. This narrow lane offers plenty of scope for drinking and occasional dancing. **Sherry** is a great drinking den, extremely popular with a young crowd; **IBEO** also stays busy till late. Farther along, **Paparazzi** attracts a slightly more pretentious young crowd. **Kaya**, Calle Alfileritos, 13, is an especially lively bar, busy till 2.30, and if you want to drink and dance to Spanish music, head for **Cuevas** at Calle Alfiteros, 4.

On from Iglesia San Vicente

Monteros, Calle Alfonso X El Sabio (opposite San Ildefonso church). Lively bar with a great collection of tapes – indie, jazz, R & B and mainstream pop. **Broadway Jazz Club**, Calle de Alfonso XII, has live jazz from 19.30 most nights.

CUENCA

Cuenca's spectacular hanging houses thrust above a deep ravine, sheer from the rock face. Carved wooden balconies jut out in tiers, one above the next, pinned to the buildings as if ready to topple into the chasm below. Dating from the 14th century, these death-defying structures are Cuenca's greatest draw, placing the town firmly on the tour-bus trail. Hanging houses aside, it is an intensely picturesque place; what's more, it offers a handful of excellent small museums and some delightful scenic walks from the old centre. All in all it is well worth a stopover en route from Madrid to Valencia, around 160 km from the capital.

GETTING YOUR BEARINGS

You are most likely to arrive in the new part of town, below Cuenca's famous historic hilltop centre. It makes sense if you are on foot to take a local bus up to the Plaza Mayor in the old town. If you arrive by bus, turn to the left as you leave the bus station and then take the second turning on your left into Avenida General Moscardó, where you can catch a No. 1 or 2 bus to the high town. If you arrive by train it is even easier: Avenida General Moscardó leads straight up from the train station. Just around the corner from the bus stop is the local tourist office in Calle de García Izcara – a handy place to pick up a local map and hotel information. Motorists will find directions to the old town clearly signposted.

DON'T MISS . . .

The Old Town

Cuenca forms a dramatic highlight in a highly charged landscape. Ravines fall either side of this ancient hilltop town to meet two rivers carving their way through the land below. Surrounding rocky hills seem to have an energy all their own, arid and raw; nearer slopes are covered in the exclamation marks of deep-green poplar trees. Narrow, twisting lanes wind up steep slopes to the Plaza Mayor, passing the Torre de Mangana on the way, formerly part of an Arab fortress, now the town's clock tower.

The pretty, cobbled Plaza Mayor forms the quiet centre of old Cuenca. A handful of cafés and gift shops nestle here behind a sprinkling of leafy young trees. Here, too, is the Gothic cathedral, a blunt, blockish building, strangely cold and quite at odds with the flavour of the place. The interior is surprisingly airy, with an 18th-century high altar by Ventura Rodríguez, kept behind elaborate grilles.

Don't miss the cathedral museum of medieval and Renaissance paintings and sculpture: it also gives access to the chapterhouse, which has a plateresque (see p. 365) doorway of exquisite, wispy stone carving, and the Honda Chapel, with its elaborate coffered ceiling.

Back out in the plaza again, follow the lane down to the right of the cathedral (as you face it) to find the town's three important museums: the Diocesan Museum, Cuenca's Archaeological Museum and the Museum of Abstract Art.

The Diocesan Museum

(Entrance 100 pesetas. Open Tuesday–Friday 11.00–14.00 and 16.00–18.00, Saturday till 20.00; Sunday 11.00–14.30.)

The Diocesan Museum houses a large collection of 18th-century Cuenca tapestries and carpets, two small paintings by El Greco and a dazzling array of church silver.

Continue down the lane to find:

Museo de Cuenca
(Tuesday–Saturday 10.00–14.00 and 17.00–19.00; Sunday and holidays 10.00–14.00.)

A thoroughly enjoyable collection of Roman finds forms the mainstay of this local archaeological museum, including some superb statuary, carved capitals and mosaic fragments, along with coins and jewellery.

Museo de Arte Abstracto
(Tuesday–Friday 11.00–14.00 and 16.00–18.00, Saturday till 20.00; Sunday 11.00–14.00.)

This museum houses sculpture and paintings by Spain's most accomplished abstract artists, including work by Chillada, Saura, Tàpies and Zóbel. It occupies part of one of the beautifully preserved hanging houses: from inside the craftsmanship of the carved balconies can be inspected at close quarters, and the views are exceptional.

Puente San Pablo
Walk under the archway by the Abstract Art Museum to the vertiginous San Pablo bridge for thrilling views of the canyon and the hanging houses.

HILLSIDE WALKS
Cuenca has delightful, sequestered hillside walks. From the Plaza Mayor follow Calle de Julian Romero, which runs up from the left side of the cathedral façade. It leads through a quiet quarter of ancient, dilapidated houses to the 18th-century church of San Pedro. From the church, follow the lanes that fall off to your left, and then turn left again on to Ronda del Júcar, a hillside roadway that heads back in the direction of the new part of town. Soon you will see a twisting pathway leading off here down towards a crumbling convent building – the Hermitage of the Virgin of Las Angustias – and then down to the river.

This really is a charming wooded walk with views across the gorge to tremendous rocky hillside scenery. Once at the river, cross the bridge, turn left and follow the road back towards the new part of town. Recross the river at the bridge next to the church of the Virgin of La Luz.

FACTFILE

Tourist Office, Calle Dalmacio García Izcara, 8 (1st floor). Tel: 22 22 31. Open Monday–Friday 9.00–14.00 and 16.30–18.30; Saturday 10.00–13.00.
Train Station RENFE information Tel: 22 07 20.

ESTREMADURA
Extremadura

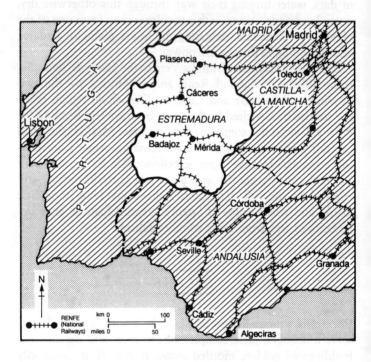

Estremadura is a huge, dry region, void of people and industry. The landscape is varied and expansive, big enough for the imagination to roam as if across a new and empty continent. Hot, hoarse winds blow chaff and dust through the clean air and vast fields of wheat stretch beneath peerless blue skies to the high sierras of Tentudía, barely visible in a shimmering watery haze. Plains of parchment-yellow grass are studded with thirsty olives; gaunt, heat-emaciated cattle shelter their bony, boot-polished forms beneath eucalyptus trees or graze at the meagre lips of precious watering holes; the occasional mule stands stone-still in a field. The scale of it all is somehow liberating; a land big enough for storks and eagles to soar, while at ground level starch-white egrets pick the fields.

Strangely, its most dramatic features are its huge lakes, fed by the rivers Tagus and Guadiana, which lie bounded by dark craggy rocks, appearing like water-filled canyons, great seams of dark water forging their way through this otherwise dry, dusty landscape. Along with agriculture they form one of the region's prime assets, irrigating the lower plains of Badajoz and providing hydroelectric power.

Estremadura reaches from La Vera to the Sierra de Tentudía, from Toledo to Cuidad Real, and is formed by the two provinces of Badajoz and Cáceres. The whole region is off the tourist trail, visited in the main by travellers heading for Portugal, yet it has some fine historic sites: Mérida (the small capital) has some superb Roman remains, while Cáceres is the conquistador town par excellence. Under-development has real advantages; this is a place where traditions are still enjoyed to the full, particularly those involving food and drink, and where some of Spain's greatest historic sites can be enjoyed free from mass commercialism.

CÁCERES

Cáceres is a uniquely special place. Its ancient city walls preserve a near-complete complex of medieval and Renaissance buildings of golden, mottled stone. It is as if an entire city has been left behind, like a forgotten cupboard of treasures, moth-eaten, dusty and wholly evocative of both its former glories and the passage of time. Proud armorial crests are supported by crumbling masonry, strong weeds grow from crevices in noble doorways, and every glorious minor palace and church of modest splendour is topped by bristling stork's nests. It seems the birds have moved in to occupy the city in the absence of human interest across recent centuries.

A wander through the lanes and alleyways at night is silent and magical; you half expect to meet a cleric in his robes, or a torch-bearing servant running from silent house to mansion doorway. There is rarely anything to spoil the illusion, and it is not just a few squares that are worthy of attention: every inch of old Cáceres rewards exploration.

Cáceres remains off the main tourist routes despite being declared a World Heritage site in 1986 and classed as the second most important monumental city of Spain by the Council of Europe. History aside, it's a surprisingly lively place for its size and has a frenzied youth scene, particularly during term time.

GETTING YOUR BEARINGS

The Plaza Mayor is the heart of the city's social life and the most obvious place to get your bearings. It's a long cobbled square that sits just outside the old city walls. At one end is the rather orderly and stately Ayuntamiento, and around three sides the low arches of colonnading provide cool walkways; above them buildings glare whitewashed in the baking heat.

The tourist office sits below the city walls here, to the right of a central flight of steps which lead up into old Cáceres. The old town itself is a series of narrow lanes linking secluded, irregular squares, closed to all but residents' traffic.

Modern Cáceres is adjacent to the old walled town, but in no way impinges on it. The lanes that run off the Plaza Mayor directly opposite the old town offer good ground for cheap accommodation and places to eat and drink. Calle de los Pintores and Calle del Alcazar shoot off the top end of the plaza as busy shopping streets. At the end of them, and beyond the church of San Juan, Calle San Pedro leads down to Avenida de España, the central spine of the modern town, a busy tree-filled boulevard with a popular *paseo*.

DON'T MISS ...

Plaza Mayor
The Plaza Mayor alongside the old town offers the perfect opportunity to sit with a cool drink and admire a length

of the city's outer defences. Cáceres has been walled for centuries: the El Christo gate on the south side of town is Roman, the mud-adobe Torre del Horno, visible here beside the Ayuntamiento, Arabic.

The plaza is the noisy hub of Cáceres life, by night chock full of young people drinking and talking, by day busy with traffic and the comings and goings of the town's people.

A Walk Through Old Cáceres

Every inch of the old town within the walls is worth exploring. Most of the palaces are now in use as civic buildings and not open to the public, but if doors are open it is worth looking inside at the inner courtyards that were such a feature of these elegant homes.

Climb the steps from the Plaza Mayor and enter beneath a broad, low arch. The lane straight ahead leads to **Plaza de Santa María**.

The cathedral of Santa María is a modest Gothic church. Inside are the worn stone tombs of the nobility and an altarpiece dating from 1551; put a coin in the slot to light up lively battle scenes and portayals of the life and resurrection of Christ.

Directly opposite the cathedral is the **Episcopal Palace**. Notice the medallions either side of the doorway: that to the left represents the Old World, that to the right the New. Wander round to the left of the cathedral (as you face it) and you will find the **Carvajal Palace**, with its round, rubble-masonry tower dating from the 12th century. Walk back and round to the right of the cathedral to continue through perhaps the most richly textured area of the old city.

Twice honoured with the visit of Ferdinand and Isabella, the **Palace de los Golfines de Abajo** is one of the most beautiful palaces in the city. It is wonderfully embellished with armorial carvings, griffins and stone balustrading. The overall Gothic style shows Mudéjar influences in its paired windows and repeated decoration.

From here the lane leads to the **Plaza San Jorge**. The majestic, crumbling façade of **San Francisco Javier**, an 18th-century Jesuit church, dominates the square. Weed-covered steps lead up to a Baroque portal flanked by dilapidated towers, each crowned by top-heavy straw nests, the dull clacking of stork's bills constantly overhead. Nearby the 15th-century **Casa de Los Becerra** lurches above an overgrown doorway, a now run-down city mansion decorated with proud armorial carving.

Climb the steps up the side of the church and at the top turn left past the **Palace de Las Cigüeñas** (Palace of the Storks), now a military building. Beyond it is Plaza de las Veletas, with the Provincial Museum (see below).

In the adjacent **Plaza de San Mateo** is the church of the same name, a mishmash of styles, with a highly dilapidated clocktower of red brick; the interior is bare but for its Baroque altarpiece.

From Plaza San Mateo wander down to Plaza de Santa Clara with its four huge, healthy palms and little whitewashed houses, and then back up through the old town just inside the city wall along the enchanting Calle de Adarve de Padre Rosalio. Continue straight ahead, passing steps to the Plaza Mayor, to the Plaza Conde Canilleros and the Casa Toledo-**Moctezuma**, a palace built by Juan Toledo Moctezuma, grandson of Tecuixpo Istlaxoohitl, a.k.a. Isabel Moctezuma, the Aztec princess.

The Provincial Museum

(Plaza de Las Valetas.
Free. Open Tuesday–Friday 9.30–14.30.)

The Casa de las Veletas, which houses an archaeology and ethnology museum, is of great interest in itself. It was built on the foundations of an alcázar and beneath ground level is an *aljibe*, an Almohade water cistern from the Moorish citadel that stood here. It is well worth seeing for the *aljibe*'s vaulted ceiling, supported by granite columns and horseshoe arches.

ALSO WORTH SEEING . . .

Casa Museo Árabe – Yussuf al-Borch

(Calle de la Cuesta a Marques, just off Plaza San Jorge.)
This is a small, private museum dedicated to Arabic studies; tours in Spanish.

The Conquistadors

Estramadura's greatest period of history was the age of the conquistadors – the adventurers who explored and exploited the New World. Cáceres took a key part in this. The city had been exempt from feudal taxes as a reward for the role it played in the Reconquest and as a result the nobility prospered. They amassed considerable fortunes and went on to provide the men and the money for the expeditions to South America that eventually changed the entire face of that continent. The wealth that the conquistadors brought back with them is visible in the palaces they built in Cáceres, Trujillo and Plascencia, as each tried to outdo the opulence of the next, and in the riches they lavished on the monastery of Guadeloupe.

OUT OF TOWN . . .

Trujillo

Trujillo, 5 km east of Cáceres, is a conquistador town seething with history. It was the birthplace of Francisco Pizarro, merciless conqueror of Peru, one of the many adventurers from Estramadura to bring back vast wealth from the New World. The town has at its centre an engaging clutter of grand 16th- and 17th-century seignorial mansions sporting lavish armorial bearings; the 13th-century Gothic church of Santa María in the Plaza Mayor is enriched by a heavily detailed 16th-century retable (which you can light up) and on the edge of town stands a 10th-century Arab fortress.

FACTFILE

Tourist Office, Plaza Mayor. Tel: 927 24 63 37. Open Monday–Friday 9.00–14.00 and 17.00–19.00, Saturday and Sunday 10.00–14.00.
   Train Station Tel: 22 50 61.
   Bus Station Tel: 21 04 95.
   The bus and train station are opposite one another some way out of town. To reach them from the centre, take a No. 1 bus from Calle de San José.
   Taxi Tel: 24 30 63.
   Swimming Pools Cáceres has two public swimming pools, both a good 15–20 minutes' walk from the Plaza Mayor, but well worth the effort in the Estramaduran heat.

The Virgin of Guadeloupe

The little village of Guadeloupe (80 km east of Trujillo) is dominated — as it has been for centuries — by its monastery. A sound Gothic structure overlaid with Mudéjar decoration, it was richly embellished in subsequent centuries. At its centre is a shrine to **the Virgin of Guadeloupe**, a black-skinned icon revered by millions across the Spanish-speaking world. Today this Romanesque statue is dressed in elaborate gowns and a glitzy crown. It is supposed to have been carved by St Luke, sent by the pope to Seville, and removed from there as the Moors swept across Spain. The story goes that in the 13th century the Virgin herself appeared to a shepherd in a vision and directed him to the spot where he unearthed the long-lost statue. After its discovery Guadeloupe became a centre of pilgrimage, and came to symbolize the *Hispanidad*, the united culture of Spain in Europe and South America. Columbus had two Indian slaves baptized in the fountain here in front of the church, and he also named an island in the West Indies after the shrine.

A guided tour takes you through the monastery, and includes a visit to the Mudéjar cloisters, a collection of canvases by Zurbaran, and an excellent embroidery museum with ecclesiastical pieces as elaborately decorated as the monastery itself.

1. Follow Calle General Primo de Rivera from Avenida de España, follow the road as it swings round to the right and then take Calle de José Luis Cotallo off to the left: the pool is at the end of this road on the left.

2. Wander from Plaza Santa Clara down Calle de Sierpes, then Calle de Colón to the Plaza de los Conquistadores. From here Calle Antonio Reyes Huertas leads to the pool. Here you can lounge under shady trees between dips.

WHERE TO STAY
Cheap to Moderate

Castilla, Ríos Verdes, 3. Tel: 24 44 04.
Goya, Plaza Mayor, 33. Tel: 24 99 50.
Los Naranjos, Alfonso IX, 12. Tel: 24 35 08.
Iberia, Pintores, 2. Tel: 24 82 00.
Alvarez, Calle Moret, 20. Tel: 24 64 00.

Smarter Option

Parador de Caceres, Calle Ancha, 6. Tel: 21 17 59. Housed in former city palace in the magical old town. Air conditioning and TV in rooms. Garden.

WHERE TO EAT

El Corral de Las Cigüeas, Cuesta de Aldana (follow signs from Plaza Santa María). Sit out in a cool courtyard with ivy-covered whitewashed walls and towering palms. Primarily a bar, this is one of the prettiest places to eat in the old town around midday or early evening. Open for drinks till 2.00 weekdays, and until 3.00 or 4.00 weekends.

Palacio del Vino, Calle Ancha. A pungent smell of garlic sausages draws you to this tiled bar; there's also a wine-lined *comedor*, a very pretty courtyard and a cheap Spanish menu on offer. Overall this is a curious blend of the charming and the relentless, very quaint but dogged by grinding pop music.

Bodega Medieval, Calle del Orellana, 1. Tel: 245458. Traditional restaurant in the quiet, old, walled city offering regional specialities such as *perdiz al estilo Alcantara* – a casserole of partridge, mushroom, red peppers and juniper berries. Medium price range.

El Puchero, Plaza Mayor, 10. Tel: 24 54 97. Sit out under the stone arcading and look across at the city's ancient fortifications. El Puchero is a good choice for plain Spanish food, offering plenty of cheap *platos combinados* – eggs, chops, squid etc.

Mesón El Asador, Calle Moret, 34. Tel: 22 38 37 and 24 38 37. Whether you want just *tapas, raciones* or a full meal, this is one of the best options in town for reasonably priced good Spanish food. They have a huge range of tasty, typical local dishes, from cheap *pinchos extrameño* – a skewer with tasty morsels of meat cooked in garlic – to *Pata Negra*, the best and priciest of local *jamónes*.

El Figón, Plaza San Juan, 14. Tel: 24 43 62. Good-quality, traditional restaurant serving typical Extramaduran food. Moderate to expensive; they take credit cards.

El Gran Mesón, Calle Gral Ezponda, 7. Tel: 24 77 26. Big bullfighting bar with cool, tiled restaurant to the rear.

Pizza Queen, Plaza Mayor, Standard chain pizzas in lively setting looking over the square.

BARS AND NIGHTLIFE

Plaza Mayor

The Plaza Mayor is the hub of Cáceres nightlife, swamped with young people eating, drinking and talking from around 21.00 until after midnight weekdays, at weekends till 3.00. The crowd are generally in their late teens and early twenties.

Local Delicacies

Try *Licor de Bellota*, a typical Estramaduran liqueur made of acorns. It is rounded, smooth and very sweet, with a warm vanilla and coffee flavour, just nudged with chocolate.

Acorns figure large in Estramaduran traditions: *Jamón Extrameno* is produced here from acorn-fed pigs – the very best cured ham in Spain.

The Old Town

If you want a quieter place to spend your evening, there are a few places to drink in the ancient part of town: **El Corral de Las Cigüeñas** is particularly popular or you might try **Palacio del Vino** (see Where to Eat above).

Calle Sergio Sanchez and Calle de Pizarro

These streets (both lead off from behind Iglesia de San Juan) offer trendier, more stylish bars, attracting an arty, slightly older crowd (mid-twenties to thirties). There's a good mix of bars and coffee houses.

La Gioconda, Calle Pizarro, 8. Chic, restrained Edwardian-style café-bar looking out over orange trees for Irish coffees, fresh fruit juices and exotic ice creams.

La Traviata, Calle Sanchez, 6. Arty bar to hear yourself think in. Jazz, reggae and an exceptional decor of huge carnival heads, turquoise palms, oak-framed mirrors and rust walls.

Montana, Calle Sanchez, 8. Perhaps the reddest bar you will ever drink in.

Habana, Calle Sanchez. Spacious bar in elegant old house, now a cool, fashionable drinking den. Vivaldi to jazz-funk.

Madrila

This is the area everybody heads for to dance from around 3.00 till morning at weekends. There are several discos (some with cover charge) and bars with dance floors (free). It all happens beneath the modern flats of this area between Calle de José Luis Cotallo and Calle de Doctor Fleming. To find it, turn off Avenida de España down Calle General Primo de Rivera, follow the road as it swings round to the right past an equestrian statue, then cut down the steps beneath the flats to the left.

MÉRIDA

Ancient Roman ruins rise from this quiet town and imbue it with grandeur. During the time of the emperor Augustus, Mérida was one of the most important towns of the Roman Empire and the sites that remain are among the very finest in Spain. It is a small place, everything is on a personal scale and the sense of history is extremely accessible.

Situated beside the broad, languorous river Guadiana, Mérida's low-rise buildings afford little shelter from the excessive heat of the Estremaduran plains: from early summer it is very hot. The chaotic Plaza Mayor is an unsettled mixture of styles and the life of the town revolves slowly around it. Surrounding streets follow the small grid pattern of Roman times, and dotted throughout its modern centre are occasional reminders of Mérida's Roman past. At a pinch the highlights can be seen in a day; classicists and archaeologists will want to spend longer.

GETTING YOUR BEARINGS

Finding your way around this small town is quite straightforward. Modern development is to the south of the river, as is the main bus station; all the interesting sites are found in the older part of town to the north. They are largely grouped together and walking is the best way to explore the town's treasures. The Puente Romano crosses the Guadiana and leads straight up, past the Alcazaba fortress, to the Plaza España (also known as the Plaza Mayor) and on into Calle Santa Eulalia. The plaza is, as ever, the very heart of things, while Calle Santa Eulalia is a busy pedestrianized street running through the centre of town. Roughly parallel to it is Calle Sagasta, a minor lane where you can stumble across the 1st-century BC Temple of Diana. Both streets lead up to Calle José Ramón Mélida, which climbs to the tourist office and Mérida's finest Roman sites: the National Museum of Roman Art, the Roman theatre, the amphitheatre and the less significant Casa Amfitheatre. Mérida's other Roman house, the Casa Mithraeum, is near the bullring; to find it, follow Calle Graciano past the Alcazaba.

The Romans in Mérida

Mérida – or Augusta Emerita, as it was then called – was founded in 25 BC as a home for veterans of the V and X legions. Their feats were evidently richly rewarded since all that was best in Roman civic entertainment is found here: a superb theatre, a huge circus for chariot races and an amphitheatre. The town was built at the junction of two main Roman roads; that between Toledo and Lisbon, and the Salamanca–Seville road, an important silver route. The town prospered and became capital of the province of Lusitania, which included much of Extremadura and southern Portugal. By the end of Augustus's reign it was one of the most important cities of the empire.

DON'T MISS . . .

Roman Theatre
(Open 8.00–22.00 daily.)
The Roman theatre is not only impressive, it is also still very beautiful: two tiers of pale-grey marble columns topped by Corinthian capitals rise from the stage, Roman statues are ranged below them, and a semicircular seating arrangement capable of holding 6,000 completes the scene, just as it did when it was given to the citizens of Mérida by Agrippa in 15 BC.

Roman Amphitheatre
(Open 8.00–22.00 daily.)
This was built around 8 BC, and here up to 14,000 citizens gathered to watch gladiators fight or to see spectacular mock sea battles, for which the arena was flooded. You can climb on to the terraces for a citizen's view of the

Entrance
Entry to most of the sites in Mérida is bought on one ticket: the Roman theatre, the amphitheatre, Casa Mithraeum, Casa Romana, and Alcazaba.

proceedings, or crawl into low, dungeon-like chambers and see where gladiators were kept before their fight to the death, close enough to smell the blood and hear the screams of men savaged in the ring before them.

Museo Nacional de Arte Romano (National Museum of Roman Art)

(Entrance 200 pesetas. Open Tuesday–Saturday 10.00–14.00 and 17.00–19.00 Sunday 10.00–14.00.)

This is one of Spain's great museums; even the building is a treat – the work of Rafael Moneo, completed in 1986. The style is strong yet unobtrusive: the spacious, oat-coloured brick interior is gently lit and walking through this purpose-built museum seems effortless.

The exhibits are equally special: exceptionally fine Roman sculptures from around Mérida, huge mosaics – look out for a particularly vivid "Escena de Cacería" (boar hunt) and for the "Rape of Europa" – and a wealth of bronze statuettes, ceramic lamps and pots. If you have an interest in classical art, expect to find this place absorbing for hours.

Alcazaba

(Open Monday–Saturday 9.00–14.00 and 17.00–19.00, Sunday and holidays 9.00–14.00)

Commanding a strategic position overlooking the river and the ancient bridge, this Arab fort was built around AD 835. Inside you can climb the battlements or follow steps down to inspect the Arab water cistern. It's an

impressive Moorish construction. Inside a low, solid building two even flights of steps lead down to the water supply. The striking vine-decorated lintels are in fact pieces of Visigothic masonry reused by the Moors.

Puente Romano

The 60 granite arches of the Puente Romano are best viewed from the river bank at Avenida de Guadiana, but to really appreciate this Roman bridge, start walking across it. It has been here since the 1st century AD; not only is it strong enough to support modern-day traffic but, being Roman, it is also dead straight. Part-way across is a slipway that provides a riverside view of the massy defences of the Alcazaba.

ALSO WORTH SEEING . . .

Temple of Diana
(Calle Sagasta.)
Ruins of the Corinthian-style Temple of Diana stand in the modern street, giving some impression of the Roman origins of the town.

Casa Mithraeum
(Open Monday–Saturday 9.00–14.00 and 17.00–19.00, Sunday and holidays 9.00–14.00.)
The best mosaic floors of this Roman house (of which only the foundations remain) are preserved in breeze-block huts: look out for an especially fluid composition of mythological figures in blue, turquoise and shimmering gold pieces.

Casa Anfiteatro
(Open Monday–Saturday 9.00–14.00 and 17.00–19.00, Sunday and holidays 9.00–14.00.)
This is the site of a Roman house, right by the amphitheatre. Excavations have revealed water courses that were fed by the San Lázaro reservoir, along with a patio, baths and mosaics. Look out for the large mosaic with designs of fish, flowers, shells and dolphins, and an exceptionally lively one portraying grape-treading.

Trajan's Arch
(Calle Forner.)
This is part of a much larger arch which stood here in what was once the main street of Mérida.

Iglesia Santa Eulalia
This Romanesque church has a typical square tower and solid carved doorway but the shrine to St Eulalia adjoined to it

is very unusual, constructed out of 1st-century columns and capitals of the old Roman Temple of Mars.

Circus Maximus

Strictly for dedicated archaeologists, this 400-metre racecourse was the scene of chariot races and held up to 30,000 spectators; very little of it remains. Find it between the railway line and Avenida Juan Carlos on the edge of town.

OUT OF TOWN . . .

Aqueduct of the Milagros

(Five km out of town, visible from the road or train to Càceres.)

This is the more impressive of two aqueducts that brought water to the town, feeding two reservoirs. The reservoir of Prosperine is now an ecological reserve.

FACTFILE

Tourist office, Calle Pedro Maria Plano. Tel: 31 53 53. (At the top of Calle José Ramón Mélida.)

Train station, RENFE Tel: 31 81 09 or 31 20 05.

St Eulalia

St Eulalia was one of the most popular Christian martyrs in Roman Spain; more villages are named after her than any other person. She lived during the time of Diocletian (early 4th century) and at the age of 12 was ordered to renounce her Christianity. Proudly defiant, she spat in the face of her judge, and was subsequently burned in an oven. Even today local people commonly pray at her shrine.

Bus station, Plg. Nueva Cuidad, Tel: 30 04 04/07.
Car hire, Rent a Car, Calle Piedad, 3. Tel: 30 16 63.
Taxi, Tel: 31 91 67.

WHERE TO STAY
Cheap to Moderate

El Arco P*, Santa Beatriz de Silva, 4–1. Tel: 31 01 07.
Nueva España HS*, Avenida Extremadura, 6. Tel: 31 33 56.
Vettonia, Calderón de la Barca, 26. Tel: 31 14 62.
Lusitania H**, Oviedo, 12. Tel: 31 61 12.
Cervantes H**, Camilo José Cela, 8. Tel: 31 49 01.
Nova Roma H***, Suàrez Somonte, 42. Tel: 31 12 01.

Smarter Options

Parador Nacional Via de la Plata H****, Plaza Constitución, 3. Tel: 31 38 00. This *parador* is housed in a converted 15th-century convent tucked behind a square lush with palms and orange trees. Central location, garden; air-conditioning and TV in rooms.

WHERE TO EAT
Cheap to Moderate

La Gamba, Calle Cervantes. Early-evening seafood *tapas*.
Antillano, Calle Félix Valverde Lillo, 11. Tel: 31 32 06. Pleasant, tiled restaurant serving traditional Estramaduran dishes. Their midday menu is particularly good value; try the *caldereta Estrameño*, a thick lamb stew, or the *soupa Estrameña*, a thin soup with hunks of bread, bacon and egg, all delicately flavoured with red peppers.
Rafal-2, Calle Santa Eulalia, 15. Tel: 31 58 54. Popular local restaurant serving traditional Estramaduran dishes. It can be moderately expensive, but there is also a cheap *menù del día* around midday. Good selection of Estremaduran wines.
Casa Benito, San Francisco, 3. Tel: 31 55 02. Excellent meaty *raciones* – as you might expect from a bar plastered wall to wall with bullfighting posters. There is a *comedor* to the rear if you want a full meal, or you

can sit out on their street side terrace. As well as the omnipresent chops, cutlets and sausages, you can try the local *perdiz estofado* – partridge stew. Cheap to moderate.

Mesón Emerita, Calle Oviedo. Worthy, plain Spanish bar for tasty *raciones*.

Galileo, Calle Piedad, 3 (off John Lennon Street). Friendly, youthful atmosphere. The pasta dishes are tasty but strangely insubstantial; pizzas are a better option here.

Restaurant Rufino, Plaza Santa Clara, 2. Tel: 31 20 01.

A good option if you want a light meal; this is a plain family restaurant for the budget-conscious.

Hong-Kong, Calle Marquesa de Pinares, 2. Tel: 31 11 63. Pleasant, airy Chinese restaurant.

Smarter Option

Restaurant Nicolás, Calle Félix Valverde Lillo, 13. Tel: 31 96 10. Traditional local dishes in grandiose setting, including a large selection of Estremaduran wines, hams and cheese.

Cafés

The best of Mérida's cafés are around the Plaza Mayor; in early evening the central garden is full of people sitting out on the terraces.

Alternatively, **Horno Santa Eulalia** on the edge of town, at the end of the street of the same name, is a *pastelerie* offering exquisite cream cakes, which you can eat outside sitting among the yucca palms.

BARS AND NIGHTLIFE
Plaza Mayor

The Plaza Mayor is a jumble of styles and full of the noise of traffic and chattering birds. It is the place to sit in the early evening and watch the light fall over its palms, orange trees and gushing fountain.

John Lennon Street

Find it off the Plaza Mayor. John Lennon Street (honest) is the centre of Mérida's youth scene and from around 22.00 onwards everybody heads here to drink and dance. It is extremely lively – which comes as a surprise in such a small town. Bars and clubs jostle for space the length of the street and this largely mainstream strip attacts a late-teens to mid-twenties crowd. There is no entrance charge for most late-openers, so it is easy to hop from one place to the next. Things keep going till 3.00 seven days a week.

John Lennon Inevitably this pub stares at you through a pair of huge neon specs; inside it is more Madonna than Magical Mystery Tour.

Titanic Suitable bar to sink a few.

Divina Decadencia Solid, non-stop dance music.

Wal Ki Ki Cool, mint-green bar with big wicker seats; mainstream pop and disco sounds.

Alternatives

Fino San Patricio Garvey, Calle Piedad, 3. Friendly, old-style bar devoted to traditional Spanish culture: *jamón*, sausages and flamenco. Catch live musicians and dancers here at fiestas and some weekends.

Jazz Bar To find it follow Calle Forner from town centre, walk under Trajan's Arch and turn right. Cool, cool jazz bar, open till 3.00.

Disco

Cacao, Calle Oviedo. A case of brain damage meets brawn damage: find this relentless, pounding disco opposite the bullring. Once you know you are looking for a club that looks like a carpet warehouse, you can't miss it. Open till 5.00 weekdays, all night at weekends; free.

PLUS . . .

- Good-quality **replicas** of Roman lamps, pots, figures and glassware are on sale all round town. If you can't find room in your travel bag for a ceramic amphora, you might pick up a tragicomic mask or two. Try the shops along Calle José Ramón Mélida.

- **La Casa de los Jamónes Estremenos,** Calle Santa Eulalia, 38, is definitely the place to shop for local **cheeses, hams and wines** – and worth a visit for the kitsch shopfront itself, all tiled with archaic adverts.

ANDALUSIA
Andalucía

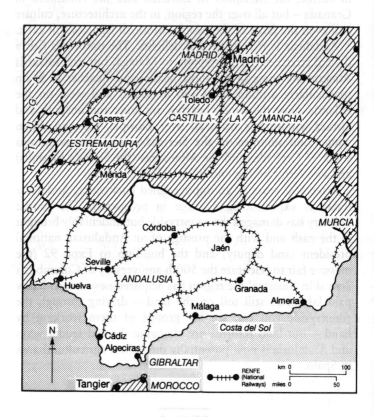

Every Spanish cliché that has ever been misappropriated for tourists can be found for real in Andalusia. Bullfights, flamenco and Gypsies all have their origins here and all can be found in abundance in one of the most culturally rich areas in Spain.

The name Andalusia comes from either of two possible sources – "Vandalusia", the land of the Vandals who occupied Spain after the Romans, or (as is thought more likely) "Al-Andalus", the name given to Spanish territory brought under the control of the Moors.

The Moorish influence is what makes the region so exciting. The outstanding monuments are in the big cities – the alcazar in Seville, the Mezquita in Córdoba and the Alhambra in Granada – but all over the region, in the architecture, culture and even the faces of the people, Moorish legacies still exist.

Andalusia is rich in natural delights. The notorious Costa del Sol stretches from Estepona to Málaga, but east towards Almería are some of the most picturesque beaches in Spain (particularly around the Cabo de Gata) and west on the Atlantic coast the windy beaches are huge and unspoilt and attract windsurfers from all over Europe. You can ski in winter and summer on the Sierra Nevada, the mountains south of Granada, and the Alpujarras (the Sierra's foothills) are wonderful hiking and horse-riding country.

After 500 years as an impoverished backwater, Andalusia today is experiencing a surge in prosperity. The tourist industry has damaged the countryside but undeniably brought in the cash and with the prestige of an Andalusian national president (and deputy) and the build-up to Expo 92 (the massive fair to celebrate the 500th anniversary of Columbus's arrival in America) the region has acquired new status. Badly paid labourers still toil on the land – driving through the countryside you can see big groups of them working by hand – but land reforms are changing the old feudal ways and Andalusia is now potentially the richest agricultural area in Spain.

SEVILLE

No other city in Spain has had so much romantic imagery attached to it. In the 12th century Seville was a rich Moorish capital, in the 16th century a gold-laden port and in following centuries Don Juan, Carmen and Figaro all put

Julius Caesar captured Hispalis, as Seville was then known, in 45 BC and renamed it Colonia Julia Romula. After falling first to the Vandals, then to the Visigoths, it was taken by the Moors in 712 and renamed Xibilie. After the fall of the Cordoban caliphate in the 11th century, Seville became capital of the Almohad kingdom. Ferdinand III captured it in 1238 and settled there with Christians from Castile. The 14th century saw some expansion and the additions made by Pedro the Cruel but the Golden Age of Seville followed the discovery of the New World. Seville became the administrative centre for overseas trade and throughout the 16th century booty-laden galleons poured into the port until the Guadalquivir silted up and commerce was transferred in 1717 to Cádiz. At the start of the Civil War, Seville was taken and used as a bridgehead by the Nationalist forces arriving from Morocco. Despite centuries of decline, and current misfortunes such as high unemployment and crime rates, Seville is still the largest city in Andalusia and fourth largest in Spain and it has been put on the political map again as being Prime Minister Felipe Gonzalez's home town.

Seville on the map. Flamenco is alleged to have started here (the city still has a Gypsy quarter across the river in Triana), its bullring is one of Spain's oldest, and modern Seville maintains old traditions with the solemnity of its Semana Santa (Holy Week) and the exuberance of its vast April Fair.

Today's Seville is also Andalusia's biggest city, with an exciting metropolitan buzz. Unemployment is high, petty crime is appalling, the drivers are the maddest in Spain, and you can cruise round trendy clubs and bars till dawn. You can also, however, still stroll through narrow white-washed streets and smell orange and jasmine in the air. The city's sights are enticing: a Moorish minaret, the Mudéjar alcazar – which in parts is as beautiful as the Alhambra – and the largest Gothic church in the world (Christopher Columbus is buried in it). Lesser monuments include the tobacco factory in which Carmen worked and the hospital for the poor founded by Seville's original (and reformed) Don Juan.

Seville is the host of Expo 92 – Spain's biggest-ever world's fair, which hopes to attract 20 million people – although no one knows if the city will be ready in time.

GETTING YOUR BEARINGS

The focal point in Seville is the massive cathedral and the Giralda tower, and you will find almost everything that is

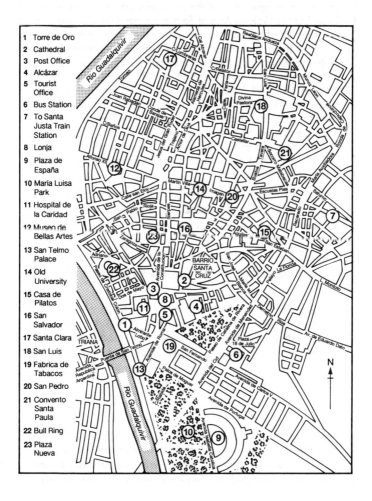

1 Torre de Oro
2 Cathedral
3 Post Office
4 Alcázar
5 Tourist Office
6 Bus Station
7 To Santa Justa Train Station
8 Lonja
9 Plaza de España
10 María Luisa Park
11 Hospital de la Caridad
12 Museo de Bellas Artes
13 San Telmo Palace
14 Old University
15 Casa de Pilatos
16 San Salvador
17 Santa Clara
18 San Luis
19 Fabrica de Tabacos
20 San Pedro
21 Convento Santa Paula
22 Bull Ring
23 Plaza Nueva

Festivals in Seville

Seville's **Semana Santa** (Holy Week that is, the week leading up to Easter Sunday) is the most important in Andalusia. Hotels are packed, pavements are crowded and roads are redirected to make way for the processions of *cofradias* (ancient brotherhoods associated with the local churches) who march through the streets each evening. The processions are a spectacular sight. Giant flower-bedecked *pasos* (floats bearing images — usually of Christ or one of the city's many Virgins) are carried through the streets on the shoulders of up to 50 men who gently march and sway in time to *saetas* (dirgelike hymns with flamenco origins) played by the accompanying band. The *pasos* are also accompanied by penitents in robes and conical hats (they look just like Klu Klux Klan members) who carry candles, chains and big timber crosses along the entire route. The processions converge at the Ayuntamiento. Details of Holy Week events can be found in all local papers.

If Semana Santa is all about excess and solemnity (even though restaurants and bars still get packed), the April Feria is all about excess frivolity. For a whole week Seville enjoys a fiesta. Everyone puts on their best outfits — the women wear brilliantly coloured frilly flamenco dresses and the men don cropped jackets and Cordoban hats — and dances Sevillanas until dawn.

The Feria started off as a livestock auction and all the events take place in a field — the Real de la Feria in Los Remedios on far side of the river — behind a giant, specially erected gateway. Hundreds of tentlike *casetas* (little houses) are put up and sponsored by families, clubs and unions who all enjoy their own little party. During the day carriages and impeccably groomed horses parade through the streets and there are bullfights and horse shows at the Maestranza. All the events in the Real de la Feria start at dusk. Just follow the crowds — they'll take you there. One small word of caution — the atmosphere at the Feria is magical but because each *caseta* is sponsored, some of them can feel exclusive. Many will let strangers in (given a bit of charm) but some keep bouncers on the door. The Feria at Jerez is much more accessible for outsiders.

Seville's other big festivals are **Corpus Christi** in June — when the cathederal altar boys put on 17th-century cassocks and do the dance of the *seises* (the sixes) — and the **feast of the Virgen de los Reyes** — when the statue of Seville's patron saint is taken from the cathedral's Capilla Real and marched through the city in procession.

interesting to see clustered in the immediate vicinity. Nearby is the charming network of narrow streets of the Barrio de Santa Cruz. Next to the cathedral, the city is bisected by the main thoroughfare, the Avenida de la Constitución, which becomes the pedestrianized shopping street Calle Sierpes beyond the central Plaza Nueva. The river Guadalquivir also runs through the city, parallel to Avenida de la Constitución, and is lined by the riverside walkway, the Paseo de Colon. On the other side of the river is the traditional Barrio de Triana and the more modern Los Remedios district. The main railway station (Estación de Córdoba) is situated in the north of the city and the smaller Estación de Cádiz is near the Maria Luisa park in the south.

DON'T MISS . . .

The Giralda

(Visited in conjunction with the cathedral. For opening times, see below.)
You can see the Giralda from almost all over Seville. The exotic former Moorish minaret towers over the city as if still intending to call people to prayer. It is the only remaining part of the mosque and for the last 400 years has stood incongruously next to Seville's huge Gothic cathedral. The Christians added its belfry but none of its exoticism has been lost – the delicate brickwork and horseshoe arches are still in excellent condition. Climb up to the top (it has ramps instead of steps so going up is easy) for beautiful views of Seville.

Originally the minaret attached to the mosque, it was built in 1184 by the Almohads of Roman stones brought from Italica and is 98 metres high. There are no steps inside but a series of 35 slightly inclined ramps – built so men on horseback could ascend it – lead to the top.

Externally, the tower is divided into three distinct sections. The central part, with lattice brickwork and Moorish horseshoe windows and arches, is the most delicate. The lower section, with its austere stonework, is more characteristic of the Almohads. It was originally topped by four golden apples but these were destroyed in an earthquake.

In 1568 the present top five storey, composing the belfry, were added. Twenty-four bells were placed inside and a revolving bronze statue of Faith (the Giraldillo – which acts as a weather vane and from which the Giralda takes its name) placed on top. The original Giraldillo now stands in the cathedral, having been replaced by a less valuable replica.

The Cathedral

(Open Monday–Saturday 10.30 to 13.00 and 16.30 to 18.30. Sunday 10.30 to 13.00. No shorts.)

"Let us build a cathedral so big that future generations will think us mad for attempting it," the chapter is alleged to have said when Seville's cathedral was still an idea. In 1506 it was finished and at 116 metres long and 76 metres wide it is the biggest Gothic church, and third largest cathedral (after St Peter's, Rome, and St Paul's, London), in the world. There's plenty worth seeing inside.

The cathedral was built on the site of what was first a Visigothic church and later an Almohad mosque. The interior follows the ground plan of the mosque and as a result the nave and transept are not immediately obvious. There is, however, a central nave, with two sets of double aisles and flanked in turn by side chapels, but the transept does not project beyond the side walls. The overall structure is more easily appreciated by looking down on the roof from the Giralda.

About 40 main columns support the vaulting, which rises to 56 metres at its highest point. The central aisle is interrupted by the *coro* (choir) with Gothic choir stalls.

The **Capilla Mayor** houses the largest Gothic altarpiece in the world – a spectacular gilt Flemish masterpiece, which took 82 years to make, depicting 45 scenes from the life of Christ using over 1,000 figures. Unfortunately the intricacy and detail of the work is hard to appreciate because it is surrounded on three sides by 16th-century *rejas*, or grilles.

The **Capilla Real** is a former royal burial chamber with a domed roof built in the Renaissance style. It is dedicated to St Fernando, king and Christian conqueror of Seville, whose remains lie in a silver and bronze shrine (a gift to the cathedral from Philip V in 1717) immediately in front of the altar.

In the centre of the altar is a clothed wooden statue of the Virgen de los Reyes, a 13th-century Virgin Mary and Seville's patron saint, which Ferdinand took into battle with him. To the left and right of the altar are the tombs of Alfonso the Wise and his mother Beatrice of Swabia.

In front of the Capilla Real, stairs descend to the **crypt,** which houses the tombs of Pedro the Cruel and his mistress Maria de Padilla, and Fernando's original coffin. There's another statue of the Virgin, this time in ivory, which Fernando also carried into battle.

The **Sala Capitular,** or chapterhouse, has a Baroque elliptical ceiling and contains paintings by Murillo.

The **Sacristia Mayor** houses the treasury among whose relics are Ferdinand's sword, a gruesome head supposedly of John the Baptist, and the *tablas Alfonsinas* – a box which accompanied Alfonso into battle and which contains such goodies as ancient bits of tooth and bone. The Gothic **Sacristia de los Calices** contains more Murillos and a Goya.

Around the cathedral, the dark side chapels contain works of art, including another Murillo in the Capilla de San Antonio and a Zurbarán altarpiece in the Capilla de San Pedro.

On the south side is the **tomb of Christopher Columbus,** whose body did almost as much travelling dead as it did when he was alive. After his death in Spain, his remains were taken to what is now the Dominican Republic, where they stayed until they went to Cuba. Here they rested at Havana Cathedral (some believe his real remains are still there) before being brought back to Spain at the turn of the century when Cuba became independent. His tomb is carried by four nobles representing the kingdoms of Spain – Léon, Castile, Aragon and Navarre. One carries a cross piercing a pomegranate, representing the Christian Reconquest (a pomegranate is the symbol of Granada), and an oar represents Columbus's journeys. His son Fernando is also buried in the cathedral near the main portal.

The **Patio de los Naranjos** is, with the Giralda, the only surviving part of the mosque. Some of the original Almohad outer walls and horsehoe-shaped arches remain. The fountain dates from Visigothic times. The Puerta del Lagarto is named after the crocodile hanging from the ceiling – a gift to Alfonso from the sultan of Egypt when he asked for the hand of the infanta. The present one is wooden but the original in 1260 was stuffed. The tusk hanging next to it is supposed to have come from the Roman ruins at Italica. On the east side of the patio is the Biblioteca Colombina (being restored in 1991) containing manuscripts, books and prints, which were a legacy from Columbus's son.

The Alcazar (Reales Alcázares)

(Open 9.00–12.30 and 15.00–17.30; Sunday and holidays, mornings only.

Admission from the Plaza del Triumfo via the Puerta del Léon. Save time queueing by having change for the ticket machines inside.)

With its decorative detail based on the Alhambra in Granada, the Seville alcazar is the most important piece of Mudéjar architecture in Spain. It might not have the romance attached to the Alhambra but it was built at the same time and by artisans lent from Granada who copied much of the artwork from its more famous model. Used as a royal palace right up to the present day, it is in near perfect condition and has beautiful, extensive gardens.

Built for Pedro the Cruel in 1366, it succeeded the much

bigger citadel and palace (built in the 11th century by the Almohads – probably on the site of a Roman praetorium) and subsequently underwent various alterations and extensions by later monarchs.

Go through a series of ivy-clad patios, separated by the original arched Moorish walls, to reach the inner courtyard with the main façade of the 14th-century palace in front, and the later Renaissance additions on either side. To the right stands the Cuarto del Almirante (also known as the Casa de Contratación or Casa del Oceano) which was commissioned by Isabella in 1503 to house the administrative offices for Spain's overseas affairs. The chapel has a model of one of Columbus's ships, the *Santa Maria*, and a painting known as "La Virgen de los Marinos" or "the Madonna of the Navigators" (Columbus is supposed to be the one on the right at the feet of the Virgin). Temporary exhibitions and Flemish tapestries are on display in the other rooms. Outside, an *azulejoed* staircase leads up to the royal apartments on the first floor (close) in 1991 but may reopen).

At far end of the inner courtyard in **Pedro the Cruel's Palace**. The narrow façade of the Puerta Principal is richly decorated with Moorish arches and arabesques. Above there is a protective wooden overhang and a Kufic inscription from the Koran stating, "There is no victor but God." The vestibule inside leads left into the central **Patio de las Doncellas** (Courtyard of the Maidens/or Maids of Honour), decorated with tiles, stucco work, paired columns and arches. An upper storey was added in the 16th century.

Across the courtyard is the most elaborate room of the palace, the **Sala de Embajadores** (Ambassadors' Hall), whose wealth of decoration rivals anything in the Alhambra. It has a magnificent cedarwood domed ceiling. The balconies and the frieze of royal portraits were added by Charles V, who married Isabella of Portugal here in 1526. Horseshoe arches lead off into the adjacent rooms: a long dining room, the apartments of Maria de Padilla (Pedro's infamous mistress), and Philip II's salon. The salon leads into the exquisitely diminutive **Patio de las Muñecas** (Dolls' Court), named after two tiny faces hidden in the carving. The columns come from the Roman ruins at Italica and some of the capitals from Córdoba and Medina Azahara, but again the upper storey are much later (19th-century) additions. Leading on to the patio are the bedrooms of Isabella and her son Juan (who was born here). Nearby is the Dormitorio de los Reyes Moros.

On the far side of the central patio we find the salon of Charles V (his motto "Plus ultra" is inlaid in the floors) and the apartments of Maria de Padilla. According to popular local legend, Maria was known as the "Queen of the Gypsies" and was accused of having bewitched King Don Pedro by giving his unfortunate queen – Blanche de Bourbon – a gold girdle which looked like a live snake to the eyes of the king.

Leave the alcazar and pass through Charles V's Palace with its tapestries and chapel to the beautiful gardens, which descend in terraces, interlaced with walkways, hedges, orange groves, palm trees, fountains and pavilions.

The Casa Lonja and Archive of the Indies

(Plaza del Triunfo. Open 10.00–14.00. closed on Mondays.)

The Lonja is the old Exchange originally built for Seville's Golden Age merchants; today it houses the Archive of the Indies. You'll find it tucked between the cathedral and the alcázar. Although the city had always been an important port, its heyday came after the discovery of the New World. Booty-laden galleons sailed into the city attracting merchants from all over Europe, who conducted their transactions in this building. Now, all the documents and drawings collected by the crown during the Age of Exploration are here and, as well as the first-ever maps of the Americas, there are letters and log books bearing signatures of Magellan and Cortes and even a diary kept by Columbus.

Before the construction of the Lonja, all business was conducted in the cathedral's Patio de los Naranjos. Not surprisingly this upset the bishop, who petitioned Philip II to build them an exchange elsewhere. Juan de Herrera, who at the time was busy on El Escorial, got the job and the Lonja, with its severe façade and stone balls on top, has similarities to his more famous work. By the late 18th century, with the decline of the American trade, Seville was less commercially important so Charles III converted the Lonja to house the Archive of the Indies.

Barrio Santa Cruz

A maze of narrow whitewashed streets with pretty flower-bedecked patios lies right beside the alcazar. This is the quintessential romantic heart of the city. Some houses still have iron grilles on their windows through which young men used to serenade their sweethearts. Until 1492 it was the Jewish quarter of Moorish Seville. Today there are plenty of attractive bars, *hostales* and restaurants, and the presence of tourists is not excessive. Among attractive squares to look out for are Plaza de Doña Elvira (where theatrical performances used to take place) and Plaza de las Cruces (which contains three crosses, including a 17th-century one in wrought iron). Among the alleyways are the Callejon de Agua (with its pretty inner courtyards) and the Calle de Mármoles (which contains three marble Roman columns).

Fábrica de Tabacos
(Calle/San Fernando.)

The former state tobacco factory, built in 1757, which today houses parts of Seville University is a huge edifice standing just South of the Alcázar gardens, on the other side of Calle San Fernando. It's the second largest building in Spain after El Escorial. At its peak, the factory employed over 10,000 women and produced three quarters of Europe's cigars. It was so huge that it had over 100 courtyards and was divided into residential and industrial zones. Its most famous *cigarrera* was Carmen, the Triana Gypsy heroine of Prosper Mérimée's novel and George Bizet's opera. Alexander Dumas was just one of several 19th-century visitors:

> It is amazing to see its pretty young work-girls all smoking in the street like veterans or chewing tobacco like old sailors . . . They are allowed to use as much tobacco as they like in working hours, and if some also finds its way into their pockets that may explain why no cigarrera is ever without her escort of a young subaltern or handsome officer of the merchant navy.

Maria Luisa Park and the Plaza de España

The beautiful gardens of Maria Luisa Park, stretching south beyond the university, were laid out in 1929 for a Spanish-American trade fair. Dozens of pavilions were erected and the Plaza de España with its towering twin spires and semi-circular colonnade was designed to be the fair's focal point. Unfortunately world economic depression meant the fair wasn't successful but today the park, with its beautiful subtropical gardens, is the perfect city escape. You can hire boats on the moat of the Plaza de España, which is crossed by pretty blue-tiled bridges. The 58 *azulejo* scenes around the pavilion represent historical scenes from all the provinces in Spain.

The Hospital de la Caridad

(Calle/Temprano. Open 10.00–13.00 and 15.30–19.00.)
The real-life model for the original Don Juan is supposed to have commissioned this hospital for the sick and the poor, which stands between the Giralda and the river. After a life of indulgence, and the death of his wife, Don Manuel de Manara joined the Caridad Brotherhood – a charity fraternity which provided Christian burial for executed criminals. In 1661 he commissioned the Hospital de la Caridad as a place of refuge, which took in the sick and the poor. He spent the rest of his life running it. The façade of the chapel is decorated with beautiful *azulejos* (said to have been designed by Murillo, a friend of Manara) representing Faith, Hope, Love, St George and St Roch. Inside are Manara's tomb, paintings by Murillo on the theme of mercy, and two by Valdes Leal on the theme of death. One is particularly gory and shows a bishop's body being eaten by worms.

The Torre del Oro

(Paseo de Cristobal Colon. Open 10.00–14.00; closed Mondays.)
There are two theories of how the waterside Torre del Oro – literally, Tower of Gold – got its name. The first is that it came from the tiles of pure gold that allegedly covered the exterior. The second is that it was a repository for gold brought back from the New World. Whatever the 12-sided tower's former glory, today it houses a small maritime museum and stands like a lost castle turret stranded on the banks of the Guadalquivir.

Like the Giralda, the Torre del Oro is a landmark of Seville. It was built in 1220 by the Almohades to protect the river, and was connected to the old alcazar. It was also connected, by a chain, to another tower on the other side of the river.

This would be stretched across if Christian boats tried to attack.

The Bullring
(*M. de Toros*), Seville's famous bullring, the Maestranza, is further up Paseo de Cristobal Colon, set back from the river Guadalquivir close to the Triana bridge. It dates from the mid-18th century and is one of the oldest in Spain. Bullfights are held every Sunday from April to October and throughout the April Feria. In Bizet's opera, Carmen was murdered here and opposite the bullring a statue of her stands by the river.

Triana Quarter
Across the Guadalquivir, the old port area on the west side of the river is the traditional working-class and Gypsy barrio and therefore home of Seville's flamenco artists and bullfighters. There is a statue of Belmonte, one of Seville's most illustrious toreros, near Triana bridge. It is also the traditional pottery area – Cerámica Santa Ana is the oldest in the citys. Its original name, Trajana, is Roman and came from the emperor Trajan. Calle Betis, which runs along the river, is a good bet for nightclubs and restaurants.

ALSO WORTH SEEING ...

Museo de Bellas Artes (Fine Arts Museum)
(Plaza del Museo, 9. Open 10.00–14.00 and 16.00–19.00; closed Mondays and Sunday afternoons.)
The former Convento del Merced, built in the early 17th century around a beautiful cloister, now houses an excellent collection of mainly Spanish art. There are 20 rooms of paintings from the 13th–20th centuries, including works by Velázquez, Goya and El Greco, and some of the best Murillos and Zurbaráns.

The Alameda de Hercules
This promenade in the north of the city was a swamp until the land was reclaimed in the 16th century. At each end are two columns. Those on the south side represent Hercules and

Caesar, the legendary founders of the city. The Alameda leads
you to the edges of La Macarena.

Casa de Pilatos
(Plaza de Pilatos. Open in summer 9.00–13.00 and 15.00–
19.00; 9.00–13.00 and 15.00–18.00.)
According to local myth, Don Fadrique, 1st Marquis of Tarifa,
returned from Jerusalem in 1519 with sketches of Pontius
Pilate's house and had his own version built in Seville. It
is an interesting mix of Gothic, Mudéjar and Renaissance
styles. The house is on two floors and, rather cheekily, they
make you buy a ticket for each one. If time and money
are limited, stick to the ground floor – the exquisite patios
are scattered with Roman statues and busts and the *azulejo*
decorations are beautiful, Upstairs you're not trusted to walk
round the interior rooms alone and must wait to be shown
round in a group.

The Archaeological Museum
(Plaza de América. Open 10.00–14.00; closed Sundays and
Mondays.)
This excellent museum down in the southern part of the
city, at the far end of Parque de María Luisa, portrays the
full history of the region – from 4,000-year-old Palaeolithic
pendants to modern flamenco dresses. There are wonderful
Roman mosaics and statues from Italica.

La Macarena Quarter
In the working-class, northern section of the city you will
find a large stretcth of the original Moorish walls and
next to the Macarena gate a church housing the famous
statue of the same name – the **Virgin of Macarena**. Known
as the Virgin of the Sorrows because of the glass tears
on her cheeks, this is one of the symbols of Seville and
star of the Semana Santa processions. No one is sure of
her origins but legend has it that Macarena was an Arab
princess. During the Semana Santa, she competes with her
two main rivals for popularity – the Jesús del Gran Poder
(sculpted by Juan de Mesa in 1620, it stands in its basilica
on the Plaza de San Lorenzo) and the Virgin known as the

Esperanza de Triana (in a chapel on called Pureza in the Triana quarter). Both Virgins have been adopted by bullfighters as patron saints.

FACTFILE

Tourist Office, Avenida de la Constitution, 21. Tel 22 14 04. Just south of the cathedral. Open Monday – Saturday 9.30–19.30, Sundays until 13.00. Get their map of the Barrio Santa Cruz. They also issue lists and maps of all *fondas* and *camas*.

Airport Aeropuerto San Pablo, Carretera de Carmona, (about 12 km out of town. Tel: 51 06 77. (Iberia, Calle Almirante Lobo, 2. Tel: 22 89 01.) There is no longer a bus link between the airport and the centre of town but it might be reinstated. The only connection is by taxi.

Trains Estación de Córdoba, Plaza de Armas, 56. Tel: 22 18 28; RENFE information, Tel: 41 41 11. RENFE office Calle Zaragoza, 29, off Plaza Nueva. Frequent departures to all major destinations (Madrid, Granada and Málaga five per day, Córdoba 12 per day). Estación de Cádiz/San Bernardo Calle San Bernardo, 13. Tel: 41 43 60. Seven trains per day.

Bus Station, Calle (Prado de San Sebastian, 1. Tel: 41 71 11. All the large companies operate out of here: Alsina Graells to other parts of Andalusia; Transportes Comes to Cádiz, Los Amarillos to Ronda, La Union de Benisa to Madrid, Valencia and Barcelona, Estación Damas on Calle Segura, 18 (Tel: 22 63 00), serves Huelva. La Estellesa on Calle Arenal, 7 (Tel: 22 58 20), serves Badajoz.

Car Hire Avis, Avenida de la Constitución, 15. Tel: 21 53 70. Hertz, Avenida Republica Argentina, 3. Tel: 27 88 87. Record Car Rentals.

Dial-a-taxi Tel: 62 04 61.

Post Office Avenida de la Constitución, 32. Tel: 22 88 80.

Telefónica Plaza Nueva, 3, Open Monday-Friday 9.00–14.00 and 17.30–22.00, Saturday 10.00–14.00. Code for Seville 954.

Consulates UK: Plaza Nueva, 8. Tel: 22 88 75. USA: Paseo de las Delicias, 7. Tel: 28 18 84.

Police Plaza de la Gravidia. Tel: 22 88 40, emergency 091.

Hospitals Hospital de la Universidad, Avenida Dr Fedriani. Tel: 37 84 00. Casa de Socorro, Tel: 38 24 61.

Lost property Calle Almansa, 21. Tel: 21 26 28.

WHERE TO STAY

Accommodation in Seville is generally more expensive than in other Spanish cities but there is plenty of it. High season is March or April during Semana Santa and the April Feria when room prices double or even treble and accommodation can be almost impossible to find.

The most sought-after rooms at any time are in the narrow alleyways and tiny squares of the Barrio Santa Cruz, the picturesque old Jewish quarter near the cathedral. A pleasant alternative is the central area on the other side of the Avenida de la Constitución, between the cathedral and the bullring and the more expensive streets below the Plaza Nueva. Surprisingly nice is the area around the Estacion de Córdoba and the Museo de Bellas Artes. There are also several *hostales* in the commercial and pedestrianized Calle San Eloy. Anything farther north of the main shopping part is usually cheaper but also more dangerous, especially around Calle Quintana and Calle Cervantes, which is the red-light district. Fortunately, Seville is easily covered on foot so no matter where you are based, everywhere is within walking distance.

The tourist office supplies lists of *hostales*, *fondas*, and *camas*. Here are a few of our new recommendations:

Santa Cruz Area

CHEAP TO MODERATE: **Córdoba** Calle Farnasio, 12. Tel: 22 74 98. Right and then left at the end of Mateos Gago. **Hostal Residencia** run by an entire family; the father even irons the sheets. It stands in a quiet alleyway with a pretty patio, and has clean modern bathrooms (showers extra). Very squeaky beds. Good value.

Casa Huéspedes Fabiola, Calle Fabiola, 16. Tel: 21 83 46. Close to the above, down a small alley off the main street. Clean but more expensive than the Córdoba. It has a nice patio and a terrace.

Hostal Residencia Monreal, Calle Rodrigo Caro, 8. Tel: 21 41 66. In the heart of Santa Cruz. Very popular owing to its location – a real Eurotravellers' hang-out. Comfortable rooms, some with neo-Mudéjar ceilings. It can be noisy at night because of all the bars outside. Prices reasonable (apart from the showers) except in high season when they become quite extortionate.

Toledo, Calle Santa Teresa, 15, off Plaza Santa Cruz. Tel: 21 53 35. One of the more reasonably priced *hostales* for rooms with en suite bathrooms in such a good, quiet location. Pretty courtyard.

Goya, Calle Mateos Gago, 31. Tel: 21 11 70. Has the appearance of a two-star hotel. Courteous staff. Most of its rooms have showers. However, prices are surprisingly lower than might be expected and a lot cheaper than some of its cheaper-looking neighbours.

Marco de la Giralda, Calle Abades, 30. Tel: 22 83 24. In a small street running north off Mateos Gago, close to the cathedral. More expensive but recently refurbished and extremely clean.

Sanchez Sabariego, Calle Corral del Rey, 23. Tel: 21 44 70. Carry on up Calle Abades and bear right. Run by a friendly and helpful lady with one of the nicest patios in Seville. Not the cheapest but not unreasonable.

Pension Archeros, Calle Archeros, 23, close to Plaza Curtidores Tel: 41 84 65. Two others in the same street. Lower-budget option but clean, simple and friendly.

Casa Diego, Plaza Curtidores, 7. Tel: 41 35 52. Simple again, with new bathrooms. Good value. There is another slightly cheaper C.H next door at No. 6.

SMARTER OPTIONS   **Murillo,** Calle Lope de Rueda, 7. Tel 21 60 95.

In the heart of Santa Cruz. A two-star establishment with simple rooms overlooking narrow streets and geranium-decked balconies. Very close to the Alcazar gardens.

Doña Maria, Calle Don Remondo, 19. Tel: 22 49 90. Opposite the Giralda, Extremely smart – it is one of the best hotels in Seville. Originally an early 19th-century private villa. Wonderful views of the Giralda from its rooftop terrace (which is complete with a tiny swimmingpool) and four-poster beds in some of its rooms.

West and Northwest of the Cathedral

CHEAP TO MODERATE   La Castellana, Calle Gamazo, 17. Tel: 22 08 95. South of the Plaza Nueva, close to both the bullring and the cathedral. A friendly, well-run family *hostal.* Good value.

Camas Romero, Calle Gravina, 21. Tel: 21 13 53. Near the station, but in a nice, relatively quiet side street in which there are many other *hostales.* Very clean, simple, pretty attic-like rooms. Spotless modern bathroom.

Londres, Calle San Pedro Martir, 1. Tel: 21 28 96. In a street perpendicular to Calle Gravina. Large *azulejoed* hall. Most rooms have bathrooms. More expensive but good value for money.

SMARTER OPTIONS   Simon, Calle García Vinuesa, 19. Tel: 22 66 60. In a street perpendicular to the Avenida de la Constitución and close to the cathedral. An 18th-century Sevillian mansion with a plant-filled patio complete with fountain. The landings are elaborately decked out with antique furniture, ornaments and mirrors but the rooms are simple and prices actually very reasonable.

Sevilla, Calle Daoiz, 6. Tel: 38 41 61. North of the Plaza Nueva in a little plaza in the centre of town. Comfortable rooms with old-fashioned furnishings and yet another lovely patio. Slightly more expensive than the Simon.

WHERE TO EAT

Eating out in Seville is not cheap. Sevillians themselves appear to prefer *tapas* and *raciones* to full-fledged meals. Restaurants, apart from the obviously tourist-oriented ones and a few expensive options, tend to reflect this preference. As an alternative to *tapas* there is always the excellent *pescaito frito,* or fried fish, from the *freidurias* for which this part of Andalusia is noted. Take it into the next-door bar or bodega and enjoy it with a beer or a well-chilled fino. It's OK to do this – everyone else does. Here are a few suggested places to eat and drink.

Town Centre

As you would expect, there are lots of predominantly tourist restaurants around the cathedral and into Santa Cruz. Some are not bad and you will often find locals in them as well. If you don't want to be surrounded by tourists, eat later on in the evening. The *tapas* bars especially overflow with young Spaniards.

CHEAP TO MODERATE   **La Abundancia/Buffet Libre**, Avenida de la Constitución, 10. Pay a set price and help yourself as many times as you like to a buffet selection of seafood, paella, salad etc. There is another restaurant of the same name near the station at Marques de Paradas, 16.

Guadalquivir, Calle García de Vinuesa, 21. Café-bar with excellent-value *platos combinados*. Good chocolate and *churros* in the mornings.

Pez Espada, Calle Hernando Colon, 18, north of the cathedral. More *platos combinados* but their speciality, as the name suggests, is fried fish. Lively, busy bar.

Alcazabar, Calle Mateos Gago, 6. One of the better tourist restaurants near the cathedral. Their *platos combinados* vary in quality but they do a good gazpacho and an excellent *espinacas con langoustinas*. Rather slow service.

Chinese Restaurant: Calle Mateos Gago, 4. A choice of single set menus on Thursdays, Fridays and Saturdays. At other times their set meal for two is good value if not particularly imaginative.

Artesano, Calle Mateos Gago, 9. Nice pizzas that are a long time coming.

Casa Diego, Plaza de Curtidores, 7. Cheap and cheerful. Good gazpacho and kebablike *brochetas* of meat and fish.

Casa Modesto, Calle Cano y Cueto, 5, near Plaza de Refinadores. Popular, friendly *tapas* bar downstairs with a wide variety to choose from. The *angulas* and *coquinas* are good. There is a pricier dining room upstairs.

El 3 de Oro, Calle Santa Maria la Blanca, 34. Near the above. Cafeteria with very nice *platos combinados* and a few house specialities. A good place for breakfasts, too (it opens at 8.00).

Bodega Góngora, Calle Albareda, 5, just north of the Plaza Nueva. Popular seafood *racione* bar with tables on the pavement outside. Ask for a *pata de fero*, the local brand of fino.

Rincon de San Eloy, Calle San Eloy, 24. Cheap, simple menus on offer in this pretty bar with *azulejos* and bullfighting posters.

Jalea Real, Calle Sor Angela de la Cruz, 37, on the corner of Calle Jerónimo Hernandez. A high-standard vegetarian restaurant with interesting, imaginative Spanish dishes. Very reasonable prices and excellent value.

SMARTER OPTIONS   **Enrique Becarra**, Calle Gamazo, 2. Tel: 21 30 49. Closed Sundays. Between the cathedral and the Plaza Nueva. Good-quality Andalusian cuisine with an excellent *tapas* bar.

El Meson, Calle Dos de Mayo, 26. Tel: 21 30 75. Closed Mondays. South of the bullring. A well-known bullfighter and tourist haunt. Its walls are covered in torero memorabilia and pictures of American celebrities. As you would expect, bull steak is a favourite dish.

El Figon del Cabildo, Calle Arfe, 8, on Plaza de Cabildo. In a pretty square between the cathedral and the bullring on two floors with an open-air terrace, it is another restaurant with bullfighting traditions, hence the *rabo de toro*. Try also the artichoke hearts with *anoulas* or the steaks with prawns. Their desserts are excellent.

Restaurante San Francisco, Plaza San Francisco, 10. Tel: 22 20 56. Housed in an 18th-century townhouse. It serves delicious *nouvelle*-Spanish food.

Don Raimundo, Calle Argote de Molina, 26. Tel: 22 33 55. Just north of the cathedral, down a flowery alleyway. The building, originally a 17th-century convent, has high ceilings with columns and chandeliers. Elaborate dishes include clam soup with pine nuts, partridge in sherry and venison in *mazarabe* sauce.

There are several quite pricey tourist restaurants in the small squares of the **barrio Santa Cruz**, for example **La Albarca**, Plaza Santa Cruz, 12 (Tel: 22 07 14), set in a lovely, atmospheric old mansion with an open-air terrace; **Hostería del Laurel**, Plaza de los Venerables, 5 (Tel: 22 02 95), primarily a restaurant but with a good *tapas* (especially ham) bar in the front; and **Meson del Moro**, Calle Meson del Moro, 6 (Tel: 21 87 96), which is a restored 12th-century Moorish bath house with specialities such as *corvina* (a local sea bass) *à la marinera* and *robalo al hinojo* (sea perch with fennel).

Across the River

The working-class Triana district has an attractive riverfront with traditional bars and bodegas behind. The youth-oriented Los Remedios district has its trendy clubs, bars and fast-food restaurants.

CHEAP TO MODERATE **Kiosco de las Flores**, Plaza del Altozano. Cross over the Puente Isabel II and it is down the stairs on your left. More of a shack than a bar, it has outside tables and some of the best fried fish in town. The prawns in particular are superb.

Bar Kiki, Calle Pages del Corro, 76. A real workers' bar with traditional and very cheap *tapas* and a *comedor* at the rear.

Sol y Sombra, Calle Castilla, 151. A very pretty bar with walls covered in faded photographs. Excellent *tapas* of squid, anchovies and *solomillo al ajo* (beef in garlic).

El Puerto, Calle Betis, 59. Tel 27 17 25. Closed Mondays. On the riverside with a terrace overlooking the Torre del Oro. The restaurant itself is not cheap but the bar has delicious *tapas* which you can take outside.

El Amanecer, Calle Asunción, 8. A Mexican bar with Mexican food which only gets going after 22.30. Young, trendy atmosphere.

Tel-Aviv, Calle Virgen de la Estrella. In a street parallel to Virgen de Lujan, off Calle Asunción. Inexpensive Jewish cuisine.

SMARTER OPTIONS **El Mero**, Calle Betis, 2. Tel: 21 53 76. On the riverfront, this popular restaurant serves slightly more up-market *pescaito frito* and other typical dishes.
La Dorada, Calle Virgen de Aguas Santas, 6. Tel 45 51 00. Closed Sunday evenings and some of July and August. One of the best seafood restaurants in Seville with specialities such as *sopa de mariscos* and *dorada* and *lubina* baked in salt. Family atmosphere.

BARS AND NIGHTLIFE

As in the rest of Spain, people in Seville get going late and carry on going even later. The young crowd of Seville pour into the narrow tree-lined streets of Santa Cruz on hot summer evenings and overflow from the many small bars on to the pavements, creating an animated and lively ambience. If you don't fancy a restaurant meal, it is possible to eat at many of these bars. These are a few of our favourites:

Central Area

Cervecería La Giralda, Calle/Mateos Gago, 3. Looks like Seville's equivalent to London's Soho Brasserie. A well-known, favourite haunt. Tables outside and Moorish stucco work and arches inside. Good *tapas* if you can read the blackboard. Touristy but also full of well-dressed young Spaniards.
Bodega Santa Cruz, Calle/Rodrigo Caro, 1. Almost opposite the former. So crowded, especially at weekends, that it is almost impossible to reach the bar. Come early and try their hot roquefort sandwich and *vino de naranja*.
La Gitanilla, Calle/Ximenez de Enciso. Right on the corner, a typical Andalusian *azulejo* bar where local university students often come and play flamenco and *sevillanas*. Some *tapas* available behind the counter.
Las Teresas, Calle/Ximenez de Enciso, 16. Placido, the proprietor, is a Sevillian institution in this old-fashioned shop and bodega. Excellent, but expensive, *tapas* of *jamón serrano* and *lomo*.
Queipiriña Calle/Rodrigo Caro. Its name might be that of a Brazilian cocktail but this is another typically Sevillian bar. Dimly lit, it is more subdued than its neighbours.
Bar Lucas, Calle/Doncellas. Get chatting to Lucas; both his French and his English are better than most people's Spanish. You might not appreciate his artwork but his tiny hole-in-the-wall bar is as charming as he is. Since he is friendly with local flamenco artists, you might be lucky enough to see some spontaneous action.
Casa Morales, Calle/García Vinuesa, 11. An ancient and run-down sherry bodega with huge butts and barrels all around and a battered

wooden counter. Bring in your *pescaito frito* from the *freiduria* opposite and sample the inexpensive house fino.

The unnamed bar farther down the same street at No. 20 is long and narrow with a room at the back with tables. Very noisy and crowded.

El Rinconcillo, Calle/Gerona, 40. On a corner opposite the Iglesia de Santa Catalina, this 17th-century establishment has hardly changed since then and is one of the most famous bars in Seville. Wonderful *azulejoed* exterior; inside, the walls are covered in bottles and there are marble-topped tables to eat your ham and cheese *tapas* off.

Bar Alicantina, Plaza del Salvador, 2. Modern, uninspirational decor but many tables outside in the square. Good seafood *tapas* and *raciones* – try their clams in bechamel sauce.

Patio de San Eloy, Calle/San Eloy, 9. In the centre of town. Large and cavernous, it has a patio and tables and gets very busy both at lunchtimes and in the evenings. Impressive plates of ham and cheese.

La Carbonería, Calle/Levies, 18. Near the Plaza las Mercedarias, off Calle/Santa Maria la Blanca at the far end of the barrio Santa Cruz. Formerly a coalhouse, it is now home to a large two-roomed bar. Each part has its own distinct character; the cosier front room has two fireplaces – one elaborately carved wood, the other a functioning stone one – high ceilings and whitewashed brick walls. The back room has more of a summer-camp or student-union feel. Outside is a lovely patio with palm trees. There are live performances of different types of music here most nights with flamenco guitar and singing on Thursdays. If you are in a group, ask for a jug of their Agua de Sevilla, the divine local concoction.

Abades, Calle/Abades, 13, to the north of the cathedral. A far more sedate and sophisticated atmosphere prevails in this 18th–19th-century mansion with its beautiful plant-filled patio, fountain and classical music. The bar serves cocktails.

El Soneto, Calle/Dos de Mayo, 10. A relaxed and comfortable cocktail bar which serves a wonderful variety of creations, including an authentic *sangría*, a delicious Agua de Sevilla, and a potent Irish coffee. Don't be put off by the tasteless neon sign outside.

Poseidon, Calle/Marques de Parada, 30, near the Estación de Córdoba. Pub/disco (no cover) in the patio of a restored town house. Gay – but less exclusively than some of the neighbouring clubs and bars on Calle/Trastamara.

Sol Jazz, Calle/Sol, 40. Formerly known as BeBop. Open 23.00–4.00, with a small cover charge. Jazz club wilt live music at weekends plus improvisation. Try their rum-based drink called *mojito*.

Blue Moon, Calle/Roldana, 5. Small and smoky jazz club.

Across the River

Most of the traditional bars in Triana are situated along Calle/Castilla and in the streets off Plaza Santa Ana. Along the riverfront on Calle Betis there are many bars and pubs and a straightforward disco – **RRIo** at No. 67. Along Calle/Salado, parallel to Republica Argentina, there is a string of bars which feature *sevillana* music and dancing. They open late with a small cover charge.

Bodega Siglo XVII, Calle/Pelay Correra, 32. A restored 16th-century building with columns and arches and old-style furniture. Local flavour.

Bar 518, opposite the Iglesia Santa Ana. The lifetime ambition of the owner of this little bar is to transform the interior into a replica of the Mezquita at Córdoba. At present the *azulejo* arches are only half-finished . . .

Los Chiringuitos, Recinto Ferial, at the end of Calle Asunción. Open for the 11½ months of the year when the Feria isn't being held. A rambling collection of outdoor bars and stalls on the fairground.

EM, farther south on Calle García Morato, opposite the bridge. An outside disco.

La Recua, farther south still on the Carretera de Cádiz, opposite the Military School and Hospital. Only open on Fridays and Saturdays. This outdoor club *discoteca* with gardens, tropical plants and swimming pool is an ideal location for the end of a hot summer night.

FLAMENCO SHOWS

Apart from the clubs you can visit to dance or watch *sevillanas* or listen to spontaneous guitar and *cante jondo*, various places offer professional flamenco spectacles or shows known as *tablaos flamenco*. The performances here are usually tourist-oriented and, though slick and colourful, lack some of the passion and intensity found in more authentic (but hard to find) locations. Nevertheless, unless you are prepared to track down local schools or *peìas*, they provide the most accessible, albeit pricey, means of experiencing this fascinating art form.

LOS GALLOS, Plaza Santa Cruz, 11. Tel: 21 69 81 for reservations. Shows begin at 21.30 but don't arrive before midnight or you will see only a pale representation of what the performers are capable of. The converted townhouse provides an ideally intimate setting. Steep cover charge includes the price of the first drink.

ARENAL/TABLAO DE CURRO VELEZ, Calle Rodo, 7. Tel: 21 64 92. Shows begin at 22.30.

EL PATIO SEVILLANO, Paseo de Colon, 11. Tel: 21 41 20. Close to the Plaza de Toros.

PLUS . . .

- On Sunday mornings in the scruffy Alameda de Hércules, there is a mini-version of Madrid's Rastro or **flea market**. Browse among the junk and "antiques". Rather a dodgy area.

- Also on Sunday mornings, in the Plaza de la Alfalfa, there is an **animal market** selling mostly birds and bunnies.

- Across the river in Triana, don't miss the **Cerámica Santa Ana** (turn right over the bridge – Puente Isabel – and you'll see the wonderful *azulejo* faade). Here you can wander among the vast selection of *azulejo* tiles, bowls etc. If you're not up to a complete set, how about a single tile of Seville's Madonna of the Macarena? All at factory prices – more expensive in the shop across the road.

- Get your **take away churros** from a little shop in Calle Arfe, 22. Ultrafresh.

- If *churros* aren't you scene, try the **cake shop** at the top end of Calle Sierpes – Confitería La Campana.

- **Burn off the calories** with a pedalo ride on the Guadalquivir and get a great view of Seville's landmarks from the water. On hire from Calle Betis opposite the Torre del Oro.

OUT OF TOWN . . .

Italica

The ruins of this twin city to Hispalis (Roman Seville) bear witness to the original size and importance of this Roman settlement, founded in the 3rd century BC. Three Roman emperors (Trajan, Hadrian and Theodosius) were born here and you can still see the remains of the third largest amphitheatre in the Roman world (it had a capacity of 30,000), some fine mosaics and the foundations of houses and street systems.

Although 9 km out of town, it is easily reached by bus which goes from just near the Plaza de Armas/Estación de Córdoba on Calle Marques de Paradas to the village of Santiponce. The site is open daily except Monday, 9.00–19.30.

Carmona

If you are en route to Córdoba, you might consider stopping off at this attractive, miniature Seville, complete with its own little Giralda. It was once an important Roman city (from which an enormous and fascinating underground necropolis remains), and subsequent Moorish occupation left behind the Puerta Sevillana, an impressive horseshoe-shaped gateway. Pedro the Cruel favoured Carmona as a summer retreat and built a palace here (it was destroyed in an earthquake in 1504). There are also some interesting Renaissance churches and a collection of fine mansions.

Carmona makes an easy day trip from Seville; should you want to stay, there is a choice between a couple of cheap *fondas* near the old gateway or the luxury *parador* in part of Pedro's old palace. It is also worth noting that, together with nearby Ecija, it is one of the hottest places in Spain.

Osuna

Halfway between Seville and Antequera, Osuna makes another interesting stop-off point. It is famous for its dukes, mansions and enormous university and Iglesis Colegiata (theological college) which overlook the town.

The Sierra Morena

This low-lying mountain range stretches across Andalusia to form its northern boundary. It is little visited but with its pretty white villages, cool air and lush scenery it makes lovely walking country or simply a pleasant excursion.

Aracena is the Sierra's main town, an attractive hillside spot dominated by the ruins of a Knights Templar castle. Its main claim to fame, however, is its truly spectacular underground cave of stalactites, stalagmites and lakes – La Gruta de las Maravillas. A guided tour takes you round the different chambers. They each have their own names – from the romantic La Pozo de la Nieve (Snow Well) to the equally appropriate Sala de los Culos (Buttock Room). Open daily 10.00–18.30.

If you want to stay in Aracena, a good bet would be the **Casa Carmen** on Calle Mesones (Tel: 11 07 64) which has a nice restaurant next door. Hotel **Sierpes** (Tel: 11 01 47) in the same street is a bit more upmarket but still good value. Restaurant **Casas** next to the caves is excellent.

It is worth remembering that this is prime *jamón serrano* (mountain-cured ham) country. Jabugo nearby is reputed to produce the best in the whole of Spain – try the acorn-fed version, the *jamón de bellotas*. Jabugo is also one of many pretty villages around Aracena that are worth exploring. Another scenic detour is to the cliff-hanging village of Zufre, just off the Seville road, which rivals both Ronda and Cuenca.

COSTA DE LA LUZ: HUELVA PROVINCE

Spain's undeveloped Costa de la Luz stretches from Ayamonte on the Portuguese border to Tarifa at the gateway to the Mediterranean. It owes its name to the luminous expanses of white sandy beaches. Almost deserted, they are washed by a clean Atlantic Ocean and cooled by offshore breezes. There is little tourist development, and what there is tends to be Spanish.

The coast is divided into two provinces – Huelva and Cádiz – and is split by the wetlands or *marismas* at the mouth of the Guadalquivir River. These cannot be crossed and connections must be made via Seville.

The city of **Huelva** itself is a mass of sprawling industrialization and is best avoided. Little remains of the old town – it was flattened by the same earthquake that destroyed Lisbon in 1755. Today vast petrochemical refineries scar the landscape, ruining what was once a beautiful estuary. The rest of the province, however, away from these eyesores, is mostly unspoiled with long beaches and pine-covered dunes. Here we take a look down the coast, starting from the Portuguese border.

Ayamonte and Isla Cristina

Both fishing villages, the border town of Ayamonte is less interesting as a place to stay than nearby Isla Cristina, a low-key holiday resort that the Spanish have been coming to for years. It has a marvellous beach backed by eucalyptus trees and several discos, cafés and *tapas* bars, especially along the pretty quayside.

Hotels are likely to be fully booked in summer – try **Hotel Los Geranios** on Carretera Isla Cristina Playa (Tel: 955/33 18 00), **Hotel Pato Azul** on Gran Va (Tel: 955/33 13 50) and **El Paraiso Playa** (Tel: 955/33 02 35). They are all quite pricey but have good facilities – the first two have swimming pools. The cheapest accommodation is **Hostal Maty** on Calle Catalanes, 7, Tel: 955/33 18 06.

La Antilla

An expanding resort with some unfortunate high-rise development and lots of private villas. Halfway between the two is **La Redondela**, a good place to stop for a picnic in the pine trees behind the sand dunes.

El Rompido

A lovely fishing village and a charming place to stop but there is only one, quite pricey, hotel – LA GALERA (Tel: 955/39 02 76) on the main road. There are many bars and restaurants in the village by the lighthouse. Farther along is probably the best stretch of the whole coast, at **El Portil**. Backed by pine trees, the beach is superb. Some private development but no facilities whatsoever.

Punta Umbria

The most built-up area in this part of the coast, Punta Umbria has long been a busy Spanish holiday resort. At weekends the road from Huelva is packed, as are the hotels, cafés and discos. Fortunately the lovely, long beach can accommodate everyone. Plenty of facilities.

The cheapest places to stay are **Pension Oliver**, Plaza del Cantábrico, 4 (Tel: 955/31 15 36) and **Hostal Casa Manuela** on Calle Carmen, 6 (Tel: 955/31 07 60). Slightly nicer is **Hostal Playa** on Avenida del Oceano, 77 (Tel 955/31 01 12). Good bus connections to Huelva, only 15 minutes away.

Around Huelva

This is Christopher Columbus country and evidence is all around. In Huelva there is a giant statue of him, donated by the USA in 1929, looking out to sea. Columbus's first voyage set off from Palos de la Frontera and at La Rábida

is the monastery where he found favour when no one else
believed in him.

Mazagon

The best thing about Mazagon is its beach. There are a few
places to stay and eat in the small town but mostly it is
one long stretch of private family villas. On the road to
Matalascanas is the **Parador Cristobal Colon** (Tel: 955/37
60 00). It is modern with a lovely clifftop setting, swimming
pool, beach and good restaurant. The long coastal road from
here on is completely undeveloped and unspoiled – look out
for eagles en route. (Only one daily bus link.)

Torre la Higuera/Matalascanas

The biggest resort and popular as a day trip from Seville
(buses – Empresa Damas from Calle Segura near Plaza
de Armas in Seville). Accommodation is expensive – lots
of high-rise tourist complexes – and impossible to find in
summer. **Camping** is a better bet since there are several
options in the dunes nearby – Camping Rocio (Tel: 43 02
38) or Camping Doñana (Tel: 37 68 89). The beachfront
at Matalascanas is lined with bars and café-type restaurants
plus lots of discos.

Beyond, the deltas of the Guadalquivir form a vast *marisma*
of marshes, dunes and lagoons which have been set aside as
the Doñana National Park.

El Rocio

On the edge of the swampland, this is probably the best place
to stay in the area (in spite of the mosquitoes) because there are
several reasonable *hostales* – **Pension Cristina** at Calle/Real,
32, Tel: 955/40 65 13 and **Hostal Velez** at Calle Rociana, 2,
Tel: 955/40 61 17.

It is a quiet, spread-out village with boarded-up cottages
and sandy roads but one week a year it hosts probably
the most important pilgrimage in Spain – the Romeria del
Rocio.

Parque Nacional De Doñana

This important nature reserve is home to many wetland species of animals, some rare, as well as being a prime resting and breeding ground for thousands of migratory birds. One theory says it gets its name from Queen Doña Ana, who favoured the area.

The park can be visited on prearranged tours (phone ahead on 955/43 02 32) from the following reception/information areas:

- La Rocina: just outside El Rocio with footpaths to the edge of the park. Tel: 955/61 40.
- El Acebuche: farther down the road with a footpath to the Laguna del Acebuche. Land-Rover tours leave twice a day from here and last about four hours.

CÁDIZ

Considering the English have been coming to Cádiz for at least 400 years, you'd think there would be more of them here today. But like most foreigners they go elsewhere in Spain for their holidays so the city is unburdened by tourists. Those Cádiz does get tend to be Spanish, which is one reason why its ancient maritime atmosphere remains refreshingly unspoiled.

The old city, a huddle of weatherbeaten white houses hiding behind 17th-century sea walls, is almost disconnected from Spain. It juts out into the Atlantic like an island and is connected to the mainland by a causeway which houses surburbs and (Spanish) holiday hotels. Although still part of the same modern city, locals talk about visiting Cádiz (or Ca-dee, as it is pronounced in Spanish) when they go into the old part of town.

One of the nicest things to do in Cádiz is to walk out to sea along the mole. There is a ramshackle old café at the end of it where you can enjoy a beer, some *tapas* and a view of the city crowned by its golden-domed cathedral, just as mariners have seen it for centuries. But there are a dozen other pleasures in Cádiz – its beaches, fried fish and nightlife are all excellent and its February carnival is the biggest in the world after those at Rio, Havana and New Orleans.

Romeria Del Rocio

At Pentecost/Whitsun thousands of pilgrims converge on El Rocio to pay tribute to Nuestra Senora del Rocio – Our Lady of the Dew, ROMERIA DEL ROCIO. The "Paloma Blanca", as she is affectionately known, was discovered in the grass by a shepherd long ago and resisted all attempts to move her from this now holy spot. The pilgrims arrive from far and wide in ox-drawn *carretas* or carts, colourfully decorated like Gypsy caravans. Many come on horseback. All are dressed in traditional Andalusian costume. From Saturday to Monday the flamenco and *sevillanas* don't stop and neither does the sherry, interrupted only by midnight Masses. The highlight is the candle-lit procession of the statue which is jostled through the crowds, culminating in an outdoor Mass to several thousands of people. Nobody sleeps for three nights.

Cádiz makes a good base for a trip west along the Costa de la Luz to some pretty Spanish holiday towns such as Sanlucar de Barrameda and Chipiona or east to the huge beaches near Tarifa. These are generally lashed by winds so they are perfect for windsurfing experts but less good for those wanting more sedate beach pleasures.

DON'T MISS ...

Cathedral
The Catedral Nueva (built to replace Santa Cruz – the Catedral Vieja next door) is an awesome Baroque block. With its golden dome of glazed yellow tiles, it was the symbol of the city's prosperity, begun in 1722 and completed in 1838. It houses a treasury containing a chalice by Benvenuto Cellini and the tomb of the Cádiz-born composer Manuel de Falla.

Museo de Cádiz (or Museo Arqueológico de Bellas Artes)
(Plaza de Mina 5. Open Monday–Friday 10.00–14.00 and 17.30–20.00, Saturday 10.00–14.00; closed Sunday.)
This building houses two museums. On the ground floor the archaeological section contains a marble Phoenician sarcophagus testifying to the city's ancient history. Upstairs the

Cádiz was founded as Gadir by the Phoenicians in 1100 BC and claims to be the oldest city in western Europe. The Romans renamed it Gades and turned it into a wealthy port but under the Moors its importance declined. After the discovery of America in 1492 it became one of the richest ports in Europe and a target for attack by the English. In 1587 Sir Francis Drake came to "singe the King of Spain's beard" (he burned the ships at bay that Philip II had prepared for the Armada) and was followed in 1596 by the 2nd Earl of Essex, who destroyed much of the city and its navy (his crew included Sir Walter Raleigh and the poet John Donne). In the 18th century Cádiz became wealthy again when the river Guadalquivir silted up in Seville and the port monopolized trade with America. This gave it much contact with Europe — there was a British factory here and a general of Irish descent (Alexander O'Reilly) became royal governor of the city. In 1805, after being defeated by Nelson at the Battle of Trafalgar, the ruined French and Spanish fleet returned to Cádiz. In 1812 the Liberal Constitution was declared here and the city became the capital of free Spain.

art museum houses some Murillos and a series of Zurbarán saints.

Museo Histórico Municipal

(Caltel Santa Ines, 9. Open Tuesday–Friday 9.00–13.00 and 16.00–20.00, weekends 9.00–13.00; closed Monday) Contains a superb, immensely detailed scale model of Cádiz made from ivory and mahogany in 1779.

Two Chapels

There are two lovely artistic surprises in Cádiz. The chapel of the **Hospital de Mujeres** (open daily 9.00–18.00) has a wonderful El Greco of "St Francis in Ecstasy" and the chapel or **Oratorio de Santa Ceuva** (open Monday–Saturday 10.00–13.00 and 16.00–18.00. Ring the bell on Calle Rosario and wait for the attendant) contains three frescos by Goya.

FACTFILE

Tourist Office; Calle/Calderon de la Barca, 1. Tel: 21 31 13. In

Plaza Mina on the far side of the old city. Open Monday–Saturday mornings only.

Trains: RENFE, Avenida del Puerto. Tel: 25 43 01.

Buses Transportes Generales Comes, Plaza de la Hispanidad, 1. Tel: 21 17 63. Serves Seville, Málaga, Córdoba, Granada and Jerez. Transportes Amarillos, Avenida Ramon de Carranza. Tel: 28 58 52. Serves Sanlucar and Chipiona. When arriving by bus, make sure you wait till you reach the terminus.

Post Office: Plaza Topete. Open 9.00 to 19.00. Post code is 11080.

Telefonica Caal/Sacramento, 44, Open Monday–Friday 9.00 to 14.00 and 18.00 to 21.00; Saturday mornings only.

Police Avenida de Andalucía, 28. Tel: 28 61 11.

WHERE TO STAY

There is plenty of good, cheap accommodation available in the narrow streets of the old town, and since Cádiz has relatively few tourists you should have no problem finding a room except in February when Carnival is on. Most of the *hostales* are situated around the main square of San Juan de Dios, the cathedral and the lovely Plaza de Candelaria.

Cheap to Moderate

Ceuta, Calle Montanes, 7. Tel: 22 16 54. Near Plaza de Candelaria. Homely and friendly with neat clean rooms and nice decorative touches. More expensive than the Barcelona opposite but showers are included so it works out about the same. Run by a helpful lady who'll phone round her friends if she's full.

Barcelona, Calle Montanes, 10. Tel: 21 39 49. Clean, airy rooms, some with enclosed balconies overlooking the church in front. Attention to details such as glasses wrapped in plastic, soap and even an electric mosquito zapper. Showers extra.

Casa Huespedes Marques, Calle Marques de Cádiz, 1. Tel: 18 58 54. Just off San Juan de Dios. Small and friendly with cool patio. Cheap but clean. Most rooms have balconies – ours did and I left some almost new shoes on it (if found please return to the publisher!). Showers extra. Avoid the more expensive and thoroughly unfriendly Pension España at No.9.

El Sardinero, Plaza San Juan de Dios, 3. Tel: 28 53 01. Right on the square next to the restaurant of the same name. Clean, friendly and very central if a little noisy. Showers extra. Good value.

Manolita, Calle Benjumeda, 2. Tel: 21 15 77. Towards the other end of town – a slightly less salubrious area. Rather dilapidated but being done up in 1991. The bathroom is clean but hot showers are only available after 10.00. OK if everywhere else is full.

Smarter Options

Centro Sol, Calle Padre Elejalde, 7. Tel: 28 31 03. Just off Plaza de Candelaria. A cut above the rest but not that much more expensive than other *hostales*. Pleasant and good value.

Imares, Calle San Francisco, 9. Tel: 21 22 57. In a noisy pedestrianized shopping street near Plaza San Francisco. Large, old hotel with a rather dark inner courtyard, marble staircase and balconies. Well-kept by friendly staff.

Francia y Paris, Plaza San Francisco, 2. Tel: 22 23 48. On the pretty little square filled with orange trees, in the heart of the old town. Slightly faded charm. Nice bar and lounge. Breakfast included. More expensive than the others.

WHERE TO EAT

There are several cheap places to eat in Cádiz, especially in and around Plaza San Juan de Dios. But what Cádiz is really famous for is its *freidurias* or fried-fish shops, the local answer to fish-and-chip shops. They do *gambas, calamares, merluza* and potato croquettes, but make sure you try the *cazon* – it is rather like swordfish but cooked in a batter with garlic and vinegar. Delicious – tastes a bit like tandoori chicken! Ask for a *papelon surtido*, a mixed bag, so you can try a bit of everything (it is sold by weight). Eat it in the café next door; the bar tender doesn't mind as long as you have a drink and they'll even give you lemon if you ask. The best are on Calle Veedor near Plaza San Antonio, and Las Flores, near the cathedral. Other good places to eat include:

La Economica, Calle San Fernando, 2, virtually on San Juan de Dios. Cádiz's very own greasy-spoon café. One of the cheapest eating places in Andalusia. Varied menu and varied clientele. Very good swordfish. Next door at Restaurante **El 9** you can have more of the same.

La Caleta, San Juan de Dios, 1. Looks like the inside of a ship. Good mushroom *tapas*.

Bar Terraza, in front of the cathedral. A lovely place for breakfasts at the tables in the square. Toast comes with jam served in a dish – a nice change. They also do some very good *tapas* and lots of different sherries.

Bar Rosario, Calle B. Diego de Cádiz, 3, near Plaza San Francisco. Again popular for breakfasts – good chocolate and *churros*. They also serve *tapas* and do ice cream and *horchata*.

Menor-Donalds, on the corner of Calle Sagasta and Calle San Pedro. Pizza and fast-food joint for teenagers and young trendies.

Punta de San Felipe, at the end of the mole skirting the harbour. A little bar that serves excellent *tapas* and *raciones* of paella, *calamares* etc. Try their *dobladillo* – the special house sandwich that most locals plump for. Wonderful view both day and night.

EL ANTEOJO, Alameda de Apodaca, 22. Tel: 21 36 39. Between the mole and the park, looking out to sea. A more expensive place, it has a downstairs *tapas* bar and a dining room upstairs which serves very good seafood and has a lovely view. Try their *tortilla de camarones*.

BARS & NIGHTLIFE

Cadiz comes alive at night. In winter the liveliest area is in the streets between Plaza Mina and Plaza de Espana, which are full of animated pubs and bars. Try **La Bodeguilla de Cadiz** on Calle San Pedro, 20, with its giant amphora above the bar, or **La Sala** on Calle Sagasta, a smarter bar for a more sophisticated set which stages exhibitions. In summer, attention switches to the Paseo Maritimo, where people cruise up and down from bar to bar. This is where you'll find most of the city's discos, such as **Metropol** on Avenida Cayetano del Toro, 25, or **Kuk** at No.42, and **Bao-Bac** at Paseo Maritimo, 5. For afternoon or early-evening drinking, try the following:

Cervecería Del Puerto, Calle Zorilla, 4. Just off the tropical Plaza Mina, in a pedestrianized side street. One of the most popular bars in town. Traditionally a beer-drinking place, it also serves tasty *tapas*. Very crowded, especially in the evenings when everyone spills out on to the street.

EL PARISIEN, Calle San Francisco, 1. Very popular local bar with good, cheap *tapas*.

BAR VELARDES PLAZA, Plaza San Juan de Dios, corner of Calle Sopranis. Big lively bar in the central square.

CERVECERÍA EL BARRIL, Glorieta Ingeniero La Cierva. Not far out of the old town, along the Paseo Maritimo facing the Playa de la Victoria. Like all the bars and *terrazas* on the seafront, this one buzzes all summer.

Meson Miguel Angel: Plaza Mina. Sit outside in the lovely square where they sometimes put on puppet shows called Tia Norica.

PLUS . . .

• In the colourful area all around the dilapidated old market building on **Plaza de la Libertad,** you will find many traditional little bars serving *tapas*. But to really capture the atmosphere, come early in the day and have fresh *churros* from the stalls for breakfast. During Carnival especially it is a hive of activity.

• Sit outside at the Salon Italiano on Calle Ancha and have one of their **delicious ice creams.** Or, if you prefer to have yours by the sea, head down the Paseo Maritimo to La Jijoneca.

• For **tea and cakes,** head to Salon de te Bonsai on Calle Brasil, 1, just off the top end of the Paseo Maritimo. For **coffee,** try Café-bar El Tinte in Callejon del Tinte near Plaza Mina.

- The exquisite local speciality in the sweet line, **turron,** a sort of nougat or marzipan, can be bought from a cake shop in Calle Compana near the cathedral.

- Buy some dried fruit, nuts or sweets from a little shop, La Barraca, in Calle Antonio Lopez, 18.

COSTA DE LA LUZ:
CÁDIZ PROVINCE

This section of the coast is quite developed around Cádiz itself but further south you'll find more deserted beaches. One of the reasons for this is the incessant winds which have made the resort of Tarifa a windsurfers' paradise. Starting at the river Guadalquivir, you'll reach towns in the following order:

Sanlucar de Barrameda

A historic port that is well worth a visit (don't be put off by the outskirts). Situated on the mouth of the Guadalquivir, it saw the launch of Magellan's circumnavigation and one of Columbus's expeditions.

Nowadays it is famous for its own delicate version of fino called **manzanilla.** Literally translated it means chamomile but tastes nothing like it; some say it has a salty taste from the sea air. Certainly its flavour *is* due to local conditions – if you bring a barrel of fino here from Jerez it will turn into manzanilla. Anyway, it is delicious, light and dry; try some in one of the many bodegas and *tapas* bars in the town. If you're feeling rich, have a huge *langoustina* to go with it – Sanlucar is famous for those, too.

The town is divided into two parts – the Barrio Alto and the Barrio Bajo. In the older streets of the Barrio Alto you will see many mansions and palaces. Down by the quayside is a good area for bars and on the river beach in August horse races are held as part of the local festival. (If you want to stay, **Hostal Blanca Paloma** on Plaza San Roque, 9, Tel: 36 36 44, has big, clean, balconied rooms.)

Chipiona

A traditional Spanish resort with lots of family-run *hostales*, a real Spanish feel and a certain dilapidated charm. How long it will last is another matter – it has just been discovered by tour operators. The best beach is the Playa de Regla, south of the lighthouse and the church of Nuestra Señora de la Regla, which has a fountain of curative water.

Most *hostales* are around here – try VIRGEN DE LAS NIEVES on Avenida del Ejército, Tel: 37 02 89, or GRAN CAPITAN on Calle Fray Baldomero Gonzalez, 7, Tel: 37 09 29. In the pedestrianized part of town there's the nice NUESTRA SEÑORA DE LA O on Calle Isaac Peral, Tel: 37 07 29.

All along Calle Isaac Peral you'll find bars and *freidurias* where you can try the local baby squid and musca-tel wine. It is best to walk, because Chipiona has an infuriating one-way system.

Good beaches extend along the coast to **Rota** with its notorious US naval base. A brasher resort in all respects, full of pizzerias and burger bars and simmering with local resentment.

El Puerto de Santa Maria

This blossoming resort would like to see itself as the Marbella of the Costa de la Luz. It is actually another sherry port; the signs to Puerto Sherry don't lead to the old quayside but to a brand-new marina with Puerto Banus aspirations. Fortunately it has got a long way to go. At the moment it still has a relatively unspoiled air with some nice beaches (although the proximity of the port detracts a little), lovely old mansions belonging to the sherry aristocracy, an important bullring and an active bar and nightlife. The liveliest zone is along the Ribera del Marisco and the Ribera del Rio, which are crowded with excellent *tapas* bars (try the **Ouke-Lele!**). You can spend the day at Aquapark Sherry, the evening at the disco Joy Sherry and sleep it off at Hostal Sherry . . .

The road then winds round the Bahia de Cadiz into the city. Turn off in Chiclana de la Frontera to the beaches of **La Barrosa** and **Sancti Petri**. La Barrosa has villas, bars and cafés in the pine trees. Sancti Petri, on the other hand, has nothing. The Famous Five would have loved it – there is a sheltered beach, a deserted village and a tiny castle-topped island. Ten years ago it thrived on tuna fishing but the local supplies ran out. Today there is only the odd squatting hippie and a small *club maritimo* – just the place for a swim, a picnic and a day's exploring.

Conil de la Frontera

A small, picturesque fishing village with an enormous, wind-swept beach, it is rapidly assuming resort proportions with development going on all around. There are *hostales* in the village but it is impossible to get a room unless you've booked up well in advance. Lots of bars, restaurants and discos and even a flamenco festival in July.

Farther south towards Cape Trafalgar are more beaches, the Trafalgar lighthouse and the small resort of Los Canos de Meca. Historical associations aside, it is a good place to visit if you want peace and quiet. There are a couple of *hostales*, a campsite, a nudist beach and lots of Germans. The cliffs are noted for the ever-decreasing waterfalls.

Vejer de la Frontera

Surprisingly, this hill-top *pueblo blanco* is off the tourist trail. Extremely scenic with great views, it is a charming village of blindingly white cobbled alleyways. Vejer is a lovely place to stay, especially if you come at fiesta time, and Vejer has lots of fiestas – both Easter Sunday and the Feria de Abril are celebrated by an *encierro* or running of the bulls through the streets; at Corpus Christi the streets are decked with flowers; at the Candelas de San Juan soon afterwards they have a miniature *fallas* bonfire; and fesivities in honour of the Virgin of the Olives take place in May and August accompanied by flamenco.

Pension La Janda on Cerro Clarinas (Tel: 45 01 42) is excellent. Failing that, several friendly women rent out rooms – ask for Dona Luisa on Calle San Filmo, 10, or Dona Isabel Lopez on Calle de Amaro; 8. There are lots of typical bars; you might be lucky enough to hear some flamenco at **Pena Flamenca Aguilar de Vejer**.

Zahara de los Atunes

As the name suggests, this little fishing village is all about tuna, just like nearby Barbate de Franco with its canneries. Zahara, however, is much prettier – it has a vast beach but fairly pricey accommodation. **Bolonia** (turn off on the way to Tarifa) has cheaper *hostales*, the interesting Roman ruins of *Baelo Claudia*, a few beach bars and a wild and wonderful beach with stray cows.

Tarifa

Even if you're not a windsurfer, you can still enjoy Tarifa, though it is unlikely you'll appreciate the ferocious wind as much as they do. It is an attractive walled town with a distinctly north African feel – Moroccans hanging around pushing dope and a market that looks like a casbah. It is also the southernmost town in Europe and on a clear day you can see Tangier across the straits. You can even take a ferry there and back in a day.

The long beach starts a little way out of town and is lined with hotels, campsites and windsurfing facilities. In town, there is a lively atmosphere in the evenings at the numerous bars and pubs, especially along Calle San Francisco and in Plaza Sancho IV. There's a great disco called **Tanakas** in an old cinema in the heart of town that is worth a visit (free entry) even if you don't fancy a dance – trendy hard rock downstairs, intimate flamenco upstairs.

For eating, try **El Patio** on Calle Nuestra Señora de la Luz just inside the walls – good salads. The restaurant **Villanueva** (under the *hostal* of the same name) on Avenida de Andalucía, outside the walls, is another good bet. Accommodation is hard to come by and expensive but the Villanueva is good. Also the Hostal **Tarik** on Calle San Sebastian, 36 (Tel: 956–68 52 40) – all rooms have sparkling modern bathrooms and there is a small bar that does breakfast next door.

A luxury option would definitely be the romantically named **Hurricane Hotel** on the main road (Tel: 68 49 19) with a lawn running down to the beach, swimming pool and balconied rooms. It has its own windsurf school, too. Whether you're staying here or not, have a drink in its pastel and palm bar.

JEREZ DE LA FRONTERA

You can smell sherry in the air as soon as you arrive. In fact, "sherry" is an English corruption of the name Jerez. The town is full of bodegas. Most of the firms are familiar household names in Britain at least and it is because of this alcoholic attraction that most people pay a quick visit to the town, if only for the free tasting sessions at the end of the tour.

But there is more to Jerez than sherry; and a day trip to the bodegas doesn't do it justice. Everything that is quintessentially Andalusian – fino, fiestas, flamenco, bulls and horses – thrives here. It is the centre of a rich agricultural area of rolling green hills, known for breeding fine *toros bravos* or fighting bulls. And even better known are its horses, the beautiful Arab stallions that perform at the celebrated Equestrian School. It is also considered to be the cradle of flamenco, which is very much alive and kicking in Jerez. Twice a year, Jerez stages its two unique festivals – the Horse Fair in May and the Sherry Harvest in September – where all these colourful traditions come together.

The town is clean and modern with a small old quarter, and it has a gentrified and prosperous feel, making it a very pleasant place to visit. It also makes an excellent base from which to explore the popular tourist routes nearby.

GETTING YOUR BEARINGS:

It is very easy to get lost coming into Jerez by car; it is poorly signposted. Once in the centre, which is the area around Plaza del Arenal, parking is not hard to find but is metered until 18.00. There is an official car park near the alcazar, close to Plaza del Arenal. If you arrive by train or bus, the stations are about a 10-minute walk from the centre along Calle Medina or Calle Diego Fernandez. The main artery is the Calle Larga, which runs north of the central plaza and leads up to the tourist office, the Equestrian School and the Avenida Alvaro Domecq with its smart hotels and fairground. The old part

> The Phoenician town of Sert or Ceret became known as Asido Caesaris by the Romans, who imported the *vinum ceretanum* mentioned by Pliny for their own use. When the Moors took it over, they called it Scheres or Xeres and built a castle and city walls. Captured by the Christians in 1264, it subsequently became one of their frontier towns, hence *de la frontera*. During the 16th and 17th centuries it flourished with agricultural and wine exports to the New World. England had been importing sack, as sherry was first known, for some time and a few aristocratic British Catholic families settled here as refugees, developing its trade. In 1608, the distinctive wine became known as sherry (derived from the town's name of Xeres) in England. When England was looking for alternatives to French wines in the 18th century, the British sherry trade really took off. Big shipping families emigrated here; many of the large sherry firms have English names and are owned by families with aristocratic landowning traditions who are descended from these British roots. English is still the second language in Jerez.

of town is to the west of the main square and north of the alcazar and cathedral.

DON'T MISS . . .

Real Escuela de Andaluza de Arte Equestre
(Royal Andalusian School of Equestrian Art), Avenida Duque de Abrantes. (Tel: 31 11 11.)
Every Thursday at noon, a dressage show is put on for the public. Set to music and in 17th-century costume, it is a spectacular form of "equestrian ballet". The entrance is fairly steep but it lasts about an hour and a half and is an incredible display of riding skill.

On other weekdays 11.00–13.00, for a small admission charge, you can watch the horses being exercised in the grounds. The stables are open to visitors at the same time – look out for the wheelbarrows full of carrots.

Fundación Andaluza de Flamenco
(Palacio Premartin, Plaza de San Juan, 1. Entrance free. Open Monday–Friday 10.00–14.00.)

Feria Del Caballo

Held annually at the beginning of May, this week-long horse fair is similar to Seville's. Everyone dresses up and celebrates with singing and dancing in the *casetas* or tents set up on the Recinto Ferial, the fairground, while horse parades and competitions take place. It is less exclusive than the one in Seville. Anyone can join in the drinking and eat *tapas* in the *casetas*. In 1990, Andalusian horses were plagued by disease and both Jerez and Seville were forced to ban horses from the fairs.

Flamenco has a high profile in Jerez. The Fundación Andaluza is study centre promoting flamenco music and dance, and every hour on the hour they run a video in Spanish telling the story of flamenco in the auditorium. Exhibitions are mounted downstairs and you can sometimes watch students practising in the classroom on the top floor.

Other Sights

The **alcázar** was under restoration in 1991. The Gothic **cathedral**, in Plaza de Arroyo, has a monumental staircase.

FACTFILE

Tourist Office, Calle Alameda Cristina, 7. Tel: 31 11 50. At the far end of Calle Larga, Open 8.00–14.00 and 17.00–20.00.
Airport, 7 km out of town on the Carretera Jerez-Sevilla. Tel: 33 56 86 or 33 43 00. Iberia, Plaza Arenal, 2. Tel: 33 99 08.
Trains The lovely station building is at Plaza de la Estacion. Tel: 33 66 82. RENFE office in town on Calle Torneria, 4. Tel: 34 96 12.
Buses, Calle Cartuja. Tel: 34 52 07. Good connections to Seville, Cádiz, Ronda, Granada and Málaga.
Post Office, Calle Ceron, 1, off Calle Fermin Aranda.
Telephones, Plaza del Banco, Code is 956.
Police, Calle Ingeneiro Antonio Gallegos. Tel: 34 35 43, emergency 091.

WHERE TO STAY

There is plenty of reasonable accommodation in Jerez, both in terms of price and quality. The only time you'll encounter problems finding a room is during its two main fairs or while the motorbike championships are being held at the end of April in the new stadium outside town.

Sherry

There are four main types of sherry — **fino**, light and dry with a delicate bouquet and drunk well chilled; **amontillado**, dry but darker and fuller-bodied with a richer bouquet; **oloroso**, medium dry with a still fuller flavour; and the **sweet** dessert wines, or *dulces*, such as Bristol Cream, made by sweetening the wine with a PX (*Pedro Ximenez*) liqueur. Another popular variety is manzanilla, a type of fino which comes only from Sanlucar de Barrameda.

The distinctive character of sherry is due to the natural conditions of the area — climate and soil. Sherry has no vintages because it is a blended wine. Uniformity and continuity are ensured by the *solera* process of ageing and blending: sherries are aged at least three years in casks above ground (humidity is maintained by sprinkling the sand around the barrels with water) and rotated and blended according to age.

Cheap to Moderate

San Miguel, Plaza San Miguel, 4. Tel: 34 85 62. Opposite the church of the same name, just off Plaza del Arenal. A lovely *hostal* in a quiet location; its patio and staircase are full of columns and statues. The owner is friendly and helpful. Excellent value.

Las Palomas, Calle Higueras, 17. Tel: 34 37 73. Just off Calle Medina, in the direction of the bus and train stations. Pretty patio, plants and parrots (well, canaries, actually). Immaculately kept with modern bathrooms. A bargain.

Nuevo Hostal, Calle Caballeros, 23. Tel: 33 16 04. Very near San Miguel, Central location. Good atmosphere with old-fashioned but very clean bedrooms. Meals available, too.

Residencia Gover, Calle Honsario, 6. Tel: 33 26 00. Just off Calle Arcos, near Harvey's bodega. Simple accommodation at reasonable rates. The best thing about it is that it has a garage.

Smarter Options

Residencia Mica, Calle Higueras, 7. Tel: 34 07 00. One of the best in the street but a little too new to be atmospheric. Very comfortable; all rooms have bathrooms and air conditioning.

Joma, Calle Higueras, 22. Tel: 34 96 89. In the same street as the above but slightly cheaper rates. If that's full up, the Hostal Avila in Calle Avila not far off is an alternative and slightly cheaper.

Bodegas of Jerez

Top of the list of things to see of course are the bodegas. They all offer tours and tastings afterwards; some are free, others charge admission. You used to have to reserve ahead but now it is normally all right to turn up on the day. However, they are only open Monday to Friday, in the mornings, and usually close in August and for the harvest and Fiesta de la Vendimia in September.

Most of the bodegas are situated fairly centrally. Maps are available from the tourist office. Tours last about an hour.

Harvey's of Bristol, Calle Arcos, 53. Tel: 34 60 00. Close to the train station so very convenient if you're pushed for time. Beautiful gardens with a pool containing a 65-year-old Mississippi alligator.

Sandeman, Calle Pizarro. Tel: 33 11 00. Next door to the Equestrian School – joint tickets available. One of the largest bodegas.

Pedro Domecq, Calle San Ildefonso, 3. Tel: 33 19 00. On the outskirts of the old part of town. Probably the most famous bodega of them all (prior reservations sometimes required). La Ina fino is extremely popular all over Spain. You will be shown the barrels laid down for Admiral Nelson and the Duke of Wellington, among others.

Gonzalez Byass, Calle Manuel Maria Gonzalez, 12. Tel: 34 00 00. Near the Alcazar, Rivals Domecq in popularity especially with its Tio Pepe fino. Apart from the sherry-fed mice, you will see a circular chamber designed by Eiffel.

William's and Humbert, Ltd, Calle Nuno de Cana, 1. Tel: 33 13 00. Next to the bullring. It has large stables and an impressive collection of coaches.

WHERE TO EAT

Jerez isn't known for its food but you can still find some good places to eat. If you want to economize there are always the *freidurias* (fried-fish shops) and the *tapas* bars. It is also worth remembering if you're touring in a car to stop off at some of the often excellent roadside *ventas* or inns.

Cheap to Moderate:

Restaurante Economico, Calle Fontana, 4. Between Calle Medina and Calle Arcos. Just that; and if that's all you want it's fine. Very good value.

Paco, Calle Arcos, 33. Near Harvey's bodega. The bar is busier than the restaurant until much later-in the evening. Gazpacho a speciality. Mid-price range.

Bar Maypa, Calle Ramon de Cala, 11. Behind Plaza San Miguel. Some of the best *tapas* in town in quite a refined atmosphere.

Bodosqui, Edif Parque Avenida. Near the Plaza del Caballo on the Avenida Alvaro Domecq. A little way out but you'll get some excellent fish here. Worth the effort.

El Boqueron de Plata, Plaza Santiago. In the old part of town. The best *freiduria* in Jerez if you're not up to Bodosqui's. Great take-away fish which you can have with a drink in the nearby bar.

Smarter Options

Tendido 6, Circo, 9. Tel: 34 48 35. Near the bullring. A high-quality restaurant with a truly excellent and enticing display of *tapas*. Very popular.

El Bosque, Avenida Alvaro Domecq, 28. One of the best-known establishments in Jerez – very stylish. You can eat out in the garden.

Gaitan, Avenida Gaitan, 3. Tel: 34 58 59. Basque and Andalusian specialities; try the monkfish casserole. Expensive, like the others.

BARS AND NIGHTLIFE

There are traditional bars and *cervecerías* all over the centre of town. Try the **Gallo Azul** and others in Calle Larga, such as the *azulejoed* alcove **La Venezia** at No. 3 or **La Moderna** at No. 65, plus a couple in Calle Cotofre off Calle Corredera. In the old town, wander round the Alameda Vieja near the cathedral. At night a very lively area is in the Plaza del Caballo and the Paseo de la Rosaleda off the Avenida Alvaro Domecq. Here you'll find several bars and disco-pubs such as **Avante, Cristal** and **Botijo**.

The star of the show when it comes to Jerez bars, however, is tucked away in a housing estate on the outskirts of town. The only way of getting there is to drive or take a taxi. Don't be put off – it is a unique experience. It is called EL CAMINO DEL ROCIO in Calle Velázquez. Dedicated to the pilgrimage of El Rocio (see box feature page 110), it is full of souvenirs and photos. There's nice food and a lively family atmosphere but at midnight you'll see why its so special. The lights go out, candles are lit in front of the Madonna and the whole place breaks out into a Gypsy version of Ave Maria. Another day is crossed off the blackboard (countdown to the next pilgrimage) and the dancing starts. This happens every night.

PLUS

• Jerez has particularly excellent **cake shops**. La Rosa de Oro at Celle Mesones, 4, and at Celle Consistorio, 7, off Plaza del Arenal, has a wonderful selection of mouth-watering delicacies. Don't worry, it even claims to specialize in *pasteleria baja en calorias*.

- Jerez is a great place to see real, untouristy **flamenco**. Apart from the Fundación Andaluza de Flamenco, you can visit one of the *penas* or dance schools and watch them practising. A good one is *Los Cernicalos* on Calle Sanchez Vizcaino, 25, almost on the outskirts of town but not that far from Plaza San Miguel. Closer is **El Garbanzo** in Calle Santa Clara, 9, also behind San Miguel). Go between 20.00 and 21.00 and if you're lucky you'll catch a rehearsal of genuine *cante jondo* and the most emotive dancing you'll see anywhere.

- If you wanted to spend more time here, you could even learn to dance the **sevillana** (the popularized form of flamenco) at one of the schools that run short courses. Fernando Belmonte in Calle Bizzcocheros, 13 (Tel: 32 29 20), is a central one. El Carbonero in Calle San Miguel, 17 (Tel: 33 67 97), is a guitar academy. Everyone shows off their skills at the Festival of Theatre, Music and Dance in August.

OUT OF TOWN . . .
The following signposted tourist routes (Full details and maps available at the tourist offices) will take you to the highlights of the region:

Ruta de los pueblos blancos (white village route)
This takes in a series of picturesque whitewashed villages starting at Arcos de la Frontera, one of the loveliest. Follow the N342 to Olivera at the end of the route. Very narrow, twisty road.

Ruta de la Sierra (hillside route)
This consists of a series of beautifully situated villages starting at El Bosque and continuing via the Natural Park of Grazalema and Zahara de la Sierra to Setenil.

Ruta del toro (bull route)
Begins at Paterna, south of Arcos, and crosses the rolling, bull-breeding countryside with its isolated *cortijos*, or estates, to the delightful Moorish and medieval town of Medina Sidonia. Continue round to Jimena de la Frontera.

Ruta del vino (wine route)
This consists of the so-called wine triangle of Jerez, Sanlúcar de Barrameda and El Puerto de Santa María, it also takes in Chipiona and Rota (see Costa de la Luz, p.106, for details).

GRANADA

Everyone arrives in Granada full of romantic expectations but nothing can prepare you for the exoticism of what you've come to see, the Alhambra. This hilltop palace-fortress, the last bastion of Moorish civilization, is the city's crowning glory, the most beautiful symbol of Islam in Spain.

In the modern city below, the Christian conquerors are entombed in their own crowning glory, the Capilla Real, so completing the historical picture. Their original intention was to be buried in Toledo, then capital of Spain, but after fulfiling their lifelong ambition and taking the keys of the city of Granada in 1492, Ferdinand and Isabella decided to make this their last resting place.

Unfortunately, there is nothing romantic about the new town. Busy roads tear through its centre and while it lacks the village feel of Córdoba it also lacks the buzz of Seville. But it still has a perfect location – at the foot of the snow-capped Sierra Nevada and above a large fertile plain – which, despite the thickness of the car fumes, gives it a cool verdant air.

Apart from the Alhambra, there are few architectural legacies of the Moors in Granada, although the Albaicin, the old Moorish quarter, retains its traditional flavour. But you will find the most perfect Renaissance cathedral in Spain and a collection of Renaissance churches – hastily constructed after the Reconquest to encourage good Christian worship.

GETTING YOUR BEARINGS

Whether you arrive by train, bus or car, your approach will be via the busy city centre. Two main arteries, the Calle Reyes

Católicos and the Gran Vía de Colon, converge at the Plaza
Isabel la Católica. Off to one side is the Plaza Nueva, at the
foot of the steep Alhambra hill and the Albaicin quarter. To
the other is the Puerta Real crossroads. Tucked away in the
new part of town below the Gran Vía lies the cathedral
and here the pedestrianized streets of the commercial sector
radiate out from the lovely, traffic-free Plaza Bib-Rambla.
Farther out in the same direction are the train and bus

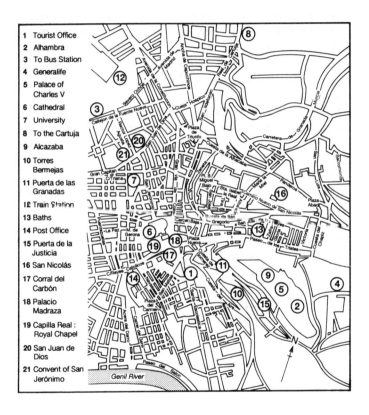

1 Tourist Office
2 Alhambra
3 To Bus Station
4 Generalife
5 Palace of
   Charles V
6 Cathedral
7 University
8 To the Cartuja
9 Alcazaba
10 Torres
   Bermejas
11 Puerta de las
   Granadas
12 Train Station
13 Baths
14 Post Office
15 Puerta de la
   Justicia
16 San Nicolás
17 Corral del
   Carbón
18 Palacio
   Madraza
19 Capilla Real :
   Royal Chapel
20 San Juan de
   Dios
21 Convent of San
   Jerónimo

stations. To get to the centre from these, take bus No. 11
and get off at the cathedral (it's not visible from the road but
look out for the fountain at the T-junction and you're near
enough). Most of Granada can be negotiated on foot, though

History

The name Granada means pomegranate in Spanish and this is often taken as the symbol of the city being frequently used in decorative motifs depicting either the city or the Reconquest. In fact it comes from the Arabic Karnattah, the name given to this strategic provincial capital by the Moors. It was here, on account of its impenetrable defensive location, that Mohammed I established the seat of his Nasrid dynasty in 1232. As the rest of Al-Andalus fell to the Christian onslaught, Granada maintained its stronghold. In 1236, Cordoba's loss was Granada's gain. The former caliphate's wealth and talent were transferred via a massive influx of refugees to Granada and for the next 250 years the city prospered economically, culturally and politically. But by the late 15th century, the kingdom's frontier towns were being taken; Ronda, Málaga and Almería all fell to successive Christian advances. In 1492, Granada stood alone in the face of external Christian offensive and internal feuding and intrigue. The kingdom had been split under Muley Hassan and his brother Al-Zagal, but civil war broke out when the sultan's wife Ayesha (annoyed by her husband's preference for a Christian convert called Zoraya), proclaimed her son Boabdil king – El Rey Chico. Allegiances were divided and Boabdil seized power amid vicious recriminations. The political repercussions were enormous; weakened internally, Granada was prey to cunning Christian manipulation and bargaining. After a series of sieges and kidnappings, Boabdil was forced to surrender the city to Ferdinand and Isabella on 2 January 1492. With the eviction of the Moors, the crusade was over. At the Suspiro del Moro pass in the mountains above Granada, the exiled king turned and cried while his mother supposedly rebuked him, saying, "You weep like a boy for what you could not defend like a man."

After the Reconquest, the code of religious tolerance by which the Moors had lived was not continued under Christian rule. Before being completely expelled, the Muslims were persecuted and their buildings destroyed. Spain's Jews, too, were slaughtered or forced to leave. The Alhambra was abandoned until interest revived in the 19th century. During the Civil War, Nationalists ravaged Granada with a massacre of over 4,000 Republicans, including one of the city's famous sons, the poet Federico García Lorca.

it's quite a climb up to the Alhambra and walking round the Albaicin.

DON'T MISS . . .

The Alhambra:
(Open daily 9.30–20.00 in summer, 9.30–17.30 Sunday and out of season. Floodlit visits twice a week from 22.00–24.00 on Saturday and one variable weekday (according to the season – check with the tourist office). It is free on Sunday after 15.00)
The ticket comes in three parts – for the Alcázaba, the alcázar and the Generalife; any unused section is valid the following day. There are two main ticket offices: one inside the Puerta de la Justicia near the *parador* and another near the entrance to the Generalife. The queues at the former are usually much shorter.

The complex is reached from the town centre via Calle Cuesta de Gomerez, through the Puerta de las Granadas (note the three pomegranates) built in 1536. Bus No.2 from the Plaza Nueva will drop you off at the top. Although the climb is steep, the alameda outside the main perimeter walls makes for a wonderful leafy approach on foot (fork left as you go up).

The fairy-tale Qalat Al-Hamra or "Red Fort", the palace-fortress of the Moors overlooking the town from its craggy perch, is *the* reason people come to Granada. The Alhambra is quite literally unique; it is the only Arab palace from the Middle Ages to remain intact and represents the zenith of Moorish architectural accomplishment in Spain. A city within a city (even now its grounds house a *parador*, a *hostal* and a restaurant), its courtyards, palaces, mosques, terraces, gardens and fortresses were once alive with scenes straight out of *The Arabian Nights* and as you wander from the Court of Myrtles to the Court of Lions and from one terraced garden to the next, those memories can still be evoked today.

Further up the hill, commanding an even better view over the neighbouring Albaicin district, is the Generalife, the sultans' summer palace. The royal entourage would retreat here to the cool gardens of cypresses and oleanders, pools and fountains, all achieved through the Moors' skillful irrigation and engineering.

Although many of the sumptuous buildings were destroyed by Charles V with the construction of his Renaissance palace, by Napoleon's ransacking troops and by centuries of neglect, and despite the fact that Moorish buildings were never built to last, the Alhambra survives as the epitome of Moorishness in Spain and is the country's greatest monument.

Enter the outer gate and walk through the shrubbery, to reach **the Puerta de la Justicial**. (Just outside you will see the Pilar de Carlos V, a Renaissance fountain whose three spouts represent the three rivers of Granada: the Genil, the Darro and the Beyro). The gate is so named after the inscription "May God make the justice of Islam prosper within her". It forms part of the inner ramparts and is made up of two arches. Over the first one there is an outstretched hand symbolizing protection against evil and representing, by means of the five fingers, the five Islamic precepts of prayer, alms-giving, fasting, pilgrimage to Mecca and the oneness of God. The tasselled key above the other arch represents the power God gave Mohammed to open the doors of Heaven.

Inside is the isolated **Puerta del Vino** (so called because it was here that wine was deposited for the inhabitants in the 16th century) and through that the open Plaza de los Aljibes, named after the cisterns that were later constructed beneath. Towering in front are the massive inner walls of the Alcázaba; behind is the Renaissance structure of Charles V's palace.

The Alcázaba is the citadel, the key defensive part of the fortress. Some of its foundations date from the 11th century, but it was in the 13th century that the military impenetrability of the Alcázaba was assured with the construction of the towers and outer ramparts. It was originally separate from the rest of the complex. Enter by the Puerta de las Armas to the inner courtyard and barracks and climb the watch tower, the Torre de la Vela, from which you get a spectacular view of the city below and the rest of the Alhambra behind. It was from this tower on 2 January 1492 that the Catholic

In 1238, after the fall of Córdoba, the first Nasrid king decided to transfer his court and seat of government to this hilltop site for obvious defensive reasons. He enlarged and reinforced the existing *alcázaba* or fortress, increasing the outer ramparts and fortifications and also diverting the river Darro into channels for use inside. Most of the palaces as we see them today, however, date from the 14th century. Yusuf I (1333–54) and Mohammed V (1354–91) were responsible for the embellishments of the Court of Myrtles and the Court of Lions respectively and it was at this time that Moorish architecture reached its peak in Granada. About the only change Ferdinand and Isabella were to make was to convert the mosque (Isabella was even temporarily buried in the Convento San Francisco – now the Parador – while awaiting the completion of the Capilla Real). Charles V, however, wreaked his usual havoc; he destroyed a large section of the Arab complex to make way for his massive Renaissance palace which was never finished, let alone inhabited. Much damage was done by an explosion in 1590 and the site was virtually abandoned until the 19th century. An attempt by French troops to blow it up was foiled and, after popularization in 1829 by the American author Washington Irving with his *Tales from the Alhambra*, restoration began in earnest.

flag was hoisted, signifying the surrender of the Moors and the completion of the Reconquest.

The Alcázar or the Casa Real is the palace proper, the heart of the complex, and here we find the richly decorated rooms and patios of the different areas and living quarters.

Behind the delicately ornate stucco tracery with its simple, geometric repetition of design, behind the beautiful coloured *azulejo* tiles, the stalactite ceilings and the arabesque arches is a flimsy assortment of rubble, brick and plaster. The Moors built for the present, not posterity; decoration (and the art of capturing the interplay of water and light) was everything and when one ruler went the next tore down his predecessor's palace to replace it with new heights of decorative splendour.

As in most Arab palaces, rooms radiate off a central courtyard. The courtyards in turn lead into each other through rooms or passageways. Each area had a designated function –

the Mexuar or council chamber where public administrative affairs were carried out; the Diwan or official state rooms with the throne room; and finally the intimate harem or private apartments.

The Mexuar, though much altered and damaged, is one of the oldest parts of the complex. It was originally where the king would deal with public petitions and administrative matters. Transformed into a chapel after the Reconquest, it still invokes the "glory of God", the "power of God" and the "kingdom of God" in its inscriptions. The small room at the end is the oratory. Next to this comes the Patio del Mexuar with its adjoining Cuarto Dorado or Golden Room decorated in Mudéjar style with Gothic motifs. The ceiling is gilded and inlaid with ivory and mother of pearl. The restored canopied façade of the courtyard opposite quotes the much favoured line from the Koran "There is no victor but God" which appears throughout the Alhambra.

The Diwan (sometimes called the Serallo) is made up of the Palace of Comares and centres on the long Patio de los Arrayanes (Court of the Myrtle Trees). In the middle is a pool filled with goldfish and carp, banked by clipped myrtle bushes, reflecting the crenellated Torre de Comares in its water. Pass through a marble-colonnaded loggia, the Sala de la Barca (Boat or Blessing Room). It owes its strange name to the greeting *baraka* or blessing which can be seen inscribed on the walls. Its ceiling, which was destroyed by a fire in 1890 and rebuilt in 1965, also has the appearance of an upturned boat.

The Sala de Embajadores (Ambassadors' Hall), the most spectacular room in the palace, was the throne room where the sultan would grant twice-weekly audiences. It has a magnificent carved and vaulted cedarwood ceiling with allegorical geometric designs (symbolizing the Seven Heavens) that rises to a height of 18 metres (60 ft). Tapestry-like stucco work and friezes from the Koran cover the walls above a band of beautifully coloured tiles. The horseshoe-shaped windows frame superb views of the hills outside, although originally the light would have been diffused through stained-glass windows of matching geometric patterns. At the far end of the courtyard is the 16th-century addition of the chapel crypt.

The almost secret passageway to the Sala de los Mocarabes makes a perfect, subtle entrance to the miniature paradise of **The Patio de los Liones (the Court of Lions)**. A colonnade of slender single and paired columns topped by lacy, fringed arcading surround the patio. In the centre of the court, which would once have been planted with trees and scented shrubs.

Twelve stone lions (representing the 12 months of the year or the 12 signs of the zodiac) support the basin of a fountain while four channels of water (the four rivers of paradise or the four corners of the cosmos) flow out to the elaborate rooms on all sides.

On opposite sides of the court are the Sala de los Abencenerajes, named after a family massacred here, and the Sala de los Dos Hermanas (Room of the Two Sisters), named

after the twin marble slabs in the floor. Both contain spectacular stalactite or honeycombed cupolas of great intricacy.
The Mirador de Daraxa or Lindaraja, the Queen's bedroom
and most intimate part of the palace, opens off this last room
and overlooks a patio of cypress and orange trees. The royal
baths below would have been reached by a staircase. At the far
end of the Patio de los Liones is the Sala de los Reyes (King's
Chamber), divided into alcoves, where paintings on the ceiling
depict courtly scenes. Human representation is forbidden in
the Koran so these were probably later additions.

Beyond the royal quarters are the lovely terraced **Partal
Gardens,** enclosed within the outer ramparts and towers.
Follow the signs round to the more recent apartments of
Charles V where Washington Irving lodged, and the Patios de
la Reja and de Lindaraja. Access to the beautifully illuminated
bath chambers underneath the harem is from here.

The Palace of Charles V
Erratic opening times. The contrast between the delicacy and
light of the Moorish palaces and the weighty sombreness of
this Renaissance mammoth could not be more striking. After
demolishing much of the original Alhambra to accommodate
it and levying taxes on the Moriscos to pay for it, Charles
never used his unfinished residence. Built in pure Renaissance
style by Pedro Machuca, a student of Michaelangelo, in 1526,
its colonnaded circular courtyard within the outer square building was once used for bullfights. It houses two museums. The
Museo de Bellas Artes exhibits 16th–18th century religious
art; the Museo Nacional de Arte Hispano-Musulman holds
a collection of Moorish artefacts including a blue amphora
known as the "Alhambra Vase".

The Generalife
The simple summer palace of the kings is nothing special
after the sumptuous rooms of the Alhambra. But the terraced
gardens with their cypress walkways, sculpted bushes, orange
trees, roses, oleanders and rhododendrons, pools, fountains and
patios are magnificent. The Callejon de los Cipreses and the
Callejon de las Adelfas lead into the inner court, Patio de la
Acequia or canal. The nearby water-filled staircase, Camino

de las Cascadas, is a feat of Arab engineering. Wonderful views extend over the Albaicin on the opposite hill.

The Albaicin

This is the old Arab quarter of the city, on the hill opposite the Alhambra, whose narrow, winding streets still preserve the Moorish feel. The hill was the site of the original fortress, and the surrounding streets expanded rapidly with the influx of refugees from other parts of the diminishing Arab kingdom. You can still see the whitewashed Moorish town houses or *carmenes*, with gardens and patios dotted with cypress and orange trees.

Take the Carrera del Darro along the river, past the Plaza Santa Ana. Note the Arab baths with their vaulted roofs which can be visited at No. 31. Climb the Calle Banuelo and lose yourself in the labyrinthine lanes. Make sure you reach the Mirador de San Nicholas by the church of the same name, where you'll get the best view of the Alhambra. It is particularly lovely at sunset, although the Albaicin is not the safest place to walk at night. Not far away is the Plaza Larga, the heart of the quarter, and a little way down, the delightful Plaza San Miguel Bajo with bars and cafés.

The Cathedral and the Capilla Real

(Open 11.00–13.00 and 16.00–19.00.)

Far more imposing than the cathedral is the earlier Capilla Real (or royal chapel).

This mausoleum swallowed up a quarter of the royal income in its construction. Although they had already built another mausoleum for themselves in Toledo, Ferdinand and Isabella decided to make Granada their final resting place, after eventually taking the city from the Moors. They are buried inside under two ornately carved marble sarcophagi, next to their daughter Juana the Mad and her husband, Philip the Fair. The actual lead coffins (plus that of the eldest grandson, Prince Miguel) lie in the crypt below. Other members of the royal family were buried here until they were transferred to the royal mausoleum at El Escorial.

The adjoining sacristy contains Isabella's fine collection of Flemish paintings, and a lovely Botticelli ("Christ on the

> In the same year work started on the cathedral, which is
> largely Renaissance in style although not finished until 1714.
> Inside note the figures of the Catholic Kings kneeling by the
> *capilla mayor.*

Mount of Olives"). It also displays the queen's crown, sceptre
and jewel box and the king's sword.

The separate Capilla Real is an impressive example of the
flamboyant late Gothic or Isabelline style of architecture. It
was begun in 1506 and completed in 1521.

ALSO WORTH SEEING . . .

Other churches

In the northern part of town, especially round the university
quarter, are other examples of Renaissance and Baroque
churches such as San Juan de Dios and Convento de San
Jeronimo. Farther out still is the Carthusian monastery of La
Cartuja – a 16th–17th century Baroque extravaganza.

Corral del Carbon

This is almost the only remaining Arab building in the new
town (the other is the Madraza or *medressa*, the former
Arab university opposite the Capilla Real). It's set back in
a side street just off Calle Reyes Católicos. Originally an
Arab hostelry, its three-storey balconied courtyard provided
stabling and accommodation for travelling merchants. It later
became a coal warehouse and in the 16th century was used as
a theatre. It now houses craft workshops.

The Alcaiceria

Next to the Capilla Real, it is a 19th-century replica of the
original Arab silk market. It now houses a collection of
souvenir shops.

FACTFILE

Tourist Information calle Libreros, 2. Tel: 22 59 90 and 22 12 22. Open
10.00–13.00 and 16.00–19.00; closed Saturday afternoons and Sunday.
Off Plaza Bib-Rambla near the cathedral. (There is another at Calle de

Pavaneras, 19.) Will provide maps of the city and the noticeboard has lots of useful information.

Airport 15 km out of town on the *carretera* Málaga/Córdoba. Tel: 44 64 11; information 27 34 00. Mostly domestic flights, Iberia, Plaza Isabel la Catolica, 2. Tel: 22 75 92. Shuttle-bus connection to the airport and back.

Trains RENFE Avenida Andaluces. Tel: 23 34 08. RENFE office on Calle Reyes Católicos, 63. Tel: 22 34 97.

Buses Alsina Graells, Camino de Ronda, 97. Tel: 25 13 58. Main bus station, serving the whole of Andalusia. Bacoma, Avenida de Andaluces, 12 (Tel: 23 18 83), serves Valencia and Catalonia, Bonal, Avenida de Calvo Soto, 34 (Tel: 27 31 00), runs excursions to Sierra Nevada, and a Madrid service.

Car Rentals Hertz, Calle Recogidas, 46. Tel: 25 16 82. Avis, Calle Recogidas, 31. Tel: 25 23 59. Atesa, Plaza de Cuchilleros, 1. Tel: 22 40 04

Post Office, Puerta Real. Open Monday–Friday 9.00–14.00 and 16.00–18.00.

Telefonica, Calle Reyes Católicos, 55, just near Plaza Nueva, Open 9.00–13.00 and 17.00–22.00. Code is 958.

Police Tel: 091.

Hospital, Avenida Dr Oloriz. Tel: 27 64 00.

WHERE TO STAY

Although there is no accommodation available in the old Moorish Albaicin quarter, the most attractive part of town, there are plenty of hotels and *hostales* centrally located in the modern districts If you've come from Seville, these will seem refreshingly cheap. For budget accommodation there are three main areas to look in:

Plaza Nueva and up to the Alhambra

The main street leading up to the Alhambra, Calle Cuesta de Gomerez, is lined with low-priced *hostales*. Although marvellously central, the road itself, lined with souvenir shops, is noisy and there is a constant stream of cars and coaches screeching their way up the hill.

Pension Britz, Calle Cuesta de Gomerez, 1. Tel: 22 36 52. On the corner with the Plaza Nueva and consequently noisy. Good views of the square but ask for a side room if you want to sleep before 3.00. Very well maintained with nicely furnished rooms and spotless bathrooms. Same management as the Hostal Lisboa (see below). More expensive than the others nearby but good value for what you get

Hostal Residencia Gomerez, Calle Cuesta de Gomerez, 10. Tel: 22 44 37. Simple, clean, friendly and one of the cheapest – hot shower extra. Don't confuse it with Huespedes Gomerez at No. 2; this is a much better option. Restaurant Gomerez does some good *platos combinados*.

Hostal California, Calle Cuesta de Gomerez, 37. Tel: 22 40 56. Farther up still, on the left. Well-kept, simple rooms, some with bath. More expensive than the above.

Huespedes Santa Ana, Calle Puente de Espinosa. North of the Plaza Nueva and Plaza Santa Ana, near the second bridge, overlooking the river Darro. The quietest and prettiest location outside the Alhambra.

Cathedral Square and Plaza de la Trinidad

This is the more commercialized central area south and west of the cathedral around the charming, pedestrianized Plaza de Bib-Rambla and the leafy Plaza de la Trinidad. It is bordered to the north by the busy Gran Vía, along which there are also many *hostales*.

Florida, Calle Principe, 13. Tel: 26 37 47. On the corner with the main square. Most peculiar entrance system – a piece of string attached to the lock going up to the first floor. Some guests haven't been able to get back in . . . Clean and characterful. Run by a lady who keeps parrots and spends a lot of the time at the hairdresser's.

Los Tilos, Plaza de Bib-Rambla, 4. Tel: 26 67 12. A charming, friendly two-star hotel right on the square. All rooms have private bathrooms. Worth the extra cost. Linger over breakfast at one of the many cafés outside.

Zacatin, Calle Ermita, 11. Tel: 22 11 55. In the alleyways next to the cathedral near the touristy Alcaicera (restored Arab market). No frills but perfectly acceptable.

Zurita, Plaza de la Trinidad, 7. Tel: 27 50 20. A long white house on the square with a pretty internal courtyard and bar/breakfast room downstairs. Slightly more expensive than others in the immediate vicinity but well maintained and very clean.

San Joaquin, Calle Mano de Hierro, 14. Tel: 28 28 79. Farther towards the station and less central than the others, this is nevertheless one of the most attractive *hostales* in Granada. A lovely old residence with three plant-filled patios, marble columns and tapestries. Simple rooms as usual, some with shower. Friendly owners who also do good meals.

Plaza del Carmen and Behind

This is the area on the other side of the main central artery, Calle Reyes Católicos. Still right in the centre and also within walking distance of the bars in the active Campo Principe district.

Lisboa, Plaza del Carmen, 29. Tel: 22 14 13. An excellent *hostal*. Ultra-clean with a lovely lounge/reading room on the top floor from which you get a view of the square and the Alhambra – perfect viewing if you're here in Semana Santa when the parades pass right in front. Everyone is very friendly and helpful right down to the singing maid.

Niza, Calle Navas, 16. Tel: 22 54 30. Close to the Lisboa and a good bet if that's full, but this is more expensive. Quieter, however.

Roma, Calle Navas, 1. Tel: 22 62 77. Farther down the same street, this is the cheapest of the three. Simple with a lively atmosphere.

Mallorca and **Princesa**, Calle San Matias, 2. Tel: 22 45 10 and 22 93 81. Both in the same building. The Princesa is the more expensive of the two but the Mallorca is good value if nothing special.

Cataluña, Calle Colcha, 13. Tel: 22 30 22. Up towards the Plaza Nueva, in a side street off Reyes Católicos. Above a reasonable bar and restaurant with cheap menus. Good location and often full.

Smarter Options

Macia, Plaza Nueva, 4. Tel: 22 75 35. Slightly characterless but good-quality modern hotel with all the comforts. Looks on to the main square.

America, Real de la Alhambra, 53. Tel: 22 74 71. For not much more you can stay right inside the Alhambra walls in this absolutely charming 14-room *hostal*. Provided you book two or three months in advance, or a year if you want to come during Semana Santa, of course. Breakfast (and dinner if you want) included, it is a bargain at the price. It overflows with plants and flowers and its shady patio is set with tables for its well-cooked meals. Idyllic once the day-trippers are gone and you can stroll freely around the gardens.

WHERE TO EAT

There aren't that many good, cheap eating-places in Granada. In the centre they are, with a few exceptions, touristy and uninspiring. Local specialities include the ubiquitous Andalusian fried fish, tortilla Sacromonte (mixed omelette), and *habas* with snow-cured *jamón serrano* from the Sierra Nevada.

Cheap to Moderate

CENTRALLY Most of these restaurants are situated round the Plaza Nueva and in the adjacent streets, especially off Calle Elvira to the west. A few are farther afield in the more modern part of town.

Bar/Restaurant Leon, Calle Pan, 3. Just off Plaza Nueva. The bar is on one side of the road, the restaurant on the other. Full of tourists, like all the restaurants round here, but quite good value all the same.

La Riviera, Calle Cetti-Merien, 5. Off Calle Elvira. It does some good *raciones* at the bar, especially the *calamares* and *gambas al pil pil*. Also an unusual peach *sangría*. But keep an eye on the prices or it ends up not being so cheap. There is a similar restaurant next door.

Reyes Católicos, Placeta Silleria, 1. Next to two youthful bars – Pendiente de Ti and Bar Baridad. It offers a wide variety of set *menús del día* with a slightly more imaginative selection than elsewhere.

Gargantua, Silleria, 7. Slightly more expensive, bistro-style decor with what tries to be refined service but ends up being very slow. Un-Spanish selection on their menus. Good salads.

Nuevo Restaurante, Calle Navas, near Plaza del Carmen. A good cheap

restaurant serving a wide selection of *platos combinados* at the bar.
Menus available in the dinning area until 23.00.

El Rincon de Juan, in an alleyway almost opposite the above. Friendly
little bar full of locals. Serves good *tapas* and *raciones*.

El Patio Andaluz, Calle Carmen, 12. Behind Plaza Gamboa. Small,
typical local restaurant with a very cheap *menú del día*. Good *sopa
de mariscos*. There is a nice cake shop opposite.

Pizzeria Verona, Calle Elvira, 108. A hole-in-the-wall-type place which
does good pizzas.

El Capillo, Calle Pescaderia, on the *placeta*. Rock-bottom prices. Cheap
and filling if nothing else.

IN THE ALBAICIN DISTRICT   **El Ladrillo**, Placeta de Fatima (Tel:
29 54 05) off Calle Pages at the top end of the Albaicin. Quite a
hike up there. Being done up in 1991 and whether it will still be as
good as before remains to be seen. Only serves fried fish, e.g. a *media
barca* for two people. Excellent quality and value. Sit outside on the
small square.

Meson Yunque, Plaza San Miguel Bajo. In a lovely, quiet, shaded plaza at
the lower end of the Albaicin. Tables outside and offering a good choice
of *raciones* and a menu. There is a restaurant run by the same people
on the corner opposite: **Martinet**. Lots of other bars in the square, of
which Bar **Laro** offers *platos combinados* and Café-Bar **Adrian** a wide
selection of *tapas* and *raciones*. A delightful place to stop for a drink.

Bar La Mancha Chica, Camino Nuevo San Nicholas, farther up the
hill on the left, towards the Mirador San Nicholas. It has an elevated
terrace on the other side of the road and offers good, very cheap chicken
and chips.

Cocetin de la Parron, Plaza Larga. Up again and slightly to the west.
More seafood and good gazpacho. Café **Casa Pasteles** in the same square
serves cakes and ice cream.

ELSEWHERE IN THE NEW TOWN   **El Amir**, Calle General Narvaez,
3. Go down the busy Calle Recogidas past all the modern hotels and it is
a street off to the right towards Plaza de Gracia. A bit more expensive,
it serves delicious and inventive Arab dishes.

Nearby in Calle La Cruz, 2, there is an excellent Indian vegetarian
restaurant, **Oriente Y Occidente**. If you've been in Spain a long time and
can't face another *plato combinado*, this is a good bet. The only other
strictly speaking vegetarian restaurant, **Raices**, is quite a long way out
of town on Calle Professor Albareda, 11, over the river Genil.

Smarter Options

Cunini, Calle Pescaferia, 9. Tel: 26 37 01. Versatile seafood is the
speciality here, cooked in a variety of styles, e.g. Basque and Catalan.

There is a stand-up *tapas* bar on the ground floor. Try their *sopa sevillana* and stuffed sardines.

Los Manueles, Calle Zaragoza, 2 and 4. Tel: 22 34 15. In a side alleyway off Reyes Católicos. This old *taberna* has two small dining rooms decorated in typical Andalusian style with *azulejos* and hams hanging from the ceiling and tables outside on the pavement. Touristy but high standards. You can always opt for the *tapas* (they do a very good tortilla Sacromonte), which are some of the best in town.

Primer Puente, Carrera del Darro. North of the Plaza Nueva; as it says, by the first bridge. Beautifully decorated little rooms with an intimate atmosphere. Expensive.

Parador Nacional de San Francisco, Recinto de la Alhambra. Tel: 22 14 93. If you feel like an enormous splurge, this is the place to do it. The restaurant's glass wall enables diners to feast on the incredible view as well as on specialities such as roast kid in garlic sauce. The Parador itself is probably the most romantic place to stay in Spain.

BARS AND NIGHTLIFE

Bars

The liveliest areas, especially at night, are in the Albaicin, around Campo Principe or along Calle Pedro Antonio de Alarcon in the new part of town.

Castaneda, Calle Elvira, 6. It is often given other addresses since it is in fact surrounded by streets on four sidea. Probably the best-known traditional bar in Granada. It has a huge, cavernous interior full of bottles and barrels. It serves mainly local wines and a good vermouth but their house speciality is called *calicasas* and tastes a little like Martini rosso.

El Fogon, Calle Navas, 27. A bar with bullfighting traditions (there is even a stuffed bull's head on the wall). It does good *tapas* – you often get one free with a fino – but is stand-up only.

Carmelo, Calle Colcha, 3. A popular local bar with a small eating area in a back alcove where Carmelo himself will propose a menu should you also want to eat. Good *rabo de toro*.

Casa de Yanguas, Calle San Buenaventura, off Cuesta del Chapiz. A classy bar in an ancient patio with exhibitions, terraces and balconies.

Flamenco

The *zambras* on flamenco shows offered by the Gypsies in the Sacromonte caves have become a notoriously expensive tourist rip-off. You will be pestered and cajoled as soon as you get anywhere near. Most of the displays aren't particularly brilliant either. A better bet for real flamenco is **La Pena Plateria**, Patio de los Aljibes, 13. It is in the heart of the Albaicin, and is a private club with a lovely patio setting which is nevertheless open to the public (temporary membership on the door) every night except Saturday when it is reserved for private members only. Highly regarded among flamenco aficionados.

Classics

Generalife *Conciertos romanticos* are held here by the Ayuntamiento on Friday and Saturday evenings during the summer and the International Festival of Music and Dance stages classical ballet here in June and July. Other concerts are put on in other parts of the Alhambra. Contact Comisaria del Festival, Calle Gracia, 21 (Tel: 26 77 42), for tickets.

Disco

Try **Oh! Granada**, Calle Doctor Guirao Gea. Three crowded dance floors with a studenty atmosphere.

PLUS ...

- **Casi de Todos**, Calle Elvira opposite Bar Castaneda. The best **bocadillos** in Granada if not in Andalusia. An enormous choice of fillings is written up behind the bar; their *jamón con roquefort* is divine or try their speciality, a hot *casi de todos* – a little of everything. Eat it there in the tiny bar or, better still, have it on the way up to the Alhambra.

- **Teterias** or **tea-houses** Calle Caldereria Nueva, off Calle Elvira, is a very trendy little street with a couple of wholefood shops. At La Rendez-Vous you can have tea, crepes and listen to classical music, Al Faguara is more ethnic and wholefoody, while As Sirat has Arab decor and huge selection of teas with a few cakes on offer as well.

- **Heladerias** For ice cream, try La Perla in Plaza Nueva at No. 16 or Los Italianos on the Gran Vía. Helados La Jijoneca is on Carrera de Genil, 97, near Galerias Preciados, or sit outside in Plaza Mariana Pineda with a *horchata* from Café Futbol.

- **Markets** The main covered market is off the Gran Vía at Calle San Augustin but in Calle Pescaderia there are lots of excellent fruit and veg stalls.

- **Churros** There is a *churreria* in the same square. Sold by the kilo, they are very cheap and very fresh. If you'd prefer to have them with chocolate, sit down at Café Alhambra in Plaza Bib-Rambla nearby.

  The convents of Santa Catalina de Zafra and of San Bernardo del Cister in the carrera del Darro make delicious **cakes and sweets** to sell.

OUT OF TOWN

The Sierra Nevada

The snow-capped peaks of the Sierra Nevada not only provide the perfect backdrop to the city of Granada but their accessibility makes them an easy day trip in summer or winter. Skiing is possible for much of the year in Spain's highest mountain range, at the ugly Solynieve resort, and in summer the flower-strewn paths and passes make it a good hiking destination. You can even take the dirt track (25 km) over the peaks to the valleys of the Alpujarras on the other side.

To reach the peak of Veleta, there is a single road from Granada which at 3,398 metres (11,148 ft) makes it the highest road in Europe. A bus service runs to Solynieve and above it to the **Parador de Sierra Nevada** from Granada every day at 9.00 (Autocares Bonal from the Fuente de las Batalhas, opposite the Diputacion) and returns at 17.00. If you want to stay, food and lodging are expensive; try the Albergue **Universitario**/Penonas San Francisco (Tel: 48 01 22) or the *parador*. Ski lifts and a cable car take you to the higher slopes and the road continues over the pass. Information and maps on hiking and skiing are available from the tourist office.

The Alpujarras

These isolated white villages scattered on the southern slopes of the Sierra Nevada were for a long time a forgotten corner of Spain with appalling low literacy levels and rock-bottom standard of living. Though they are still poor, tourism has brought some improvements, fortunately without ruining the beautiful tranquillity and simplicity of the picturesque villages. They make an idyllic mountain retreat where visitors can hike or, better still, go on one of the marvellous horse-riding tours on offer.

Historically and geographically cut off, these valleys were inhabited first by Berber and then by Moorish refugees. The Moors introduced a system of terrace farming and irrigation on the fertile slopes and they contended themselves here until the Christian conquest. When the Arabs were expelled, the valleys declined – although they were later popularized by the British writer Gerald Brenan in *South from Granada*.

There are two main approaches: one via the spa town of Lanjaron from the turn-off on the Granada–Motril road, the other from the direction of Almería. As the majority of visitors come by bus (Alsina Graells runs three per day to Lanjaron and Orjiva, where you can pick up connections for the higher villages. One direct bus leaves Granada at 13.30) or car from the Granada road, the western High Alpujarras are consequently more touristy and developed. If you have your own transport, a quieter, more authentic approach is from Ugijar in the east. Here you will pass through lush valleys planted with vines and orange trees.

Yegen is one of the most typical Alpujarran villages, with wonderful views all round. Its steep, cobbled streets and fountain remain almost as they were in Brenan's day, when he lived in the house with the plaque. There's a tiny, nameless pension on the main road which is very cheap and has great views. You can eat at the Bar Nuovo in the village, which also has rooms.

Berchules; surrounded by chestnut glades and grassy meadows, is a slightly bigger village, which still maintains its Moorish carpet and rug-making traditions. Fonda Rafael overlooks the canyon while Bar-Restaurant Caravol on the main road also has cheap rooms.

Trevelez; Spain's highest inhabited town, is famous for its snow-cured hams (*jamón serrano*) which can be bought all over the village and even direct from the factory. Situated at the head of a valley on the slopes of Mulhacén, the Sierra's highest peak, it is not the prettiest town in the Alpujarras but still displays the characteristic features such as division into a lower and upper town and traditional houses with stables underneath. There is lots of accommodation, of which the best is the Hostal Fernando on the higher road into town; cheap, modern and ultra-clean. Eat at its sister bar and restaurant a little higher up where they do a wonderfully hearty *plato alpujarreno* of fried ham, sausages, eggs and potatoes – just the thing to warm you up in the chilly evenings.

Portugos and Pitres are two very characteristic and unspoiled villages right in the heart of the best walking country. They have a much more unrefined feel and atmosphere than some of their neighbours. The Hostal Mirador de Portugos on the main square is excellent if more expensive than the good

Fonda Sierra Nevada in the main square at Pitres. (There is also a campsite here and one at Trevelez.)

Bubion and Capileira are on the edge of the spectacular Poqueira gorge. These two picturesque white villages have received the brunt of the tourist invasion and on Sundays and holidays a never-ending stream of cars and coach tours winds its way up the narrow mountain road. The tiny villages are having difficulty making space for them and unfortunately quite a lot of development is going on. If you really want to escape the crowds, the Spanish-Tibetan Buddhist monastery of Al Atalaya provides a Centre of Transcendental Meditation and offers lectures on Buddhism and retreats.

If that is not for you, Meson-Hostal La Poqueira in **Capileira** offers nice, clean rooms and a good menu. Casa Ibero on calle/Parra is also a good place to eat, as is Casa Teide in **Bubion**.

Alternatively, accommodation can nearly always be found in the lower, bigger towns such as **Lanjaron** and **Orgiva**.

East from Granada – Guadix
Guadix and Purullena are famous for their bizarre, white-washed cave dwellings. No longer inhabited by Gypsies, some of these residences are quite sophisticated with all mod cons. The caves in Guadix are more authentic and are situated in the Barrio de Santiago behind the church. For a good view of them, climb up to the Moorish alcázaba. If you want to stop over night, there are several places to stay; the Hotel Restaurante Comercio on Calle Mira de Amezcua, 3, in the centre of town is one of the best. There are good bus connections with Granada (Empresa Autodia).

ALMERÍA

Images of Almería province are familiar to us all. Its desert landscapes with their hot, dry climate and intensely strong sunlight have proved the perfect setting for films such as *Lawrence of Arabia, Conan the Barbarian* and a succession of spaghetti Westerns. Former Wild West film sets are open as tourist attractions.

The Province of Jaén

The province of Jaén is isolated and almost undiscovered. It comprises the area between Andalusia and Castille with the Despenaperros Pass through the mountains, and its name comes from the Moorish word *geen*, meaning caravan route. It is Spain's olive-growing region *par excellence*; the low hills are silver with millions of olive trees. If you want to take some olive oil home, one of the best brands to look out for is Oro de la Loma.

Hiding in the olive groves are two of Andalusia's treasures — the twin towns of Ubeda and Baeza. Both fell early to the Christian Reconquest and prospered in peace, leaving behind a legacy of numerous Renaissance buildings, making an interesting contrast to the rest of Andalusia.

There are two main squares in **Ubeda**, the "Salamanca of Andalusia" — the triangular Plaza del General Saro, with pavement cafés, in the newer part of town; and the monumemtal **Plaza Vazquez de Molina**, a large Renaissance square lined with such mansions as the Casa de Cadenas, and some fine churches. The whole effect is very impressive. Behind are the narrow, cobbled streets of the old town. Look out for the church of San Pablo in Plaza 1 de Mayo. Monuments apart, Ubeda is a lively town and a good place to browse round craft shops, especially in Calle Valencia.

If you fancy spending the night, there is plenty of cheap accommodation near the bus station — Hostal Sevilla in Calle Ramón y Cajal, 9 (Tel: 75 06 12), is one of the cheapest options. The only place to stay in the old quarter is the wonderful **Parador Nacional Condestable Davalos** (Plaza Vazquez de Molina, 1, Tel: 953/75 03 45) in a restored 16th-century ducal palace — definitely worth it if you feel like splashing out. As well as being one of the loveliest *paradores* in Spain it also has an excellent restaurant.

East of Ubeda, after about 45 km, you come to the beautiful mountain scenery of the **Sierra Cazorla** with its national park. The town of **Cazorla** itself is a pretty maze of steep streets, dramatically set against the backdrop of the mountains.

West of Ubeda, about 9 km away, is the little town of **Baeza**. En route you will pass the enormous Hospital de Santiago, nicknamed the "Andalusian Escorial".

Smaller and more compact than its neighbour, Baeza also centres on two main squares. The cobbled **Plaza de Leones** has a two-storey, open colonnade, its namesake lion fountain and a shady paseo. The **Plaza de Santa Maria** in front of the cathedral has a triumphal arch of a fountain – the symbol of the city. Wander round the labyrinth of alleyways and keep your eyes open for the many seignorial mansions, such as the Palacio de Jabalquinto.

Baeza is a lovely place to stay. Unfortunately, there is not a lot of accommodation but since it's off most tourist routes you should be able to find a room. Try the Fonda **Adriano** on Calle Conde Romanónes, 13 (Tel: 74 02 00), near the Plaza de Leones, which is an old mansion and is delightful. If not, there are a few other choices, including the smarter Hotel **Juanito** on Avchida Arca del Agua (Tel: 74 00 40) on the outskirts of town, which has a good restaurant.

Despite receiving more sunshine than anywhere else in Spain – an average of 320 days a year, which makes it worth visiting in winter – the coast of Almería has remained comparatively undeveloped (largely because of the lack of water). West of Almería city, the view along the coast is generally one of market-garden vegetables under plastic – most of Spain's winter produce comes from here. There are tourist towns such as Aguadulce and Roquetas de Mar. East of Almería, however, lie some lovely unspoiled spots, such as the area around Cabo de Gata.

The hot, dusty port of Almería gets on to few tourists' itineraries. However, Almería was once an independent kingdom and the most important Moorish capital in Spain.

The city "is like a bucket of whitewash thrown down at the foot of a bare greyish mountain" (Gerald Brenan) and is crowned by an impressive Moorish alcázaba. There are few other reminders of its past glory. But with its narrow streets and colourful cave dwellings – the fisherfolk's Barrio de la Chanca – the city still has a particular Arabic atmosphere.

Its name comes from the Moorish *Al Mariya* which means the mirror of the sea.

DON'T MISS . . .

Alcázaba

(Open 10.00–14.00 and 16.00–20.00 in summer, 9.00–14.00 and 15.00–19.00 in winter.)

The Phoenicians were the first known Almerían settlers, Carthaginians, Romans, Visigoths, then Arabs followed. Between 1035 and 1091, after the fall of Córdoba, Almería became an independent kingdom. In 1091 it was taken by the Almoravides and in 1147 Alfonso VII, king of Castille, and Ramon Berenguer, count of Barcelona, conquered but only held it for ten years. The Moors reconquered it in 1157 and ruled it pirate-fashion until the city fell to Ferdinand the Catholic in 1488. In 1490 the Moors were expelled and afterwards Almería declined. For much of the Civil War it was a strong Republican base.

An old saying goes: "When Almería was Almería, Granada was but its *cortijo* [farm]." The strongest Moorish fortress in Spain, Almería's 10th-century alcazaba towers above the city. During its peak it contained beautiful gardens and palaces. Unfortunately much was destroyed in an earthquake in 1522. But views of the city are wonderful and the gardens over the ruined fortifications make a cool escape from the hot streets below.

Cathedral
(Open 8.30–12.00 and 17.30–20.00)
With its four massive towers and fortresslike construction, the cathedral looks as though it was built more for war than for prayer. In fact it fulfilled both military and religious functions, and its four towers did once hold cannons.

The cathedral was built in 1524 after the destruction of its predecessor – a former mosque – in the 1522 earthquake. Its fortified construction was made necessary by Barbary pirates who periodically attacked Almería.

FACTFILE

Tourist Office, Calle Hermanos Machado. Tel: 23 06 07.
Trains, Carretera de Ronda. Tel: 25 11 35.
Buses, Plaza de Barcelona. Tel: 22 10 11.
Ferry A daily six-hour crossing operates to Melilla. It is signposted the Transmediterránea.
Post Office, Plaza J, Cassinello.
Telephones, Calle Navarro Rodrigo, 9, Open Monday–Saturday 9.00–13.00 and 17.00–21.00. The code is 951.

> The alcázaba dates from the 8th century but of the original palace only the foundation walls remain. The best remains are the keep built by Ferdinand and Isabella – you can see their arms above the Gothic gateway – and the Mozarabic chapel of San Juan. The building is linked by a wall to the hill of St Cristobal and the ruins of a Knights Templar castle.

Police, Avenida del Mediterraneo. Tel: 22 37 04.
Hospital, Calle Hospital. Tel: 23 05 04.

WHERE TO STAY

All quite central:
Casa La Francesa, Calle Narvaez, 18. Tel: 23 75 54. Run by a woman who speaks excellent French. The rooms are clean and simple and the price of the shower is included.
Andalucia', Calle Granada, 9. Tel 23 77 33. Clean but not very inspiring. Some rooms have their own bath. You can eat here, too. Good value.
Casa Universal, Calle Puerta de Purchena, 3. Tel: 23 55 57. Very central location. Spacious rooms with or without bath. Front rooms are noisy.
Maribel, Avenida Federico García Lorca, 153. Tel: 23 51 73.
Within walking distance of the bus and train stations. Cheap but reasonable.
Nixar, Calle Antonio Vico, 14. Tel· 23 72 55. Close to the Puerta de Purchena. Slightly more expensive than the others. Well-kept and friendly. Most rooms have private bath. Worth the extra.

FOOD AND DRINK

Almería isn't a brilliant place for eating out. Nevertheless, you will find several acceptable places in the little streets perpendicular to the Paseo de Almería. Otherwise, try these;
Bodega la Botas, Calle Fructuoso Perez, 5, Atmospheric, lively place with good food.
Bar Bahia de la Palma, Plaza de la Constitucion, near the Ayuntamiento, Excellent *tapas*.
Tabla La Blanca Paloma, Calle Federico de Castro, 1, Busy bar with tasty *tapas*, *Trigo*, a hearty soup or stew, is the local speciality.
Pizzeria Augusto Cesares, Parque Nicolas Salmeron, 12. Situated in the park next to the port. Good, reasonably priced pizzas. Have a beer in the bar **El Barril** nearby.
   A trendy drinking area is that around Plaza de Masnou, which is crowded with pubs and bars. **Pedraforca** and **El Porron** are two of the best known. At the latter, drinks are served in glass *porrones*, spouted drinking bottles.

EAST OF ALMERIA

Cabo de Gata (literally, Cape Cat, but the place name derives from Cabo de Agata, or agate, because semiprecious stones used to be found here) can be reached by bus from Almería main bus station. The entire tip of the peninsula is wonderfully unspoiled with one of the best beaches in this part of the Mediterranean. The long strech of windswept sand begins at the small town of **El Cabo de Gata** (where some accommodation is available but is likely to be full in summer) and runs for 5 km to the salt pans at Las Salinas. The lagoon behind is a haven for flamingos. At the far end the road climbs perilously up the cliffs to the *faro* or lighthouse.

Farther round the coast is **San José**, which is a much more developed, but still low-key, resort (lots of cars from Barcelona). It is set against a wide, sandy cove. The beach isn't that nice but the water is good. Haphazard private development is taking place and there are several fairly expensive places to stay; try Casa Huespedes **Costa Rica** for the cheapest option. **Camping La Tau** is set in trees behind the beach. The seafront quay on the far side of the bay offers a selection of eating places; it is especially nice at night.

Working round the coast, you'll reach **Los Escullos**, which has a good beach, followed by the tiny, as yet unspoiled fishing village of **La Isleta del Moro**. This is an idyllic spot if you want to do nothing. It has a small beach nearby but the main attraction is peaceful simplicity. The main square is unpaved and the women still mend nets and do their washing communally here. A single, well-run *hostal* with a bar and restaurant, where you can eat the freshest fish imaginable, provides delightful rooms overlooking the fishing boats: Hostal **La Isleta** (Tel: 951/36 63 13).

Inland, **Nijar** in the hills has several places to stay, and offers attractive pottery and rugs.

Carboneras is the next resort along the coast. Not wonderfully attractive (Agua Amarga is prettier), it nevertheless has several *hostales*. The cheapest is **La Marina** on Calle/General Mola, the most expensive **El Dorado** on Playa de Carboneras, tel 951/45 40 505. The beach out of town to the north is empty and unspoiled.

The road continues along the cliffs to **Mojácar**; though

passable, it is a rough drive but is being improved. At the time of writing it is quicker to go back via the main road.

Mojácar is a fully fledged resort, though more tastefully developed than most. The town with its white sugarcube houses is set back in the hills while the narrow beach at its foot is backed by a busy road and lined with restaurants and trendy beach bars. Packed out in summer, the only relatively cheap places to stay are the Fonda **El Africano** (Tel: 951/47 80 10) and the Hostal **El Puntato** (Tel: 951/47 82 29), both on the beach road, **Camping El Cantal** by the sea is a good if popular choice if you have a tent.

La Garrucha, further north, isn't anything special but has several *hostales*.

CÓRDOBA

Every day hundreds of people miss Córdoba's biggest delight. They drive for miles to see the Mezquita, have a look around and get back in their car or their coach – all of them missing out on the real pleasure of just staying in the city.

You almost can't fail to find pretty accommodation in Córdoba. Most of it is in the narrow whitewashed alleyways of the old Jewish quarter within a few yards of the historic Mezquita. But it is the beautiful flower-drenched patios that make most *hostales* and *fondas* so exquisite. Every May there is a competition for the city's prettiest patios. Nearly all buildings have one and all year round everyone seems to be competing.

Today's Córdoba is a fusion of cultures and the evidence of these cultures is still tangible. The city's oldest bridge has Roman foundations, its cathedral was built as a mosque and Spain's oldest synagogue outside Toledo still stands in the Juderia.

Córdoba's ancient crafts of shoemaking and silversmithing continue in the old part of the city while the modern part of town, experiencing a recent boom under its communist mayor, has a relaxed atmosphere less frenzied than that at Granada or Seville.

GETTING YOUR BEARINGS

Córdoba's train and bus stations are in the modern part of town to the north, which is a shame, because the best way to approach Córdoba is from the south, across the Puente Romano, with the view of the Mezquita in front of you. The Judería, the delightful maze of streets forming the old Jewish quarter, flanks the giant mosque. The Alcázar of the Reyes Católicos, the column of San Rafael and the triumphal arch built for Philip II all cluster together nearby. To the east is the charming Plaza del Potro. Beyond lies the decaying 17th-century Plaza de la Corredera, which was once used for bullfights. Further north, around the Plaza de las Tendillas, is the clean modern town which has grown up on the centre of the old Roman settlement, and here you'll find a restored, almost complete Roman temple.

DON'T MISS ...

The Mezquita
(Admission charge. Open 10.30–13.30 and 15.30–18.00.)
A labyrinthine forest of endless Roman columns and double red and white Moorish arches, the Mezquita was the most beautiful mosque ever built by the Moors in Spain. It was so revered that it became a place of pilgrimage almost equal in importance to the mosques at Mecca and Jerusalem.

For 750 years it has officially been Christian and for the last 500 it has housed the addition of a cathedral right in its heart. But despite Charles V's accusation that "you have built here what you might have built anywhere else but have destroyed what was unique in the world", most of the original Mezquita still stands and in parts you can ignore the incongruous Christian addition. The building remains the most sumptuous monument built by the Cordoban caliphate and one of Spain's great architectural treasures.

Córdoba was originally called Kartuba, a Phoenician name which means rich and beautiful city. The Romans conquered in 152 BC and renamed it Corduva. After the civil war between Caesar and Pompey, the city was left almost ruined. Augustus reconstructed it and Corduva flourished to become the biggest city in Baetica, or southern Roman Spain. It was the birthplace of Seneca the elder and his son Seneca the younger, a philosopher and teacher of Nero.

The Moors invaded in AD 711 and, by the 10th century, under the Omayyads, the city had become the capital of the independent caliphate, reaching the peak of its cultural and political brilliance. The economy and agriculture boomed (there was a sophisticated irrigation system outside the city), the riches of the empire poured in, and Córdoba boasted a population of over half a million, with universities, schools, libraries, palaces, baths and several hundred mosques, the grandest of which was the Mezquita. In short, it was one of the great centres of the medieval world, with a civilization rivalling those of Constantinople and Damascus. In the 11th century, on account of bitter squabbling among the different Moorish factions, the caliphate splintered into separate states or *taifas* and Córdoba's glory declined, Moorish power shifted to Seville, although throughout the 12th century Córdoba's intellectual life continued to flourish – Averroes, the Moorish philosopher (who made Aristotle's works famous in the West) and the Jewish scholar Maimonides both lived in the city at this time. In 1236 the Christians conquered under Ferdinand III.

Two and a half centuries later it was in Córdoba that Queen Isabella gave her consent to Columbus's voyage which led to the colonization of America. Nevertheless, under the Catholic Kings and their successors the city waned. The Judería was left deserted in 1492 with the expulsion of the Jews.

Córdoba fell early to the Nationalists in the Civil War but in 1979 returned a communist mayor and is now experiencing a newfound prosperity.

Yet, in spite of the impression of uniformity created by the endless rows of columns and canopies, many of the 850 pillars are different. A few are Visigothic but most are Roman, some having been brought from as far away as Carthage and Constantinople. Marble, jasper, onyx, granite and even wood have been used; some are smooth, some ribbed, some spiralled. The capitals are also of mixed origin, supporting the tiered arches which in turn support a ceiling of larch.

The central axis from the Puerta de las Palmas directs you to the focal point of the original mosque, the sacred Mihrab, now tucked away in an almost forgotten corner. This is the niche which indicated the direction of Mecca. Its magnificent shell-shaped dome amplified the imam's prayers. In front and to the side is the Maksourah, the caliphs' enclosure. Surrounded by multilobed columns and covered in a wealth of shining mosaics of gold, turquoise, red and blue, complete with friezes from the Koran, it is an awesome relic of a former Spanish civilization.

Built on the site of a Visigothic church, the original mosque dates from 785. It was begun by Abd Ar-Rahman I and completed in 790 by his son. At this stage it formed a square made up of 11 horizontal and 11 vertical aisles. After some minor alterations by his predecessors, Al Hakam II (961–76) expanded it considerably to the south and added the present Mihrab (Muslim prayer niche). In 990, under Al Mansur, it was extended again, this time to the east, and its internal symmetry was distorted. Although it was converted to Christian worship after the Reconquest, it was not until the 16th century that the cathedral made its intrusion.

From outside the periphery wall you enter through the Puerta del Perdon. This is the 14th-century Mudéjar gateway next to the belfry where the minaret once stood. You pass into the Patio de los Naranjos, the original Moorish courtyard still full of its namesake orange trees, with the Moorish fountain (the Al Mansur basin) in the middle. Opposite is the Puerta de las Palmas, originally the mosque's central doorway when it was only 11 aisles wide.

On first entering the Mezquita it is almost possible to be disappointed. It is cold and dark inside without an obvious focal point. But it wasn't always like this. Before they were blocked up and turned into side chapels by the Christians, light flooded in through the 19 doorways, so the interior was illuminated from all directions. With no separating wall between them, the forest of columns inside the mosque appeared as an extension of the trees outside, and the distinction between the secular patio (where social meetings took place) and the holy interior was blurred. The original intention was to create an open, airy atmosphere and structurally this was achieved by the sophisticated architectural technique of superimposing the columns with two sets of horseshoe-shaped arches. The effect was one of height and spaciousness with a feeling of meditative unity and harmony.

The Puente Romano and Torre Calahorra

The ancient-looking Puente Romano – literally, Roman bridge – crosses the river Guadalquivir just a few paces from the Mezquita. The bridge is not really Roman at all. It was built in the 8th century by the Moors on Roman foundations after the original bridge was destoyed by the Visigoths and has subsequently been much restored. Downstream are the

It is hard to be dispassionate about the **cathedral** since it has such an effect on the Moorish purity of the Mezquita. Construction went ahead in 1523 against the wishes of the city council (Charles V gave his permission, then regretted his decision) and to make way for the *coro* and the *capilla mayor*, a central part of the roof and 63 columns were removed. It was built in a mixture of styles – the transept and apse are Gothic, the arrangement of the walls is Renaissance and much of the decoration is Baroque. The inaccessible remains of a Mudéjar chapel, the Capilla de Villaviciosa, can be seen just south of the *coro*.

To get a good picture of the overall layout of the building, climb the bell tower for a bird's-eye view.

remains of the Arab water wheels, including one, in front of the Alcazar which Isabella had destroyed because it disturbed her sleep. **The Torre Calahorra** (Open 10.00–14.00 and 17.30 to 20.00; 10.00–18.00 in winter; Sunday 10.00–14.00 Closed Monday), on the other side of the Puente Romano, was formerly the guardian tower of the bridge. It now houses a complicated high-tech museum, not very visitor-friendly, which does, none the less, possess one gem. As you go in you're given a cordless headset which has been tuned in to the language you require. You proceed through a series of rooms, triggering off a commentary as you enter each one. Music plays, lights go on and off. It would all be very marvellous were it not for the technical hiccoughs. My headset occasionally picked up German as well as English and some exhibits refused to work. Persevere, however, because the room on the top floor houses a model Mezquita, the way it appeared at the height of the Cordoban caliphate. The model demonstrates perfectly how the great mosque was designed to look. Here the lights really come into their own – shining into the building and passing uninterrupted through the forest of columns. It makes you wonder how the Christians could ever have messed it up.

Alcázar de los Reyes Católicos
(Open 9.30–13.30 and 17.00–20.00, 16.00–19.00 in winter. Free on Sundays.)

The best thing about this alcázar, where Ferdinand and Isabella sometimes held court, is the beautiful terraced gardens, interlaced with cypresses and pools containing goldfish and carp. At night they are floodlit. The fortress-palace itself, rising from the Guadalquiver's north bank a couple of hundred metres down from the Puente Romano, was built in the 14th century on the site of an earlier Arab construction and contains some original Moorish courtyards, large Roman mosaics and a sarcophagus. Between 1490 and 1821 it served as the headquarters of the Spanish Inquisition.

The Judería

Get beautifully lost in the maze of white lanes north of the Mezquita, but look out for a few important landmarks. By the Almodavar gate in the old Moorish walls you will come across one of the few legacies of the former occupants of this barrio. The tiny Mudéjar-style synagogue in Calle Judios (open 10.00–14.00 and 15.30–17.30; closed Mondays and Sunday afternoons) bears witness to the contemporary climate of tolerance. You can still see remains of the stucco decoration and the Hebrew inscriptions plus the unusual women's balcony. Nearby is the statue of the Jewish religious scholar and philosopher Maimonides.

Don't miss the exquisite **Calleja de las Flores** north of the Mezquita, which affords a flower-framed view of the cathedral belfry. And in the surrounding streets the patios of virtually every house make it hard to resist stopping to have a quick look.

ALSO WORTH SEEING . . .

Museo Arqueologico

(Plaza Paez/Alta de Santa Ana. Open Tuesday–Saturday 10.00–14.00 and 17.00–19.00; closed Sunday afternoons.) Housed in a Renaissance mansion on the edges of Judería, this is the largest archaeological museum in Andalusia and the third largest in Spain. It contains Roman mosaics, early Christian art and a fine collection of Moorish artefacts including items from the site of Medina Azahara. The museum itself was under restoration in 1991.

Museo de Arte Taurino

(Plaza de Maimonides. Open 10.00–13.00 and 17.00–20.00; 16.00–19.00 October–April; Sundays mornings only; closed Mondays.)

Dedicated to the art of *tauromaquia* with rooms devoted to Córdoba's most famous bullfighting sons, this Municipal Museum is over on the opposite side of Juderia, near the synagogue. Crammed with Manolete memorabilia, it has pictures of his last fight, his death mask and the carcass of the bull that killed him.

Museo de Bellas Artes and the Museo Julio Romero de Torres

(Plaza del Potro.)

The square itself with its colt-topped fountain (*potro* means colt) is more enticing than the museums. The 14th-century inn or *posada* in the square is mentioned in *Don Quixote* by Cervantes and now displays artisan work. The Fine Art Museum houses some canvases by Zurbarán and Goya among others, while Julio Romero de Torres was a turn-of-the-century Córdoban painter of romantic nudes.

OUT OF TOWN . . .

Medina Azahara

A palace town of immense proportions, the ruined Medina Azahara is another example of monumental Moorish architecture. It stands about 8 km west of town. It was built for Caliph Abd Ar Rahman's favourite wife, who was called Azahara, meaning orange blossom. Begun in 936, it was probably the most luxurious palace Spain has ever seen but it only lasted 80 years before being destoyed by rebellious Berber mercenaries. For centuries it was plundered as a quarry (parts of Seville's Alcázar came from here) until 50 years ago excavations and restoration began.

The complex was built on three levels – on the lowest were the mosque, municipal buildings, accommodation and stables, in the middle were the gardens and on the upper level was the alcazar itself. A small museum shows some of the treasures found on the site but to appreciate the scale and grandeur of the palace, let your imagination run riot.

The site is open Tuesday–Saturday 10.00–14.00 and 16.00–18.00; Sundays mornings only. To reach it from Córdoba, take the Villarubia road and simply follow the signs. A free bus tour operates from the Alcazar on Wednesdays and Fridays at 10.00. Alternatively, Autotransportes San Sebastian from Calle de la Bodega runs five buses a day past the crossroads 2 km from the site.

CÓRDOBA FACTFILE

Tourist Office Calle Torrijos, 10. (Tel: 47 12 35.) This is the provincial office and is situated on the west side of the mosque. Open Monday–Friday 9.00–14.00 and 17.00–19.00, Saturday 9.30–13.30. The municipal office is at Plaza Juda Levi, (Tel: 29 07 40) and is open Monday–Friday 9.00–14.00. Ask for a map of the Judería.
Airport, 6 km from city centre, domestic flights only, Iberia, Ronda de los Tejares, 3. Tel: 47 26 95.
Trains Avenida de América. Tel: 47 82 21, information 47 93 02. RENFE office, Ronda de los Tejares, 10.
Buses Alsina Graells Sur, Avenida Medina Azahara, 29 (Tel: 23 27 34), for Granada, Málaga, Almería, Cádiz, Empresa Urena, Avenida de Cervantes, 22 (Tel: 47 23 52), for Seville and Jaen, Autocares Priego, Paseo de la Victoria, 29 (Tel: 29 01 58), for Madrid, Valencia and Barcelona.
Post Office Calle Cruz Conde, 21. North of the Plaza de las Tendillas. Post code is 14001.
Telefonica, Plaza de las Tendillas, 7. Open Monday–Friday 9.00–13.00 and 17.00–21.00. Code is 957.
Police, Avenida del Dr Fleming, 25. Tel: 47 75 00, emergency 091.

WHERE TO STAY

Head immediately for the Judería, the picturesque streets around the mosque, where you'll find the prettiest accommodation in Spain – small, well-kept *hostales* with simple rooms looking on to gorgeous patios or narrow whitewashed alleyways.

Cheap to Moderate

Pension Martinez Rucker, Calle Martinez Rucker, 14. Tel: 47 25 62. In a small street to the east of the mosque, this immaculately kept *hostal* has sweet little rooms, ultra-clean modern bathrooms (showers included), a delightful patio and a friendly woman owner. Quieter than some of the others nearby. Excellent value.
Fonda Rey Heredia, Calle Rey Heredia, 26. Tel: 47 41 82. In a long street almost parallel to the eastern side of the mosque. Nice patio

decorated with colourful ceramics. Rooms only have washbasins but there are modern bathrooms on the landing and showers are included in the price. Slightly more basic than the others.

Pension La Milagrosa, Calle Rey Heredia, 12. Tel: 47 33 17. Smarter and consequently more expensive than the above with yet another lovely arcaded patio. Some rooms have bathrooms; if they don't, then showers are extra. Spotless.

Seneca, Calle Conde y Luque, 5. Tel: 47 32 34. The street is parallel to the north side of the mosque. Efficiently run by two women – one Spanish, one French – who have both put their heart in the *hostal*. It is one of the most popular in Córdoba. Beautifully decorated and full of personal touches. The charming patio overflows with plants and flowers. Not all the rooms have showers but the bathrooms are modern and very clean. Breakfast (with good coffee) is available in the small breakfast room. Slightly more expensive than its counterparts. Worth booking ahead.

Luis de Gongora, Calle Horno de la Trinidad, 7. Tel: 29 53 99. On the northern edge of the Judería, near the synagogue. A quiet, very pleasant, well-run hotel that is good value for money. On a par with the Seneca and the Milagrosa but less expensive than their top-price rooms. A good option.

El Leon, Calle Cespedes, 6. Tel: 47 30 21. In a tiny street just north of the mosque. Run by a friendly chap who speaks French and spends a lot of time mending his motorbike in the rather untidy patio (which features an earless bull's head). It has a larger capacity than some of its neighbours, which puts a strain on the single bathroom. Breakfast available in the patio if you give notice the night before. Some of the rooms facing the street can be noisy late at night.

El Portillo, Calle Cabezas, 2. Tel: 47 20 91. Off the lower and of Calle Rey Heredia but still only five minutes from the mosque. This typical Córdoban house has a marble patio surrounded by old *azulejos* and with a stained-glass window. Simple rooms. Showers extra.

Mari, Calle Pimentera, 6 and 8. Tel: 47 95 75. Just south of the above. Hard to find if you're looking for the street but the *hostal* is signposted. It has a pretty garden and the cheapest prices in town.

Fonda Augustina, Calle Zapateria Vieja, 5. Tel: 47 08 72. Close to the above. It also has rooms in Calle Cardenal Gonzalez, 48, which are more modern. Cheap, clean and cheerful. There is a dining room in the old part where the owner lets you eat your own meals.

Smarter Options

El Triunfo, Calle Cardenal Gonzalez, 79. Tel: 47 63 76. Excellent situation on the south side of the mosque. Each of the 45 rooms has bathroom and phone and is spotless. The rooms overlooking the patio are the quietest. The *hostal* has a good restaurant and bar downstairs but the menu doesn't vary a great deal.

Marisa, Calle Cardenal Herrero, 6. Tel: 47 31 42. Superbly situated hold right opposite the mosque (which means the noisy bells can be a bit of a problem). Quite small – it has 28 well-furnished rooms, all with bath. Breakfast available but not included in the price. More expensive than the Triunfo. Reservations recommended, but you might be lucky out of season.

WHERE TO EAT

There isn't an abundance of good, cheap restaurants in Córdoba, although there are a lot of mediocre tourist eating places around the Mezquita. Just a few of these aren't too bad and also attract locals. Some of the *tapas* bars in the Judería are good and you will also find a couple of the town's best restaurants here. If you get the chance, try the local versions of gazpacho – a white one made from almonds – or *salmorejo*, a thicker version of the usual with egg and ham on top.

Cheap to Moderate

Don Manuel, Calle Cardenal Gonzalez, 19, southeast of the Mezquita. A lively, family-run restaurant that is open all night. It offers several very reasonable menus and if you eat late you might see some live flamenco. Quite touristy but not exclusively so.

Restaurante LaLaLa, Calle Cruz del Rastro, 3, on the corner of the riverfront road, between the Mezquita and the Plaza del Potro. Excellent salads as well as a good selection of well-priced menus. Try their watermelon *sangría*. Very good value.

Bar Juda Levi, Plaza Juda Levi, opposite the tourist information. Excellent, well-prepared *tapas* and *platos combinados* which you can eat outside in the square. Lots of young Spaniards come here for just a beer and an ice cream.

Bar Mesón Rafae, Calle Deanes (corner of Calle Buen Pastor). Northwest of the Mezquita. Open all day, it offers a good dish of the day as well as a list of cheap *raciones*. You'll find lots of locals in here with the tourists. Traditional atmosphere.

Casa Pepe de la Judería, Calle Romero (corner of Calle Deanes). Close to the above. One of Córdoba's most popular bars, serving good *tapas*. A traditional Andalusian *taberna* with patio. It is being renovated.

El Extremeño, Plaza Benavente, 1. Very central location. The menus are a little steep but it does good Estremaduran specialities. Reasonable *platos combinados*.

Restaurante Cafeteria Halai, Calle Rey Heredia, 28. A sort of Islamic community centre with a restaurant. In the makeshift dining room you can choose from three set menus, including couscous and *harira*, or opt for just tea in the Eastern-style front room. Makes an interesting change.

Taberna El Potro, corner of Calle Lucano and Calle Enrique Romero de Torres, Good-value *menú del día* and a selection of *tapas* that you can eat outside at the lower end of the pretty Plaza del Potro.

Smarter Options

El Churrasco, Calle Romero, 16. Tel: 20 04 39. Right in the heart of the Judería. Specializes in grilled meats with hot pepper sauce but the *rape en salsa de pinones* (monkfish in pinenut sauce) is also delicious. Set in a lovely old building with an arcaded patio complete with fountain. One dining room is downstairs as are the bar and open grill; upstairs it is more formal. Enticing display of *tapas* at the bar. Closed Thursdays and in August.

El Caballo Rojo, Calle Cardenal Herrero, 28. Tel: 47 53 75. Just north of the Mezquita down a flowery passageway. One of the smartest, most expensive restaurants in Córdoba. The old *mesón* has three levels with bars, a terrace and several dining rooms. Inventive cuisine; its specialities include *rabo de toro*, *rape mozarabe* and *cordero a la miel*. Or try the *cazuela de pescado al Pedro Ximenz* – assorted fish in sweet sherry. They also do a white gazpacho made from almonds and apples.

La Almudaina, Plaza de los Santos Martires, 1. Tel: 47 43 42. Near the alcazar. This renovated school with its lovely courtyard is considered to be one of the most attractive restaurants in Andalusia. Fish is their speciality – try the salmon crepes. Not quite up to the standard of the Caballo Rojo, though.

BARS & NIGHTLIFE

The Sociedad de Plateros is an association of *tabernas* scattered throughout the Judería offering their own selection of wines. One of the nicest, with a big patio, is in Calle Barros near the Museo Julio Romero de Torres. Otherwise there are plenty more little bars and bodegas all over the Judería where you can sample the local very dry fino known as Montilla.

Most of Córdoba's nightlife centres on the streets near San Hipolito church, and in Calle Reyes Católicos and Calle de Osario, north of Plaza de las Tendillas in the new part of town. Lively pubs and bars include **Epoca**, **La Buhardilla** and **Los Turnos**. Another popular area is out of town on the Carretera del Brillante – try **La Luna** (live music), **Sherezade** or **La Torre**. Some other favourite bars:

Bar Santos, next to the Mezquita, by the north corner. Famous for its excellent *tortilla de patatas* – get there early or it runs out.

Bar Mezquita, Calle Cardenal Herrero, 24. Tiny, traditional bar (one of the oldest in Córdoba) with nice *tapas*. Right next to the Mezquita.

Café-Bar Coronas, Calle Blanco Belmonte, just north of the Mezquita. Sit outside and soak up the atmosphere in this charming corner while you listen to the dance school next door practising flamenco.

Mesón Cabezas, Calle Cabezas, in the patio of an old house with great big wood and leather seats.

Bodega Campos, Calle Lineros, 32, near the Plaza del Potro. Full of barrels of the local sherries, some bearing signatures of the celebrities who have been here over the years (it opened in 1908). Try the Montilla fino or the Moriles from the nearby towns of the same names.

PLUS . . .

Varsovia, Calle Romero, 6. Disco bar in the Judería – youngish crowd.

- **Flamenco** La Buleria, Calle Pedro Lopez, 3. Tel: 48 38 39. Near the Plaza Corredera. Touristy flamenco shows on offer every night, except Mondays, from 21.00. No cover and a lot cheaper than Seville. There is also a National Flamenco Contest held every three years in May. At other times, flamenco festivals are held during the summer. (Go to the *caseta* in Plaza San Hipolito or ask at the tourist office).

- **Live concerts** International Guitar Festival hosts concerts from July to October (for details, Tel: 48 02 37 or go to the box office at the Gran Teatro on Avenida del Gran Captain, 3). Sunday concerts are often held in the gardens of the alcazar.

- Every morning all Córdoba's street pedlars, tinkers and traders gather to do business in Plaza de la Corredera, a dilapidated but still charming square. It's a real people's **market** – hardly a tourist in sight. You'll find herbs, cheap clothes, live birds and rabbits and some of the cheapest *churros* in Spain. Adjacent is a covered food market and the surrounding streets are full of artisan workshops.

- **La Flor de Levante,** in Plaza de las Tendillas, is one of the many excellent **heladerias** in the city centre (others include Siena Bar with a terrace and Gran Café) where grannies come to spoil their grandchildren with 45-cm long ice-cream cones (*barquillas*). Great *horchata* and *granizados*.

- The **Zoco** is a restored Arab souk, close to the synagogue, which has been turned into a crafts market. Interesting souvenirs on offer.

Good-quality leather items also available at the Leatherworkers' Guild in Calle Encarnacion.

MÁLAGA

Of the thousands of tourists who fly into Málaga airport each year, most give Málaga a miss. It has no decent beaches, it is surrounded by ugly high-rise buildings and is famous for its high unemployment and crime rates. Nevertheless, there are considerable pleasures to be had here, and it makes a good base.

Unlike the holiday developments that surround it, Málaga is a proper Spanish city where you can soak up an atmosphere entirely different from that in most places on the Costa del Sol. There are excellent fish restaurants where you can sample Málaga's famous fried fish, and plenty of ancient bodegas where you can taste the city's own sweet wine – known as Málaga. And there is an elegant tree-lined seafront promenade. If you have just flown in without accommodation, Málaga has many cheap options in the old town and if you want to move on there are good connections to other parts of Spain.

Málaga also has a few things to see – the one-armed cathedral is curious if not splendid (it only has one finished tower), and the fortresses of the Alcázar and Gibralfaro make good introductions to Moorish architecture in Andalusia. The Museo de Bellas Artes contains early sketches and paintings by Picasso, who was born here in 1881.

If you come just before Easter, Málaga's Semana Santa is on a par with that at Seville (following a centuries-old tradition, prisoners still carry one of the floats in a Maundy Thursday procession) and around the first week of August a big city celebration commemorates the Catholic Kings' victory over the Moors with parades and bullfights.

GETTING YOUR BEARINGS

The easiest way to get from the airport to the town centre is to take the suburban electric train. On leaving the arrivals lounge, go through the car park and follow the signs to the

Málaga was a Phoenician, Carthaginian, then Roman port. It became an episcopal seat in the 4th century but was taken by the Moors in 711. Later it became the main port for the Nasrid dynasty at Granada but in 1487, after a long siege, it was taken by Ferdinand the Catholic. It flourished again as a trading port with the acquisition of Spain's overseas colonies but declined when she lost them at the end of the 19th century.

During the Civil War Málaga was a Republican stronghold until the Nationalists took it in 1937. Violent reprisals followed and thousands of Republicans were executed. Many of its historical buildings were destroyed at this time.

ferrocarril. The trains run every 30 minutes and are very cheap. Málaga is the last stop going east (in the other direction they run to Fuengirola via Torremolinos and other resorts). You arrive at a small separate station – the RENFE and main bus terminal are a short walk up the road. It is about a 20-minute walk into the centre (bus No. 3 takes you to Plaza de la Marina). Coming back, it is worth noting that there are two airport stops – one *nacional* and one *internacional*. Buses (Empresa Portillo company) also run from the airport to the city every 30 minutes and drop you off at Calle Córdoba near the alameda. They return from the same place.

The main throughfare is the tree-lined Alameda Principal which becomes the Paseo del Parque after the Plaza de la Marina. At the far end loom the Alcázaba and Gibralfaro. The main commercial area lies to the north of the Alameda in the network of old narrow streets off Calle Marques de Larios and Calle Granada. The cathedral is also here.

DON'T MISS . . .

Alcázaba and Gibralfaro
(Open 10.00–13.00 and 16.00–19.00, Sunday 10.00–14.00.)
The **Alcázaba** is Málaga's best sight and even if you're only killing time before moving on elsewhere, it is definitely worth a quick visit.

Although the main structure was built in the 8th century, the fortress is Roman in origin and marble Roman pillars blend in with the Moorish brickwork. (There is also a partly covered Roman theatre near the entrance to the Alcázaba.) The palace, with two decorated patios (11th and 12th century) and Moorish-style *artesonado* ceiling (20th century), has been restored as an archaeological museum and contains a good collection of Moorish ceramics from the 9th to 15th centuries.

Farther up the hill is the ruined **Gibralfaro** castle (*gibralfaro* means lighthouse hill) connected to the Alcázaba by a double wall. You can walk up through the beautiful gardens of bougainvillea, honeysuckle and jasmine, a bit of a hike, or drive along the road which leads to the nearby *parador*. The view from the top is wonderful.

Cathedral

(Open 10.00–13.00 and 16.00–17.30. Entrance fee unless you're coming to pray.)

Málaga's cathedral, heart of the old quarter of town, is most famous for its incomplete tower. The little stump on the south side is known as la Manquita – the missing one. The cathedral was begun in the early 16th century and is built in the Renaissance style. Its most outstanding feature inside is the elaborately carved choir stall, which took over 60 years to make. The Capilla de los Reyes contains statues of Ferdinand and Isabella and a gilded statue of the Virgin – reputed to have been carried into battle during the Reconquest. Outside there is an Isabelline door on the Calle Santa Maria side of the building.

Museo de Bellas Artes (Fine Arts Museum)

(Calle Augustin, 6. Open 10.00–13.30 and 17.00–20.00, 16.00–19.00 in winter. Closed Mondays and Sunday afternoons.)

Exhibits in this former palace of the Moors close to the cathedral display some of Picasso's earliest works, as well as an assortment of items from the family home of Málaga's most famous son.

Mercado Central,

The main doorway to the market, just north of the Alameda Principal is a horseshoe-shaped arch from the original Moorish city walls. Inside is a bustling modern-day version of an Arab souk.

FACTFILE

Tourist Office, Calle Marques de Larios, 5. Tel: 21 34 45. Near Plaza de la Marina. Open Monday–Saturday 9.00–14.00 and in summer 16.00–20.00 as well. Closed Sunday. They provide maps of the centre and lists of *fondas*.

Airport About 9 km out of town. See directions above. Domestic and international flights, Iberia, Calle Molin Lario, 13. Tel: 22 76 00. Airport enquiries, tel: 31 60 00.

Trains The main RENFE station is on Calle Cuarteles. Tel: 31 25 00. There is an office in the centre of town at Calle Strachan, 2 (Tel: 21 31 22) near the cathedral. To Madrid (four trains per day) takes about 8 hours, to Barcelona (two trains, per day) about 14 hours. Connections to other Andalusian cities. You often have to change at Bobadilla junction.

Buses Central bus station at Paseo de los Tilos, behind RENFE. Different bus companies serve different destinations. Alsina Graells (Tel: 31 04 00), Portillo (Tel: 22 73 00) and Los Amarillos (Tel: 21 35 29) serve most of Andalusia. Granada 9 buses per day/takes about 1½ hrs; Ronda 11 per day/takes 3 hrs; Córdoba 2 per day/2½ hrs; Almería 3 per day/4½ hrs (stops along the coast). Buses also run to Madrid (Portillo-3 per day/9 hrs); Barcelona (3 per day/18 hrs), Alicante and Valencia (11 hrs) – all with Empresa Bacoma (Tel: 32 13 62).

Car Hire Numerous companies offering good deals line the walls at Málaga airport. Benelux has reasonable rates.

Post Office, Avenida de Andalucia. Tel: 35 91 07. Open Monday–Friday 9.00–14.00 and 16.00–18.00, Saturday 9.00–14.00. Post code is 29070.

Telefonica, Calle Molina Larios, 11, next to the cathedral. Open Monday–Saturday 9.00–21.00, Sunday 10.00–13.00. Code is 952.

Consulates UK Edificio Duquesa, Duquesa de Parcent. Tel: 21 75 71. USA Edificio El Ancla Apt, 502, Calle Ramon y Cajal. Tel: 47 48 91.

Police Tel: 21 50 05, emergency 091.

Medical assistance Tel: 22 44 00.

WHERE TO STAY

Most *hostales* are located centrally in the streets just to the north of the Alameda Principal and the Paseo del Parque. However, Málaga accommodation, although plentiful and cheap, is shabby and generally lacks charm. Definitely avoid the seedy dives near the station.

Cheap to Moderate

Chinitas, Passaje de Chinitas, 2. Tel: 21 46 83. In a pretty alleyway near the Plaza de la Constitución. Eccentric, kitsch reception full of mirrors and fish tanks. Clean and friendly. Pricier *hostal* than the others but worth it.

Buenos Aires, Calle Bolsa, 12 Tel: 21 89 35. On the second floor of a building that has very confused numbering. Quite expensive compared to some of its neighbours but still good value: well-kept and friendly. Avoid the Hostal Moran downstairs.

La Palma, Calle Martinez, 3. Tel: 22 67 72. In a street full of *hostales*, parallel to the Alameda Principal. Run by a friendly couple. Much better than the squalid Hostal Europa in the same building.

Pension Ramos Calle Martinez, 8. Tel: 22 72 68. Very reasonable prices and rooms. The Pension Rosa is less friendly but has better bathrooms.

Fali, Calle Marques, 4. Tel: 21 02 15. North of the market. Rather dingy but very cheap.

Smarter Options

El Cenachero, Calle Barroso, 5. Tel: 22 40 88. Left at the bottom of Calle Córdoba near the seafront. Named after a popular Málaga character, an itinerant fish vendor whose statue stands in the Plaza de la Marina. A small, modern hotel, very clean and friendly. All rooms are carpeted and have a shower.

Derby, Calle San Juan de Dios, 1. Tel: 22 13 01. On a main square in the centre of Málaga. It is on the fourth floor and some of the rooms have views of the port and sea. More expensive than the above.

FOOD AND DRINK, NIGHTLIFE

There are lots of inexpensive places to eat in the town centre around Plaza de la Constitución and Plaza del Siglo. Another popular area is a couple of kilometres out of town at Pedregalejo and El Palo along the seafront (take bus No. 11 from the Paseo del Parque and get off at Restaurante El Tintero Dos). You'll find some superb fish restaurants and stalls as well as most of Málaga's nightspots. The city centre also has several good bars.

El Tormes, Calle San Jose, 2, near Calle Granada. Opposite the Museo de Bellas Artes. Closed in the evenings. Large choice of menus. Generous portions.

The Costa Del Sol

Spain's sunshine coast runs for 300 km from Gibraltar to Almería. Cheap land and an abundance of sunshine led to its development in the 1950s and it is still developing today.

West of Málaga are the sprawling major resorts of **Torremolinos**, **Fuengirola** and **Marbella** (in ascending order of smartness), and the rather tacky places in between. It is worth remembering that perfectly ordinary non-resorty Spanish towns lie just a short distance inland. There are also some quite pleasant smaller resorts in the hilly backcountry, **Mijas**, for example.

East of Málaga, the coast hasn't yet fallen prey to concrete, at least not on the scale of the western sector. There are some exceptions, such as the mini-Torremolinos of Torre del Mar, but the coast road has attractive views of the rugged cliffs and there are a few interesting stop-off points where you get an idea of what life was like before package holidays. Beaches are grey and coarse.

A focal point for beach holidays east of Málaga is **Nerja**. It is a large, but low-rise, development, and still retains some of its old village streets, has pleasant coves nearby and good nightlife. It is famous for its limestone caves and its Balcon de Europa jutting out into the Mediterranean. Accommodation is plentiful enough but expensive and extremely difficult to get hold of in July and August. Hostal **Florida** on Calle San Miguel, 35 (Tel: 52 07 43), near the bus station, is the cheapest; Hotel **Cala-Bela** on Calle Puerta del Mar, 10 (Tel: 52 07 00), is smarter and more expensive and has a good restaurant. The restaurant of the **Portofino** next door is excellent. You'll also find the tourist office here.

The much-visited caves near Nerja (buses every 30 minutes) are ultra-touristy, with piped music and photographers; but still spectacular with enormous stalactite and stalagmite formations. Open 9.00–21.00 in summer, 10.00–13.30 and 16.00–19.00 September–April.

Maro is a pretty, unspoiled village close to Nerja, as is **Frigiliana** in the hills behind. En route to Salobrena, however, there is not much to see – the corniche road has good views from Cerro Gordo but Almunecar is full of unattractive high-rises.

Salaboreña, a whitewashed, castle-topped village set in a sea of sugar cane, cannot conceal its Moorish legacy. The long beach at the foot of the village is grey and gritty but

La Tarantella, Calle Granada, 61. Pizzas and salads followed by the house speciality digestif – amaretto, port, sugar and something mysterious.

La Cancela, Calle Denis Belgrano, 3. Also near Calle Granada. Sit outside in the peaceful, flowery alleyway. Very good *sopa de mariscos*.

El Boqueron de Plata, Calle Bolsa, 8, and at Calle Alarcon Lujan, 6. Very popular *cervecería* that does some of the best seafood *raciones* in Málaga. Have a beer and a plate of prawns even if you don't have anything else.

Bar Lo Gueno, Calle Marin Garcia, 11. One of several good bars in this street. Very busy. Specializes in hams and cheeses. Tables outside.

La Tasca, Calle Marin Garcia, 12. Similar to the above but much better known. If you can survive the chaos, have some of their delicious *croquetas y pinchos*.

La Campana, Pasaje de Chinitas. Bodega where you can try Málaga's famous sweet muscatel wine. If the taste grabs you, other local wines include Pedro, Lacrima and Vino de Competa.

Antigua Casa de Guardia, Alameda Principal, on the corner of Calle Pastora. One of Málaga's oldest and most atmospheric bodegas. This really is the place to come and sample some of the dozens of wines in the casks. The old boys, either those serving *or* those drinking, are always ready to advise. If you don't fancy asking, start with the sweet Parajete or the drier Trasanejo or *seco anejo*. Or stick to a muscatel.

OUT OF TOWN

Inland to Antequera

The main reason for a visit to Antequera is to explore the surrounding countryside. The town itself is unremarkable but provides a useful base (Hostal **Manzanito** on Calle Calvo Sotelo, 31, is a good choice). From here you can visit the three **dolmen** caves nearby (Cueva de Menga is the most impressive, on the Málaga road). More spectacular are the **National Park of El Torcal** and **El Chorro Gorge**. The former Mozarab settlement of **Bobastro** with a basilica carved out of rock also makes an interesting detour.

El Torcal's surreal landscape of eroded limestone and rock formations is an excellent place for hiking. It is 13 km out of town on the C337 (a bus will take you as far as Villanueva de la Concepcion). There are several trails indicated by yellow arrows for the shorter route and red arrows for the longer one.

El Chorro: Must be counted one of Spain's greatest natural wonders. It is a narrow gorge with sheer walls over 200 m deep. A railway tunnel cuts right through the rock and skirting the cliff is a dilapidated concrete walkway – the Camino del Rey. Although dangerous in sections, it is still open, but extreme care should be taken. El Chorro can be reached by train on the Antequera–Málaga line – the view from the train isn't bad. Get off at El Chorro and follow the signs to the La Garganta.

RONDA

Villages and towns hanging on the edge of cliffs are a Spanish speciality. You'll find them all over the country and Andalusia has its share. Ronda is one of the most spectacular. Split in half by a 150-m gorge, it sits precipitously surveying the surrounding countryside. One side of the ravine is the old Cindad, on the other side is the modern section of Ronda.

The gorge itself, Tajo, is spanned by an impressive feat of 18th-century engineering – a three-arch bridge complete with sentry box underneath. Its caged-in vantage points afford dramatic views of the deep ravine and river below with the remains of the Arab mills. At sunset you can watch the kestrels and martens swooping and gliding in the air currents.

Ronda is often referred to as the birthplace of present-day bullfighting. Like Seville, it has one of the oldest and most beautiful bullrings in Spain. It was here that the rules of combat for modern corridas were laid down between the 17th and the 18th century by successive generations of the Romero family.

Ronda has also attracted a succession of celebrities. Bullfighting aficionado Orson Welles loved the place and his ashes are buried on a bull farm outside the town. Ernest Hemingway spent time here and in his novel *For Whom the Bell Tolls* describes such Civil War atrocities as victims being thrown off the bridge alive. Earlier still, the Austrian poet Rainer Maria Rilke

Salobrena makes a pleasant place to stay. **Pension San José** on Calle Cristo, 96, is one of the best. Pension **Mari Carmen** on Calle Nueva, 30 (Tel: 61 09 06), is another good, cheap bet with great views. Likewise the Pension **Arnedo** at No.15. Bar **Pesetas** near the church does *tapas* and meals which you can eat while overlooking the village.

Castell de Ferro, small and unspoiled, has a good beach and good accommodation. The little **Hostal Bahia** on the main Plaza de España, 12 (Tel: 64 60 60), is well worth trying to get a room in — they're clean and modern with private bathroom and balcony. The restaurant next door is very good. It is the nicest spot on the whole coast.

wrote his "Spanish Trilogy" here. Much more recently, Frederico Rosi used the bullring in his filming of the opera *Carmen*.

Its proximity to the Costa del Sol makes Ronda perfect for day-trippers. After the coaches and crowds have gone, however, it assumes a different atmosphere altogether – well worth waiting for.

GETTING YOUR BEARINGS

Ronda is divided into two by the narrow gorge and linked by three bridges. On one side is the original Moorish settlement with its characteristic streets known as the **Cuidad**. Most of the towns historic monuments are located here. Across the Puente Nuevo is the **Mercadillo** district, which grew up after the Reconquest. The bullring is in this part, close to the Plaza de España, as is the commercial centre around Plaza del Socorro and Carrera Espinel. Farther out still are the bus and train stations.

A GUIDED TOUR

Start from the **Plaza de Toros** (Close to the tourist office), a beautiful colonnaded bullring dating from 1781/5, rivalling Seville's as the oldest in Spain. By area, it's one of the largest in the country. You can wander round the ring and visit the small but interesting Museo Taurino. Every May *corridas goyescas* are held in 18th-century costume.

History

Ronda is one of the oldest towns in Spain. Known as Arunda to the Romans, it was later taken by the Moors and used as a regional capital. Because of its almost impregnable site, it remained in Moorish hands until 1485, when it fell to Ferdinand the Catholic. Many of its monuments were destroyed, first by the Christians and later by Napoleonic troops. The surrounding hills have always been a smugglers' and bandits' paradise, especially during the Civil War, when Ronda was scene to many horrors. Today there is still a large military garrison here.

Walk along Calle San Carlos, pass through Plaza de España, to the **Puento Nuevo**. The name means "New Bridge", and it *was* new – in 1740, when it was built to replace an earlier version that collapsed. It was finished in 1788 and has been in use ever since.

Cross the bridge into the Ciudad. Turn left on the far side to discover the **Casa del Roy Mor** (Calle Marques de Pavaela, 17). Despite its name and Moorish foundations, this mansion dates from the 18th century. In the garden 365 steps forming an underground stairway called the *mina* descend to the bottom of the gorge.

Farther down the street, **Palacio Marques de Salvatierra** is an elegant Renaissance mansion with two carved stone figures above its door. They supposedly represent Inca Indians. Guided tours every half-hour.

Facing the building are the **Puente Viejo** and **Puente San Miguel**. The first bridge has horse shoe-shaped arches and was built in 1616 on Roman or Arab foundations. The latter is single-span and looks Roman in origin.

The domed roof of the **Arab baths** is visible beside the river. Although they are being restored, they can still be visited – apply to the caretaker. Farther along the outskirts of town are the ruins of the alcázaba.

Take any turning into the heat of the Ciudad, and you'll soon reach the **Iglesia de Santa Maria**. Built on the site of the mosque, it still retains some Moorish features – there is an arch inside the entrance and its bell tower was the former minaret. The rest is a mixture of Gothic and

Renaissance styles. It is set in the lovely Plaza de la Duquesa de Parcent.

Round the corner, **Palacio Mondragon** is a mansion that was once a Moorish palace but was later converted for the use of Ferdinand and Isabella. Inside there are lovely arches and courtyards and a pomegranate tree in the garden. Opening times are erratic while restoration is in progress.

RONDA FACTFILE

Tourist Office, Plaza de España, 1. Tel: 87 12 72. Open Monday–Friday 10.00–14.30.

Trains, Avenida de Andalucía. Tel: 87 16 73. Two trains daily to Seville, Málaga, Granada.

Buses, Avenida de Concepción Garcia Redondo, 2. Empresa Los Amarillos (Tel: 87 22 64) to Seville and Malaga. Empresa Comes (Tel: 87 19 92) to Jerez and Cádiz. Costa del Sol (Tel: 87 22 62) to Marbella.

Police, Calle Espinel, 38. Tel: 87 13 70.

Telephone code: 952.

WHERE TO STAY

Most visitors to Ronda come only for the day so finding a room is not usually hard. *Hostales* are situated in the new town, off Carrera Espinel.

Cheap to Moderate

La Espanola, Calle José Aparico, 3. Tel: 87 10 52. Down the alley next to the Turismo. Kept by friendly women, it has two floors of spartan rooms – the ones at the back have lovely views. Bathrooms are modern but weren't quite clean when we were there. Cheap.

Rondasol, Calle Cristo, 11. Tel: 87 44 97. Near Calle Sevilla. Run by another nice woman. No views but very clean and central.

Biarritz, Calle Cristo, 7. Tel: 87 29 10. Near the Rondasol. Simple, clean and well-kept. Slightly more expensive but still good value.

El Tajo, Calle Doctor Cajal, 7. Tel: 87 62 36. Off Carrera Espinel in the heart of the new part. More expensive again but everything is comfortable, clean and new – it even has a lift. There is a restaurant downstairs with a reasonable menu.

Bullfighting

Despite the growing awareness of bullfighting as a barbarous practice, and the position of football as the country's most popular spectator sport, bullfighting still plays an undeniable role in Spanish culture. Most towns have a bullring and during the season, from Easter to October, most hold a bullfight (or corrida) each week. During big fairs, such as those at Seville and Jerez, corridas may take place every day.

A foreigner may wish to attend a bullfight to satisfy curiosity. The event is a display of great pageantry but it is also a display of a few Spanish men dressing up like peacocks to slaughter an animal for the danger and spectacle. The slaughter is highly ritualized, but many tourists feel they haven't seen Spain until they've seen a corrida.

Smarter Options

Polo, Calle Mariano Soubiron, 8. Tel: 87 24 47. Close to the Plaza del Socorro. Quite a luxury option, but good value. Very professional atmosphere with a nice restaurant.

Reina Victoria, Calle Jerez, 25. Tel: 87 12 40. The smartest hotel in town, British-built at the turn of the century, it was a popular retreat for officers from Gibraltar. The poet Rilke stayed here in 1912 and his mementos have been preserved in one of the rooms. There are spectacular views from all the rooms, some of which have a private terrace, and there is a swimming pool in the garden. It also has an excellent restaurant. In Hemingway's opinion an ideal honeymoon hotel.

FOOD AND DRINK

The area away from the Plaza de Espana is more authentic. At night the Plaza del Socorro becomes very lively.

El Patio, Calle Espinel, 100. Towards the top end of the street. A *cervecería* and *marisquería* with a good menu and a lovely patio with *azulejos* and plants.

Cafeteria Dona Pepa, Calle Marina, 5. Cheap menu and *platos combinados*. Good place for breakfast.

Mesón Santiago, Calle Marina, 3. Next door to the above and same management but much more up-market. The lunchtime menu is pricey but good value. Nice patio.

Pizzeria Piccola Capri, Calle Villanueva, 18. Pizza with a view.

Bodegas Jimenez, Calle Sentenil at the end near Calle Bola opposite the bullring. An atmospheric bar with good wines. Evenings only.

Don Miguel, Calle Villanueva, 4. Right by the bridge. The restaurant is expensive but go there for a drink on the terrace to enjoy the lovely views. You can also have *tapas*.

Bridge Bar, in the middle of the bridge, in the former sentry box and prison, reached from the Plaza de Espana. It opens erratically.

Las Catacumbas, underneath the church of Santa Maria in the old town. Nighttime only – a lively bar, popular with young Rondonians.

PLUS . . .

- Enormous **churros** for breakfast at Café Alba; Calle Espinel, 44.

- Gestoria Harillo, Calle Espinel, 36. **Wonderful cake shop** famous for its crystallized orange. Another great cake shop is Las Campanas, Plaza del Socorro; try their *Yemas del Tajo*.

- Heladeria Rico, Calle Espinel, 40, has delicious **ice creams**.

CASTILE and LEÓN
Castilla y León

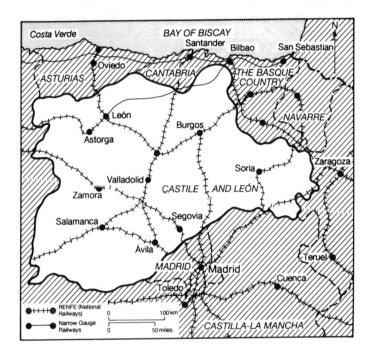

Scorched red plains burn beneath the heat, endless wheat
fields stretch to distant horizons, straight roads disappear
to nothing: the sense of space is awesome, almost ghostly.
The autonomous region of Castile and León sits on the north
meseta, one of two huge plateaus that form the great central
tableland of Spain, with Madrid at its centre. The sluggish
green Duero River cuts across it east to west, the only incision

in a landscape void of shade and shape. Remotely dotted over this vast area are towns steeped in the history of the region. From the road you would never guess; few people visit Castile and León for the scenery.

The fusion of these two kingdoms formed the foundation of modern Spain. Warriors from the region played a key role in the Reconquest when Alfonso VI of León and El Cid took Toledo in 1085. The rows of castles built along the Duero and in a second line of defence at Avila, Segovia and Salamanca were crucial in the consolidation of Christian power. The marriage of Ferdinand of Aragon and Isabella of Castile in 1479 enlarged the power base further, and signalled the beginning of the centralized Spain we know today.

The wealth of the dynasties that controlled this huge area is evident in the richly embellished university town of Salamanca, with its Renaissance and medieval architecture, in the museums of Valladolid, and in the defences of Zamora, Avila and León. Throughout the Middle Ages, pilgrims en route for Santiago de Compostela passed through the north of the region, and magnificent Gothic cathedrals at Burgos and León, along with a trail of Romanesque churches, remain as outstanding monuments to the power of the shrine.

LEÓN

León is an immensely enjoyable city. For centuries it has been an important stopping place for pilgrims on the road to Santiago, and the cathedral and the Basilica San Isidoro rank among northern Spain's top historic sites. Both are rich in decorative detail and together they pull a bustling tourist crowd. Sizeable segments of the old city walls stand nearby, most impressive at Plaza Puerta Castillo; the modern city is neatly spliced alongside in a well-planned series of avenues, leaving old León the space it deserves, and generating a vibrant social atmosphere quite independent of tourism.

A short walk from the cathedral, things seem quite different. Around the Plaza Mayor runs a charming and evocative series of quiet old squares and shabby lanes, silent as a ghost town.

Bound on all sides by traditional colonnading, and dominated by a grandiose Ayuntamiento, even the Plaza Mayor seems strangely deserted. From here a warren of little lanes and alleyways run to Plaza San Martín and Plaza Santa María del Camino, the original point of entry to the city for pilgrims on the road to Santiago. It feels like an abandoned film set with its intriguing crooked lanes, overhanging and bulging old buildings, and the occasional rusty, ornamental street lamp jutting out from a faded ochre wall, somehow placed with the kind of casual poetry more typical of Hollywood than of real life. It is as if the whole area is waiting for something to happen; it does. At night these streets become a riot of activity, with bars, bodegas and restaurants appearing as if from nowhere. The neighbourhood is so renowned as a drinker's paradise that it has been nicknamed *Barrio Húmedo* – the humid quarter.

GETTING YOUR BEARINGS

León sits on a huge, open plain beside a broad river that neatly runs north to south. The train and bus stations are across the water on the edge of town. Arriving here affords an expansive sense of León's location, exposed to the scorching summer heat and the icy winds of winter; the snow-dusted mountains of Asturias are visible in the distance.

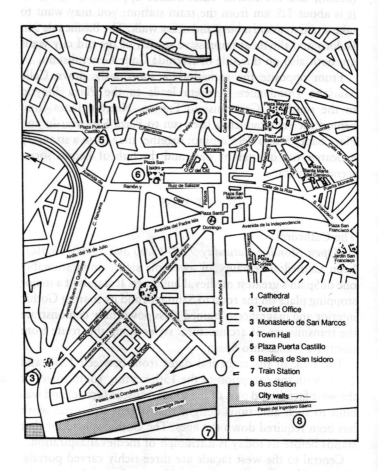

1 Cathedral
2 Tourist Office
3 Monasterio de San Marcos
4 Town Hall
5 Plaza Puerta Castillo
6 Basílica de San Isidoro
7 Train Station
8 Bus Station
City walls ⌒⌒⌒

An orderly arrangement of regular, straight avenues radiating from traffic islands form the modern centre of town. Here buildings are largely unattractive apartment blocks, with little of interest for the visitor. The bridge from the railway station feeds straight into this network along Avenida de Ordoño II,

León's main thoroughfare, bisecting the city east to west. At Plaza Santo Domingo it becomes Generalísimo Franco and cuts into the heart of the old city.

The cathedral is at the top of this long road to the left (north), and the tourist office stands opposite its entrance. It is about 1.5 km from the train station; you may want to take a taxi to avoid a busy and noisy walk. The Basílica de San Isidoro and the most impressive stretch of the old city walls are both also on this side of Avenida Calle Generalísimo.

From opposite the cathedral, a short walk down Calle Mariano Domínguez Berrueta leads to the Plaza Mayor, to the south of Generalísimo Franco. Narrow lanes from behind the Ayuntamiento here run to Plaza San Martín and Plaza Santa María del Camino: together they form a strangely evocative old quarter by day, and the hub of León's social scene by night.

DON'T MISS . . .

The Cathedral

(Open Monday–Saturday 9.30–13.00 and 16.00–18.30.)
León Cathedral remains an awesome sight, unquestionably one of Spain's greatest medieval buildings. It stands at a major stopping place on the road to Santiago, and its soaring Gothic interior and magnificent stained glass powerfully demonstrate the transmission of architectural styles along this route from northern France into Spain.

The bulk of the cathedral dates from between 1258 and 1303 (with the exception of the 15th-century south tower of the west façade and part of the south transept façade) and was built to such ambitious designs that urgent structural work has been required down the ages. The Gothic splendour that stands before us today is a triumph of medieval aspiration.

Central to the west façade are three richly carved portals. Tired and hungry pilgrims arrived here to be met by a simple, frightening Christian message in stone: the Last Judgement. Here is the weighing of souls, clear for all to see: graphic and gruesome scenes of long-toothed demons devour the damned, while the saved rejoice in processions of Christian celebration. Above all this detail sits Christ in his glory.

After such a heavy moral lesson, pilgrims stepping into the showering splendour of coloured light inside the cathedral must have been moved as if by a vision of heavenly beauty. Soaring pillars pull your eyes skywards and between them burn vast curtains of stained glass – flame reds, golds and yellows. Taken in three stages, the windows represent the natural, social and celestial worlds: the lower windows show local plant life; the middle windows are decorated with heraldic devices; and saints and angels glow up in the clerestory. Even the massy choir with its heavy, elaborate carving does not detract from the sight. The diocesan museum, housed off the cloisters, seems a rather down-to-earth collection by comparison and offers little competition to the excitement generated by the cathedral itself.

Basílica de San Isidoro

(Entrance 200 pesetas. Open Tuesday–Saturday 10.00–13.30 and 16.00–18.30, Sunday and holidays 10.00–13.30)

The Romanesque Basílica San Isidoro is sumptuously embellished with 18th-century decoration, reaching its most flamboyant in the Santiago Matamores figure that rides triumphant above the robust 11th-century portal, celebrating the victory of Christians over Moors.

A monastery built here in the mid-9th century was dedicated to St John the Baptist; subsequently the relics of St Pelayus were transferred to León and the basilica became his shrine. Destroyed by the Moors, once recaptured it was rebuilt in the early 11th century, and a pantheon was added to house the royal dead of León.

The pantheon is the highlight of the whole complex: vaults are supported by boldly carved capitals of griffins, grotesques and Gospel scenes, and decorated with Romanesque frescoes dating from the late 12th century. The frescoes are among the most impressive in Spain and include seasonal scenes of medieval life and stories from the New Testament.

The basilica itself is a spacious, barrel-vaulted structure. Its museum is well worth visiting for the exceptional ecclesiastical treasures it holds: an exquisite 12th-century Limoges enamel reliquary, an 11th-century agate chalice and an 11th-century Romanesque ivory chest are the highlights.

ALSO WORTH SEEING . . .

Plaza Mayor

Dominated by a stately 17th-century *ayuntamiento* and colonnaded in a grandiose fashion, the Plaza Mayor is oddly
neglected. It lies in the most eerily evocative part of old León,
with nearby deserted streets and squares of a faded, ancient
character. A short lane away Plaza San Martín is the centre
of León's manic drinking scene at night, yet the Plaza Mayor
remains strangely on the edge of all this. Only on Sunday
mornings is the peace broken and the square comes to life
in a vibrant, colourful market. It is like the sudden flowering
of a desert: the huge, dusty expanse of the Plaza Mayor
bursts teeming with life with stalls selling vegetables, junk
and clothing; Plaza San Martín is engulfed with bales of
flowers and herbs; and passionate flamenco blares from hi-fi
stalls. The market starts at around 8.00; a great atmosphere
and well worth catching.

Plaza de Santa María del Camino

Low, antiquated houses supported by rough-hewn wooden
porticoes create an easy, almost too perfect charm within this
secluded cobbled square. The plaza was the entrance to the city
for pilgrims en route to Santiago, and has an ornamental cross
and babbling fountain. The yellow stone and warm, red-tiled
roof of a 12th-century Romanesque church stand nearby.

Monasterio de San Marcos

The monastery of San Marcos is decorated with a profusion
of carved medallions, fruit, garlands and scallop shells, a
gorgeous flourish of plateresque craft skill. A monastery was
first built here in 1168 for the Knights of Santiago, giving
food and shelter to pilgrims on their way to Santiago de
Compostela. The present building is overall a Renaissance
design, begun 1514 and altered well into the 18th century.
It is now a national *parador* hotel. Ask at the reception to see
the elaborately decorated choir stalls of the adjacent church.

Iglesia San Marcos

The church of San Marcos stands alongside the monastery, covered in the scallop-shell motifs of the pilgrims. Visit the small local archaeological museum inside to view the exceptional 11th-century Carrizo crucifix.

OUT OF TOWN . . .

Astorga

Astorga sits on a low hill 50 km west of León surrounded by Roman town walls. In medieval times it was a small but busy stopping place along the road to Santiago, thronged with pilgrims; today it dozes quietly with just a couple of historic monuments to absorb the attention of visitors passing through. A real mishmash of styles, its late-Gothic cathedral parades an elaborate Baroque façade at its west front, while its east end bristles with buttresses. The interior is cold and uninviting, but does harbour a fine Renaissance high altar. Nearby the Episcopal Palace is a fanciful fairy-tale affair designed by Antoni Gaudí – though completed long after his death – housing a small pilgrimage museum.

If you are near the Plaza d'España on the hour, look out for the couple of mechanical figures who chime the bell on the Town Hall clock. Their costume is based on that of the Maragatos, a north African tribe who settled in Astorga around the 8th century and maintained a culture quite distinct from the local population well into the 20th century. They made their living as muleteers and were real specialists in transportation until modern times.

LEÓN FACTFILE

Tourist Office, Plaza de Regla, 3. Tel: 23 70 82. Opposite the Cathedral. Open Monday–Friday 9.00–14.00 and 16.00–17.30; Saturday 10.00–13.00.
Train Station, Avenida de Astorga. Tel: 22 37 04.
Bus Station, Avenida Ingeniero Sáenz de Miera. Tel: 21 10 00.
Taxi, Radio Taxi León. Tel: 24 12 11 or 24 24 51.
Telephone Code: 987.

WHERE TO STAY
Cheap to Moderate

NEAR THE STATION   Oviedo, Avenida Roma, 44. Tel: 22 22 36.
Covadonga HR*, Avenida de Palencia, 2. Tel: 22 26 01.
La Barra HR*, Avenida de Palencia, 2. Tel: 22 10 84.

AROUND TOWN   Carmina HR*, Avenida Independencia, 29. Tel:
25 28 12.
Reina HR*, Puerta de la Reina, 2. Tel: 20 52 12. Off Avenida
Independencia.
Reino de León HR**, Martín Sarmiento, 10. Tel: 20 32 51.
Hotel Paris, Avenida Generalísimo, 20. Tel: 23 86 00.

Smarter Options

San Marcos H*****, Plaza San Marcos, 7. Tel: 23 73 00. National
parador housed in superb Renaissance monastery.

WHERE TO EAT

Head down Calle de Mariano Domínguez Perrueta towards Plaza Mayor
and San Martín for eating and drinking. The dry air and the narrow
streets of the old town seem to trap wafts of delicious food from the
bars and *mesóns* tucked within its lanes.
Casa Lorenzo, Calle Mariano Domínguez Berrueta. Cheap café-bar
serving delicious traditional food; popular with a young crowd.
Catedral, Calle Mariano Domínguez Berrueta. Plain Spanish restaurant
with middle-aged clientele and very good food.
El Tizon, Plaza San Martín. Friendly, cheap, traditional restaurant
offering the omnipresent *merluza* (hake) any style.
Droguerie & Perfumeria, Plaza San Martín, 12. This isn't really a
drugstore – it's just they haven't changed the sign yet. It conceals a
casual, trendy bar with a fine array of *tapas*.
Mesón El Escudo, Plaza San Martín.
Café-bar with seafood and draft cider.
Rancho Chico and Mesón San Martín, Plaza San Martín. Both
traditional, down-to-earth café-restaurants offering good-value basic
menus and local wines.
   On the other side of town there are:
Casa Merino, Ramón y Cajal, 5. Tel: 248924. Extremely popular
restaurant with a wide-ranging traditional menu.
Mister Pib, Ramón y Cajal, 1. Popular, down-to-earth café, a handy
option for cheap tortillas and fish dishes.
El Llager, Fairly upmarket, strait-laced *marisqueria* and cider house
serving very good food.
Parada de Postas The bus-station café-restaurant serves delicious basic
meals, though the atmosphere is rather clinical.

BARS AND NIGHTLIFE
Plaza San Martín and Calle de la Misericordia

The very best of León's nightlife is generated in and around Plaza San Martín, where you will find a huge range of bars and *mesóns* packed with people. Try the ancient bodega at Calle de la Plegaria, 12, for a glass of vino in a traditional setting, then explore the little alleyway off here (between El Gaucho and La Norta bars) and uncover a hidden seam of bars and cafés.

Bar Vaticano, Plaza San Martín. Tucked in the corner of the square. There are actually three bars in this building two on the ground floor and a huge, lively purple-neon rock bar upstairs.

Aliarmar Bar, Calle de la Misericordia. Raunchy, atmospheric rock bar with sumptuous decor including intensely ornate, heavily carved wooden ceiling and Mudéjar-style arches.

La Brasa, Calle de la Misericordia. Clean, modern tiled interior and very loud music. This bar is popular with late teens and early twenties.

Mesón La Patata, Calle de la Misericordía. Quaint and cute bar gaily festooned with garlic and heaving with funk; attracts a young crowd from early evening, i.e. 21.00 onwards.

Calle Santa Cruz

A very busy lane running from the bottom of Calle de la Misericordia back up to Plaza Mayor. There are a couple of poky traditional tiled bars with a lively, young crowd: try **EM Bar**, **Quiloche**, the especially festive **El Húmedo**, or **El Bazin**, one of the tiniest bars in the world. At the junction of Calle Santa Cruz and Calle Tarifa there is a nameless bar and dance floor with great Latin music and excellent atmosphere.

La Pianola Café is a friendly, young bar playing good, solid rock music and R & B, popular with a conspicuously clean young crowd.

Plaza Mayor

Universal, Plaza Mayor, 1. Trendy bar for stiff drinks under the colonnading of the Plaza Mayor. Tasteful, burnt-orange walls effectively recall the near-desert around León, creating a thirst for the huge range of liqueurs on offer.

El Cafetin, Calle Mariano Domínguez Berrueta, 13. Rough walls plastered with a great collection of old posters. Raucous Latin sounds and a young and arty crowd. Plenty of atmosphere.

Plaza de Santa María del Camino

The plaza remains quiet in the evening, so if you want to savour the spirit of the old city as night falls, take a drink in the tiny Bar **El Grano** and imagine that you are back in the 18th century, or try the Taberna **Asturiana** on Calle de la Capilla, near the church.

North of Avenida Generalísimo Franco

There are few interesting bars in the streets to the north of this main thoroughfare.

El Gran Café, Calle Cervantes. This is a modern bar with a fine, old-world elegance. Very popular with a relaxed, young crowd.

La Radio, Calle Recoletas, off Calle del Cid. Loud, young bar playing very middle-of-the-road pop music.

PLUS . . .

For traditional souvenirs, *La Casa Los Telares*, Calle Mariano Domínguez Berrueta, is an excellent basket-work and crockery shop.

Calle Serranos has a small, wacky art gallery, *Trafico de Arte*, open till around 21.00. The street also has a couple of interesting, off-beat art/craft/clothes shops.

BURGOS

Burgos is overwhelmed by its massive cathedral, just as it has been since medieval times. It was a major stopping place on the road to Santiago and the cathedral is a Gothic masterpiece. Its cold iron-grey stone confers a northern European flavour, and Burgos's harsh winters add to the steely qualities of the place. (It is worth remembering, if you are travelling in spring, that snow is not uncommon as late as April.) Lit up at night, the cathedral turns ghostly pale, and the whole magnificent structure seems to float amid the town's domestic buildings like a vision.

This is very much a one-stop tourist town; hordes come to see the much-prized cathedral and move on, which is a pity, because there are several other medieval monuments worthy of exploration. Burgos itself is home to the military, a small, orderly place. Gardens are well-kept, trees grow in regular rows and the atmosphere is fairly conservative. The traditional evening *paseo* centres on the Paseo de Espolón, flanked by regimented avenues of pollarded limes, while weeping willows flow over the adjacent riverbanks. Follow any of the flat, even stretches of parkland out of town and yet more orderly poplars and pines accompany you along the way.

GETTING YOUR BEARINGS

Burgos sits beside the river Arlanzón dominated by its cathedral: both act as landmarks for getting your bearings. To the south of the river are the bus station, just off Calle de Madrid, and the train station, at the end of Avenida Conde Guadalhorce. Head for the centre of town crossing the Arlanzón from Calle de Madrid and you pass through the Arco de Santa María to the cathedral. Entrance to this great Gothic building is via Plaza de Santa María, a flagged pedestrian square. From here, stepped lanes climb the hill, retaining the medieval scale of the town centre; those immediately above the plaza take you to the church of San Nicolás and then on to that of San Esteban.

Below the east end of the cathedral Calle Huerto del Rey and Calle Laín Calvo form the bedrock of Burgos's young bar scene, alive with people at weekends. From here Calle Segura leads to Plaza José Antonio, a rather disappointing square carved through by traffic, linked by pedestrian lanes to the Paseo del Espolón.

The Paseo del Espolón runs alongside the river, from the Arco de Santa María to Puente San Pueblo, an orderly strip of a riverside park and the scene of the evening *paseo*. At Puente San Pueblo a ferocious statue of El Cid charges with sword drawn at full tilt, ready for any oncomers from Madrid. Stretching away from behind him, Calle Santander soon becomes Avenida del Cid Campeador; the tourist office is tucked in a small square to the left off here. Call in and pick up a map.

Calle Juan and Calle Pablo run off the broad Calle Santander to converge at a little bridge across a tributary of the Arlanzón and the Plaza San Juan, a quiet square flanked by the **Iglesia de San Lesmes** and the **Museo de Marcelione Santa María**. Beyond this brief Gothic interlude, Calle las Calzades and Avenida General Yagüe form the Bernardas area of high-rise apartments and late-night discos.

Most of Burgos's sights are grouped around the cathedral and are easily explored on foot: the **Monasterio de las Huelgas** and the **Cartuja Miraflores** are two exceptions. The Monasterio de las Huelgas is 1 km away: follow the signs heading west along the southern bank of the river. The

History

A fort was built beside the river Arlanzón in AD 884 and the growth of the surrounding settlement was swift; it soon became the town of Burgos. In the middle of the following century Fernan Gonzalez made it the capital of Castile. It was during the Reconquest that Burgos really flourished, playing a key role in driving out the Moors and being subsequently recognized as the most important Christian town in Spain. At the same time it continually received pilgrims at its hospitals and lodging houses, as a key stopping place on the pilgrimage route to Santiago de Compostela. The town prospered, alive with commercial, religious and political activity.

In 1087 the Castilian court was moved first to Toledo and then to Valladolid, and Burgos lost its former political power. None the less the wool trade here was excellent and a prosperous merchant class continued to develop the town. Evidence of this can be seen in the 16th-century remodelling of the Arco de Santa María: statues of warriors and civic dignitaries hark back to Burgos's more illustrious political and military past, but the work was paid for by wealthy traders.

Only at the beginning of the 17th century did Burgos fall into a gradual general decline, from which it has only begun to emerge during the last hundred years. For a while it was the Nationalist capital during the Spanish Civil War, and it was in the chapterhouse of the Monastery de las Huertas that Franco first assembled his government. It remains a very conservative city, with the church and the army still much in evidence. It also continues to draw thousands of visitors each year to the doors of its magnificent cathedral.

sequestered Cartuja de Miraflores is 4 km away in the opposite direction: follow the signs out of town heading east along the southern bank of the river.

DON'T MISS . . .

The Cathedral

Burgos Cathedral is a magnificent fusion of French and German Gothic styles, dripping with decoration and stunning from all angles. Its sheer size is also outstanding. Twin towering spires flank the west façade, two octagonal lantern towers are crowned with intricate, lacy decoration and to the rear a mass of flying buttresses flail like spiny insect legs. Crazy, delicate spires and pinnacles seem to issue from every point and there is a stately unity to the whole pile that is quite extraordinary. Its exterior alone could keep you absorbed for hours. Inside it is just as exhilarating.

As you enter the cathedral, the first chapel on your right contains one of Spain's most gruesome statues of Christ. It is covered in some kind of undetermined animal skin and has a beard of human hair. Folklore has it that the beard still grows – and has done for the last 500 years – and needs trimming every eight days. Next to this, the Capilla de la Presentación contains a fine alabaster Renaissance tomb.

The soaring octagonal tower at the crossing of the nave is studded with glorious decoration and topped with a star-vaulted roof. Light floods in through the windows on all sides. Below it is a simple slab – the tomb of El Cid.

The cloisters are 13th and 14th-century Gothic and in their adjacent rooms are tapestries and reliquaries. Placed high on one wall is a simple iron-bound wooden casket, supposedly the chest of El Cid.

At the extreme east end of the cathedral is the Capilla del Condestable, an exquisite expression of the Isabelline Gothic style. It was built as a chapel for the burial of Pedro Fernandez de Velasco and his wife Mencia de Mendoz. Its star-shaped arrangement of windows and its airy lantern tower were the inspiration for the larger central tower.

Walking back down the church towards the entrance, you pass the ornate Escalera Dorada, or Golden Staircase, by Diego de Siloe, one of the earliest pieces of Spanish design to show the influence of the Italian Renaissance.

Just before leaving the church, look at the 14th-century clock high on the wall: a grotesque figure called Papamoscas swats flies – and strikes the hour.

Building began on the cathedral in 1221 and progress was swift; by the middle of the century most of the cathedral was completed. The work was heavily influenced by the French Gothic style, one of the new ideas transmitted along the road to Santiago. A second spate of building came in the late 15th century, this time under the direction of the de Colonias, a family of German origin, and it was they who added the central lantern tower.

San Nicolás

This unassuming church conceals an elaborate altarpiece that completely fills the end wall, as if the sculptor tried to cram as much frenzied, lacy detail into this tiny church as there is on the vast cathedral nearby. It is the work of Simon and Francisco de Colonia, begun in 1505, and shows scenes from the life of St Nicholas. Find a switch on the column by the entrance to illuminate the church. Notice, too, the unusual large medieval wood carvings on the door outside.

Arco de Santa María

In the 14th century this chunky monumental gateway was built as part of the city's defences. In the 16th century it was remodelled to please Emperor Charles V. His statue stands to the left of centre surrounded by nostalgic figures from Burgos's glory days as a fighting city: El Cid stands to the right of centre.

Cartuja de Santa María de Miraflores
(Open Monday–Saturday 10.15–15.00 and 16.00–18.00; holidays 11.20–12.30 and 13.00–15.00 and 16.00–18.00.)

Built of ghostly silver-grey stone, this Carthusian monastery lies in a secluded spot surrounded by pines; there is a palpable tranquillity about the place. Founded in 1442, it has a simple Gothic exterior; inside is a wealth of medieval carving.

The alabaster tomb of John II and Isabel of Portugal is the real highlight of the monastery. It was completed towards the end of the 15th century, the work of Gil de Siloe, a Flemish sculptor. The monarchs lie on a star-shaped tomb in all their finery, the folds and beaded brocade work of their robes a rich and meticulous celebration of their earthly glory. The figures carved around the sides of the tombs include lions, dogs, winged creatures and biblical characters sporting a fascinating array of medieval costumes.

Nearby, to the left of the altar, is the similarly elaborate tomb of the Infant Alfonso. Kneeling in prayer, the prince wears a richly carved gown, a large ornamented hat swung almost fashionably over his shoulders, his tomb lavishly detailed with cherubs, small animals and birds weaving their way in and out of entwining foliage. Alfonso's early death ensured the ascension of his sister Isabella the Catholic to the throne of Castile, an event that was radically to alter the history of Spain.

The altarpiece displays a profusion of biblical scenes and is covered in the first gold to have come from the Americas.

ALSO WORTH SEEING . . .

Monasterio de las Huelgas
(Entrance 350 pesetas. Open Tuesday–Saturday 11.00–14.00 and 16.00–18.00, Sunday 11.00–14.00.)

Having been both a royal palace and a Cistercian abbey, this religious complex displays a mixture of styles. There are Gothic and Romanesque cloisters, and the church, which holds tombs of the Castilian aristocracy, is decorated with

17th-century French tapestries. The convent has a considerable amount of Mudéjar workmanship, in particular the ceilings of the cloister and of the Capilla de Santiago.

Museo Marceliano Santa María
(Plaza San Juan. Open Tuesday–Saturday 10.00–14.00 and 17.00–20.00, Sunday 10.00–14.00.)
Housed in the splendid Gothic cloisters of the remains of a Benedictine monastery, the museum displays a large collection of paintings by a local artist, Marceliano Santa María (1866–1952). His canvases show picturesque scenes of local village life in a light and colourful Impressionist style. Look out for painting No. 52, which shows the church of San Lesme (just outside in Plaza San Juan) as it once was in a rural setting.

Casa del Cordón
(Plaza de Santo Domingo de Gusman, just behind the statue of El Cid.)
There is no public access to this late-15th-century city palace, but the façade is distinguished by a weighty rope carved in stone surrounding the entrance – the *cordón* of Franciscan monks. It was in this building that Ferdinand and Isabella received Columbus after his second voyage to the Americas.

Casa Miranda: Museo Arqueológico
(Entrance 200 pesetas. Open Monday–Friday 10.00–13.00 and 16.45–19.15, Saturday 11.00–13.00.)
Archaelogical museum displaying prehistoric, Roman and Visigothic finds.

OUT OF TOWN . . .

Monasterio de Santo Domingo de Silos
(60 km southeast of Burgos. Open Monday–Saturday 10.00–13.00 and 16.30–18.00.)
The 11th-century Benedictine monastery of Santo Domingo de Silos is worth seeing for its superbly decorated Romanesque cloisters. Capitals are carved in wonderfully animated detail with plants and animals, and pillars show a range of biblical

El Cid

El Cid (1026–99), the hero of popular legend, was born 6 km from Burgos at Vivar. Celebrated in epic poems and song as the champion of Castile, expelling the Moors from the land, El Cid was in fact a mercenary and fought both for and against the Christian cause. His exploits in battle during the Reconquest were so outstanding that Alfonso VI became jealous of the glory heaped upon him and banished him from the kingdom, despite the fact that El Cid was married to Alfonso's cousin Ximena. Or did Alfonso fear for his throne? Whatever the reason, El Cid was forced to seek his fortune far away from his home and the Christian cause; he found it with the enemy, the king of Saragossa. In 1094 he led a Moorish army and captured Valencia after a siege of nine months. Again his strength, skill and bravery were astounding. El Cid was to switch allegiances again, and he was finally defeated by the Moors at Cuenca. His body was buried in a monastery 10 km from Burgos, but was moved to the cathedral in 1921.

scenes: Christ on the road to Emmaus, the Annunciation and the Ascension. You can also visit the monastery's 18th-century pharmacy and a small ecclesiastical museum, but most worthwhile of all is to hear the monks' Gregorian chants. These can be heard at morning Mass at 9.00 or at vespers at 19.30 (at 20.00 Thursdays during the summer).

Men wishing to make a retreat are welcome at the monastery; arrangements should be made in advance. Tel: 38 07 68.

BURGOS FACTFILE

Tourist Office, Plaza de Alonso Martínez, 7. Tel: 20 31 25 and 20 31 25. Open Monday–Friday 9.00–14.00 and 16.30–18.30, Saturday 9.00–14.00.
Train Station RENFE, Moneda, 21. Tel: 20 91 31 and 20 35 60.
Bus Station, Calle Miranda, 4. Tel: 20 55 75.
Telephone code: 947.

WHERE TO STAY
Cheap to Moderate

Victoria HRS*, San Juan, 3. Tel: 20 15 42.
Ansa P, Calle Miranda, 9. Tel: 20 47 67.
Castellano HS*, Llaín Calvo, 48. Tel: 20 50 40.
Ambos Mundos HRS*, Plaza Vega, 27. Tel: 20 61 30.
Norte y Londres HR**, Plaza Alonso Martínez, 10. Tel: 26 41 25.

Smarter Options

Del Cid H***, Plaza Santa María, 8. Tel: 20 87 15. Superb, quiet location overlooking the cathedral. TV in rooms; garage facilities.
Cordón HR***, La Puebla, 6. Tel: 26 50 00. Central location. TV and video in all rooms.
Corona de Castilla H***, Calle Madrid, 15. Tel: 26 21 42. Central location. TV in rooms; garage facilities.

WHERE TO EAT

Restaurants in Burgos tend to reflect the style of the city's medieval past, so you can expect to eat beneath oak-beamed ceilings and wrought-iron candelabra. They also tend to be slightly overpriced because of the steady flow of tourists they cater for; the few exceptions to this are noted below.

Calle Gonzalez, which overlooks the back of the cathedral, has a handful of pleasant, cheap places to eat, particularly if you want a *menú del día* around midday.
Speios, Calle Segura. Popular, down-to-earth café-bar serving delicious *tapas*.
Bar Royal, Calle Huerta del Rey. This bar serves gargantuan sandwiches, including the Spanish equivalent of a BLT – a three-tier creation with additional olives and gherkins. Beer comes in the kind of mugs that Desperate Dan probably likes to use on holiday. All comes accompanied by loud rock and roll.
Encarna, Calle Huerta del Rey. Another bar for cheap meals and loud rock music. There is sawdust on the floor, huge barrels to rest your beer on and a good selection of *platos combinados, pinchos* and of course *tortilla*.
Prego, Calle Huerta del Rey. A cavernous witch's den of huge, shaggy tapestries against rough slate walls. This is a popular Italian restaurant with a cosy, youthful atmosphere.
Angel, Calle Gonzalez. One of the smartest of the cheap places to eat in Burgos, with many regional dishes on offer, including *lechargo asado* – roast suckling lamb – a local speciality.
Mesón de los Infantes, Corral de los Infantes. Tel: 20 59 82. Tucked besides the Arco Santa Maria. Hearty, medieval and fun, this is one of the friendliest places to eat in town. There is a crisp, smart restaurant and a simple *comedor*, decorated with stuffed wild boar's heads, for cheaper meals.
Mesón del Cid, Plaza Santa Maria. A superb location, overlooking the cathedral. The atmosphere is set by oak benches, carved doors, old stone walls and tasteful medieval trappings. Highly convivial. The menu offers traditional Castilian food, including a good range of fish dishes.
Mesón La Cueva, off Plaza de Santa Maria. Cosy atmosphere. Extensive menu, including the chance to try *leche frita* – a delicious deep-fried milk pudding.

Don Nuño, Calle Nuño Rasura, 3. Newly furbished café restaurant with squeaky clean traditional tiling and piped Muzak. Terrace seating offers good views of the cathedral, and prices are high accordingly. However, the *menú del día* is reasonably priced, and a good range of tasty *tapas* is available throughout the day.

Rincon de España, Nuño Rasura, 11. Tel: 20 59 55. Nouveau-medieval restaurant geared to tourists. Fairly pricey traditional Castilian menu, worth considering if you want to sit out on the cobbles and admire the cathedral.

Bon Fin, Calle Nuño Rasura. Self-service cafeteria offering good-value *platos combinados*. It does not have a view of the cathedral and you can expect to pay half the price you would in the restaurants opposite.

BARS AND NIGHTLIFE

Burgos has a surprisingly active weekend social scene once you know where to find it.

The traditional *paseo* is as strong here as anywhere in Spain and takes place early evenings along the Paseo del Espolo. It is a very civilized affair, with people strolling beneath the avenues of limes or sitting among the topiaried yews and yucca palms.

Sit out on the terrace of Restaurant **Pinedo,** beneath the tall chestnut trees, and take it in.

Around the Cathedral

Immediately round below the east end of the cathedral are some of Burgos's busiest streets for drinking and occasional dancing, till midnight or 1.00.

Calle de la Llana de Afuera harbours a clutch of hard-rock drinking dens, many hijacked by pubescent youth doing their best to maintain Burgos's warlike image. Here too is **Tearoom Oliver,** not a tearoom but a very comfortable lounge serving all manner of whiskies and Irish coffees.

La Espaderia, Llana de Adentro, is reached through a low stone archway directly opposite the **Gonzalo** bar on Calle Llana de Afuera. Attracting an older class of headbanger, this loud rock bar is full of curiously clean metal fans. Medieval suits of armour stand as decoration, useful to fall against and make rather obvious heavy-metal jokes about as the night wears on.

Calle Huerta del Rey and Calle Laín Calvo

These streets are particularly good for the variety of places to drink, eat and dance; if the road is still dug up, don't be put off. Alive till 24.00 or 1.00.

Okapi, Calle Huerta del Rey. Very loud, screaming jazz and funk bar; crowded, fashionable and convivial. The place is wonderfully done out with Egyptian wallpaintings and hieroglyphs. A place to drink and be seen.

Bar Royal, Calle Huerta del Rey. Pink walls splattered with photos of Hollywood greats. This is an excellent, rowdy bar playing rock, R & B and pop, and serving great snacks.

Kiss, Calle Huerta del Rey. Straightforward modern bar, popular for dancing.

Trantos, Calle Huerta del Rey. Good down-to-earth disco bar, wholly unpretentious and great fun.

Café España, Calle Laín Calvo, 17. Something of a rarity in this town – a relaxed and trendy jazz café-bar with vaguely hip, intellectual overtones.

Café Antigüedades, Calle Edward Martínez del Campo, 4. Antique-filled café-bar attracting a civilized, arty crowd. Find it on the west side of town, off Avenida Generalísimo Franco.

Calle de San Juan and Calle de la Puebla

These two streets run like a pair of pincers to meet at a little bridge that crosses over to Plaza de San Juan. Both are excellent for lively bars until 24.00 or 1.00.

In Calle San Juan, try **Mythos** or **Gueldo** for dancing and drinking. In Calle de la Puebla, try the deceptively small bar at No. 17 for R & B, rockabilly and rock music. Alternatively, **Vinoteca** attracts a more sedate, fashion-conscious crowd for drinks and chat.

Bernardas

Late-night drinking and dancing continues after 1.00 in an area known as Bernardas: Calle las Calzadas, the parallel Avenida General Yagüe and the streets that run between them. To find Bernadas, pass through the stone archway to Plaza de San Juan, and head for Calle las Calzadas straight ahead. It is a new part of town, full of uninspiring high-rise blocks, but the bars and discos here stay open till around 4.00 at weekends. Most of them are very new, very modern and play straight, mainstream disco sounds. Dress codes seem a bit confusing: it can feel a bit like a New Romantics convention at times, but fun none the less. Try **Besame Mucho** and **Pub la Sarandula** on Calle las Calzadas; **No-Do** disco bar and **Cgpax** and **El Cielo Puede Esperar** on Calle de Marco.

VALLADOLID

Valladolid is home to one of Europe's finest sculpture museums; the best reason to visit the city. Enjoying Valladolid itself can seem like hard work. Ugly modern development and congested roads have carved up this historic town so that its fine monuments can rarely be appreciated to the full. Instead of meandering leisurely between great churches and museums, it is advisable to target a particular site and head straight for it. Valladolid is a tricky town to negotiate and it is easy to lose your way.

Valladolid has recently been confirmed the capital of Castile – a distinction it has held off and on down the centuries as home to the Castilian court and much of the nobility. The marriage of Ferdinand and Isabella, that landmark in Spanish history, took place here, and Philip III also lived here for a while. During the 16th century it was the most aristocratic city in Castile, and even to this day is considered the place where the purest Spanish is spoken. The city has long been an episcopal See: the Holy Week celebrations here are famously solemn and impressive. Many fine, ancient church buildings remain and there is a handsome 16th-century Plaza Mayor, yet, despite all this, Valladolid lacks any really satisfying historic centre.

GETTING YOUR BEARINGS

On arrival, Plaza Zorrilla makes a good point from which to explore Valladolid. It is well signposted and serves as a linchpin between the old and the new city. The tourist office is here too, worth calling in to pick up a map. Calle de Santiago leads off Plaza Zorrilla, soon becoming pedestrianized, to the Plaza Mayor and the Ayuntamientio.

To find Plaza San Pablo and the sculpture museum, face the Ayuntamiento and find Calle Especería Cabaderia, which runs at a tangent to its far right corner. Follow this lane, turn left down Calle Platerias, passing Iglesia de la Cruz, and continue straight ahead down Calle Felipe II. To find the sculpture museum, face the façade of San Pablo and then follow the little lane down its right-hand side.

To find Plaza de la Libertad, face the Ayuntamiento and find Calle Especería Cabaderia, which runs at a tangent to its far right corner. Follow this lane, turn left down Calle Platerias, and then take the first right down Calle Cantarranas.

To find the Oriental Museum; Paseo del Campo Grande is a broad avenue that runs from Plaza de Zorrilla along the side of a wedge-shaped park. Follow this avenue to Plaza de Colón and find Paseo de los Filipinos, off to the right, running along the bottom of the park. The museum is along here, housed in an 18th-century Augustinian monastery.

DON'T MISS . . .

The National Sculpture Museum
(Calle Cadenas de San Gregorio, 1. Tel: 26 79 67. Admission 200 pesetas. Open Tuesday–Saturday 10.00–14.00 and 16.00–18.00, Sunday 10.00–14.00.)
This outstanding museum will absorb sculpture vultures for hours. It is housed in San Gregorio College, one of the finest monuments in Valladolid, built by Alonso of Burgos, confessor to Isabel the Catholic. The Isabelline-Gothic façade is wholly arresting: covered in stone carving it manages to be both strangely rustic and disturbing. Clambering thickets full of chubby babies support a fabulously ornate heraldic shield; large folkloric figures, chained, bearded and covered in twirly body hair, flank the doorway. This remarkable entrance is almost certainly the work of Gil de Siloe. The fine plateresque courtyard inside is likewise exceptional, decked with tall spiral columns and heavily decorated arches.

The museum contains a superb collection of religious sculpture, chiefly large-scale wood-carving taken from Castilian church buildings. It includes pieces from the 13th to the 18th centuries, with an emphasis on the Renaissance and Baroque. The 16th-century work is particularly fine, especially that of Alonso Berruguete, and can be inspected here at unusually close quarters. Rare subtleties are achieved in the modelling of wood as flesh and the fine gold paintwork of robes reaches the intensity of burnished metal. Three rooms are dedicated to Berruguete's work.

Look out for the overdemonstrative figures of Juan de Juni's "Burial of Christ" in Room XV, designed to create impact from afar, and for a busty and defiant "Mary Magdalene", a religious piece of dubious spiritual inspiration. In Room XIII a minor polychrome panel describes a particularly unsavoury narrative: a white nobleman is having a leg transplant, his "new" leg having been chopped off a black man who lies bleeding by his bedside. The noble seems pleased at the fit despite the mismatch of flesh.

Church of San Pablo
(Plaza San Pablo.)

Heavy Isabelline-Gothic decoration fills the façade of San Pablo, the 15th-century church of a former Dominican monastery. Carved stone posts bearing lions and heraldic shields lend the approach further dignity. The disappointing interior was revamped in the 17th century.

The Cathedral
(Plaza de la Libertad.)

Monumental and imposing, the cathedral looms with all the cold severity that typifies the work of Juan de Herrera. It was Herrera who designed El Escorial for Philip II, and the monarch commissioned the cathedral in Valladolid from him in 1580. Doubtless neither of them would have approved of the later additions by Alberto Churriguera, an architect with a far more flamboyant sense of grandeur. Carvings of St Peter and St Paul stand in small niches either side of the entrance, while above them monumental stone carvings of the four apostles strike swashbuckling poses. Inside, a powerful austerity proves a sombre setting for Juan de Juni's brilliant gilded altarpiece, dating from 1551.

Santa María la Antigua
(Plaza de la Libertad.)

This church is an odd combination of cool Gothic, with flying buttresses of white-grey stone, and warm Romanesque, with a tall, square tower capped by a red-tiled roof. Together they form a highly distinctive church.

Muséo Oriental
(Paseo de los Filipines, 7. Tel 30 69 00. Entrance 300 pesetas. Open Monday–Saturday 16.00–19.00, Sunday 10.00–14.00.)

All manner of Chinese art is on display here, from fine porcelain and lacquerware to embroidery and watercolours, along with a collection of 18th-century Spanish-Filipino ivory work.

Cervantes and Valladolid

Miguel de Cervantes (1547–1616) is Spain's greatest literary figure, creater of *Don Quixote*, the novel about the mad knight who sets out to champion goodness, truth and honour. Cutting a ludicrous figure in a rusty suit of armour astride a clapped-out steed, he tilts his lance at windmills under the illusion he is tackling giants. His delusions symbolize the folly of his quest and the knight errant becomes a comic dramatization of all human aspiration. We put our ideals in motion on the basis of a belief in the reality we see with our own eyes – despite experience telling us that that picture we hold as reality will shift and shift again, and that certainty is forever elusive.

It is not known how long Cervantes worked on the book, but it was published in Valladolid in 1605 and was an immediate success. Cervantes became famous throughout the Spanish-speaking world: within the space of a year puppets of Don Quixote, Dulcinea and Sancho Panza – main characters in Cervantes's novel – had appeared in fiestas as far away as Peru.

Cervantes had spent a couple of years in Valladolid as a small boy. His family had moved there in pursuit of honour and prosperity; finding neither, they soon left, but Miguel was to return in later life and enjoy his greatest celebrity in the city.

In 1601 the royal court of Philip III moved from Madrid to Valladolid as a result of politicking by the powerful Duke of Lerma, who wanted to remove the king from the influence of the royal grandmother, Maria of Austria. When the court moved, the businesses of the former capital moved too, including publishers and booksellers. In 1604 Cervantes followed and a year later published the first book of *Don Quixote*. His novel coincided with Valladolid's brief period of national importance, a time when the city was the centre of Spanish political life and awash with great wealth and great poverty. Just five years later the king, court and the economic life that revolved around it made the 200-km journey back to Madrid, where it remains today.

Cervantes's House Museum

(Calle Rastro, 7. Tel 30 88 10. Admission 300 pesetas. Open Tuesday–Saturday 10.00–15.30, Sunday 10.00–15.00.)
Cervantes lived in this house around 1605, at the height of his fame. At that time the place was a slum, not far from

the abattoir, and had a rowdy bar beneath it. The museum has been kitted out with furniture of the period along with maps, books, a painting of the Battle of Lepanto and one of Cervantes's manuscripts. It all makes for an interesting picture of how a 16th-century noble might have lived, but it certainly does not reflect just how cramped and unsavoury life here would have been for Cervantes and his family and friends.

VALLADOLID FACTFILE

Tourist Office, Plaza de Zorrilla, 3. Tel: 35 18 01. Open Monday–Friday 9.00–14.00 and 16.00–18.00, Saturday 9.00–14.00.
Train Station RENFE, Estación del Norte. Tel: 30 35 18.
Bus Station, Puente Colgante, 2. Tel: 23 63 08.
Airport Villanubla Airport. Tel: 25 92 20. Iberia Airlines, Gamazo, 17. Tel: 30 07 88.
Telephone code: 983

WHERE TO STAY
Cheap to Moderate

Avenida HsR*, Acera Recoletos, 23: Tel: 22 19 17. This avenue runs alongside Paseo del Campo Grande, beside the park.
Miño HsR*, Plaza Mayor, 9. Tel: 35 36 61.
Greco HsR**, Calle Val, 2. Tel: 35 61 52.
Colón HsR**, Acera Recoletos, 22. Tel: 30 40 44.
Paris HsR**, Especería, 2. Tel: 35 83 01.
Enara HR*, Plaza de España, 5. Tel: 30 03 11.

Smarter Options

Mozart HR*** Menéndez Pelayo, 7. Tel: 29 78 88.
Lasa HR***, Acera de Recoletos, 21. Tel: 39 02 55.

WHERE TO EAT

Many of the best places to eat and drink in Valladolid are 1980s reconstructions of traditional bars. Although their newness feels somewhat unauthentic, the food can be very good.
Taberna Carralito, Calle de la Antigua, 6, opposite the church of Santa María Antigua. Brand-new bar and restaurant done out in a traditional tile-and-beam style. Clean and modern. There is plenty of good *tapas* on offer and a cheap *menú del día* around midday.
La Solana, Calle de la Antigua. Cheerful *mesóntaberna* with hams and garlic swinging from the rafters; a popular traditional eating house.
El Sarmiento, Plaza de Portugalete. Rather weak on atmosphere, but a cheap *menú del día* makes this a handy option for the budget-conscious.

Pan con Tomate Plaza Mayor, 19. *Taberna* with a new "traditional" interior offering a great range of *raciones*. For a full meal, there is a moderately priced restaurant upstairs.

Lion d'Or, Plaza Mayor. Extravagant *fin-de-siècle* swirls of polished wood, ornate mirrors and lamp-bearing Classical statues make this the finest café-bar for a coffee or a beer.

SALAMANCA

Salamanca is easily one of the most enjoyable cities in Spain. It is stunning to look at, packed with history and very, very lively. Two cathedrals vie for space in the heart of the old quarter, but the real jewel of Salamanca is the Plaza Mayor at its centre, arguably Spain's finest town square. Salamanca's university was founded in the 13th century and the city retains a wealth of ancient college buildings along with medieval and Renaissance convents, churches, cathedrals and squares. Delicate, intricate carving decorates doorways, walls and windows in a style known as "plateresque", the hallmark of Salamancan architecture.

The elegant grandeur of the Plaza Mayor, coupled with the cathedrals and university buildings, suggests a city of size as well as stature. In fact it is quite a small place, everywhere is easily accessible on foot, and this is a real bonus if you want to make the most of the city's excellent nightlife. The university and the international language schools here ensure a vibrant youth scene and the place has an abundance of great bars, clubs and discos. There is never any problem finding somewhere lively to spend the evening, and on Thursdays, Fridays and Saturdays things don't stop till around four in the morning.

GETTING YOUR BEARINGS

Most places of interest are within Salamanca's compact centre – a great source of charm. The Plaza Mayor is at the very heart of the city and the most obvious focus for visitors. You can pick up a free street map from the tourist kiosk here; more comprehensive tourist information is available at the Turismo on the Gran Vía.

Rua Mayor runs south from the Plaza Mayor into the most

rewarding area of the city, leading to the ornate Casa de las Conchas – literally the "house of shells", – the Baroque church of La Clerecia and into Calle Libreros with its ancient university buildings. Here is the quiet and stately Plaza de Anaya alongside the two cathedrals. If you fancy walking farther south, you can reach the Roman bridge and cross it for superb views of Salamanca's jumbled skyline of domes, towers and flying buttresses.

A short walk east of the Plaza de Anaya leads to the Plaza del Concilio de Trento and the church of San Esteban, a piece of Salamancan plateresque architecture that's every bit as impressive as the New Cathedral. Nearby stands the Dominicas Dueñas with its fascinating Grotesque cloisters. Calle de España (also known as the Gran Vía) runs from beside San Esteban the length of the city centre, by day an important main road and home of the Turismo and the post office, by night a riot of drinking, dancing revellers. It meets Plaza de España at its north end and feeds into Paseo de la Estación; the train station is just off here.

West from the Plaza Mayor, Calle del Prior leads to the Plaza de las Agustinas and the Palacio de Monterrey, Iglesia de la Purísima, and Convento de las Úrsulas. An area of less intense historic interest, it is pretty none the less, and worth exploring at night for a handful of very lively bars. Beyond Plaza de las Agustinas, Calle Ramon y Cajal heads past the Renaissance Colegio del Arzobispo Fonseca to Calle Fil Villalobas and the bus station on the edge of town.

DON'T MISS ...

The sights in this section are listed in the order in which you come across them if you start at the Plaza Mayor and head south down Rua Mayor. If you are really short of time, the highlights are the Plaza Mayor, a walk past the Casa de las Conchas, the two cathedrals, and the church and convent of San Esteban.

Plaza Mayor

The Plaza Mayor is a glorious sight; built of the warm, honey-coloured stone that is found throughout the city, its rows of rounded colonnades create a beautiful, rhythmic symmetry. Over 20 arches span each side of the square and above them, in perfect proportion, are three storeys of windows, each with louvred shutters and iron balconies. The Town Hall at the centre of the north side is the work of Andrés Garcia de Quiñones, an integral part of the overall design. The plaza was begun in 1729 and completed in 1755, the masterly planning of Alberto Churriguera.

Bullfights were held here well into the 19th century and today the Plaza remains the centre of Salamancan life. It is alive with people throughout the day, and the scene of the traditional *paseo* in the early evening. The wood-beamed ceilings of its colonnaded walkways amplify the sound of people talking as they stroll beneath them, so that a constant hum rises from the square, as if it were a huge, human drum. All in all it really is the kind of sight you could never tire of. You are bound to pass through the Plaza Mayor more than once a day: make sure you find the time to sit out at one of its cafés on bars and soak it all in.

Casa de las Conchas

(Calle de la Compañía. Closed for restoration 1991–92.)
Row upon row of *conchas* – the scallop shells of the pilgrims of Santiago – cover the external walls of this solid town mansion. It belonged to Dotor Talavera Maldonado, a knight of Santiago, and was built in 1493; windows and doorways are decorated in the elaborate Spanish Gothic style typical of the era of the Catholic Kings.

La Clerecía

(Open Tuesday, Thursday and Friday 11.00–13.00.)
The view of this imposing Baroque church is somewhat hampered by surrounding buildings: none the less it remains a powerful monument. It was begun in 1617 as a Jesuit school by Philip III and his wife Margaret of Austria. The lower part of the façade is austere and restrained; a statue of St Ignatius presides over the entrance. The upper section, added over a hundred years later, is a far more wordly affair, heavily decorated and topped with a couple of hearty, hefty Baroque towers.

Inside, a massive, gold-coloured Baroque altarpiece barely relieves the sour grey gloom. A glimpse of adjacent cloisters hints at more appealing interiors nearby, but unfortunately the rest of La Clerecía is inaccessible to the public.

Once outside the Clerecía again, take Calle Serranos, passing the refined simplicity of the church of San Isidoro, and turn left into Calle Libreros. Wander down here to the Plazuela Universidad.

The University
(Open Monday–Saturday 9.30–13.30 and 16.00–18.30, Sunday 10.00–13.00.)

Salamanca's old colleges sit around a quiet square. The entrance to the main building is a superb example of the plateresque. The façade is a riot of intricately carved flowers, foliage, beasts and flowing urns. There is a frog hidden somewhere among all this too, but you need sharp eyes to find it. Medallions of the Catholic Kings, Charles V's coat of arms, two-headed imperial eagles and St John are among the key figures in the overall design. Above these range carvings of Hercules, Venus, the pope and cardinals.

Take a stroll around the cloister inside beneath its coloured, panelled ceiling and look out for the Renaissance staircase, busy with frolicking swains performing all sorts of antics to impress pedestal-bound maidens. The women look rather pleased with themselves.

For a glimpse of more restrained aspects of university life, visit the lecture rooms. Some are grandiose with huge, vaulted ceilings, tapestries and paintings, but university life was far from comfortable: painfully narrow, splinter-ridden benches line the lecture room of Fray Luis de León's scholars.

In the far corner of the *plazuela* is the Escuelas Menores.

Las Escuelas Menores
Across the Plazuela Universidad the Escuelas Menores sports a fine plateresque doorway, bearing the three imperial coats of arms. Inside is a very elegant cloister and one of the lecture halls has an impressive fresco of the zodiac, moved here from the library.

El Museo Provincio: Palacio de Abarca
(Patio de las Escuelas, 2. Tel: 21 22 35.)
This late 15th-century palace, adjacent to the Escueles Menores, houses a small collection of paintings, sculpture and archaeological finds.

New Cathedral
(Plaza de Anaya. Open 9.00–15.00 and 16.00–20.00 every day.)
The New Cathedral is a late-Gothic masterpiece iced with Renaissance and plateresque decoration. Biblical scenes above the portal form the focus of the overall design of the main façade, but it is the surrounding detail that has real impact. From a distance it looks like delicate lace; close up, tiny detail shows animals weaving their way in and out of succulent vines. The obsessive complexity of it is mind-boggling.

The interior is less magnificent – largely because so much money was lavished on the exterior. Most of the building was completed between 1513 and 1560, though additions were made over the following 200 years. The ornate 18th-century choir stalls are particularly worthy of attention, designed by Alberto Churriguera, the Salamancan who also planned the Plaza Mayor.

Old Cathedral
(Plaza Juan XXIII. Entrance through the New Cathedral – same opening times.)
The distinctive Torre del Gallo of the Old Cathedral, a Romanesque-Byzantine ribbed dome, seems lost against the decorative exuberance of the New Cathedral shoved up against it. In fact this peculiar arrangement was necessary: the Old Cathedral, built in the 12th century, was after 400 years in danger of collapse, and the new one was built right next to it to give it structural support.

The Romanesque interior of simple, bold lines can be enjoyed unimpeded: solid columns are topped by capitals carved as griffins and snarling beasts; tombs bear traces of the bright paintwork with which they were originally covered,

Plateresque

The plateresque style is typified by minutely detailed, intricate stone carving used to embellish doorways and windows. Flowers and foliage, delightful small animals and hideous grotesques are usual decorative motifs, set against smooth, plain walls. The effect is like an elaborate embroidery in stone. The larger carvings at the heart of all this decoration are often strangely crude, almost folksy, by comparison.

A uniquely Spanish style, fashionable in the late 15th and early 16th centuries, the plateresque reaches its most splendid concentration in Salamanca. Here the local sandstone proved an excellent material for the most intricate of designs, and its glorious golden colour ensured a harmony to the overall effect of smooth walls and complex decoration. Many of the stone carvers who developed the style were former silversmiths — *platero* is Spanish for "silversmith" — so the plateresque can truly be considered the hallmark of Salamancan architecture.

and most impressive of all is the altarpiece. Fifty-three tablets depict scenes from the lives of Christ and the Virgin Mary, painted by Nicolás Florentino in the 15th century. The central copper-covered statue, the "Virgen de la Vega", dates from the 12th century, its throne decorated with Limoges enamel. Above this looms an ominous, lurid painting of the Day of Judgement. Tucked away at the west end of the nave is the chapel of San Martín, covered with 13th- and 14th-century frescoes.

Off the cloister, the El Salvador chapel (12th century) has a fine Mudéjar vault beneath which the Mozarabic Mass was celebrated. The Diocesan Museum here also contains evidence of the Christian Moorish presence in Salamanca; most notably, the 16th century Salinas Organ, covered in Mudéjar designs. The collection of paintings here includes works by Fernando Gallegos, Salamanca's most famous painter, and an outstanding triptych by Juan de Flanders (1506).

Church and Convent of San Esteban
(Plaza del Concilio de Trento, 1. Tel: 21 50 00. Open 9.00–3.00 and 16.00–20.00.)
The golden sandstone façade of this 16th-century church

drips with intricate carving, a monumental celebration of the plateresque style. A relief of the stoning of St Stephen takes centre place and statues of saints and clerics are studded all over the surrounding stonework.

Entrance is via the adjacent convent building. The elegant, broad arches of the Renaissance cloisters are decorated with medallions of the prophets. A range of rooms off here include the Panteón de los Teólocos (Pantheon of the Theologists), a small and suitably plain mausoleum, and a chilling, overbearing chapter house.

Sinous grotesques writhe beneath the arches of the cloister's upper storey, access to which is via a heavily embellished Renaissance staircase. There are good views of the families of herons nesting on the church roof, too, and a door off here marked *Coro* leads into the upper choir of the church. It is a great place from which to appreciate the sheer size of the nave and to inspect a fresco by Palomino showing "The Triumph of the Church through the Dominican Order". To get downstairs you need to retrace your steps back through the cloisters.

Phantasmagorical flying horses and wheezing dragons decorate the inside of the doorway from the cloister to the nave, easily missed since back in the church again the huge altarpiece demands attention, a wholly extravagant Baroque masterpiece by José de Churriguera, constructed in 1693.

El Convento de las Dueñas

(Plaza del Concilio de Trento. Tel: 21 54 42. Open 10.00–13.00 and 16.00–19.00.)

Exceptional two-storey Renaissance cloisters form the core of interest in this 16th century convent. The stonework is creamy and smooth, the irregular five-sided garden is lush with potted yuccas and the overall scene is deceptively charming. Take a closer look: the capitals are carved with nightmarish grotesques; those on the upper storey portray hideous characters from Dante's *Divine Comedy*, and a portrait of the poet. Notice, too, the Mudéjar doorway as you step out on to the upper level from the small collection of religious paintings housed here.

Torre del Clavero

If you head back towards the Plaza Mayor from the Convento de las Dueñas, look out for the octagonal 15th-century tower with fairy-tale turrets that stands on Calle Consuelo.

SALAMANCA FACTFILE

Turismo, Gran Vía, 39. Tel: 24 37 30. Open all year Monday–Friday 9.30–14.00 and 16.30–19.00, Saturday 10.00–14.00. Holy Week open Thursday only.
Train Station, off Plaza España. Information Tel: 22 02 95 and 22 57 42. RENFE travel office, Plaza de Libertad, 10. Tel: 21 24 54.
Bus Station, Avenida de Filiberto Villalobos, 73–83. Tel: 23 67 17.
Telephone code: 923.

WHERE TO STAY
Cheap to Moderate

Tormes HS*, Rua Mayor, 20. Tel: 21 96 83.
Laguna HS**, Consuelo, 19. Tel: 21 87 06.
Orly HsR**, Pozo Amarillo, 3. Tel: 21 61 25.
Gran Vía HR*, La Rosa, 4. Tel: 21 54 01.
Pasaje H**, Espoz y Mina, 23, 25. Tel: 21 20 03.
Condal HR**, Santa Eulalia, 3–5. Tel: 21 84 00.

Churrigueresque

The Churrigueras were a family of sculptors and architects from Salamanca whose overwhelming, flamboyant style
became influential throughout Spain in the 17th and 18th
centuries and gave rise to the term "Churrigueresque". The
retablo in the church of San Esteban is a perfect example
of what this name came to signify. The altarpiece is a
monumental affair: juicy, gold vines hung with clusters of
fruit and foliage writhe and wrap themselves around huge,
swirling pillars; golden cherubs sweep back gold-tasselled
curtains, while high above the altar angels perch with open
wings, as if preparing to launch themselves down into the
main body of the nave. It is the work of José de Churriguera.
Strangely, though, the style to which the family lent its name
is not representative of the very best of their work. After
all, Alberto Churriguera, José's brother, designed the Plaza
Mayor, arguably the most superbly balanced and tasteful work
of the period in all Spain.

Smarter Options

Alfonso X HR***, Toro, 64. Tel: 21 44 01.
Parador de Salamanca, Teso de la Feria, 2: Tel: 26 87 00.

WHERE TO EAT

One of the best areas to start looking for places to eat is around the Plaza
Mayor, particularly in those streets between it and the Gran Vía.

Cheap to Moderate

Bar Felix, Pozo Amarillo, 10. Tel: 217281. Cheerful, unpretentious
bar with a *comedor*, serving tasty, cheap meals in generous helpings.
For a starter try their *consommé de Jerez* – a deceptively filling and
potent soup.
Isidro, Pozo Amarillo, 19. Tel: 262848. Plain, spacious restaurant, a little
lacking in atmosphere, but very friendly and good value for anything
from just a beer and a tortilla to a full meal. A cheap *menú del día* is
available around midday.
Dulcinea, Pozo Amarillo, 5. Tel: 217843. This restaurant is plain,
not in the least bit fashionable and very, very popular. The food is
good, reasonably priced and there is a sizeable wine list. Try their
pimentos rellenos – tasty stuffed peppers – or some mouth-watering
fresh salmon.
El Bardo, Calle de la Compañía, 8. Tel: 21 90 89. Round the corner from
Casa de las Conchas. Crumbling, ancient stone walls and oak-beamed

ceilings foster an olde-worlde atmosphere. Downstairs a lively little bar pumps out loud music; the restaurant is on two upper levels. The set menu at midday is extremely good value, and there is even that rarity, a vegetarian menu – making this one of the most popular places among young people to eat in Salamanca.

El Trigal, Calle Libreros, 20. Another option for vegetarians in Salamanca. The homely café has comfy, big wicker armchairs and serves savoury wholefood snacks, fabulous ice-cream and just about every type of fruit juice imaginable. Open Monday–Thursday 9.00–16.00, Friday, Sunday and holidays 10.00–23.00.

The restaurant offers good-value, wholesome vegetarian meals. Open daily 13.00–16.00, and for evening meals 20.00–23.00 Friday, Sunday and festivals.

Smarter Options

Bermeo, Pozo Amarillo, 5. Tel: 21 95 19. Quiet, smart, polished and conservative, this place specializes in seafood. There is a very good selection, but remember if you are ordering shellfish that it is sold according to weight: fresh lobster or crawfish can work out quite pricey.

El Candil, Calle Ventura Ruiz Aguilera, 10. Tel: 217239. Cheerful restaurant for a hearty meal, popular with a middle-aged crowd. It has a grandiose, antique atmosphere with red velvet walls and wood-panelled ceilings. Traditional Castilian dishes include *cochinillo* – suckling pig. The stuffed bull's head and the bullfighting posters behind the adjacent bar should tell you that the menu features plenty of steaks.

La Riojana, San Pablo, 1. Tel: 27 01 77. This is an intimate little restaurant with a pretty, shell-pink interior. It offers excellent Castilian cuisine, and plenty of fish. Try their hake in either crab or salty anchovy sauce.

La Sablon, Espoz y Mina, 20. Tel: 26 29 52.
La Sablon has a conservative, subdued atmosphere and serves some quite exquisite dishes, like monkfish with crawfish sauce, salmon with honey sauce, and *codornices con vias y pinones* – quails with grapes and pinenuts.

BARS AND NIGHTLIFE

For a restorative drink after exploring the university and the cathedrals, Calle La Latina (which crosses the southern end of Calle Libreros) has plenty of bars for you to choose from. **Café Tosoa** generates a fashionably relaxed atmosphere beneath its slowly whirring fans. On Calle Libreros itself, **Corral de Guevara** at No. 44 is a very ordinary bar, except that it serves excellent pots of tea. Also in this area is **El Café Aldaravan**, next to El Bardo in Calle de la Compañía, a convivial place where students gather to drink, chat, play chess and listen to jazz. It also has a very useful "What's On" noticeboard. But the best place to sit and have a drink in the middle of the day is at a table in the Plaza Mayor.

Salamanca has an excellent nightlife. Things tend to get going around 22.30 or 23.00 and carry on until 3.00 or 4.00. Salamanca has an astounding array of discos, bars, live venues and jazz clubs for its size. As in most Spanish cities, bars and venues tend to cluster together and there is generally no cover charge, so it is easy to move from bar to bar, disco to disco until you have found what you are looking for.

The Gran Vía has innumerable discos and the place really comes alive at weekends with flocks of people out in search of a good time. Many bars and discos are busy during the week too.

If you want loud and lethal rock music, the narrow streets between the Gran Vía and the Plaza Mayor are worth exploring. Alternatively you might try the *Platería Par Café*, Rua Mayor, 3, a lively rock bar that occasionally wanders into skanking reggae and ska.

If you want to mix with a young crowd but don't want heavy rock or disco music, the quieter, laid-back little bars along Calle la Latina might be just what you are looking for.

Ambiente, Salamanca's weekly What's On guide, is available in bars, though it can be hard to track down; the tourist office also has information on live bands and theatre.

Café Novelty, Plaza Mayor. Authentic, old-style café with a long marble bar, black and white marble floor, bentwood chairs, and elegant old mirrors. Lively atmosphere, well worth savouring with the help of a *copa de cava* – a glass of affordable, drinkable Spanish champagne.

Salon Comedor, Plaza del Corrillo, opposite Iglesia de San Martín. Excellent, battered old bar where raw "n" rowdy jazz gets elbowed out by loud, mainstream pop videos as the night wears on; trendiness intensifies too. Cheap, simple meals are available during the daytime.

El Corrillo, Cerrada del Corrillo. Relaxed, atmospheric jazz cellar beneath Salon Comedor, attracting a young crowd. It often has live music; occasional cover charge.

Teatre Juan del Engina, Calle El Tostada, 2. Bands, theatre, classical concerts and avant-garde films shown here are advertised around town and at the tourist office, though this is not a regular venue. Find it tucked in the lane that runs off Plaza de Anaya towards the Gran Vía.

Calle El Tostado, 9. Vast, cavernous, nameless student bar, jam-packed at lunchtime.

El Savor, Calle de San Justo, 34, off Gran Vía towards Plaza Breton. Hot spot for rumba, salsa and samba. Live Latin dance bands most nights (and very occasionally jazz). Usually starting around 22.30–23.00 and going on till 2.00, after which a disco takes over. Generally no cover charge.

Submarino, Calle de San Justo, 25; opposite El Savor. This disco has to be seen – the interior actually *is* a submarine. Extremely disorienting and great fun; after a few in here, you get the ocean motion thrown in for free.

Mescal Bar, Calle Carmen, near RENFE office off Plaza Libertad. Live jazz bar.

Camelot, Calle Bordadores, 3. Very trendy bar inside former 16th-century religious building; the conversion caused something of a furore at the time. Ancient walls are draped with huge medieval flags, the bar is modern and stylish and there is plenty of dancing. Great atmosphere, one of the happening places in Salamanca.

Gatsbys, Bordadores, 16. Tel: 21 73 74. Opposite Camelot. A lively, popular bar with choked dance floor. Gatsbys and Camelot sit either side of a pretty little square of old stone walls and high trees – an excellent place to sit out at a terrace café into the evening before throwing yourself into the mayhem of the dance floor.

Bibliotecha, Calle Monroy (off Toro). Lined floor to ceiling with learned tomes, this disco and bar is popular with students hell-bent on dancing. Seems they just can't drag themselves away from those books. Great atmosphere.

Birdland, Gran Vía/Plaza de España. Tatty yet refined jazz bar, with traditional tiled walls, Moorish arches and balcony seats overlooking the Gran Vía; a relaxed place for drinking and talking from around midnight.

El Puerto de Chus, Plaza de San Julian, 8. Halfway up Gran Vía. While the rest of Europe is pretending theme parks should be in some way educational, the Spanish are using them to drink and dance in. Great idea. This disco and bar is done out like an antique waterside street with a little sailing boat, ornamental iron railings and street lamps, and an olde-worlde bar tucked behind crocheted curtained doors. Quaint, but great fun. Things get going around 22.00 and go on into the early hours.

El Callejón, Gran Vía, 68. Another "living museum" disco, this time done out as an authentic traditional Spanish village, all rustic rooftops and pitchforks. Unashamedly raucous.

Tum Tum, Calle Caldereros, 13, off the south end of the Gran Vía. You won't hear any English or American sounds in here – it's strictly wild dancing and drinking to Spanish rock and disco music. Another great place to party until everyone drops at around 3.00 or 4.00.

ZAMORA

Dusty Romanesque churches of blond-gold stone and warm poppy-red roofs give this ancient place a strange poetry and unity of colour. For the most part Zamora is a sleepy, modern town with large, dowdy shops and pedestrianized streets that lend it all the appeal of a mid-seventies shopping precinct. However, the large number of Romanesque churches sprinkled through its lanes, along with its unique Romanesque Byzantine cathedral, make Zamora well worth a day's visit.

Once a walled town, Zamora stands on a rocky, bare outcrop that cuts alongside the river Duero. The centre is long, rather flat and exposed, and exploring it you can get the odd sensation that you are walking across a gigantic tourist map. It was fortified in the 9th century: Zamora was the most westerly defence post along the river Duero, heavily involved in the battles of the Reconquest. The outstanding Romanesque churches that remain bear witness to the renewed confidence of Christian powers here in the 12th century.

A WALK THROUGH ZAMORA

Arrive by bus, train or car from Madrid or Valladolid and you will find yourself at the east end of town. From here Calle Santa Clara forms the spine of historic Zamora, a pedestrianized street, punctuated by occasional minor squares, which feeds into Calle Ramos Carrion and heads directly to the cathedral, lodged in a commanding position at the western end of town.

Pick up a map from the tourist office at Calle Santa Clara, 20, and it's easy enough to take in many of the city's Romanesque churches as you head west. The street cuts past Plaza de la Constitución and the church of Santiago del Burgos; in the next side street off Santa Clara the elegant Casa de los Momos comes into view, a gracious Isabelline-Gothic town mansion dating from the 16th century, now used as a courthouse.

The Plaza Mayor is modestly distinguised by a restrained 16th-century town hall and the weighty Romanesque church of San Miguel. A couple of medieval lanes run away from the plaza, tempting exploration beside the river: ignore them and continue straight on along Calle Ramos Carrion as it feeds into the heart of the old town.

Two stately city palaces stand facing one another either side of the desolate Plaza de Viriato: the palace of the Counts of Alba and Aliste, a Renaissance palace (now a *parador* hotel) that harbours a superbly sculpted double-galleried courtyard, and the 17th-century Hospital de la Encarnación, now council offices. Behind the *parador*, lanes heading towards the river lead to the Palacio del Cordón, a stately palace with a stone *cordón* around its entrance, housing a small provincial museum. Lanes that run from the Plaza de Viriato in the opposite direction lead to the church of Santa Maria la Nueva and the Holy Week Museum, both behind the Hospital de Encarnación.

West of Plaza de Viriato, Zamora dwindles into a backwater of dusty, insignificant lanes and low houses, barely evocative of the medieval town. Suddenly the cathedral lurches into view.

The Cathedral

A fish-scale ribbed dome tops the cathedral, a suitably unusual finale to a building that musters a real hotch-potch of styles. The Romanesque-Byzantine dome is supported by pointed arches and surrounded by four cupolas, which all add to its eastern flavour. The cathedral was built between 1151 and 1174. Numerous fires down the ages made alterations to the whole building inevitable: the El Salvador Tower is a 13-century addition, the north front is Neo-classical and the cloister dates from the 17th century. The Puerta del Obispo of the south front remains the cathedral's boldest pure Romanesque feature.

Inside, the carved choir stalls offer an earthy source of amusement, displaying rather less than spiritual goings-on between monks and nuns.

Housed in the cloister, the **Cathedral Museum** (open 11.00–14.00 and 16.00–20.00) prizes among its exhibits a collection of superb 15th- and 16th-century Flemish tapestries. Especially impressive are those showing the Trojan War and Tarquinius Priscus; action-packed, colourful and fantastically detailed, they are a remarkable record of medieval life.

Once you have seen the cathedral, wander along the cobbled lane that leads away from its south entrance for views over the broad river below, with its weir and 12th-century bridge, and back along the length of Zamora to admire yet more ancient church buildings clinging to the side of this long narrow town.

Museo de la Semana Santa
(Holy Week Museum)

Holy Week in Zamora is celebrated in a huge traditional festival that dates from the 14th century. The atmosphere is very solemn: 42 processional floats depicting scenes from the New Testament are pulled through the streets by members of 16 brotherhoods, all clothed in fairly sinister white-hooded robes. The museum has the large-as-life carvings on display all the year round.

Find it adjacent to the church of Santa Maria la Nueva; take Calle Barandales opposite the *parador*.

ZAMORA FACTFILE

Tourist Office, Calle Santa Clara, 20. Tel: 53 18 45.
Train Station RENFE, Tel: 52 19 56 and 52 26 91.
Bus Station, Calle Monsalve, 1. Tel: 52 12 81 and 52 12 82.
Telephone code: 988

WHERE TO STAY

Sol HsR**, Benavente, 2–3. Tel: 53 31 52. Off Calle Santa Clara, just west of the tourist office.
Chiqui HS*, Benavente, 2. Tel: 53 14 80.
Aranda HsR*, Avenida, Alfonso IX, 5. Tel: 53 12 96.
Hosteria Real de Zamora H***, Cuesta de Pizarro, 7. Tel: 53 45 45.

BARS AND CAFÉS

There are a handful of places where you may want to sit outside and take some refreshment from the dry, dusty heat of the old town, and one or two lively youth-oriented areas in the evening – but it has to be said that Zamora is a quiet, small town.

Café Plaza Mayor and **Mesón Peromato** in the Plaza Mayor offer the chance to soak in the best of historic Zamora over a cool drink in a traditional setting. Between here and the Romanesque tower of the church of San Vicente, the tiny Plaza del Fresco has far trendier options: **Principal**, the most chic of new café-bars, and **Bar Jaliso** which draws a fashion-conscious crowd with its gangster-theme decor and loud funk. Less dressy, equally lively alternatives can be found in Calle Viriato, off the end of Calle de Santa Clara just before it hits the Plaza Mayor. Here **Café de Viriato** is very popular day and night, a cavernous, old bar decorated with huge, dusty pink landscapes, the perfect accompaniment to the well-worn, tarnished feel of the place.

Near the cathedral, **Café Galleria Cache** on Plaza de los Ciento is a a cool, shaded place to take a breather during the day, though you pay over the odds for its arty interior; **Bar Mesón El Castillo**, just round the corner on Calle de Magistral Erro, is a more down-to-earth alternative and serves good plain *tapas* throughout the day.

THE BASQUE COUNTRY, NAVARRE AND ARAGÓN
País Vasco, Navarra y Aragón

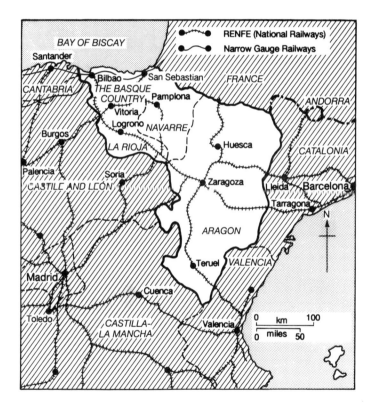

The Basque country offers great seafood, excellent beaches and beautiful countryside. Pine-covered mountains drop sheer into the turbulent steely-grey Atlantic and jagged cliffs lurch to isolated bays. The sea-torn coast is relieved by beaches of fine yellow sand, scoured clean by the pummelling of the waves, rinsed new with the ebb of each tide.

Heavy rainfall gives this north coast its vivid colours; the area is often referred to as "Green Spain". Water in the air tinges the forested mountain slopes with mist and turns the atmosphere in industrial Bilbao to a salty mugginess, but banana trees and yuccas grow among rain-soaked pines in the squares and boulevards of San Sebastián, creating a uniquely refreshing mix of the cool, fresh and exotic. Bad weather may spoil your trip but when the sun shines, it pulls the colours out from the landscape: the greens of the mountains and pastures, the iron-red rooftops of farms in the valleys, and the deep blues of the churning sea. High rainfall also means that beaches can be enjoyed free of mass, crass commercialism. If you can relax with the possibility of rain, then the Basque country is a great region to head for.

In any case a downpour can be the perfect excuse to shift your enjoyment of panoramic views of the coast and countryside to equally varied vistas indoors: the *tapas* bars. Basque cuisine is for many the very best in Spain, and the busy fishing ports all along this coast daily trawl a salty catch that goes straight to the restaurants and bars. Bilbao and San Sebastian both offer ample opportunity to savour the very best of the region's food, and for many it is reason enough to come here.

Not surprisingly, San Sebastián gets the lion's share of visitors. It is a fine *belle époque* resort, popular with wealthy Madrileños seeking cool, green relief from the oppressive southern summer heat. Bilbao, heavily developed around 50 years later, has among its weighty 19th-century architecture a handful of grand Art Nouveau buildings, reminders of its economic pre-eminence around the turn of the century when it could afford to be part of the great pan-European avant-garde movement of the day. It is the region's industrial capital, busy, noisy and congested, with a tremendous life and energy in its bars and cafés.

Inland the country reaches the wild mountain scenery of the Pyrenees, an awesome chain of snow-capped peaks. They

form Spain's natural northeast boundary and offer some
of the best walking and climbing in Europe. Pamplona,
Navarre's sleepy, provincial capital, bursts into life once a
year in the fiesta San Fermín – a fortnight-long bullfighting
bonanza that pulls crowds from all over the world. Foothills
spread from here to the fertile vineyards of Navarre and the
varied, empty landscapes of Aragón. Broad, ruddy rivers
muscle their way between hulking, rocky outcrops; tall,
swaying grasses shield fields of maize; and lowlands give
way to the neat rows of mixed orchards. Pyrenees aside,
Aragón is not an obvious tourist destination. Zaragoza,
its capital, is a busy industrial city, but it does have a
striking centre founded round the Basílica de Nuestra Señora
del Pilar. Moreover, Francisco Goya, arguably the greatest
Spanish artist of all time, was born at Fuendetodos, 45
km from the city; enthusiasts should earmark Zaragoza's
Museo Camón Aznar to view the very best of his etchings.

BILBAO

Grimy, damp and industrial, Bilbao is all that its reputation
declares it to be: you'll either love it or hate it. First and
foremost a working city, it enjoys a culture deeply rooted
in a tradition whose clearest expression is in the Basque
language and the cuisine, arguably the best in Spain. It's a
place with guts, where strong flavours satisfy strong tastes,
and the best way to get a feel for all this is by wandering its
streets and sampling the rich life of its bars and restaurants.
Bilbaoans work hard and play hard: bars and clubs heave
with people, the *tapas* here is as good as you'll find anywhere
in Spain, and amid the hectic grind of the city glimmers
a sprinkling of Art Nouveau café-bars with superb period
detail.

Physically, too, Bilbao's robust character is unique: the
place has a gritty, heavy beauty. Bold 19th-century buildings
line broad avenues, their weighty monumentality punctuated
by the loaded curves and ponderous swirls of occasional

The Basques

The Basque country defies modern national boundaries. Crossing the Pyrenees, it unites part of France and three Spanish provinces: Guipúzcoa, Vizcaya and Álava and part of Navarre. Its people share a culture far older than either of the two recognized European nations, and Euskara, believed to be older than any other European language, has baffled linguists. One theory is that it evolved among the earliest cavedwellers of the region. Basque people have quite a distinct physique from other French and Spanish people, too. Whatever their origins, their character has been formed by the toughness of the mountain environment, their strength and bravery engendered by generations of seafarers, and their political resilience honed against the onslaught of homogenizing centralized powers.

The desire to preserve Basque political independence is centuries old, but the current strength of feeling owes much to the treatment that the Basques received at the hands of Franco, still very much alive in the memory of a large percentage of the population. The language was banned and the suppression of Basque nationalism was most brutally epitomized by the bombing of Guernica in 1937 during the Civil War.

Today feelings among Basques remain strong in this heavily politicized region. A desire to secede from French and Spanish control and form an entirely independent state remains and finds its most violent expression in the bombing campaigns of ETA (Euskadi ta Azkatasuna). But there has also been progress through peaceful channels. Spain is divided into 17 autonomous regions, of which the Basque country (closely followed by Catalonia and Galicia) is the most strongly independent. They have separate laws, collect a separate Basque tax, Euskara is taught in many schools, and there is a Basque police force — visible in the streets of Bilbao in their red berets.

For the visitor, the two most prominent aspects of this unique culture are found in the language and the food. You can expect to find both Basque and Castilian Spanish written in public places; Basque is widely spoken, but most people are bilingual, so you should not have too much trouble in being understood. As for the food, expect to eat as well here as anywhere in Spain: the cuisine, which includes plenty of seafood, is renowned.

Art Nouveau

Art Nouveau is a term used to describe a style that became prominent in the last decade of the 19th century and remained influential well into the 1930s. All areas of design were affected, including furniture, jewellery, poster art and architecture. The style can be seen today in the entrances to the Paris Metro, for example, and in the posters of Toulouse-Lautrec and Alfonse Mocha.

It imitates the curves and sweeping lines of plants: solid stone, wrought metals and carved wood are made to look organic and alive. Doorways, windows, balconies and carved masonry echo the forms of stems, bulbs and leaves in bold, heavy and extravagant swoops and curls; wispy trails of decorative ironwork look like delicate tendrils being blown across solid stone.

Stained glasswork was also popular. Tiffany of New York was famous for using this medium, but Bilbao has plenty of its own that is impressive. Clambering flowers and foliage flow across windows and mirrors; intricate designs in coloured glass show idyllic scenes. In Bilbao the glasswork was also used to portray the working life of the city in such buildings as the stations and the market.

Barcelona is the Spanish city most famous for this style because of its wealth of buildings by Antoni Gaudí, but there are real gems of the period embedded in cities throughout northern Spain, especially in Bilbao. Here Art Nouveau café-bars still form an important part of the city's social scene.

Art Nouveau façades. Similarly unexpected are the colourful flashes of turn-of-the-century stained glass found in such workaday settings as the train stations and the market, echoing the dazzle of Tiffany's more famous and costly brilliance, here celebrating the ordinary life of the city.

Bilbao is surrounded by steep, strangely peaked mountains. Walk down the most central of streets, turn a corner and they swing into view. The city sits on a pinch of land between taut, sinuous curves of the river Nervión, which drags in its wake a trail of salty air so that you can taste the Atlantic on your lips. The coast is less than 15 km away and splendid beaches are easily accessible.

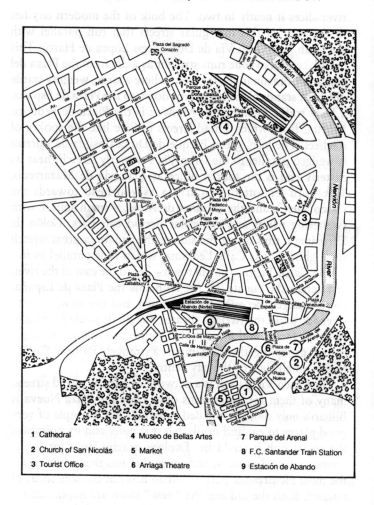

1 Cathedral
2 Church of San Nicolás
3 Tourist Office
4 Museo de Bellas Artes
5 Market
6 Arriaga Theatre
7 Parque del Arenal
8 F.C. Santander Train Station
9 Estación de Abando

GETTING YOUR BEARINGS

Bilbao is an easy place to find your way around. It is small,
readily negotiated on foot and the only time you are likely to
need any form of public transport is in the early hours of the
morning, when a taxi is your only option. The city is situated
inland, well upstream on the river Nervión; the bend in the

river slices it neatly in two. The bulk of the modern city lies to the west of this in regular streets that run parallel with the Gran Vía (Gran Vía de Don Diego López de Haro). This broad, central avenue runs straight as a die from the Plaza del Sagrada Corazón in the far west, where a large, weighty statue of Christ stands blessing the city, down to the Plaza de España, a busy traffic interchange. Midway is the Plaza de Federico Moyua, from which broad streets radiate like the spokes of a wheel. The lush, green Parque de Doña Casilda de Iturriza is wedged parallel to the Gran Vía's westerly stretch; near its easterly end is the tourist office at Alameda de Mazarredo, 12A (turn left off the Gran Vía as you head towards the Casco Viejo), and the Jardines de Albia, a small square with sweltering palms and some fine period café-bars. Colón de Larreátegui runs along the side of the square, a great stretch for nightlife, as is Calle Ledesma, which runs parallel to it.

The *Casco Viejo* – the old town – lies to the east of the river, just across the Puente del Arenal below the Plaza de España. Here, wedged between the old town and the new, a small riverside park, the Arriaga theatre, the fin de siecle Santander railway station and a restrained eighteenth-century Baroque church group together and impart a strangely Parisian flavour to this small slice of the city centre.

The Casco Viejo itself is a network of narrow paved streets, many of them for pedestrians only. Here the Plaza Nueva is Bilbao's only old, colonnaded square. It has a couple of very good places to eat and drink, but it is quiet and by no means the social hub it could be. Explore nearby lanes for lively, young bars and mesóns, and remember too that while this is the most picturesque part of Bilbao it is not the sole focus of interest. Both the old and the "new" town are important for the city's main activities – eating, drinking and dancing.

DON'T MISS . . .

Café-Bars

The city's stylish turn-of-the-century café-bars are classics of their kind, combining the twin delights of Bilbaoan culture: Art Nouveau decor and delicious seafood *tapas*. Sit at a solid marble bar admiring leaded windows dripping with stained glass while savouring superb *tapas* – maybe an anchovy wrapped snugly round an olive and soaked in extra-virgin olive oil, a hunk of tuna laced up with straps of green and red pepper or a morsel of toast covered in shrimp meat and dotted with ink-black caviar. For decor and atmosphere, the best of these period pieces include **Café Iruña, Café El Boulevard, Café Arriaga, La Concordia, Café Bilbao** and **La Granja**. See "Eating, Drinking and Nightlife" below.

Museo de Bellas Artes de Bilbao (Fine Art Museum)
(Parque de Doña Casilda Iturriza, Tel 441 95 36 and 441 01 54. Open Tuesday–Saturday 10.00–13.30pm and 16.00–19.30, Sundays 10.00–14.00).
This gallery houses a very mixed collection of paintings. Among a host of lesser works are really impressive paintings by El Greco, Velázquez – particularly his portrait of Philip IV – Ribera and Zurbarán. There is also a large collection of Flemish Primitives and 17th-century paintings from the northern part of the Spanish empire – including works by Van Dyck, Teniers the Younger and Brueghel.

Art Nouveau Bilbao: A Short Walk

Along with café-bars, Bilbao has a healthy smattering of Art Nouveau buildings that form an important part of the character of the city. This short walk locates a sample of the city's hidden architectural treasures.

Parque del Arenal The bandstand of this riverside park is worthy of close inspection. Its glass ceiling is a kaleidoscope of colour: nude, muscular angels with tobacco-brown skin fly like a group of formation swimmers against a vibrant indigo background.

Follow the river upstream around the side of the Casco Viejo to the market.

The covered market was sited beside the river so that produce (especially seafood) could be unloaded from boats; at the end of the day the whole place could be cleaned out, and bits of refuse washed back into the river. Nothing special at first glance, but after a peep at the fabulous array of seafood on the ground floor, climb the stairs to the second level: here a huge window of decorative coloured glass sends showers of dappled light across the market hall.

Walk back to the Puente del Arenal. **F.C. Santander railway station** is visible on the shoulder of the hill above the bridge, similarly fancifully decorated with yellow and green ironwork.

Estación de Abando, the station just behind It, lias a plain enough exterior, but a dazzling tapestry of coloured glass stretches above the platforms inside, celebrating the dignity of labour in strong, romantic images of people working in the fields, on the railway, and at sea in great fishing boats.

Walk out of the station, cross Calle Hurtado de Amézaga (which runs off Plaza de España) and turn right into Calle Bertendona. At No. 3 you will find **Campos Albia**. This theatre is an exuberant collision of Art Nouveau and the memory of the Moors; built in 1901, it is now an unmissable peppermint green.

ALSO WORTH SEEING . . .

Museo Arqueológico, Etnográfico e Histórico de Bizkaia
(Located in the Colegio de San Andres de la Compania de Jesus in the Casco Viejo. Cruz, 4 Tel: 415 54 23. Open

Tuesday–Saturday 10.30–13.30 and 16.00–19.00, Sundays 10.30–13.30.)

This museum of Basque culture demonstrates the various folk-art traditions of the region and includes collections of ceramics, statuary and wood carving.

OUT OF TOWN . . .

Beaches

The Basque coast between Bilbao and San Sebastián is green and dramatic: craggy cliffs backed by thickly forested hills plunge into little bays and inlets, the rocky coast relieved

Guernica

Guernica (Gernika)

On 26 April 1937, Nazi German allies of Franco's Nationalist forces launched the first aerial bombing of a civilian centre the world had ever seen on the little town of Guernica in the heart of the Basque region. Within three hours, 2,000 people were dead. The bombing came to epitomize the horror and brutality of the Civil War and is commemorated in Picasso's most famous painting, "Guernica", which was returned to Spain only after the fall of Franco; it now hangs in the Casón del Buen Retiro of the Prado museum in Madrid.

Today Guernica is a plain, modern town; its historic centre was wiped out by the attack. The Tree of Guernica remains the enduring Basque symbol of liberty. From the Middle Ages Basque lords held their court and parliament under a great oak in the centre of the town. The tree that stands in Guernica today is a descendant of the original oak.

every few miles by occasional sandy beaches and busy fishing harbours. Powerful waves make for excellent surfing and exciting seascapes.

Playa Las Arenas is the best beach for a day trip from Bilbao, only 10 km away; the beach at *Sopelanu* (20 km away) is another popular option. If you have transport it is well worth exploring farther along the coast. East of Bilbao, **Bermeo** is a thriving fishing port with several good seafood restaurants. **Mundaca** (45 km from Bilbao) has an excellent beach for surfing.

BILBAO FACTFILE

Tourist Office, Alameda Mazarredo, 12 A, 48001 Bilbao.
Tel: 424 48 19. Open all year Monday–Friday 9.00–13.30 and 16.00–20.00.
Airport Tel: 453 13 50, info Iberia 453 20 24 and 453 13 50. Bilbao airport is 10 km from the city centre and there is a bus approximately every 20 minutes from Plaza San Nicolás, Arenal. Enquiries Tel: 475 82 00. A taxi to the airport costs around 1,100 pesetas.
Train Stations There are several train stations in Bilbao.
Estación de FEVE (with "FC. de Santander a Bilbao" over the entrance), Calle Bailén, 2. Tel: 423 22 66. Services to Santander and to Valmaseda and León.

Estación del Norte (RENFE, also known as *Estación de Abando*), Plaza España, 2. Tel: 423 86 36 and 423 86 23, reservations (91) 501 33 33. Services to Barcelona, Madrid, Levante, Galicia and Andalusia.

Estación de San Nicolás (ET/FFVV), situated behind the church of San Nicolás in the Casco Viejo. Tel: 416 14 11. Services to Algorta, Plencia, Larrabasterra.

Estación de Atxuri, situated east beyond the market and next to the river. Tel: 433 95 00. Services to Bermeo, Guernica, Amorebieta and San Sebastián.

Bus Stations ANSA, GETSA and VIACAR lines, Autonomía, 17. Tel: 444 31 00. Services to Burgos, Madrid, Barcelona, Reinosa, Santander, Asturias, Galicia, Valencia, Alicante, London.

Turytrans, Calle de la Ribera, 10, just off Plaza Arraiga. Tel: 41 52 119. Services to Santander, Gijón, and Oviedo.

ENATCAR (RENFE), Autonomía, 4. Tel: 444 00 25. Services to Irún, Zamora, Orense, Palencia, Valladolid, Cáceres, Badajoz.

Intercar, Alameda Recalde, 68. Tel: 444 48 58. Services to Orense, Vigo, Tuy.

Car Hire Atesa, Sabino Arana, 9. Tel: 442 32 90. Avis, Dr Areilza, 34. Tel: 427 57 60. Autoarega, Licenciado Poza, 10. Tel: 443 60 33.

Taxi Radio Taxi Bizkaia. Tel: 416 23 00. Radio Taxi Bilbao. Tel: 443 52 00.

Post Office, Alameda de Urquijo, 19.

Telephone code: 94. Cashier-served public telephone booths are located at Barroeta Aldamar, 7 (just off Colón de Larreátegui), open Monday—Saturday 9.00–14.00 and 16.00–20.00.

WHERE TO STAY
Cheap to Moderate

La Estrella HS*, María Muñoz, 6. Tel: 416 40 66.
Ibarra HsR*, Ribera, 6. Tel: 415 82 68.
Gurea HsR**, Bidebarrieta, 14. Tel: 416 32 99.
Arana HsR**, Bidebarrieta, 2. Tel: 415 64 11.
Ripa H*, Muelle Ripa. Tel: 423 96 77.
Cantábrico HR**, Miravilla, 8. Tel: 415 28 11.
Vista Alegre H**, Pablo Picasso, 13. Tel: 443 14 50.
Zabálburu H**, P. Martínez Artola, 8. Tel: 443 71 00.

Smarter Options

Avenida HR***, Avenida Zumalacárregui, 40. Tel: 412 43 00.
Conde Duque HR***, Campo Volantín, 22. Tel: 445 60 00.
Nervión HR***, Campo Volantín, 11. Tel: 445 47 00.
Aranzazu HR****, Rodríguez Arias, 66. Tel: 441 32 00.
Ercilla HR****, Ercilla 37. Tel: 443 88 00.

EATING, DRINKING AND NIGHTLIFE

The crossover between eating, drinking and nightlife is great in this city, so to prevent unnecessary repetition the venues are grouped together here, area by area. Bilbao's weekly What's On guide *La ría del ocio* is available at newsstands.

Casco Viejo

This is the area to head for if you want traditional meals in cheap, down-to-earth and often scruffy *mesóns* and cafés. It is also where you'll find Bilbao's student bars, the remnants of its punk scene and loud rock bars, particularly in the streets off Plazuela Santiago (by the cathedral), in Calle Pelota and along Calle Barrencalle. Casco Viejo also has a couple of classic stylish café-bars.

Victor Montes, Plaza Nueva, 2. Tel: 415 16 78. Wine-lined walls, up-beat jazz-cum-cabaret music and excellent fishy *tapas* make this stylish little restaurant and bar extremely popular.
Amaya, Calle de la Ribera. Modest period café-bar with coloured glasswork and fancy chandeliers. Sandwiches, snacks and good, cheap *platos combinados*.
El Boulevard, Paseo del Arenal, just over Puente Arenal. Bilbao's finest classic Art Nouveau café-bar. The decor is highly reminiscent of the work of Gustav Klimt: small geometric shapes of dull gold and muted creams create asymmetric designs against sage and slate-green walls; gilt-framed mirrors reflect the marble pillars and highly polished bar. Undoubtably the most elegant place to drink in the city.
El Elbo, Paseo del Arenal. An opulent, though rather tarnished, nod to the stylistic perfection of the café El Boulevard a few doors up. A less classy, more exuberant little bar.
Arriaga, Plaza Arriaga, below the theatre. Chic period café-bar in the grandiose theâtre building. In fine weather you can sit out on the cobbled square and look at the passing scene: the stylistic frippery of the Estación Concordia across the river, people strolling in the tree-filled gardens nearby, and the weirdly peaked mountains encircling the city.
K2, Calle Somera, 10. Trendy young bar pumping out relentless rock music.
Café Wholdea, Calle de la Ribera, 10. Lively bar throwing out good, wholesome rock and reggae. Attracts students and laid-back, tatty trendies. Good atmosphere.
Café Miar, Laid-back, spacious, vaguely studenty café-bar for Smiths fans.
Akelarre, Pelota, 6. Café pub offering happy ska, rock and reggae mix and sometimes dancing.
Café Nervión, Calle Dos de Mayo, across Puente la Merced from the Casco Viejo. Down-to-earth, murky drinking den. Traditional tiled walls crawling with fabulous flower motifs and decorated with

grim copper pans. The bar is heaved into life by throbbing rock music.

Colón de Larreátegui and Buenos Aires

Masses of fashionable disco bars pumping out mainstream disco sounds and swarming with people make this an extremely lively area for nightlife. Here, too, are some of Bilbao's finest old café-bars, a handful of decent restaurants and *comedors* offering straightforward, cheap meals – generally more middle-aged than in the Casco Viejo, they also seem cleaner and less tatty.

Café Iruña, Jardines de Albia. One of Bilbao's finest café-bars and a prize period piece. The Café Iruña has two rooms. The huge bar has traditional blue and white tiling, the restaurant alongside it is heavily decorated with Mudéjar carving, cusped arches and ornamental lamps of bulbous, ruby-red glasswork hanging from the ceiling. All this considered, the *platos combinados* are surprisingly cheap. In the evenings there is a great atmosphere, often with live music – occasionally including flamenco.

Bilbao 1901, Jardines de Albia. Classy turn-of-the-century bar, gleaming with old mirrors and highly polished woodwork.

La Granja, Plaza de España, 3. Classic old-style Bilbaoan bar that knows how to party. Live music, great atmosphere.

Toledo, Buenos Aires, 12. No-nonsense restaurant serving possibly the best value *platos combinados* in the city. Highly recommended for the hungry and budget-conscious.

Maider, Colón de Larreátegui. Decent and reasonably priced restaurant, specializing in seafood.

Arlanza, Colón de Larreátegui. Straightforward café and restaurant serving cheap *platos combinados* – including plenty of hake.

La Concordia, José María Olávarri, 1, off Calle Navarra. Heavy, embossed crustaceans decorate the grandiose marble bar; squat classic columns support the ceiling, and dingy mahogany cabinets are crammed with kitsch knick-knacks. This dusty turn-of-the-century drinking hall is a real favourite, popular with all age groups.

Calle Ledesma

A lively strip for young, fashionable drinking and dancing. Bars and *mesóns* are shoulder to shoulder here and so full it barely matters which one you go to; you'll probably end up drinking on the street wedged between parked cars along with everybody else.

Magic, Calle Ledesma. Disco packed with people dancing to heart-rending Spanish ballads and mainstream disco sounds.

Calle de Iparraguirre and around

This area has some of the city's greatest *tapas* bars, restaurants, and discos that go on till 4.00 or 5.00am. To find it, walk down the Gran

Vía from Plaza de Federico Moyua – Calle Iparraguirre is the first road to cross this main avenue: turn left up it to find the liveliest area round here.

La Vina del Ensanche, Calle Diputacion, 10. Wine bottles climb the oak-lined walls and forests of hams hang from the ceiling. This is a very popular and fairly smart bar serving almost exclusively *jamón tapas*.

La Olla, Calle Diputacion, 10. Another great ham joint, decorated with earthy blown glasswork and old copper pans, antique engravings and a riot of *jamónes* and *salchichóns*. A tasty early-evening venue.

Mamma Mia, Marqués del Puerto, 10. Tel: 416 58 72. Very cheap and very cheerful pizzeria. Plenty of pizzas, pastas and wines from Navarre at half the price they charge for Italian plonk. Open till 24.00.

Lepanto, Plaza de Eguileor, 2. Tel: 415 04 26. Upmarket, conservative restaurant serving traditional Basque cuisine.

Drugstore, Calle Telesforo Aranzadi. Restaurant, bar and dance floor on three levels. Bar done out with dull grey-green scaffolding poured over with a layer of soft soul and MOR disco sounds, very definitely a place for young, fashion-conscious danceaholics from around midnight till about 5.00. There's also a café with snacks and light meals.

The restaurant upstairs is pretty pricey but quite an experience: walls, ceilings, tables, *everything* is covered with a rosy apples print; a kind of acid-crazed scrumping nightmare.

Tripoli, Calle Telesforo Aranzadi. Fabulous copper-green, brutal disco, starting at 1.00 and going on till 5.00.

CUA, Calle Telesforo Aranzadi. Lively little bar with dancing downstairs along with wall paintings of monstrous, mischievous cartoon nuns.

El Soplete, Licenciado Poza, 6. Another lively cramped bar with dancing downstairs. Round the corner from CUA.

Sabin-Etxea, Alameda de Recalde, 60. Tel: 443 50 76. Tiny oak-beamed bar with tartan walls and sawdust on the floor. Just a few little tables are squeezed in here – get one if you can, this place does excellent cheap *raciones*. Try their succulent garlic-soaked broad mushrooms with a glass of *rosada*. This is quite a secret place and well worth unearthing.

Urraca, Alameda de Recalde. Smart, yuppie disco bar with lots of flashing neon, shiny surfaces and very MOR pop music.

Casa Jesus, Gordononiz, 6, off Iparraguirre. Another good *tapas* place for early-evening *jamón*, olives and aperitifs. Popular with a mixed young crowd.

Hong Kong, Alameda de San Mamés. Pretty Chinese restaurant complete with paintings, paper lanterns and a range of dishes to suit most pockets.

Yonemar, Alameda de San Mamés. Live lobsters beckon you fatally from their tanks in the windows. This is an extremely popular *marisquería* for its à la carte menu and its seafood *tapas*.

Onkalada, Alameda de San Mamés, 42. Tel: 431 19 27. Another great place for local seafood dishes.

Urdazpi, Alameda de Urquijo, 48. Tel: 4321182. Good-quality *tapas* bar and restaurant. Hung with *jamónes*, the bar is a vegetarian's nightmare, but in fact the real speciality here is seafood – fabulously displayed along the bar.

The restaurant is fairly expensive: tanks of live lobsters, crabs etc. ensure it is all fresh. Name your shellfish and watch the chef go in for the kill.

Serantes, Licenciado Poza, 16. Tel: 431 21 29. There's no escaping the two specialities of this bar: dense rows of *jamónes* swing from the ceiling, while prawns and shrimps lie pink and fresh in iceboxes on the bar.

Balear, Gran Vía, 56. Classic modern bar that reinterprets some of Bilbao's old, traditional stylishness – except in the menu, which offers honest-to-goodness hamburgers and sandwiches.

Café Toledo, Gran Vía, 56. Lots of comfy black sofas, potted palms and polished mirrors. This is something of a respectable, middle-aged institution, but handy for excellent coffee in the centre of town.

SAN SEBASTIÁN

A stunning bay, perfect sandy beaches and a chic, upbeat nightlife make San Sebastián one of the best seaside resorts in northern Spain. It has been firmly established as just that for over a hundred years and the broad avenues of the 19th-century resort give it a stately grandeur and an air of cultivated, fashionable wealth. At the same time the atmosphere is never really exclusive – although accommodation does tend to be more expensive than in other Spanish seaside towns. The only note of caution must be about the weather: like the rest of this northern coast, San Sebastián has considerable rainfall throughout the year. You can be unlucky, but during the summer the sun usually shines, with an average temperature of 22°C.

GETTING YOUR BEARINGS

San Sebastián breaks up into easily defined segments and getting your bearings does not take long. The statue of the Sacred Heart on the top of Monte Urgull is a key landmark. To the west of it is San Sebastián's superb bay and Playa de la Concha and Playa de Ondarreta, the best of its beaches; to the east, the broad river flows into the sea.

Around the base of Monte Urgull are the harbour and the

old quarter of narrow lanes, full of excellent *tapas* bars and seafood restaurants. Filling out inland from the old town, and in contrast to the curves and sweeps of the beaches and the hilly coast, the "new" (19th-century) part of town follows a grid plan alongside the river. Find the tourist office on the west bank of the river at the corner of Calle Reina Regente and Paseo Argentina.

Ondarreta beach, at the far western end of the bay, backs on to a quiet suburb of well-tended hotels and gardens. Beyond this is Monte Igueldo, where you can take a funicular railway up its wooded slopes.

DON'T MISS . . .

The Beaches

The bay at San Sebastián has the perfection of a circle, ringed by beaches of golden sand. It sits between green, tree-covered hills which, along with the wooded island of Santa Clara at its mouth, protect it from the open sea, leaving the clear blue water as calm as a millpond. **Playa de la Concha** is the finest of its beaches, a huge curve of creamy yellow sand swooping from the harbour right round to the Palacio Miramar. Beyond this is **Playa de Ondarreta**, equally popular for its tennis courts and access to the funicular railway that climbs Monte Igueldo to the funfair at the top. San Sebastián's third beach is **Playa de Gros**, far on the eastern side of town. It is sandy and good for sunbathing, but strong currents make it unsafe for swimming.

The Old Town

The old town huddles at the base of Monte Urgell. At its centre the ancient Plaza de la Constitución still bears the numbered balconies of its former days when it served as the local bullring. Bound by squat colonnading, it is a small, workaday plaza, not at all the social hub you might expect. None the less good, earthy *tapas* bars lurk among its butcher's shops and grocery stores and more are to be found in the surrounding network of narrow lanes. If you want to sit out at a pavement café and enjoy the old town, Plaza de la Trinidad is your best bet, a quiet niche wedged

beneath the tangled foliage of Mount Urgell. Nearby the exuberant little church of Santa María del Coro is squeezed in between the tall buildings of Calle V. Coro. It is a masterly Baroque extravagance in golden sandstone. Turn your back to its façade for a clear view the length of Rua Mayor and beyond to the 19th-century cathedral Buen Pastor in the "new" part of town – a sharp and spiky Neo-Gothic design and a complete contrast to Iglesia Santa María's curves and flounces.

The **Museo de San Telmo** is tucked round beneath the east side of Mount Urgell, a collection of local paintings and artefacts housed in a 16th-century Renaissance building. It opens Mondays–Fridays 9.30–13.30 and 15.30–19.30; Sunday and holidays 10.30–14.00. The wooded hill can be climbed from here, affording great views of the bay.

The Harbour

The old stone harbour lies in a crook of land with its back to Mount Urgell, sheltering from harsh Atlantic storms. A stroll along the quays takes you past the busy coloured fishing vessels and the whistling masts of moored yachts; beyond them lie San Sebastián's magnificent beaches and the island of Santa Clara in the mouth of the bay. Boats leave here for the island during the summer: there is little to see once you get there, but it is a nice spot for a picnic. Seafood restaurants line the old harbour, offering the best atmosphere to enjoy a meal out of doors. The **Aquarium** sits at the far end of the quays, not at all a collection of fish, but a nautical museum. Open Monday–Saturday 10.00–13.30 and 15.30–19.30 (20.00 in summer); closed all day Monday from mid-September to mid-March.

The Modern Town

The modern town has a flavour quite different to that of the old. Its broad avenues and streets are elegantly planned, and the place has a sophisticated, cosmopolitan air akin to the French Riviera. Its shops, coffee houses and occasional restaurants are up-market and conservative.

San Sebastián first became a summer resort for the rich and fashionable after 1845, when it was visited by Queen Isabel, and the "new" part of town takes its stylistic cue from this period. It was clearly laid out on a grand scale, and this can be fully appreciated by walking along the *paseos* beside the river from the sea inland. The mood of monied confidence is set by the grandiose Hotel Christina

History

The harbour was the key to the early growth of San Sebastián. Originally its inhabitants made their living from fishing and are known to have gone as far as the waters of Newfoundland during the Middle Ages for whaling and cod-fishing. It has continued to be an important part of the economy down the ages, trawling a delicious gastronomic tradition in its wake – available all over town.

In the 16th century San Sebastián became Navarre's key port, exporting oil and wine to France, Flanders and England. A castle was built on Mount Urgell and the town became a strategic border stronghold. Napoleon's troops occupied San Sebastián from 1808 until 1813, when an Anglo-Portugese army took and destroyed the town. Eventually the slow task of rebuilding began.

In 1845 San Sebastián was visited for the first time by Queen Isabel, who appreciated its magnificent beach. Her patronage turned the town into a highly fashionable resort; the broad boulevards and grand hotels of that era remain today.

and the regally ornamented **Santa Catalina Bridge**, with its flamboyant, gold-coated statues. A few streets away, the **Plaza de Guipuzcoa** is the town's finest, its little colonnaded square thick with green foliage and luxuriant, swaying palms.

Back beside the river, the *paseo* extends deep inland, running along the back of the large 19th-century town houses that were built here with heavy and opulent grandeur. For Art Nouveau enthusiasts it is worth making a detour off the Paseo de los Fueros at the Maria Christina Bridge to the huge gushing fountain of Plaza de Bilbao to take a look at the windows and doorways of the bookshop Donosti on the plaza, and at superlative examples of the style in Calle de Prim at Nos. 10, 17 and 25.

The affluence of the area continues to this day and in the triangular wedge of streets that runs between the cathedral, the top of Calle de Prim and Plaza de Bilbao you will find a late nightlife as chic and lively as any in Spain.

SAN SEBASTIÁN FACTFILE

Tourist Office, Calle Reine Regente and Paseo Argentina. Tel: 48 11 66 and 67/68/69. Open Monday–Saturday 9.00–14.00 and 15.30–19.00; closed Saturday afternoons off-season.

Train Stations *RENFE*, Estación del Norte, Paseo de Francia. Trains to Irun and Madrid.

  FEVE, Estación de Amara, Calle de Easo. Trains to Bilbao.

Bus Station, Plaza Pio XII.

Car Hire Atesa, Anton de Luzuriaga, 2. Tel: 27 22 86. Avis, Calle Triunfo, 2. Tel: 46 15 27 and 26 15 56.

Taxi Radio Taxis. Tel: 46 76 66.

Telephone code: 943.

WHERE TO STAY
Cheap to Moderate

La Perla P**, Loyola, 10. Tel: 24 81 23.
Gran Bahia HsR*, Calle de Embletran, 16. Tel: 42 38 38.
Fernando HsR**, Plaza de Guipúzcoa, 2. Tel: 42 55 75.
La Concha P**, Calle de San Martin, 51. Tel: 45 03 89.
Alameda HsR**, Alda. del Boulevard, 23. Tel: 42 16 87.

Smarter Options

Pellizar HR**, Boulevard de Intxaurrondo. Tel: 28 12 11.
Codina H**, Avenida Zumalacarregui, 21. Tel: 21 22 00.
Niza H***, Zubieta, 56. Tel: 42 66 63.

WHERE TO EAT
Tapas Bars

Early evening the *tapas* bars of the old quarter of San Sebastián are busy with people. Hopping from one to the next can be as filling – and as much fun – as sitting down to a meal in a restaurant. In any case, many of these bars also have a *comedor* to the rear where you can sit and enjoy a full meal.

In the **old town**, Plaza de la Constitución has a couple of good bars: try **Bar Ambrosio** or **El Astelena**. Calle 31 de Agosto, just two streets away towards Mount Urgell, has several more: **Gaztelu** at No. 22 and **La Cepa** at No. 7 are both good bets. Calle Fermin Calbeton also has a couple of very popular places: **El Bartolo**, where you can try *cazuelas* – quails – and **Beti Jai**, which offers **txangurro** – spider crab – among its tantalizing array of seafood.

In the **modern town, Casa Valles,** Calle Reyes Católicos, 10. Tel: 45 22 10. Large, wood-panelled eating emporium. Sawdust on the floor, solid wood benches, and hams hanging from the rafters; a good, cheap, meaty option if you don't want a full meal.

El Rincon, Calle Reyes Católicos, 20. Tel: 45 05 58. Another good choice for meaty *raciones*; similar set-up to Casa Valles.

Bodegan Ardandegi, Calle Reyes Católicos, 7. Tel: 46 74 77. Good basement *tapas* bar for early-evening eats; attracts a young, well-heeled crowd.

Basque Cuisine

The Basque country has arguably the best regional cuisine in Spain. There is no shortage of excellent *tapas* bars and restaurants in San Sebastián or Bilbao in which to sample the local specialities. Naturally seafood is at the heart of this cuisine, and the busy Atlantic fishing ports along this coast ensure a daily catch. But it is not just the freshness of the raw materials that makes the food here special. Fiercely proud and competitive *Sociedades Populares* play a major part in this living tradition. These are long-established, exclusively male clubs that meet with the sole purpose of preparing food and eating as well as possible. The gastronomic excellence they promote ensures that an ever-improving repertoire of culinary treats is available all over the region.

Look out for:

angulas – baby eels
bacalao a la Vizcaina – cod
merluza à la Vasca – hake
chipirones en su tinta – squid cooked in their own ink
marmitako – a stew of tuna fish
anchoas – anchovies
txangarro – spider crab
txacoli – Basque white wine, tangy and slightly fizzy; produced in Guipúzcoa.

Cheap to Moderate

There are several restaurants along the quays of the old harbour where you can enjoy your meal sitting out and taking in the whole scene: fishing boats, beaches and the surrounding hills. Expect to pay a little more for the great setting.

In the old town, we recommend the following:

La Cueva, Plaza de la Trinidad. Tel: 42 54 37. Traditional old restaurant with low-beamed ceilings and rough stone walls. It is in a lovely location in the old quarter; sit out on the terrace in the cobbled square and soak in the atmosphere.

Clery, Plaza de la Trinidad, 1. Tel: 42 34 01. A prime location in the heart of the old town; straightforward, traditional menu.

Captain Palo, San Vicente, 7. Tel: 42 45 76. Pretty, intimate seafood restaurant alongside Iglesia San Vicente. Moderate to expensive.

Finally, if you don't like seafood at all, there are a couple of Chinese restaurants in the new part of town:

Palacio de China, Calle Larramendi, 11. Tel: 45 19 68.

Taiwan, Calle Reyes Católicos, 6. Tel: 47 09 55.
Italian food is available at:
Oquendo, Calle Oquendo, 8. Tel: 20 00 04. Cheap and very cheerful
pizzeria-cum-trattoria bar.

Smarter Options

Pachicu Quintana, Calle San Jeronimo, 22. Tel: 42 63 99. Elegant,
up-market restaurant in the heart of the old town; excellent seafood menu.
Akelarre, Calle Igueldo. Tel: 21 20 52 and 21 40 86. One of San
Sebastián's top restaurants, serving exceptional Basque cuisine.

NIGHTLIFE

In early evening most Donostiarras head for the *tapas* bars of the
old quarter. After about 23.00 these bars tend to close, and San
Sebastián's night scene shifts to a small wedge of streets in the new
part of town, just behind the Catedral Buen Pastor. Calle Sanchez
Toca, Calle Larramendi and Calle Reyes Católicos have the very
best of the bars. Chic, classy and often pretty pricey, they are
lively until around 2.00 – and much later during the summer and
at weekends.
Café Kalima, Calle Larramendi, 5. An animated place for drinking and
talking. Cluttered little bar with primitive masks on the walls, and
slow-whirring fans churning the air and debate rising from a relaxed,
arty crowd.
Arena R Bar, Calle Larramendi, 4. Wacky, minimalist, post-modern bar
with darts board.
Copco Bar, Calle Larramendi, opposite Arena R and Café Kalima. The
brutalism of its iron and copper façade is worth seeing; this bar seems
to attract beautiful, pouting nihilists.
Baviera, corner of Calle Reyes Católicos and Calle Larramendi.
Cuckoo clocks, Gothic candelabra and earthenware flagons make
this an obsessively Teutonic little drinking den.
Azul Cristal, Calle Reyes Católicos. Crumbly walls, milk churns and
huge wheat sheafs tumbling on to the floor; a rustic retreat for quiet
drinking accompanied by restrained pop music.
Larramendi, Calle Larramendi. Raucous, cavernous, deep-red disco bar
for unpretentious danceaholics. Starts early (around 22.30) and goes on
into the small hours.
Udaberri-Berri, Calle Larramendi, 8. Tel: 45 15 38. Strangely trendy
yet earthy bar. Great selection of Latin and indie sounds and highly
convivial atmosphere; it even has a counter on to the street to serve
the hordes that cram the pavements.
Splash, Calle Sanchez Toca, 7. Big, stylish street-corner café-bar
attracting a mixed, arty crowd. All very tasteful and well behaved,
and with a great selection of jazz, R & B, soul etc.
El Cairo, Calle Reyes Católicos, 7. Less restrained, less tasteful and

frankly more fun than some of the chicer bars around; a spanking new bar with hot salsa sounds.

Contraste, Sanchez Toca, 4. Rather plastic atmosphere, but if you like things uncompromisingly modern and you fancy spending the night beneath a red palm tree, this could be the place.

Carajillo, Sanchez Toca, 3a. Arch-minimalist, style-conscious bar animated by a surprisingly varied record collection.

Pokhara, Sanchez Toca, 1. Tel: 45 50 23. High designer chic for a relaxed, soul-loving, fashion-conscious crowd.

Jazz Bars

San Sebastián's jazz bars all cluster round the fringes of the old town.

Altxerre, Calle Reina Regente, 2. Tel: 42 40 46.

Be Bop, Calle Paseo de Salamanca, 5.

Etxekalte, Calle Mari, 21, just beside the harbour.

PLUS...

Argitan, at the corner of Reina Regente and Paseo de Salamanca. Walking past, the powerful aroma of molten chocolate may well drag you in for coffee and superb cream cakes; a good place from which to appreciate the riverside walk and the grandiose scale on which 19th-century San Sebastián was laid out.

Casa Casla, Calle Idiaquez Legazpi, 6, and Plaza de Guipúzcoa. Step into another era: this ancient *charcuteria Francesca* is an elegant period piece selling all manner of local cheeses, sausages, crystallized fruit, liqueurs and wines.

Lagun Librería, Plaza de la Constitución, 3/7. Tel: 42 20 07. **Bookshop** with a varied selection of books in English.

PAMPLONA

SAN FERMÍN: THE RUNNING OF THE BULLS

For 50 weeks of the year Pamplona remains a quiet, provincial town in the foothills of the Pyrenees. Between 6 and 14 July it explodes with people as thousands arrive from all over the world to witness and take part in the madness of the fiesta of San Fermín. It is a festival swamped with riotous drinking and music: the ritual at its centre is violent and often bloody.

The excitement starts at 8.00 each day, when half a dozen bulls are let loose through the streets between the Town Hall and the bullring. The town's young men – along with hundreds of tourists – run with them, thus, traditionally, proving their manhood. Driven by bravado, fiesta adrenalin and usually a fair amount of alcohol, they run among the roused and frightened bulls. Hysteria takes a hold and fear is palpable above the noise and fury of the thundering beasts and screaming crowds. It is an infectious madness and without doubt one of the most exciting sights in Spain, but it is also a bloody affair: every year people are gored and there are sometimes deaths. It is not a festival for the squeamish.

If you survive the thrills of the morning, you can go to watch the same bulls fight to the death in the bullring in the early evening. The drama and ritual are rousing and spectacular if you have a stomach for the gory fight that goes with it. Tickets are at a premium since the fights attract the top matadors in the country.

The fiesta was first internationally popularized by Ernest Hemingway, the American writer and bloodsports enthusiast, who visited the San Fermín celebrations in the 1920s and described them in his book *The Sun Also Rises*. Nearly 50 years later, in *The Dangerous Summer*, he was to bewail just how touristy the fiesta had become. There is a street here named after him and a bust of the writer stands outside the bullring.

ZARAGOZA

Zaragoza (Saragossa in English) has an air of purpose and sophistication way beyond that of a provincial centre. Large, abstract sculpture; bold, decisive planning and a handful of imposing historic buildings imbue the city with a strong, memorably distinct character. It's the capital of Aragón and one of the biggest industrial cities of northern Spain – hardly a typical tourist destination – yet to pass through without taking in what it has to offer would be a mistake. There are two cathedrals, a unique Arab palace, and its small museums harbour fine Roman antiquities and a collection of superlative Goya etchings. What's more, Zaragoza has a famously boisterous nightlife.

GETTING YOUR BEARINGS

Plaza del Pilar sits alongside the river Ebro, the hub of Zaragoza. It's dominated by the massy Basílica de Nuestra Señora del Pilar, which puts the older La Seo cathedral, tucked across the street at the far end of the square, somewhat in the shade. Directly opposite the basilica is a block of apartments and alleyways, in places near-derelict and strangely deserted, that extends into the area of El Tubo – an old and dingy quarter by day, renowned for its tapas bars and clubs by night. Running away from the Plaza either side of this block like the prongs of a fork are the two main thoroughfares of the old part of town: Calle de Alfonso 1 and Calle Don Jaime 1, both of which eventually meet Calle del Coso, a busy road that acts as a kind of buffer between the city's old core and the new part of town. Midway along Calle del Coso the Plaza de España feeds traffic into Avenida de la Independencia and the commercial heart of modern Zaragoza.

If you have arrived by train you will find yourself quite a way from the city centre and it's worth taking the bus to Plaza del Pilar: leaving the station walk down Calle General Mayandia, turn right onto Paseo María Agustín and take a number 21 bus.

Call into the tourist office in Calle de Don Jaime 1 and pick up a street map. You will find most places of interest (with the exception of the Aljaferiá Palace) within easy walking distance of the Plaza. To find the Aljaferiá Palace from the centre of town follow Calle Conde Aranda from the junction of Calle del Coso and Calle Cesar Agusto; the palace is beyond Calle Aranda's intersection with Paseo María Agustín.

DON'T MISS

Plaza del Pilar

Plaza de Nuestra Señora del Pilar is uncompromisingly modern. Backed by a near-derelict block of the old town and dominated by the 17th-century Basilica, the square is a striking use of civic space and should be seen. It's a bit like walking into one of de Chirico's surreal dreamscapes:

History

Zaragoza's name is a corruption of *Caesaraugusta*, as it was known in 25BC when it became a home for veteran Roman soldiers. In those days it was a walled town and had public baths, a theatre and a forum. Impressive Roman finds are now kept in the Museo Bellas Artes. The vision of the Virgin of El Pilar in AD40 resulted in the building of a basilica, and the town has remained a place of pilgrimage ever since.

In the 8th-century the town fell to the Moors, and after the dissolution of the Caliphate of Córdoba in 1031 Zaragossa came under the rule of the Banu Had family, who built the Aljaferiá Palace. During the Reconquest Zaragoza was taken by Alphonso 1 in 1118. The town grew as an important commercial centre, voting itself the most democratic Fueros (rights) in Spain, and continued to prosper into the 16th-century.

In 1808–9, during the War of Independence, Zaragoza was the scene of two hideous sieges. After tremendous resistance on the part of the Spanish, the French eventually took the city in scenes of horrific brutality, leaving 54,000 people dead.

at one end some minor continent appears to be sliding into

the square, sheets of water continually tearing across it, and a huge globe of similar matter seems to have escaped and rolled some way off into the vast Plaza. At the other end flat expanses of water perpetually flow across broad stretches of marble, watched over by a commanding statue of Goya (who lived nearby), and neo-Fascist copper lighting pillars flank the entire length of the plaza.

There are pleasant terrace cafés here where you can sit with a drink and ponder on what you think of the rather crude statue of Goya, and on what Goya might think of the array of artefacts that lie before him.

Don't miss a second look at the Plaza by night when the Basilica is lit up like an iced-sugar palace and the whole place is haunted by people out for an evening stroll.

Basílica de Nuestra Señora del Pilar
(Daily 5.45am–8.30pm.)
The Basilica stands on the site of a haloed shrine: on January 2nd, 40 AD the Virgin Mary, standing on top of a marble pillar, appeared to St James. The Pillar remained as proof of the vision and the spot soon became a place of veneration and pilgrimage, and so it remains. Several churches have stood on this site; the massive Basilica that stands today was designed by Francisco Herrera the Younger around 1677. The distinctive skyline of colourfully tiled lanterned cupolas is the result of additions a century later.

The interior is spoiled by a rather unreverential powder-blue and magnolia finish, but worth appreciating for the sheer size of the structure and for the 18th-century frescoes: those in the Chapel of San Joaquin are the work of Goya.

The Gothic statue of the Virgin, decorated in Pilasta medals, is found in a niche to the right of the Lady Chapel. Thousands come each year to kiss the column on which the statue stands.

Basilica Museum, Basílica Nuestra Señora del Pilar
(Tel 29 12 31. Daily 9am–2pm and 4pm–6pm).
Accessible from inside the Basilica.
Visiting the Basilica museum is a bit like walking into an ancient gift shop; it's crammed with medals of the Virgin of El Pilar, along with the opulent, fulsome baubles of the

18th and 19th century Aragonese aristocracy. It's the kind of jewellery you either love or hate, with gems and pearls worked into convoluted designs: a frog on a swing of diamonds, birds in flight, bejewelled bows, buckles and badges. Whatever else you think of them, there's no denying the ingenuity of the designs. Some of Goya's working drawings for the Basilica frescoes are also housed here, though fans of his work are better off spending their time in the *Camón Aznar* museum (see below).

La Seo: The Cathedral of San Salvador

A fascinating jumble of Moorish and Gothic styles are squeezed into this small cathedral, lodged beyond the statue of Goya at the end of the Plaza del Pilar. Originally a mosque, the main body of La Seo was built between 1119–1550, and the belfry dates from the 17th-century, ethereal figures tumbling around its clockface.

Wander down the lane to to the left of the entrance to admire the Mudéjar east end – a gingerbread confection of pale brick and blue and white ceramic patterning. Zaragoza was markedly tolerant of its Moorish citizens after the Reconquest, which is why flashes of Mudéjar decoration light up the tawny brick churches of the city. It was a tolerance that lasted: inside La Seo the dazzling Mudéjar-style cupola surprisingly dates from the 15th-century. Put a coin in the slot to light it up for full effect. The coloured alabaster altarpiece and the chapel of San Miguel Arcángel both display elaborate Gothic workmanship, and there is yet more richly embellished 16th-century carving around the tiny cathedral.

Museo de Tapices: Catedral de la Seo
(Plaza de La Seo)
The museum should be open daily 9.00–14.00 and 16.00–18.00, though in Spring 1992 it may still be temporarily closed. Tel 29 12 38. The exceptional Brussels tapestries on display here date from 15th to the 17th-centuries. They form one of the most important collections in Spain, as rich in their detail of period costumes and customs as in their refined workmanship.

Lonja de Mercaderes

Alongside the Basilica, this imposing exchange building is the most important piece of Aragonese Renaissance architecture. Dating from the mid-16th-century it shows obvious Italian influences, especially in the ringed pillars and the medallions and grotesques that decorate the interior. The Lonja is now used for temporary art exhibitions and consequently opening times vary.

Museo Camón Aznar

Espoz y Mina, 23. Tel 39 73 28.
Open Tuesday–Friday 10.00–14.00, Saturday 10.00–13.00 and Sunday 11.00–14.00.

Head straight for the collection of Goya etchings housed on the third floor. This museum contains the very best prints of this great Spanish artist: four series of etchings unsurpassed in the history of print-making.

The series known as *Los Caprichos* are here, biting, satirical pieces on the vice-ridden power-mongers, politicians and clergy of the day. Goya's vision encompasses all of humanity and the ignorant and dispossesed are scrutinised as ascerbically as the rich and powerful. The *Disparates* (Follies) series display fantastical and allegorical pictures, at times nightmarish, including the famous "The sleep of reason produces monsters". There's a series showing 18th-century bullfighting scenes too – the *Tauromaquia* – magnificent in composition and draftsmanship. Finally, the gruesome scenes recorded in *Los Desastres* (The Disasters of War) remain as horrible and moving as any full colour photographs of war today.

If you have any time left, there are paintings worth taking a look at on the lower floors, cutting across a huge range of styles and periods.

Aljaferiá Palace

Open Tuesday–Saturday 10.00–14.00 and 16.30–18.30. Summer Tuesday–Saturday 10.00–14.00 and 16.00–20.00; Sunday 10.00–14.00. Restoration work has been in progress for some time, which means that much of the palace may be closed. Access to the patio should be assured, but it is worth checking with the tourist office before setting off on the 30 minute walk from the Plaza del Pilar.

High outer walls, a moat and defensive towers form an imposing exterior: within is a courtyard of intricate and elaborate Moorish decoration. It comes as a real surprise to find a Moorish palace so far north and in the centre of an industrial city. It was built by the Banu Hud family and remains a unique example of Hispano-Arabic architecture; after the Reconquest it was taken over by the Catholic Monarchs who added the Church of San Martín in the 15th century. The upper storey, remodelled by Ferdinand and Isabella, and the opulent coffered ceiling of the throne room also remain from this period.

ALSO WORTH SEEING

Museo Pablo Gargallo

Plaza San Felipe 3. Tel 39 20 58.
Open Tuesday–Saturday 10.00–13.00 and 17.00–21.00, Holidays 11.00–14.00. Worth calling in as much to take a look at the Italianate courtyard of this old palace as to view the collection of 20th-century sculpture. Look out in particular for "Kiki de Montparnasse", an elegant Modernist bronze of 1928.

Museo Belles Artes

Tuesday–Saturday 9.00–14.00, Sunday 10.00–14.00.
200 pesetas

The museum has a collection of Roman finds from around the city, including some particularly enjoyable mosaics. There's a wealth of medieval religious art here too, and 14th and 15th-century altarpieces can be inspected at close quarters. The three portraits by Goya are worth looking out for: compare those of Charles IV and Queen María Luisa with the artistic maturity obvious in the much later portrayal of the Duke of San Carlos. Finally, don't leave without visiting the courtyard here, with its exhibits of plateresque and Gothic doorways.

Iglesia Santa María Magdalena

Found to the rear of the cathedral of La Seo.

The church displays some of the most distinctive Mudéjar workmanship in Zaragoza, most notably in its square brick tower decorated with regular blue, green and white ceramic tiling, very similar in style to La Seo.

WHERE TO STAY
Cheap to moderate

Las Torres HsR**
Plaza del Pilar, 11. Tel 21 58 20.
Navarra HsR**
San Vicente de Paul, 30. Tel 29 16 84.
Plaza HsR**
Plaza del Pilar, 14. Tel 29 48 30.
Hotel Sauce H**
Calle Espoz y Mina, 33. Tel 390100.

Smarter options

Europa HR***
Calle Alfonso 1, 19. Tel 39 27 00.
Ramiro 1 H***
Calle del Coso, 123. Tel 29 82 00.
Via Romana H***
Calle de Don Jaime 1, 54 & 56. Tel 39 82 15.

WHERE TO EAT
Tapas

There are excellent tapas bars in Zaragoza – try the area of *El Tubo* that backs onto Plaza de España; Calle Libertad; Calle de Cuatro de Agosto; Calle de los Martires and Calle de Jordan de Urries (off Calle de Don Jaime 1).

Cafés and Restaurants

If you are just looking for standard platos combinados the terrace cafés on Plaza del Pilar serve reasonable food, though you will pay a little over the odds for the setting.

Los Goyos
Calle San Vicente de Paul, 29. Tel 291373.
Plain restaurant with a good, cheap menú del día.

La Nicolasa
Plaza San Pedro Nolasco.
Stylish, young café-bar: sit out on the pavings or beneath the slowly whirring fans of the Victorian interior for raciones, salads or sandwiches. Excellent atmosphere.

Café Ortega
Calle Prudencio
Clean and basic café for cheap platos combinados.

El Caseron
Calle de Blason Aragones, 4. Tel 23 19 50.
Low, cavernous bar hung with cowbells and bulls horns offering good traditional Aragonese cooking. Hearty atmosphere.

Casa Ordovás
Calle San Lorenzo.
Standard, cheap café-restaurant. Fairly middle-aged in character; a good place if you just want a light meal – raciones and sandwiches.

El fuelle
Calle Mayor, 59. Tel 39 80 33.
A barn-like room hung with pitchforks and harrows; a huge stone oven at one end with chops and sausages sizzling away. Aragonese bodega and restaurant; one of the best places for tasty traditional food.

Tragantua, Calle de Jordan de Urries.
Popular, smart seafood restaurant.

Zaragoza Factfile

Tourist Offices: Calle de Don Jaime 1 (tel 29 75 82). Monday–Saturday 10am–2pm and 4.30pm–8pm, Sunday and holidays 10am–2pm. There is also a small tourist information office at the railway station, and another at the far end of Plaza del Pilar, at the opposite extreme to the statue of Goya.

Train Station Estación del Portillo, Avenida Clavé, s/n. Tel 21 11 66.

Bus Stations: *La Oscencia*, Paseo María Agustín, 84 (for Valencia and

Alicante; *Agreda*, Paseo María Agustín, 7 (for Barcelona, Daroca, Lleida).
Car Hire: *Hertz*, Calle Luis del Valle, 26–28. Tel 35 34 62.
Telephone Code: 976.

WHERE TO DRINK

Zaragoza boasts a lively, down-to-earth nightlife, with a strong emphasis on tapas and drinking. The area known as El Tubo hidden in the warren-like lanes that run between and off Calle de Alfonso 1 and Calle de Don Jaime 1, is one of the city's most popular, a dingy area well worth exploring.

Calle San Jorge: The buildings seem dangerously near-derelict, but this street harbours some raucous bars. Try Café *La Infante* with its tatty, tarnished mirrors, or *Zirod* at Calle San Jorge, 26 for Irish coffees and the chance to choose from over 74 different types of licqueur.

Calle Refugio: *El Monaguillo* and *Bar Bonanza*, a couple of lively young bars.

Calle Contamina: *the* place for infectious Latin rhythms – try *Karma*.

Calle Temple Semi-derelict buildings concealing lively, trendy bars for wild drinking and dancing. Try *La Pianola*, in a state of virtual collapse: probably Spain's scruffiest piano bar. Great atmosphere.

For more restrained drinking try *Espeio* in Calle Santiago, a laidback, young bar with clean and fanciful tapas, or *La Latina*, Calle Estebanes, a chic little café bar full of kitsch 50s cosmetic ads and ephemera. For pleasant terrace seating try the café-bars of Plaza San Felipe and Plaza del Pilar.

CANTABRIA, ASTURIAS AND GALICIA

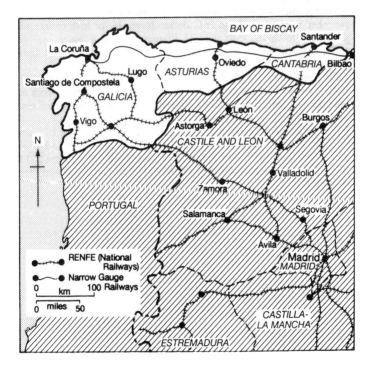

The regions of Galicia, Asturias and Cantabria all enjoy a mild, wet climate, ensuring an exceptionally lush and agriculturally rich landscape. They share, too, a coast of intense beauty. Santander offers the classiest of resorts, as it has done since the late 19th century, and green hills conceal quieter beaches nearby. Beyond here is the heavily indented coast of Asturias and remote Galicia. Fiord-like inlets surge deep inland between craggy heights and pine-covered slopes; granite cliffs rise over broad strips of bright yellow sand, and the whole sea-battered coast becomes more fragmented the farther west you go. Heavy rainfall prevents the whole region from becoming a popular tourist destination, so if you have the time to explore it and can cope with the possibility of rain, it offers some exhilarating scenery.

Lodged way up in the gentle, green Galician hills is Spain's greatest religious shrine. Santiago de Compostela has been drawing visitors to the doors of its magnificent cathedral for the best part of a thousand years. It is one of the country's historic, cultural highlights and reason enough to travel to this far northwest corner of Spain. Dusty-red Romanesque churches dot the valleys on the pilgrims' route to Santiago, which runs through a rural landscape of delightful variety. Traditional, small-scale farming is still a way of life in Galicia: a field of maize, a vine-covered slope and a clutch of fruit trees grouped round crumbling old farm buildings form a typical scene in its sheltered, twisting valleys. Cattle draw solid-wheeled carts bringing freshly cut hay from the fields, and on the edges of villages you will see *bórreos* – small stone barns that stand on stilts, keeping them free from pests and damp, usually protected by a holy cross.

The Asturias and Cantabria countryside is equally captivating: quiet vales shelter apple orchards, source of the *sidra* drunk throughout Asturias, and lush dairy pastures give way to the formidable Picos de Europa inland, a staggering range of snow-capped peaks that afford some of the best climbing and walking to be had in Europe.

SANTANDER

Santander flanks a bay that reaches deep inland; the setting is one of inescapable grandeur. A quayside promenade backed by elegant gardens and rows of stately Victorian apartments looks out over panoramic views of mountains across the water. Huge and lovely, they provide a stunning scenic backdrop.

The town is an assured, confident seaside resort and the commercial and cultural centre of the Cantabria region. The docks generate the life of the busy town centre so that it is more than just a summertime resort. The prettiest parts of the old town lie in the narrow streets that run parallel to the seafront, lacing together little squares, their exotic palms battered by sea breezes. Tall, glass-balconied apartments line the streets, a traditional feature along this coast, and these too are somehow all the more charming for the scant protection they appear to give against blustery Atlantic winds.

As the town peters out towards the open sea, a beautiful headland flicks the coastline just around the mouth of the bay, offering fresh walks with expansive views of seascapes, beaches, bays and mountains. Beyond this, on the Atlantic coast, is the resort and suburb of **El Sardinero**. It is Santander at its most polished and urbane, with stately villas set in well-tended, sprinkler-green gardens. Best of all, it has some of the finest sandy beaches in northern Spain.

Santander is just the place if you want a traditional resort holiday. Here you can relax and enjoy swimming, sunbathing and long walks around the coast. It makes an excellent touring centre, with endless possibilities for day trips: drive to the mountains nearby, explore some of the many sandy coves hidden along this lush and indented green coast, or simply take the ferry across the bay to yet more popular sandy beaches.

The local cuisine is excellent, largely because of the rich and plentiful farming and fishing that is such a part of the region's identity. The old town has bars, bodegas and restaurants to suit all pockets and satisfy most tastes (the big exception being the problems for vegetarians). If you like seafood, you will find no better place to eat it than in the **Barrio Pesquero**, tucked between the town and the docks.

As a seaside resort, the overall flavour is a rather reserved and conservative one, but the bustle of the modern town ensures there is entertainment beyond the clatter of roulette wheels in El Sardinero's ritzy casino. Popular squares, bars and discos full of young people offer a busy nightlife, especially during the summer season.

History

The very earliest known history of Santander is as the Roman town of Portus Victoriae, but it is only from the 11th century that the picture becomes clearer. At this time Santander grew under the protection of the abbey of San Emeterio and the castle of San Felipe, and probably had fewer than 2,000 inhabitants. It was an important trading port from the Middle Ages onwards, and eventually came to develop its greatest business with America towards the end of the 19th century. From this period of growth and prosperity, today's Santander takes its character. Even though much of the town was destroyed by fire in 1941, the typical glass-fronted balconies that line the narrow streets date from the end of the last century, as do the grand hotels. Around the same time Alfonso XIII built his royal palace on the Magdelena peninsula, with its stunning views across the bay, and with this Santander's future as a fashionable resort was assured. The development of the elegant El Sardinero suburb soon followed and became a showpiece playground for the rich and aristocratic, offering gambling, dancing, polo, golf and tennis.

GETTING YOUR BEARINGS

Santander is a big town that seems to be rolled out like a length of cloth along the coast, from its docks deep inland to El Sardinero farthest out. On the way it unfurls through a hectic commercial centre, through old streets that run parallel with the waterfront, and around the headland where the bay on which it is built meets the open sea. Two fine, sandy beaches make it a popular resort: Playa de la Magdalena is the nearest to town, sheltered by the wooded headland; the beach at El Sardinero facing out into the Atlantic is equally popular.

Getting your bearings is easy enough, but because of the spun-out nature of the place, the kind of aimless wanderings that can be so relaxing in many seaside towns can become a source of irritation here. It makes sense to have a fair idea of what you want to do with your day before you leave your hotel; remember not to underestimate the distances between the beaches and the town centre. A bus runs through this long thin town from Avenida de Calvo Sotelo through to El Sardinero, well worth getting to know. It is easy to use since you are always aware of where you are, with the sea generally in sight.

If you arrive by bus or train, you will find yourself at the west end of the town in the busiest quarter. The stations face one another either side of Plaza Estaciónes. From here walk down Calle de Cádiz until you face a small park. Turn left up Calle Alfonso XIII and straight ahead is the Plaza Porticada, where you will find the tourist office; call in and pick up a map. The most interesting part of town spreads east from here, following the lengthy quays.

Avenida Calvo Sotelo is the town's main thoroughfare, slicing past Plaza Porticado and soon becoming the Paseo de Pereda, which runs along the seafront. The main streets of the old town are parallel with this quayside avenue, and link a series of pleasant squares: Plaza José Antonio, with palms and café-bars, and Plaza Cañadío, a key focus for Santander's young night scene.

DON'T MISS . . .

The Bay and the Ferry

Even if you do nothing else remotely energetic, *do* walk along the quays. Views across the choppy waters of the broad bay are superb: slate-blue and iron-grey mountains, snow-covered until Easter, form a magnificent range of peaks; green woodlands tumble down to the sea to meet a fine fringe of beaches along the shore. This perfect picture-postcard scene is especially good in the evening when huge, burnished-pink clouds scud across the sky sending changing ragged patterns of light across the distant slopes.

A ferry plies around the bay during the summer months, calling at La Magdalena, El Sardinero, and then to the beach of Somo, directly across the water from Santander. Somo has a popular sandy beach and makes an excellent afternoon's excursion; you might even try windsurfing here. From early July to September, ferries leave the Embarcadero on the seafront every 15 minutes between 10.30 and 20.30. Tel 21 67 53 and 21 66 19.

The Old Town

Explore Santander's prettiest old streets, which run immediately behind the Paseo de Pereda. The severe, dignified colonnading of the Plaza Porticada hosts open-air ballet and classical-music concerts during the summer. A short walk up from here, Calle Arrabal has some of Santander's best craft and souvenir shops, where you can by all manner of traditional Spanish and ethnic ceramics, rugs, jewellery, masks and satirical puppets. Plaza Cañadío and Plaza José Antonio nearby are both delightful spots to sit out in the sunshine at a café table and watch the passing scene. Behind the grandeur of the 19th-century seafront, the little lanes east of here all have the character of an older, friendlier seaside town, with little *tapas* bars, bodegas and restaurants.

El Sardinero

El Sardinero offers the perfect opportunity for swimming, sunbathing and walks around the nearby headlands. It really is a fabulous beach of golden sand and crashing waves, and if you follow the coast west there are more secluded, equally special beaches to discover. The suburb itself is one of broad avenues and grand summer residences set in carefully nurtured green gardens. At its centre is the plush old Gran Casino setting the overall tone; a place for the holidaying rich with money to burn.

ALSO WORTH SEEING . . .

Museo de Prehistoria

> (*Calle de Juan de la Costa, 1. Open Tuesday–Saturday 9.00–13.00 and 16.00–19.00, Sunday 11.00–14.00.*)

This small museum has a sizeable display of Roman finds, including stele, amphorae and oil lamps. Along with these there are samples of medieval Spanish jewellery and finds from prehistoric caves in the region.

OUT OF TOWN . . .

Castro Urdiales

Castro Urdiales, 70 km east of Santander and 35 km west of Bilbao, is a quiet little resort wrapped snugly around a traditional fishing village. There is a sizeable fleet here, the

colourful vessels filling the old stone harbour and ensuring a daily supply of fresh fish for the local restaurants. The promontory overlooking the town is dominated by the Church of the Assumption, with red-tiled roofs and flying buttresses, one of the best pieces of Gothic architecture in Cantabria. A walk around it offers exhilarating views of the jagged hills and sudden bays that characterize this coast.

The town is a popular seafood centre: sit out at one of the bars of the colonnaded Plaza del Ayuntamiento or eat at a restaurant in Calle Ardigales. There is a beach here, too – tucked neatly on the east side of town, a short strip of golden sand.

Comillas

Comillas is a small resort town, 50 km west of Santander, worth taking in for its unusual architecture. Like so many spots along this coast, it has a couple of very good beaches, too. The town itself is set back from the sea, a strange collection of avant-garde and modern buildings: the cemetery in the former 16th-century parish church has some interesting Modernist mausoleums, there is a huge Neo-Gothic university, and most enjoyable of all is El Capricho, a gaudy Gaudí fantasy piece that looks like something straight out of Disney World.

Santillana del Mar

Couched in a rolling, rural green setting 30 km from Santander, Santillana del Mar is the real historic highlight of Cantabria, and one of Spain's best preserved ancient towns. It dates from the 9th century when there was a monastery of St Juliana here – hence the name Santillana. Wander through cobbled lanes and quiet squares to take in its rich fusion of styles. The palace of the Velardes is the best of the Renaissance mansions here, lodged in the Plaza de las Arenas. From here a lane cuts through the town lined with ancient buildings. Around the nearby Plaza Ramón Pelayo (Plaza Mayor) the Gothic fortified houses of El Merino and Los Borja vie with the Baroque Barreda Palace for attention. The Barreda Palace is now a national *parador* hotel. On the edge of town are the 17th-century convents of Regina Coeli (now the diocesan museum) and San Ildefonso.

San Vicente de la Barquera

A coastal town that offers a smattering of history in a stunning setting, San Vicente de la Barquera is famed for its seafood and its festival of *la Folía*. It may have been a Roman settlement; what is certain is the importance it gained between the 13th and 15th centuries. The church of Santa María de los Angeles dates from the 13th century and contains some interesting tombs and a 17th-century altarpiece; dotted around the town are the late-Renaissance house of the Inquisitor Antonio del Corro, the tumbling ruins of a 16th-century convent and the Hermitage of the Virgin de la Barquera. *La Folía* is celebrated here on 22 January: a statue of the town's patron saint is carried from the hermitage, first to the parish church and then to an altar by the harbour. Singing and dancing ensue, and eventually the image is taken on board a boat and returned to its shrine by sea.

If you stay in the town it is worth trying out the delicious local dish known as *sorropotúri* – a fish stew of tuna, potatoes, onions, tomatoes, peppers, bread, olive oil and salt.

SANTANDER FACTFILE

Tourist Office, Plaza Porticada. Tel: 31 07 08. Open all year Monday–Friday 9.00–13.30 and 16.00–19.00; Saturday 9.00–13.30. Also on the seafront at Jardines de Pereda. Tel: 21 61 20.
Airport Parayas Airport, Santander–Bilbao road, Tel: 25 10 04. Daily flights to Barcelona, Madrid, Pamplona (via Barcelona). Information Aviaco, Tel: 25 10 07 and 25 10 09. *Iberia*, Tel: 22 97 00.
Train Stations *RENFE*, Plaza Estaciónes, Tel: 21 02 88. *FEVE*, Plaza Estaciónes. Tel: 21 16 87.
Bus Stations, Plaza Estaciónes. Information Tel: 21 19 95. Different bus companies serve different regions, but most of them depart from the main bus station. The following numbers are for specific carriers:
   Turytrans, Tel: 22 16 85, serve Gijón, Irún, Oviedo, Pamplona, Ribadesella, San Sebastián and Vitoria.
   Fernandez, Tel: 22 10 41, serve León, Asturias, Galicia and Astorga.
   C. Auto, Tel: 22 53 18, operate services to Burgos and Madrid.
   Alsa, Tel: 22 10 41, operate international services; destinations include Brussels, Paris and London.
Ferries, Estación de Ferrys, Tel: 21 45 00 and 22 00 00. Ferries for Plymouth, England. May–September: depart Tuesdays and Thursdays. Rest of the year: depart Mondays and Wednesdays.
Car Hire Atesa, Avenida Alfonso XIII. Tel: 22 29 58. Avis, Nicolás Salmerón, 3. Tel: 22 70 25. Ital, San Luis, 8. Tel: 23 84 85.
Taxis ranks: Paseo de Pereda, 13. Tel: 21 24 63. Plaza de Estaciónes. Tel: 22 20 46. Paseo Canalejas, 97. Tel: 27 30 75 (nearest to El Sardinero). Radio Taxi. Tel: 33 33 33.
Post Office Alfonso XIII. Tel: 21 26 02.
Telephone code: 942. *Locutorio*, with booths and seperate cash desk, at Hernán Cortés, 37. Tel info 003.

WHERE TO STAY

If you envisage late nights spent drinking and dancing in the main part of town, then it makes sense to base yourself there, even though this is some distance from the beaches; it is far easier to travel by bus or walk to the beach during the day than it is to cover the same distance at night. If access to the beach is your key priority, one of the quieter hotels at El Sardinero might be more suitable.

Santander town centre

CHEAP TO MODERATE
Arenal HsR**, Calle Emilio Pino, 7. Tel: 22 24 50.
Cándido HS**, Calle Emilio Pino, 4. Tel: 22 91 63.
México HR**, Calderón de la Barca, 3. Tel: 21 24 50.

The Picos de Europa

Stretching from the far west of Cantabria into Asturias are the superb Picos de Europa — a range of jagged, rugged peaks of awesome beauty, equal to any in Europe. Largely snow-covered right into early summer, the Picos offer excellent opportunities for walking and climbing; concealed in intensely pretty valleys are ancient monastic houses and Romanesque churches. All in all, if you enjoy the great outdoors, there is enough in the Picos alone to more than fill an entire holiday.

The chief tourist centre is Potes, capital of Liebana, where the Tower of the Infantado, part of a 15th-century palace, dominates the old town. A few kilometres from Potes the monastery of Saint Toriba of Liebana commands a breath-taking location. Well restored, the 8th-century Romanesque monastery became an important religious centre when an alleged fragment of the True Cross was brought here from Jerusalem. The Lignum Crucis, as it is called, is now kept in the monastery's Baroque chapel.

A huge range of scenic walks tempt you into the mountains, but for *the* exciting view of the Picos, head for Fuente Dé, where you can take a cable car to outstanding panoramas. For walkers Peña Vieja and El Pico Tesorero are the range's two most easily accessible peaks, both exhilarating and rewarding climbs.

Alisas HR**, Nicolás Salmerón, 3. Tel: 22 27 50.

SMARTER OPTIONS
Bahía HR****, Alfonso XIII, 6. Tel: 22 17 00.

El Sardinero
CHEAP TO MODERATE
Carlos III HsR**, Avenida Reina Victoria, 135. Tel: 27 16 16.
Colóo HR*, Plaza de las Brisas, 1. Tel: 27 23 00.
Castilla HR*, Avenida Joaquín Costa, 43. Tel: 27 22 00.
Las Brisas HR*, Trav. de los Castros, 14 Bis Chalet. Tel: 27 09 91.

SMARTER OPTIONS
Sardinero HR***, Plaza de Italia, 1. Tel: 27 11 00.

Roma H***, Avenida de los Hoteles, 5. Tel: 27 27 00.

WHERE TO EAT

The best area for restaurants is the streets of Daoiz y Velarde, Calle Peña Herbosa and Calle Hernán Cortés, all of which run parallel with Paseo de Pereda; the pretty, narrow lane of Calle Río de la Pila; and for seafood, the Barrio Pescadores, found some way west of the town, down beside the docks. The huge variety of seafood on offer usually includes angler fish, barnacles, crab, lobster and *rabas* – squid fried in batter – and is prepared fresh from the day's catch.

La Casona, Calle Cuesta, 6. Lively, popular, good-quality seafood restaurant.

Los Arcos, Calle de Medio. Sit out on the terrace under the colonnades to enjoy your meal; one of the nicest places to eat out in the centre of the city.

Jauia, Calle de Medio. Clean, plain and simple, this is a cheap, traditional restaurant tucked in a quiet haven in the noisy town centre. Extensive seafood menu.

Los Caracoles, Calle de Medio. Good-value, plain traditional restaurant.

Cañadío, Plaza Cañadío. Convivial, popular bar with a good range of *raciones*.

Bodega Cigaleña, Calle Daioz y Velarde. Heavy on atmosphere, with wine-lined walls, *jamón*-filled ceilings and all sorts of medieval trappings. A highly enjoyable, fairly expensive restaurant.

La Casa de la Cerveza, Daioz y Velarde. Popular with a young crowd, a lively bar for serious drinking downstairs and cheap, tasty *platos combinados* upstairs.

Mesón Goya, Daioz y Velarde. Cosy, traditional seafood restaurant. Good atmosphere.

Bar Marisquieria, Calle Peña Herbosa. Basic *marisquiería* serving an astounding array of seafood.

Bodegan Mazon, Calle Hernán Cortés, 57. Wonderful old bodega full of huge, well-seasoned barrels. Serves wines, sherries and *tapas*.

Cruz Blanca, Calle Lope de Vega. Cavernous, medieval-style beer-cellar, curiously Anglo-Saxon in feel. Loud, lively and popular with a young crowd. Serves irresistable *tapas*.

La Mayor, Calle Juan de la Cosa. Down-to-earth bar and restaurant; though it lacks instant atmosphere, this is more than made up for by the superb range of seafood on offer. Moderately priced.

BARS AND NIGHTLIFE

As elsewhere in Spain, café-bars are open throughout the day, and many of those listed here offer a lighter midday alternative to a restaurant meal:

Along the seafront

There are plenty of cafés where you can sit out during the daytime and early evening and enjoy a view of the mountains across the bay. Try **Café Zorba**, **Café Pareda** and **Erypsia** at Nos. 17, 18 and 19 Paseo de Pareda. **Café Suiz** at Paseo de Pereda 28 offers elaborate ice creams and crêpes.

Plaza Cañadío

This square is a favourite evening haunt for a young crowd; it is surrounded by lively bars and a couple of restaurants.

La Columna, Plaza Cañadío. Tiny, traditional bar jam-packed with people; plays loud rock music.

Café de Pombo, Calle Hernán Cortés (backs on to Plaza Cañadío). Stylish café-bar with Chinese rugs, potted palms and very pleasant terrace seating; one of the classier places to drink in Santander.

Around Town

Bar Solarzano, Calle Daioz y Velarde. Excellent, down-to-earth local watering hole, always busy with the clatter of conviviality.

La Pimla, Calle Peña Herbosa. Cavernous drinking den full of abstract paintings and intellectual pretensions. A gregarious crowd.

Sibonet, Castelar, 7 (a little alleyway off the seafront). A cocktail bar that manages to be both stylish and down to earth. They play good Latin and jazz, swing and salsa sounds. If you don't want to drink alcohol, their freshly squeezed fruit juice is particularly good, though a little pricey. Young and maturing crowd. Slick.

La Luna, Calle Gran Mola. Grey-black stone, white walls and abstract paintings, all under disorienting neon of violent violet. Loud and lively popular bar that keeps going till 2.00 or 3.00.

OVIEDO

Oviedo takes a unique place in Spanish history as capital of the ancient, tiny kingdom of Asturias, the only area in the whole country to remain Christian during the Moorish conquest. The Moorish campaigns from north Africa began around 711 and their progress was swift, but in 718 the Visigoth king Pelayo defeated a Muslim army at the battle of Covadonga, around 80 km from Oviedo in the mountains of Asturias. Pivotal in Spanish history, this small victory signalled the beginning of the Reconquest. Pelayo was succeeded by Alfonso II, who transferred the Asturian capital to Oviedo. Three architectural

monuments remain from this period in Oviedo, remarkable in
their distinct pre-Romanesque style.

GETTING YOUR, BEARINGS

Oviedo is a congested, industrial city, but it does hold surprises
beyond its three famous churches. At the centre of town is the
Parque de San Francisco, a big, green, open space alongside the
remnants of the old city. The best place to get your bearings
is at Plaza Alfonso II, where you will find the cathedral and
the tourist office. Calle Santa Ana and La Rua Cimadevilla,
which run away from here, head into Oviedo's charming old
quarter. Wander through to the tangled skein of streets that
fall behind the cathedral. The area is best experienced on
Saturday morning when it comes to life with a series of highly
entertaining markets.

Plaza Daoiz y Velarde and Arco de los Zapatos form the
centre of activity. Stalls emerge from beneath rough-hewn
porticoes as if they have done so for hundreds of years:
knife-grinders, light-metal workers and *zapateros* – the shoe
repairers – all still do business. The dusty old square becomes
a riot of colour as great tubs of flowers are dragged across
the flags, sacks of beans are weighed in ancient scales and
everywhere are mounds of the lushest vegetables you will see
anywhere in Spain, the product of Asturias's high rainfall and
a reminder of why food in the simplest of restaurants here is
so good. Follow the lanes between overhanging, clinker-built
houses and precarious tall, glass-balconied windows through
to the covered cast-iron meat market. Tucked behind the
heavily ornamented *ayuntamiento* nearby is the little square
of Tras Corrales, yet more charming houses and at its centre
the old stone fish market.

DON'T MISS . . .

Santa Cámara

(Accessible via the Gothic cathedral. Open Monday–Sat-
urday 10.00–13.00 and 16.00–18.00).
Severely damaged during the Civil War, the Santa Cámara
has been greatly restored. The 8th-century inner chapel was
built by Alfonso II; the rest of the structure is Romanesque,

including some exceptionally expressive 12th-century carved figures.

The **cathedral** itself is a small and fairly unremarkable Gothic structure, built between the 14th and the 16th century, but its treasures includes the cross which Pelayo carried into battle at Covadonga, covered in gems and precious metals which were added later in commemoration of the Christian victory.

Santa María del Naranco and San Miguel de Lillo

(3 km northwest of town off Avenida de los Monumentos, behind the train station. Open May–mid-October 10.00–13.00 and 15.00–19.00; till 17.00 in winter.)

Santa María del Naranco originally formed part of the palace of Ramiro I, successor to Alfonso II. It is a building of refined elegance with balconies along the upper storey looking out over fine views of Oviedo, suggesting far more leisurely pursuits than prayer. Nearby, the church of San Lillo was Ramiro I's chapel. It is a small but monumental building, exquisitely carved inside. Both date from the mid-9th century.

Museo Bellas Artes

(Calle Santa Ana, 1. Tel: 21 30 61. Entrance free. Open Tuesday–Saturday 11.00–13.30 and 16.00–19.00, Sunday 12.00–14.00.)

Small, interesting collection of 19th- and 20th-century paintings, largely scenes of rural life and sentimental portraits. Even if you are not thrilled with the genres, the gallery itself is worthy of interest – a tastefully restored Renaissance mansion with a central atrium overlooked by balconies at all levels and massive oak-beamed ceilings.

Archaeological Museum

(Housed in the former monastery of San Vicente, behind the cathedral. Open Monday–Saturday 10.00–13.30 and 16.30–18.30, Sunday 11.00–13.00.)

This museum displays reproductions of the Asturian-Visigoth architectural decoration unique to the area, including altars, reliefs and columns similar to those at Santa María del Naranco and San Lillo, along with smaller original finds.

Sidra – Cider

A visit to a local *sideria* is a must. The cider produced here from Asturian orchards is a light drink, not too alcoholic. In Oviedo they pour it from a great height, often straight on to the stone floor of the bar, and watch it closely for impurities before settling down to the business of drinking. It is part of a great, popular tradition, and you will have no difficulty in finding somewhere to try some. Traditional *siderias* around the old town include:

El Mesón del Labrador, Calle Jovellanos, 3.

La Gran Taberna, Calle Eusebio González Abascal, off Plaza Alfonso II.

El Betiro, Calle Peso, beside the Ayuntamiento.

Sideria Manolo, Calle Altamirano. Probably the only cider house in Spain with that ultimate game-shooter's trophy – a stuffed giraffe's head with at least 2 metres of neck!

OVIEDO FACTFILE

Tourist Office, Plaza Alfonso II (Plaza de la Catedral). Tel:21 33 85. Open Monday–Friday 9.00–14.00 and 16.00–18.00 and Saturday 10.00–14.00.
Bus Information Plaza Primo de Rivera, 1. Tel: 28 12 00.
Trains *RENFE* for trains to Barcelona, Madrid, Gijon. Tel: 24 33 64.
FEVE narrow-gauge trains for Gijón and Avilés. Tel: 28 01 50.
Car Hire Atesa, Ventura Rodríguez, 8. Tel: 25 94 11.
Europcar, Independencia, 24. Tel: 24 43 57.
Taxi Radio Taxi Tel: 25 00 00
Tele Taxi 25 25 00.
Telephone code: 985.

SANTIAGO DE COMPOSTELA

Santiago Cathedral towers above a huge square, an exuberant mass of golden stone, the climax to any journey to the city. It holds the shrine of St James, Spain's most important place of pilgrimage. For over 1,000 years millions of pilgrims have travelled to this site, and even today a real sense of celebration rings through the city's streets. Whether you are Christian or not, there is a palpable feeling that you have arrived somewhere very special.

This sense of elation has always been here, for as well as being one of the greatest shrines Christian Europe has ever known, for centuries the location itself held a magical significance: the region was once known as *Finis terrae*, literally considered to be the very end of the known world. The story of the shrine of Saint James secured that magic and the legend is a crucial part of enjoying Santiago to the full. It makes a lot of sense to explore the cathedral through the eyes of the pilgrims, tracing their footsteps.

The cathedral and its story are reason enough to come here, but there is more. Santiago is one of *the* great tourist cities in Spain and stores a lavish history in its museums, monasteries, churches and university. While the story of the pilgrims is largely medieval, the character of Santiago is 18th-century Baroque, one of the most perfectly preserved historic towns in the country. The walls and pavings of the narrow streets are all of hard, yellow granite and cut through the town like cold canyons; occasional tiny squares trap scorching sunlight. The whole city is remarkably evocative and merits lengthy exploration. As if all this were not enough, an abundance of Galician restaurants, hosts of café-bars and a lively, albeit small, night scene all combine to make Santiago a difficult place to leave.

The story of the pilgrims of Santiago is one of the most astounding testimonies of the power of Christian faith in Europe. Its history reveals layer upon layer of stories: how the relics came to be here; the pilgrims and the commerce and customs they brought with them; the personal adventures they had along the way, and the part the church played in "encouraging" the legend at times of political weakness.

St James

The story goes that St James came to Spain to try and convert the peninsula to Christianity. He failed and returned in AD 44 to Palestine, where he was beheaded by Herod Agrippa. Various stories tell how his relics came to be in Galicia: one version claims they were brought here by two of his disciples; another that his remains were intitially buried in an Egyptian temple, and then brought here by Coptic monks on their way to Ireland. However they came to be here – if you believe they are here at all – they were discovered in 813 by a priest, and a shrine was soon established. The cult caught on and Santiago grew as a place of spiritual pilgrimage.

Christianity and Islam

During the 9th century Christianity in Spain was under threat from Islamic forces. The church adapted the cult of St James in the hope of strengthening people's fervour against the Moors, inventing a new role for the saint; he became *Santiago Matamores* – St James the Moorslayer. The story this time was that in 844 he appeared at a battle against the Moors and led the Christians to victory. He can be seen in this form in carvings and paintings on many religious buildings in Spain: a bishop on horseback wielding a sword. As expected, the popularity of the cult grew.

At the end of the 10th century Islamic forces attacked and destroyed Santiago and its cathedral, though they left the shrine itself well alone, fearing its magic. Once peace was restored, pilgrims flocked back in even greater numbers; Santiago became a Christian rallying cry to combat the forces of Islam, and there was yet another surge in the number of pilgrims visiting the shrine after the defeat of the Moorish kingdom of Granada in 1492.

The Pilgrims

Most of the early pilgrims were from France and the route became known as the *Camino Frances* (French Way). It became an important commercial and social thoroughfare: pilgrims brought with them their customs and ideas. Architectural styles were also transported along these roads and can be seen at their most splendid in the cathedrals of Burgos and León. Pilgrims would carry scallop shells with them, the symbol of St James; in the Middle Ages artisans began to carve them from jet and these became popular charms. You can still buy them as souvenirs today. The scallop-shell motif can also be seen in the decoration of buildings along "El Camino Santiago" all across northern Spain.

By the 18th century, the shrine was attracting pilgrims from as far away as Holland, Germany and even Scandinavia. The roads were difficult and dangerous and pilgrims travelled in groups of about 30 for safety against robbers and wild animals. Travelling on foot or on horseback, they would be away from home for at least four months, some would be away for years, and some would never return.

The pilgrims came in search of spiritual renewal: at Santiago they would be awarded a *compostella*, which was not just a certificate of their achievement, but also a plenary indulgence – a kind of voucher that would lessen their time in purgatory after death. Approach the cathedral with all this in mind for a full idea of the drama of the pilgrims' experience and to read the carvings and ritual of the building.

GETTING YOUR BEARINGS

Santiago de Compostela is a remarkably compact city and most of the streets of the old town are paved, excluding traffic. If you arrive by car it makes sense to leave it at one of the car parks on the edge of town rather than battle your way for one of the few spaces in the centre. It also allows for a suitably dramatic approach to the city. Santiago is actually very small, so finding everywhere of interest on foot presents few problems.

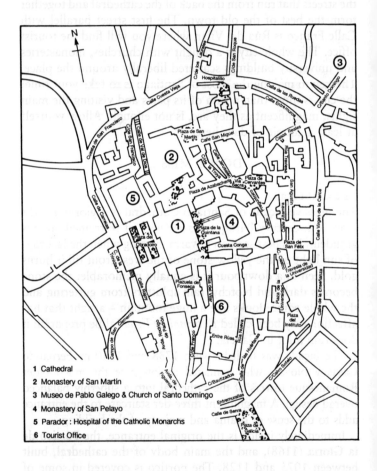

1 Cathedral
2 Monastery of San Martin
3 Museo de Pablo Galego & Church of Santo Domingo
4 Monastery of San Pelayo
5 Parador : Hospital of the Catholic Monarchs
6 Tourist Office

Since the cathedral dominates the town you will have no problem finding it. It is huge and has several fabulous façades, but the one to head for is the magnificent westerly entrance that looks out over the Plaza de Obradoiro, a vast square flanked on all sides by ancient buildings. Head straight here, like all pilgrims, and soak up its glory.

If you stand facing the cathedral front, the lane leading off to your right is Calle Franco. The old town climbs a gentle hill in paved granite lanes parallel to this. These lanes meet the streets that run from the back of the cathedral and together form the best of the old town. The first street parallel with Calle Franco is Rúa del Vilar, where you will find the tourist office. The whole city is a delight with churches, monasteries and university buildings scattered liberally around the place. The key to making the most of Santiago is to take your time: the city is more than a sum of its parts and visiting the main sights, magnificent as they are, is not enough. Allow yourself at least a couple of days here.

DON'T MISS . . .

The Cathedral

The massive **façade** of Santiago Cathedral is a glorious sight – an 18th-century Baroque masterpiece of restrained, joyous grandeur. It is best seen on a warm evening when the last rays of sun light up the yellow stone of the west front till it burns gold. Seen in a downpour it is equally memorable: the stone becomes dark and blotchy, rain splutters from guttering and the whole edifice looks like a huge fountain – a sight that has affectionately been called *El orinal de España*! Be prepared: it does rain a lot in Galicia.

The façade was built between 1738 and 1750 by Fernando Casas y Nóvaa, who managed to integrate the much older Romanesque towers of the cathedral into a superbly balanced overall design. A magnificent three-tier staircase to the entrance adds to the sense of drama and majesty of the building.

Immediately inside is the original entrance, the **Pórtico de la Gloria** (1168), and the main body of the cathedral, built between 1075 and 1128. The portico is covered in some of the most exceptional Romanesque carving in Europe, the work of Master Mateo. The sculptures held a very clear message for the medieval pilgrims, showing heaven and hell in vivid detail. There can be no doubt about the horrible fate that awaits sinners: demons sink their teeth into some, while others are thrown into bubbling cauldrons. After their exhausting, dangerous journeys, it is not hard to imagine the pilgrims' heightened awareness of sin and mortality at seeing these images.

But for Christians there is a way out: Christ will redeem them. At the centre of the portal is a solid figure of Christ in his glory. By praying to the saints it is possible to gain spiritual purity and ultimately have a life with Christ, and of course St James himself can intercede on the pilgrims' behalf; not surprisingly he takes a central place in the design, on the column immediately below Christ. The faces of surrounding apostles and angels are animated, as if they are still having a chat, and originally would have been painted to look even more realistic. Notice, too, the carvings around the top of the arches showing the 24 Elders of the Apocalypse, all carrying wonderfully detailed medieval musical instruments.

At the Pórtico de la Gloria pilgrims would put their hands on the feet of the statue of St James in thanksgiving for their safe arrival: you can see that millions have done so by the worn marks of the stone. The figure at the foot of one of the columns looking towards the altar is that of Mateo himself, and there is yet another custom whereby people knock their heads against his in order to take on some of his talent. Pilgrims would then enter the cathedral.

An excessively flamboyant altarpiece fills the end of the solemn, lofty nave, more like an elaborate fairground ride than a holy shrine. Huge, swirling, candy-twist columns decked with bulbous grapes and foliage are all carved from wood and painted in vigorous gold. In the centre is the shrine, beneath a canopy supported by colossal carved angels.

The pilgrims would walk towards it, round to the steps at the left-hand side and down to a crypt under the altar. Here the relics of St James are kept in a silver coffer. Having knelt and prayed, they would climb the steps on the right-hand side up into the very heart of the altar. It is an amazing experience: you find yourself actually inside the altar beneath a gold fluted dome right behind a statue of St James. Here pilgrims would kiss his richly embellished, gem-studded robe. From up here you also get a saint's eye view of the congregation. Having completed this ritual, the pilgrims would have been presented with their *compostellana*. This is a routine no visitor to Santiago should miss.

Tesoro y Museos – treasury, cloister, archaeological museum and crypt
200 pesetas.
(Entrance Open Monday–Saturday 10.30–13.30 and 16.00 –18.30, Sunday 10.30–13.30.)
The cathedral museum includes cabinets of elaborate church silverware, crucifixes, reliquaries, archbishop's capes of embroidered gold brocade, statuary and wood carving. The library has a wealth of ancient manuscripts depicting St James on horseback and here you can also see the "Botumfumera" – a massive incense holder that is swung by the cranelike contraption in front of the high altar. To see it in action you need to be here on feast days. Reckless though it looks, you can comfort yourself with the knowledge that it has only ever swung off its chain twice, and no one was hurt. There is a large collection of 18th-century tapestries here showing rural Spanish life in scenes of bullfighting, picnics and the *paseo*, and beyond the rooms where they hang you

can gain access to balconies overlooking the vast Plaza del Obradoiro.

Around the Cathedral

The cathedral's many façades are all worth exploring. Stand in the **Plaza del Obradoiro** with your back to the cathedral: to your left is the College of San Jerónimo, a solid 16th-century building with a 15th-century portal which was brought here from a pilgrims' hospital. Directly opposite the cathedral is the Neo-Classical façade of the Rajoy Palace, built in the 18th century as a confessor's seminary; notice the carved figure of St James the Moorslayer. The Hospital of the Catholic Monarchs completes the fourth side of the square, a splendid building founded by Ferdinand and Isabella in 1492 to provide accommodation for invalids and pilgrims. Decorated with royal coats of arms, the plateresque doorway is typical of the period; balconies and windows show subsequent Renaissance and Baroque additions. The hospital is now a national *parador* hotel.

Artisans would sell carved charms in the **Plaza de la Aza-bachería (also known as Plaza Immaculada)** in front of the doors of the cathedral; *azabacheros* means "jet craftsmen". This was once a main entrance and pilgrims would cleanse themselves in a fountain here before going into the cathedral. The façade that stands today was completed in 1738 by Casas y Nóvaa and is wholly in keeping with the Obradoiro façade. Directly opposite is the monastery of San Martín Pinario (see below).

Wander round the back of the cathedral and head back down into **Plaza de la Quintana.** This broad square, divided by a flight of steps, offers yet more excellent views of the cathedral towers.

In **Plaza de Platerías** you can admire the very oldest entrance to the cathedral, fabulously decorated with Romanesque carvings.

Monastery of San Martín Pinario

The severe 18th-century façade that looks out over the Plaza de la Azabachería conceals a huge, older monastic complex. Inside the church here is an outrageously ornate high altar by Casas y Nóvaa, incorporating the equestrian figures of

St Millán and St James crushing the Moors. Take a look too at the 17th- and 18th-century cloisters and the curious old pharmacy.

ALSO WORTH SEEING . . .

Museo de Pablo Galego
(Open Monday–Saturday 10.00–13.00 and 16.00–19.00; free.)
This very enjoyable museum of Galician folk culture includes particularly good displays on costume, farming methods and musical instruments. Throughout the museum the emphasis is on demonstrating *how* things were made: the section on sea fishing and boat-building is fascinating, and don't miss either the highly unusual triple-spiral staircase that leads up to the second floor.

Casa de Parra
(Plaza de la Quintana, Free. Open Monday–Saturday 12–14.00 and 18.30–21.00.)
It is easy to forget we're in the 20th century after a day or so in Santiago. The Casa de Parra gallery offers the perfect antedote if you have OD'd on history; it is a stylish and accessible gallery showing changing exhibitions of modern art.

OUT OF TOWN . . .

Lugo
Lugo is most famous for its remarkable Roman city walls. This is hardly surprising: they are 10–15 metres high, have no fewer than 85 towers and stretch over 2 kilometres in their circuit. These exceptional defences have stood here for over 1,700 years; they date from the 2nd century AD. To appreciate just how massive they are, climb on to them via the deceptively low slope at Plaza Pio XII behind the cathedral and once you are on them turn right and keep walking.

Because the encircling walls are so complete, the town centre has an ancient feel, though the complex of streets inside is young by comparison – only medieval and 18th century! The cathedral is a stately yet sombre mixture of Romanesque, Gothic and 18th-century Neo-Classical styles. The cloister and Baroque chapel were designed by the architect of the cathedral at Santiago, Casas y Nóvaa. The **Provincial Museum** is housed in the Iglesia de San Francisco. Largely devoted to archaeological finds, it also shows modern art exhibitions. (Open Monday–Saturday 10.30–14.00 and 16.30–20.30; Sunday 11.00–14.00.)

Aside from its walls, this sedate town is nothing out of the ordinary, but it has got two extremely pleasant central adjoining squares. One has magnificent, headily scented magnolia trees; the other, Plaza España, has a central bandstand that comes alive with local musicians at summer weekends. Sit out at a table on the square with a coffee; it is all very civilized.

SANTIAGO DE COMPOSTELA FACTFILE

Tourist Office, Rúa del Vilar, 43. Tel: 58 40 81. Open Monday–Friday 9.00–14.00 and 16.00–19.00; Saturday 9.00–13.00.
Airport Labacolla Airport. Tel: 59 74 00. 12 km from Santiago de Compostela on the N544.
Train Station RENFE, Calle del Hórreo. Tel: 59 60 50.
Bus Station, off Plaza de los 25 Anos de Paz. Tel: 58 77 00. A No. 10 bus from Plaza de Galicia will take you to the bus station about 1 km out of town.
Car Hire Hertz de España, Avenida Lugo, 145. Tel: 58 34 66.
Car Parks, For those arriving from Lugo or La Coruña, the best to use is Aparcamiento Juan XXIII. If you arrive from Vigo, use the one in Plaza de Galicia.
Taxi Estación Autobus. Tel: 56 10 28.
Telephone Code: 981.

WHERE TO STAY
Cheap to Moderate

Hostal Moure, Calle de los Laureles, 6. Tel: 58 36 37.
Hospadie Mera, Calle de la Fuente de San Miguel, 15.
Barbantes HsR, Calle Franco, 3. Tel: 581077.
Mapoula Hsr**, Entremurallas, 10. Tel: 58 01 24.
Iacobus HsR**, Entremurallas, 10–1. Tel: 58 40 89.
Suso HsR**, Rúa del Vilar, 65. Tel: 58 66 11.
El Rapido, Calle Franco, 22.
Cantabrico HS**, Calle Franco, 13. Tel: 58 57 11.
Mafer HsR*, Calle Franco, 22. Tel: 56 57 12.

Smarter Options

Hogar San Francisco HS***, Campillo de San Francisco, 3. Tel:
58 11 43.
Los Reyes Católicos HS***, Plaza de España, 1 (Plaza del Obadoiro).
Tel: 58 22 00.

WHERE TO EAT
Cafés

The narrow streets of the city often remain chilly even on hot days, so
the few tiny squares that do get the sun also have the liveliest daytime
café scenes. One of the prettiest places to drink outside in Santiago is
Barbantes, Calle Franco, 3, a tiny, tulip-filled square. The junction of
Calle de Franco and Calle Bautizados forms a popular daytime meeting
place with lively terraces, despite its proximity to a noisy road.

Plaza de la Universidad has a couple of good café-bars, with terrace
seating looking across to the grandiose, granite Faculty of History
building; a good spot to have a beer or a coffee and mill with the
crowds. The extremely pretty **Café Derby Bar** is on Calle Calvo Sotelo
nearby. Grey marble bar, panelled walls, decorated moulded ceilings
and quaint little chandeliers: this is an elegant period piece for a light
breakfast, coffee or a beer.

Café Paradiso, Ra del Vilar. Charmingly dingy, quiet student café-bar
with huge tarnished mirrors and comfy, battered leather seating. Tatty,
slow, hassle-free and pleasant for coffee or beer.

Calle de la Troya

A handful of café-restaurants and bars cluster round a quiet square on
Calle de la Troya.
Los Sobrines del Padre basic, down-to-earth café-bar, very popular with
the locals, it is in a lovely setting and you can sit out well into the
evening. The speciality here is *pulpos* – octopus, a Galician favourite.
Restaurante Rey Plain and popular, just the place to to try some of the
local specialities like *cáldo Gallego*, a very fatty pork and vegetable
soup, and *tarta de Santiago*, a sweet almond tart.
Atlantico friendly bar offering beer and Bob Dylan – still attracting a
relaxed, young crowd after all these years.

Plaza de San Roque

This is pretty, tree-lined square with a large stone fountain at its centre.
Sit out at a table of the bar **Jardin** and soak up the sun. Following the
street straight ahead brings you to:
La Bodeguilla de San Roque, San Roque, 13. An animated little bar
with plain oak stools, marble-topped tables and good music; rack upon
rack of good Riojas and Gallego wines line the walls, along with some

mythical tales told in coloured glass. Excellent **raciones** available here. Try their *pimentoes piquillo* – tasty pimentoes stuffed with sardine meat in a hot tomato sauce. Open throughout the day and night until about 0.30.

Calle Franco

Exploring Calle Franco is a bit like plunging into an aquarium: tendrilled creatures of the deep beckon from the windows of restaurant after restaurant. Definitely a place for the courageous and strong of stomach.

La Cigala de Oro, Calle Franco, 10. Tel: 58 29 52. Excellent range of ferocious, tasty seafood.

Bombero, Calle Franco, 57. Tel: 58 11 91. Good and inexpensive place to eat; the speciality is octopus.

Ribadavia, Calle Franco, 16. Cheap, straightforward place for the full range of rubbery meals from squid to octopus, with shellfish alternatives.

Bodegón Xulio, Excellent seafood restaurant.

Plazuela de la Universidad

Cafeteria Candelejas Popular with students intent on heated discussion and good food. A good option during the daytime.

Asesino, Tel: 58 15 68. Extremely popular restaurant serving excellent food. Good value.

Smarter Options

Don Gaiferos, Rúa Neuva, 23. Tel: 58 38 94. Strong on style with an imressive, brutal exterior, this is one of the very best restaurants in town. Pricey à la carte menu with an emphasis on beef: specialities include **éntrecôt marchand de vin,** steak **poivre** and steak tartare.

Retablo, Rúa Neuva, 13, Tel: 56 59 50. Conservative in feel, with marble floors and medieval carvings, this is a superbly appointed, reasonably – priced restaurant.

BARS AND NIGHTLIFE

Café-Bar Rúa Neuva, Rúa Neuva, 36. Trendy student hangout that mixes modern paintings, Latin music and a lively café scene. During the day you can sit out on the street; evenings there is music, sometimes poetry and a very useful What's On notice board detailing gigs and theatre events around town.

Carballeira, Rúa del Vilar, 41. Pleasant venue for early-evening cocktails out on the flagstones in the heart of the old city.

Bar Quintana, Plaza de Quintana, 1. Sit and drink out on the square and look out over the cathedral, while listening to the strains of Vivaldi float through the air from the bar. Probably the most elegant place to end your day in Santiago.

O' Galo D'Ouro, Cuesta Conga, 14 and 15. Lively, cavernous stone bar playing salsa, jazz, etc. Extremely popular.

Modus Vivendi, Plaza de Feijoo, 1, at the top of Calle de la Conga. Small, tartan-walled basement bar with hip sounds and occasionally live bands, sometimes jazz; open till 0.30.

Teatro Principal, Rúa Neuva, 19. A lovely small theatre under the old stone arches of Rúa Neuva. Film, music and a very varied programme of modern drama.

Café Metate, Calexón de San Paio. Traditional coffee and chocolate house in cool stone basement with original heavy wood-beamed ceilings and ancient stone coffee and chocolate grinders. Good, young atmosphere with music till around 3.00 at weekends.

Joam Airas, Rua Traversa, 11. Relaxed café-bar with lots of gilt-framed mirrors; attracts an arty crowd. This is also a venue for student plays and exhibitions.

Casa de Crechas, Via Sacra, 3. Animated, noisy student bar.

PLUS . . .

• Superb traditional **cake shop: Pasteleria Las Colonias Confiteria**, Rue das Orfas, 30.

• There are gift shops all over town, but if you want to uncover excellent modern arts and crafts Rúa Neuva is an excellent place to look: street–traders selling leatherware, trinkets and jewellery fill the lane; the shops are far more imaginative.
Amboa, Rúa Neuva, 44. Tel: (981) 58 33 59.
Particularly good for traditional jet and silver work and modern pottery. Visit the gallery to the rear of the shop for its high-quality modern exhibitions.

Sargadels, Rua Nova, 18. Innovative, imaginative and colourful ceramics plus arts bookshop.

Ceramic Típica, Calle de la Conga, 4. Large selection of traditional ceramics.

Lunula, Rúa Neuva, 4. Excellent modern jewellery and other gifts.

Libreria Vetusta, Rúa Neuva, 40. Antiquarian and second-hand **books**, postcards. Excellent browsing.

Manuel García Torres, Casas Reales, 30. In an inspired piece of tourist merchandising, this tiny shop sells nothing but *La Compostelana* chocolate *a la taza* – drinking chocolate (in powder or block form) in an irresistibly kitsch wrapper.

CATALONIA
Cataluña

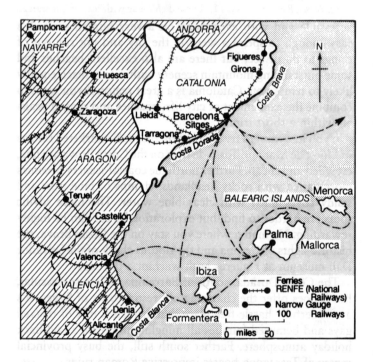

The city of Barcelona and the sand-fringed Costas are Catalonia's most popular tourist destinations – and with good reason. Barcelona, the dynamic regional capital, packs style, history, great bars and some of Europe's most outlandish architecture all into a compact centre. Continually vying with Madrid as Spain's most cosmopolitan, go-ahead city, Barcelona is easily the more manageable of the two, down-to-earth,

---

Catalan

Catalonia, like so many Spanish provinces, has its own language – Catalan (Catalá in Catalan, Catalán in Castillian Spanish). It's widely used both in speech and on street signs. It looks a bit like a mixture of French and Spanish (and it's still spoken by some French people in the Pyrenees), though when spoken it has a harsher, gutsier sound to it. In the guide Catalan names are given to correspond with what you will experience in the streets.

---

accessible and with everything on a very human scale. It's easy enough to spend a week in the city and not run out of things to do or see, but there are also excellent beaches and some outstanding mountain scenery within easy reach equally likely to tempt you. Catalonia is a great region if you want to combine the excitement of city life, beaches and rugged peaks all within a short trip.

If you just want to fry on a beach, the mass-marketed resorts of Lloret de Mar and Tossa de Mar on the Costa Brava are fine, crowded and cheap. Further north the coastal scenery becomes more varied with rocky headlands, clumps of pine trees and sandy coves filled with clear blue water. The more idyllic spots are harder to find, but exploration by car can be highly rewarding. No matter where you stay on the Costa Brava, the historic sights of Gerona and the riotous cheek of the Salvador Dalí museum at Figueres both warrant a daytrip.

The Costa Dorada, south of Barcelona, is less spectacular, but it does offer the charming old resort town of Sitges. It's a wonderfully hassle-free place that attracts a mix of relaxed gays and bemused families all mingling to create a laid-back holiday atmosphere. Farther south still, the busy provincial centre of Tarragona boasts impressive Roman ruins.

BARCELONA

Strikingly cosmopolitan, Barcelona is one of Spain's most exciting cities. As a major Mediterranean port it has always been open to influences from abroad (even during the stultified years of Franco), and it has long led the whole country in terms of style, art and vitality. Mention Barcelona and Spain's most innovative and original artists immediately spring to mind: Miró, Dalí, Picasso.

Barcelona's gothic core is protected by a mesh of bold 19th-century architecture, studded with flamboyant Art Nouveau masterpieces. The idiosyncratic buildings of Antoni Gaudí scattered around the city are emblematic of the free–spirited creativity that has been a hallmark of Barcelona for decades. But it's not just an experimentalism confined to grandiose buildings and art galleries (though no one should miss the best of these); there's an energy too in the city's café-bars and fashion houses, and a vitality to the streets themselves. The famous Ramblas is the epitome of this, a broad, tree-lined boulevard, one of the world's most culturally energized thoroughfares. You can take an interest in style here without ever being afraid of mellowing into cosy predictability. While Barcelona is daringly modern, the city's history as a port gives it an earthy seaboard exoticism.

The city offers a legendary nightlife to match all these impulses, with bars and clubs that stay up and kicking all night long.

Along with all this, the city has pretty unpleasant social problems: hard drugs are evident in the streets, accompanied by a full dose of petty (and not so petty) crime, and prostitution is prominent in many of the most touristed areas. If possible, don't carry anything of value (and keep an eye on what you do carry), leave nothing visible in a parked car, and take note of threatening areas highlighted in the guide.

GETTING YOUR BEARINGS

Barcelona's most famous street – the Ramblas – runs from the Plaça Portal de la Pau, down by the harbour, right up through the heart of town, providing a handy north–south axis. It's *the* place to get your bearings since most places of interest are in adjacent streets. It's also the most obvious place to head for if you want an immediate taste of the city. If you have arrived by train, take the metro to Liceu and you'll

History

From earliest times Barcelona has been an important port. In 218 BC the seafaring Carthaginians founded a settlement here, the ruling Barca family giving it the name Barcina. It was in 133 BC taken by the Romans who rigorously developed the town: remains from those times are still visible around the cathedral and in the bowels of the City History Museum. The Moorish occupations of the 8th and 10th centuries were swift and impermanent, and it was during the 12th to 14th centuries that the city developed a strong power base and lasting cultural identity. The capital of Catalonia, it was allied with Aragón, and both regions prospered by working together while retaining their own distinct laws, languages and rights. At one stage they jointly ruled the Balearic Islands, Valencia, Sardinia, Corsica and even parts of Greece.

This progressive state of affairs came to an end during the 15th century when the Catholic Monarchs brought Catalonia under their centralized government. As well as losing its political autonomy, the city saw its economic fortunes dwindle as commercial interest switched from Mediterranean trade to the precious metals being brought back from the New World.

Only during the 19th century did the city's prosperity begin to match that of the medieval period. The boom was largely due to the cotton industry, and the wealth of the city's industrialists is evident everywhere in the grandiose private houses and public buildings that they commissioned. At the forefront of advances in artistic taste, the city flaunts a wealth of Art Nouveau buildings, the most outlandish being those of Antonio Gaudí. The late 19th century also saw a rebirth in interest in the Catalan language, sparked off by the publishing of a Catalan poem in one of the daily papers. Catalanism became an important movement in all aspects of public life, embraced by both the left and the right of political opinion, and remains today a key part of the region's identity. It's quite different to Castilian Spanish, but you can expect to find both languages spoken.

During the Civil War the city became an important Republican centre, and it was here that the Republicans were finally beaten by Franco. Like the Basques to the north, Catalans saw their culture brutally suppressed by Franco, with Catalan books burned and the language banned from all areas of the media and education.

Catalan public protest against the Fascist regime was marked by the campaigning of communists and anarchists during the 1940s and 50s, an activism still alive in the memory of the city today.

find yourself midway down the Ramblas. Those sights that aren't within walking distance from here are easily accessible by metro or bus.

1 Cathedral	10 Sant Felip Neri	19 Església de la Mercé I Sant Miguel
2 Marès Museum	11 Palau Episcopal	20 Museu de Cera
3 Plaça del Rei	12 Generalitat	21 Palau Güell
4 City History Museum	13 Santa Maria del Pi	22 Palau Centelles
5 Sants Just I Pastor	14 Santa Agata	23 Gran Teatre del Liceu
6 Galeria Catalans Illustres	15 Llotja	24 La Boqueria Market
7 Ajuntament and Tourist Office	16 Santa Maria del Mar	25 Maritime Museum
8 Post Office	17 Museu Picasso	Ⓜ Metro
9 Museu del Calçat	18 Museu Textil	

It's a good idea to think of Barcelona in terms of its distinct areas before you begin your explorations – not least so that you can decide which areas you want to avoid. To the east of the Ramblas (i.e. to the right if you have your back to the ocean) is the old medieval quarter known as the Barri Gòtic (Barrio Góthico in Castilian), an area of narrow lanes and tiny squares best explored on foot; Via Laietana is a busy, heavily trafficked road that, like the Ramblas, runs roughly north–south, and it marks the outer limit of the Barri Gòtic.

Linking these two main thoroughfares is Carrer de Ferran, off the Ramblas, which passes through Plaça Sant Jaime and becomes Carrer Jaime 1 before meeting Via Laietana. The cathedral is just off to the west of here.

While the Barri Gótic is intriguing by day, parts of it can be threatening by night – especially in the narrow lanes around the Plaça Reial and Carrer dels Escudellers. Down by the sea on this side of town you will find pleasant harbourside cafés that run parallel with Passeig de Colom, and the area of Barceloneta, famous for its seafood restaurants. It's now possible to walk right the way along from Barceloneta to the Olympic village.

A large portion of the area to the west of the Ramblas is known as the Barri Xinès (Barrio Chino in Castilian), roughly from Carrer de Hospital right down to the port, with the broad Avinguda Parallel as its outer boundary. The Barri Xinès can be pretty unpleasant during the day as well as the night-time, and there is little of interest to bring you here anyway.

On the edge of the city, beyond Avinguda Parallel, is Montjuïc, a fort-topped hill with gardens, a funfair, Olympic stadia and museums, accessible by bus or cable car.

Barcelona is a big city and you will need a detailed map: pick one up for free at one of the tourist offices (see Factfile).

DON'T MISS . . .

The Ramblas
The Ramblas is the exotic spine of Barcelona, a broad avenue plunging beneath a tunnel of plane trees through the heart of the city. It's constantly alive, crowded with stalls selling caged birds and lush plants, buskers from the world over, and the constant clamour of people strolling, haggling and sitting in animated discussion at the terrace cafés. Day or night you can expect to find the Ramblas alive with people.

La Boqueria
(Just off the Ramblas by Liceu metro.)
Take a walk round Barcelona's colourful market to view an astounding array of seafood.

Barri Gòtic – the Gothic Quarter
The Barri Gòtic (Barrio Góthico in Castilian) is a densely packed area of narrow lanes that readily conjure up the layout of the city in medieval times.

Its most exotic square is the Plaça Reial, an elegant arcaded space lined with tall, swaying palm trees. There are plenty of café-bars with terraces out in the square – fairly pleasant by day, though this area is not recommended after dark.

The area around the cathedral harbours a mixture of medieval and stately Renaissance buildings – make sure you wander through the Plaça del Rei and Plaça de Sant Jaume.

The Cathedral
The Gothic cathedral was largely built between the 13th and 15th centuries, though the west face and spire are 19th-century reconstructions of the original. Inside the cathedral is some exceptional Gothic carving and a 16th-century white marble choir screen of note.

Visit the chapterhouse museum or simply stroll round the cloisters – one of the most refreshing spots in this dusty, noisy city – lush with trees and inhabited by a gaggle of large white geese.

Museu d'Història de la Cuitat: City History Museum
(Entrance 200 pesetas. Tuesday–Saturday 9.00–14.00 and 17.00–20.00, Sunday 9.00–14.00.)
The museum traces the growth of Barcelona from earliest times and includes the excavated Roman and Visigothic foundations of buildings that once stood here. Visit, too, the Chapel of St Agatha here and view the stained glass.

Museu Marès

(Entrance 200 pesetas. Tuesday–Saturday 9.00–14.00 and 16.00–19.00, Sunday 9.00–14.00.)

This museum has a fascinating collection of Spanish medieval polychrome woodcarving. In odd contrast there's a collection of ephemera too.

La Sagrada Família Cathedral of the Holy Family

(Metro Sagrada família. Entrance 300 pesetas. Open daily 9.00–19.00.)

The Sagrada Família (1883–1926) is an amalgam of weird fantasy and Gothic impulses, unquestionably Gaudí's most famous – and most bizarre – piece of architecture. It has to be seen. Although work commenced in 1883, it's still incomplete, and building is likely to carry on into the next century – amid controversy over how Gaudí's original designs should (if at all) be interpreted.

Honeycombed, tapered pinnacles tower like mutant fingers over the unfinished nave, their points topped by ceramic symbols glowing like bubble-gum beacons. Flying buttresses strain like the reptilian legs of mythological beasts, and doorways rise and droop with phantasmagorical sculptures. You may not like the building, but you will certainly remember it.

Oddly, the sculptures are fussily realistic due to Gaudí's idiosyncratic methods: he made plaster casts of ordinary living people, plants and animals before undertaking any stone carving, hoisting them up on to the building to see how they would look. Even the weary donkey of the "Flight into Egypt" group over the east doorway is the result of this cast-then-carve method. There is a small museum inside the building that records the architect's life and work.

Climb one of the towers (or take the lift) for vertiginous views and, on your way up, ask yourself the question: How could he have made this just that little bit weirder?

Palau Güell: The Güell Palace

(Calle Nou de la Rambla, 3. Open Monday–Saturday 11.00–14.00 and 17.00–20.00.)

The parabolic doorway that leads straight off the street heralds

Antoni Gaudí

Antoni Gaudí (1852–1926) is Barcelona's most famous
architect. He coincides with the *Modernisme* movement of
the late 19th century, a form of Art Nouveau distinct to
Catalonia (for Art Nouveau see p.365). Of all the architects
working in Barcelona, Gaudí was unique, and his buildings
are weird fantasy pieces that go way beyond the usual
terms of reference. He shares with Art Nouveau designers
a preoccupation with natural, organic forms, but in the work
of Gaudí this reaches disturbing proportions: exploring many
of his interiors is like wandering through the internal organs of
a living beast. Repulsive though it may seem at times, there's
no denying the sheer exuberance and technical brilliance of
his greatest work.

Gaudí, like others of the Art Nouveau movement, employed
a huge range of materials to create and decorate his buildings
– stone, iron, glass, ceramic tiles – lavishing attention on the
minutest of details and even designing the furniture to go
in them. Despite the wholly flamboyant and idiosyncratic
character of his work, Gaudí remains ponderously Gothic too,
most obviously in the Sagrada Família and the Güell Palace.

Gaudí worked for most of his life in the city of Barcelona,
for the last forty years becoming so devoted to the Sagrada
Família project that he actually lived on the site. He died in
1926, knocked down by a tram, and was mourned all over
Catalonia. Even the fate of his corpse may have been bizarrely
ignominious: during the Civil War part of the Sagrada Família
was bombed, and Salvador Dalí recorded a tale of how
Gaudí's body was dug up from the rubble by a couple of
children who tied a rope round its neck and dragged it around
the city streets.

a dense, decorative fantasy in stone, wood, glass and metals.
The Güell Palace, built 1885–95, houses a small theatre
museum and consequently is one of the most easily accessible
of Gaudí's domestic buildings in Barcelona.

The interior is heavily decorated – very similar to the
19th-century Gothic buildings found all over Europe – but
the style throughout is resoundingly Gaudí, with plenty of
weighty echoing of organic forms.

From the ground floor a stone spiral stairway, broad enough
for horses, leads down to stables below. On the first floor a

central sitting room is crowned with the decorative centrepiece of the whole building: a honeycomb-tiled dome reaching up through several floors to the roof. The deep-blue dome is covered in stars and pierced for natural light to filter through by day and lit by electricity by night. Look out too for the minstrel's gallery here and a tiny chapel hidden behind wood and ivory doors.

Up on the roof are crazily patterned ceramic chimney pots.

Casa Milà

(Passeig de Gràcia, 93 (at its intersection with Calle de Provenza. Metro: Diagonal and Passeig de Gràcia. Access to the roof: Tuesday–Saturday at 10.00, 11.00, 12.00 and 13.00.)

The Casa Milà was designed 1906–10 by Gaudí as a series

of apartments curving round 90 degrees. The oceanlike movement and fluidity of this massive corner building is matched by the smooth curves of the immediate detail. The façade undulates like stylized ocean waves and the balconies are decorated with curled iron-ribbon twists that flow and rustle like lead-grey seaweed. The style is very typically Art Nouveau. Inside, the wave theme is continued in gently rolling floor surfaces.

Climb on to the roof to inspect the fanciful chimney stacks and air vents, ranged like dumpy gingerbread pieces.

Casa Batlló

(Passeig de Gràcia, 43.) Metro: Passeig de Gràcia

A fantasy house for those with a taste for all things sweet and twinkling. It was built in 1875–77, but totally remodelled by Gaudí in 1904–06. Its balconies undulate smoothly in an elegant Art Nouveau style, the façade sparkles with sugary mosaic patterning and the whole building wears a snugly tiled and turret-topped roof.

Parc Güell

(Metro: Lesseps. Entrance free. Open daily May–August 10.00–21.00; winter daily 10.00–19.00.)

Take a stroll in the Parc Güell to escape from the noise and heat of the city. The park was designed by Gaudí between 1900 and 1914 and its most famous feature is the ceramic mosaic seating which snakes colourfully around the rim of an open terrace. Walk underneath this promenade to explore yet more innard-like arches by this prolific, zany designer.

The park was originally to be the garden of a fashionable suburban housing development; of the sixty houses planned only two were completed, and the whole project was cut short by Gaudí's death in 1926.

Picasso Museum

(Carrer de Montcada. Entrance 400 pesetas. Open Tuesday–Sunday 10.00–20.00.)

The Picasso Museum is housed in a charming medieval palace, worth visiting in itself. Picasso lived in Barcelona between the ages of fourteen and twenty-three, and the collection includes some of his early paintings, including "Harlequin" and the "Las Meninas" series based on the famous painting by Velázquez. There are also a great many etchings, drawings and engravings.

Maritime Museum

(Placca Portal de la Pau. Entrance 150 pesetas. Open Tuesday–Saturday 9.30–13.00 and 16.00–19.00, Sunday 10.00–14.00.)

The maritime museum shows the history of sailing through a range of detailed models; the real highlight is the life-size replica of the *Real*, the ship in which Don Juan of Austria sailed to the Battle of Lepanto 1571.

Montjuïc

Topped by a fortress, Montjuïc offers panoramic views over the city: on a clear day you can even see the Costa Brava. There's a funfair up here, all sorts of gardens – from dainty ornamental flowerbeds to spiky cactus plots – and you can see the glass dome of the new Olympic stadium. Barcelona's earlier stadium was built in 1929 and used for the anti-Nazi Games of 1936. For details of the museums here, see the box below.

There are several ways to tackle Montjuïc: take the metro to Paral.lel Espanya and either take the bus or walk up Avinguda de la Reina Maria Cristina – but be warned, it's a stiff climb on a hot day! Alternatively, for a more thrilling view of the city, take a cable car from Barceloneta. Finally, you could go to Paral-lel metro and take the funicular railway to a second, shorter cable-car ride.

OUT OF TOWN

Montserrat

The monastery of Montserrat, 40 kilometres north of Barcelona, is lodged high in the weirdly shaped Sierra de Montserrat, a range of mountains which rise sheer from the plain like fairy-tale peaks. The bus from Barcelona takes you right up to the monastery, 1,000 metres above sea level, a white-knuckle trip round hairpin bends hugging the mountainside. The driver points out the wreckage of buses that have plunged over the edge on the way up – definitely not for the weak of stomach. Alternatively, if you thrive on this sort of thing you can take the train from Barcelona and do the ascent by cable car. It is possible to walk back down from the monastery to the train station: it involves stumbling through a very dark tunnel for the first few hundred metres, takes a good four hours and is tough going in the baking heat. None the less it can be exhilarating: ask for specific directions at the tourist office at Montserrat.

Montserrat has long been a place of pilgrimage due to the discovery of a carved wooden icon – the Black Madonna – around which the monastery was first founded in the 9th century. The present buildings date from the 19th century. It's worth hearing the choir that accompanies morning mass, the salve (at 13.00) and vespers, famous for a singing tradition rooted in the 13th century.

The best reasons to visit are the spectacular views, rides on the funicular railway or the cable car, and the varied walks immediately accessible. While you are here, sample some of the liqueur made by the monks here – warm, thick

Museums of Montjuïc

Museu d'Art de Catalunya
(Entrance 400 pesetas. Open Tuesday–Sunday 9.00–14.00.)
This is a major museum and includes an outstanding collection of Romanesque frescoes taken from churches in the Pyrenees, along with Gothic altarpieces and paintings by El Greco, Tintoretto and Zurbarán.

Museu Arquelògic
(Entrance 100 pesetas. Open Tuesday–Saturday 9.30–13.00 and 16.00–19.00, Sunday 10.00–14.00.)
This museum contains Greek and Roman finds from Ampurias, Barcelona and the Balearic Islands.

Fundació Joan Miró
(Entrance 400 pesetas, students 200 pesetas. Open Tuesday, Wednesday, Friday and Saturday 11.00–19.00, Thursday 11.00–21.30, Sunday 10.30–14.30.)
A huge, fun exhibition of Miro's paintings, sculptures and tapestries.

Museu Etnològic
(Entrance 200 pesetas. Open Tuesday–Saturday 9.30–20.30, Sunday 9.00–14.00 and Monday 15.00–20.30.)
Collections of artefacts from South America, Turkey and Japan.

and flavoured with a blend of mountain herbs.

You can spend the night at Montserrat, though it's not cheap. Unless you are camping (there's a site), accommodation is best booked in advance: for information on this and bus times, ask at a tourist office in Barcelona.

Trains to connect with the cable car depart from the **Ferrocarriles Catalanes** station, Plaça de Espanya, Barcelona. (Metro: Espana.)

Beaches
The gay resort of Sitges offers the best beaches within a day trip from Barcelona. The train journey takes about 40 minutes; see the Costa Dorada below.

BARCELONA FACTFILE

Tourist Offices Gran Vía de les Corts Catalanes, 658. Tel: 301 74 43. Open daily 8.00–20.00. Estació Central Barcelona-Sants. Tel: 410 25 94. Open daily 8.00–20.00. Poble Espanyol. Tel: 325 78 66. Port. Tel: 317 30 41. Airport. Tel: 325 58 29. Open daily 8.00–20.00.

Airport Information Tel: 301 39 93. Airport train departs Estació Central Barcelona-Sants every 30 minutes 6.00–22.30.

Ferries Trasmediterránea, Via Laietana, 2. Tel: 319 82 12. For sailings to the Balearic Islands.

Train Station Estacío Central Barcelona-Sants. Tel: 322 41 42.

Bus Stations Estació del Norte, Avinguda Vilanova for buses south and to Madrid; Empresa Sarfe, Passeig de Colom, 3, for the Costa Brava; Iberbus, Avinguda Parallel, 116, for international routes.

Car Hire Hertz, Carrer Tuset, 10. Tel 237 37 37.

Taxi Tel: 386 50 00; 330 08 04; 321 88 33; 300 38 11; 358 11 11 or 212 22 22.

Post Office, at the bottom of Via Laietana on Plaça Antoni Lòpez.

Telephone Telefónica pay booths at Sants station, Plaça de Catalunya and Avinguda de Roma.

Telephone Code: 93

Hospital For emergency doctors Tel: 212 85 85; for ambulance Tel: 300 04 22.

Police Emergencies Tel: 091 or 092.

WHERE TO STAY

There's no shortage of accommodation in Barcelona, but it is expensive. Although hotels are graded just like everywhere else in Spain, this is no guarantee of quality.

You should think carefully about the area of town you intend to stay in, since a lot of the city is threatening and even dangerous after dark. As a guide, consider the comments under Getting Your Bearings. Avoid the following areas: Bari Xinès, Carrer del Carme, the lower part of the Ramblas (towards the docks) and the Barri Gòtic. This said, if you are travelling on a budget you may well end up having to stay in the Barri Gòtic, where there are dozens of *hostales* for you to try. These lists include a few, but if they are full, or you want to check out others (and plenty are OK), remember to avoid narrow lanes and alleyways, and in particular the Plaça Reial and Carrer dels Escudellers.

Barri Gòtic

CHEAP TO MODERATE
Hostal California, Carrer Raurich, 14. Tel: 317 77 66. Off Carrer de Ferran.
Hostal Rey Don Jaime, Carrer Jaume I, II. Tel: 315 41 61.

Hostal Cervantes, Carrer Cervantes, 6. Tel: 302 51 68.
Hostal Mavoral, Plaça Reial, 3. Tel: 317 95 34.
Pension Colom 3, Calle Colom, 3. Entrance in Plaça Reial.

The Ramblas

MODERATE
Hotel Flor Parks, Ramblas, 57. Tel: 318 13 24.
Hotel Lloret, Ramblas, 125. Tel: 317 33 66.
Hotel España, Carrer Sant Pau, 9. Tel: 318 17 58. Just off the Ramblas, a tolerably short walk into the otherwise unadvisable area of the Barri Xinès.

SMARTER OPTIONS
Hotel Internacional, Ramblas, 78. Tel: 302 25 66.
Hotel Turin H*,** Carrer Pintor Fortuny, 9–11. Tel: 302 48 12. Just off the Ramblas.
Hotel Oriente, Ramblas 45. Tel: 302 25 58.
Hotel Montecarlo, Ramblas, 124. Tel: 317 58 00.

Plaça de Catalunya

At the top of the Ramblas, this is one of the better areas to stay in – but prices are higher, too.
Residencia Australia, Ronda Universitat, 11. Tel: 317 41 77.
Hostal Alicante, Ronda Universitat, 4. Tel: 318 34 70.

WHERE TO EAT

If Catalunya has great cuisine, then Barcelona is a gourmet's paradise. There are places to suit every palate and every pocket. At the top end of the scale it has restaurants that rival the best in Paris, with prices to match; if you're not up to that, you can get a three-course meal from as little as 400 pesetas. In between you'll find the whole gamut of trendy and traditional bars and restaurants. Fast-food joints and tourist restaurants have sprung up everywhere too and, as in any big city, standards vary enormously, The bargain *menú del día* is not usually available in the evenings, so if you're watching your budget, follow the same eating pattern as the Barcelonians – have a hearty lunch. As in the rest of Spain, restaurants are always empty before 22.00 (most also close on Sunday nights and in August). To fill any gaps there are always the cafés and the marvellous Catalan cake shops, not to mention the pre-dinner stop-off for *tapas* and a glass of champagne.

East of the Ramblas

The most traditional and atmospheric area (including the Barri Gòtic and the La Ribera area around the Picasso Museum) with a broad cross-section of every type of place to eat, from rock-bottom *comedores* to some very smart establishments. There are lots of interesting old bars serving *tapas* (see bar listings) although the *tapeo* isn't as popular as in Madrid. Carrer Avinyo is lined with places offering uninspiring tourist menus.

CHEAP

Conesa Xarcuteria, Carrer Llibreteria, 1 (Plaça San Jaume). Great place for a quick snack or meal. Specializes in hot toasted sandwiches – 27 different types to choose from, all made to order. Take-away pizza by the slice too. Always busy.

Breakfast Bar Santa Clara Xocolateria. Carrer de la Libreteria, corner of Plaça San Jaume. Workers' breakfast and snack bar serving good coffee, thick hot chocolate and a large, inexpensive selection of croissants, brioches, madeleines, cakes and sandwiches.

If you want a take-away breakfast, our favourite bakery is the **Forn de Pa Sant Jordi** at Carrer de la Llibreteria, 8. While this one's nearly always packed the one opposite hardly seems to do business. The best bet for breakfast, if there are two of you, or if you're really hungry and alone, is a 12-inch *croissant gegante*. (If you're poor but too proud to sneakily consume it in a café, there are comfortable steps on the pleasant and often musical Plaça del Rei.)

Bar Haiti, Carrer San Jaume, 3 (off Plaça San Jaume). Ordinary-looking but popular little bar thanks to its house specialities: good *butifarra* sausage and the best tortillas in this part of town. Try the tortilla *espigalls* (asparagus). Also serves organic wine! Closes 20.00, Saturday lunchtime and all Sunday.

Bar España, Carrer Montcada, 2, near the Picasso Museum. Incredibly cheap menu in a simple café with marble-topped tables. Good paella and *sangría*. Closes Sunday and Monday.

Casa José, Plaça San Josep Oriol, 10. A Barcelona institution: it's been going for years and still produces an amazingly priced menu – you can't get any cheaper than this. Come here to fill up: the food is basic to say the least but at those prices, who cares? You will find lots of tourists there, though.

El Portalon, Carrer Banys Nous, 20. Barrels all around, nicotine-stained pictures on the crumbling walls, ancient *chorizos* hanging from the ceiling and a waiter with a muck-spattered apron. Great fun – cheap dishes chalked up on a blackboard, mixed clientele and a wonderful atmosphere. Not for the faint-hearted.

Bar El Tropezon, Carrer d'en Cignás, 20. At the lower, seedy end of Carrer Avinyo in the Barri Gòtic. Animated *tapas* bar with a nice client blend. Older regulars stick to the bar; noisy, young crowds hog the tables. House speciality is the enormous *pinchos*.

The parallel streets Carrer Ample and Merce are also good for *tapas*. Dodgy at night.

MODERATE

Xarcuteria bar **La Pineda**, Carrer Pi, 16. Three generations old, this famous charcuterie was founded at the turn of the century. There are two tables at the back – you can sample *tapas* of olives, cheese, *boquerones*, etc, there or just nip in for a sandwich.

Casa Esteban, Carrer Montcada, 22. An old-style, traditional *xampan-yeria* (see bar listings) with the best seafood *tapas* in Barcelona. Founded in 1929 by the father of Esteban (the big, jolly one), who carries on the family tradition in great spirit. You'll have to fight to get to the bar – try the delicious anchovies and the exquisite *almejas majas*. The *xampanyet* flows nonstop and they also serve fresh cider.

Plaça de la Garsa, Carrer Assaonadors, 13. Parallel to Carrer Princesa. A *bar formatgeria* serving plates of cheeses and patés which come complete with gherkins and crispy bread. A good selection of wine to go with it. Wonderful but lethal cast-iron staircase to the toilets . . . Intimate atmosphere, open very late.

Pizza Nostre Carrer Montcada. Pizza restaurant boasting double mozzarella with every choice. Discreetly lit; most of the tables are for two. Trendy/young, waitresses serve trendy young Barcelonians.

El Corte Ingles Bar Terraza, Plaça Catalunya. Top-floor restaurant with wonderful views of the city. A definite must at least once, though the decor is straight out of a Benidorm hotel with matching piped music. Help-yourself buffet in the restaurant – extra cheap between 10.00 and 11.00.

La Govinda, Plaça de Madrid, 4. It calls itself an Indian vegetarian restaurant but by British standards it's completely inauthentic. The music is piped Mozart and Vivaldi, the waiters are Spanish and there are pizzas on the menu. But many of the dishes are delicious; for example, the potatoes and aubergines in coconut cream and the cabbage leaves stuffed with cheese and nuts. The pizzas are also excellent.

Bar Brasseria Llivia Carrer Copons, 2. A little street near the cathedral, on the corner of Carrer Ripoll. Small with an upstairs dining room. Specializes in fresh pasta (made on the premises) and barbecued meats, both of which sometimes make it to the *menú del día*. Reasonable prices but can get expensive à la carte.

Brasserie Flo, Carrer Junqueras, 10, off top end of Via Laietana. Airy and elegant with Parisian overtones. Not cheap at all but there is a *menú del día* or you can just opt for a starter. Don't miss the desserts – they are superb.

Bar Barretina, Carrer Sagristans, 9, near Plaça Nova. More of a restaurant than a bar and more for late evenings than lunches. Specializes in post-prandial tarot and astrology sessions. Reasonable menu as well as ham and cheese *tapas*. Good fun.

Los Caracoles, Carrer Escudellers, 14, off lower Ramblas. Very famous and very, very touristy but still atmospheric. The spit-roast chicken and snails are good. **La Parilla** nearby is an offshoot.

EXPENSIVE

Senyor Parellada, Carrer Argenteria, 37 (Tel: 315 40 10), off Via Laeitana. Cool modern and minimalist Catalan restaurant with chic waiters and chic clients. Dishes named after politicians, plus lots of lovely vegetables.

Café de l'Academia, Carrer Lledo, 1 (Tel: 315 00 26), Plaça de Sant Just. Small but excellent. Refined atmosphere with classical music. Menu exclusively in Catalan and lots of regional specialities. Lunchtimes only.

Can Pescallunes, Carrer Magdalenes, 23, (near Plaça Nova). Upmarket but homely local favourite specializing in French and Catalan cuisine. Try the *rap amb cloises a l'all cremat* (monkfish with clams and toasted garlic). Few foreign clients, but apparently popular with French and Argentinians. Seasonal variations. Ask for the menu in Catalan because new dishes take time to make it to the English version.

La Odisea, Carrer Copons, 7 (Tel: 302 32 92), off Carrer del Dr Joaquim Pou. If you want to splash out in style, try this converted 19th-century warehouse. More like an art gallery than a restaurant, the bar where you have your aperitif is crammed with modern paintaings and sculpture. The dining room is behind; no compromise here – turbot, salmon and caviar are typical dishes while the extravagant four-course menu is a special chef's surprise.

El Gran Café, Carrer Avinyo, 9 (Tel: 318 79 86). Right in the heart of the Barri Gòtic, Marvellous *Modernista* decor and innovative Catalan cuisine. Old-world style and service.

Agut d'Avignon, Carrer de la Trinidad, 3 (Tel: 302 60 34), in an alley off Carrer Avinyo. Very smart, very expensive, very popular and very good indeed. Multi-level cosy, cottagey rooms with beamed ceilings, fireplaces, tiles, pots and plants. Excellent food – try the Catalan speciality *pollo con gambas* or the *oca amb peres* (goose with pears). Reservations essential.

West of the Ramblas

A good area (including the Ramblas themselves and the streets round the Plaça de la Universitat, above the Barri Xinès and across Avinguda Parallel) for budget eating with lots of snack and *tapas* bars around the Universitat. South of Carrer de Hospital you hit the red-light district.

CHEAP

Egipte, Carrer Jerusalem, 3, behind the Boqueria market. If you're only spending a few days in Barcelona, it's tempting to eat here every lunchtime. Everyone else thinks so too, so be prepared to queue up with students and businessmen alike. For an absurdly small sum you can choose from a huge *menú del día* that includes some quite sophisticated dishes – the *tarta de marisco* is delicious. Hectic atmosphere, slightly quieter in the evenings when it's twice the price but still a bargain.

La Garduna, Carrer Morera, 17. In the Boqueria market, at the back. A quiet sanctuary away from the frenzy. Join the stallholders and fishwives for *tapas* or a cheap *menú del día*. Freshness guaranteed.

Sitjas, Carrer Sitjas, 3, just off the Ramblas. Proud of its *precios economicos* and very cheap *menú del día*.

La Tasca d'Oli, Carrer Pintor Fortuny, 25. A street perpendicular to the Ramblas. Clean and well-kept with good-value hot and cold sandwiches and *tapas*. Also serves a copious *menú del día* and more expensive à la carte dishes such as Brazilian palm hearts and brains in batter.

Biocenter, Carrer Pintor Fortuny, 24. New Age-ish vegetarian restaurant at the back of a wholefood shop. Its speciality is its self-service salad bar and vegetable pies. Good choice of infusions and organic fruit juices; nice gazpacho, too.

Los Toreros, Carrer Xucla, 3–5, off Pintor Fortuny. Bar and bullfighting club. Covered in bullfighting memorabilia and full of old boys – hardly a woman in sight. Does a cheap and varied *menú del día*.

Horchateria Fillol, Plaça de la Universitat, 6. Everything you could possibly want to eat or to drink – *tapas, platos combinados, bocadillos*, strawberries and cream, *crema catala, horchatas, granizados, batidos* – in this popular, traditional bar.

Bodega Quimet, Carrer Poeta Cabanyes, 25. Further afield between Avinguda Parallel and Montjuic. Tiny local bodega packed with people (particularly on a Sunday). Mainly seafood *tapas* but several interesting house specialities. Ask for a *bicicleta* (a sort of cannelloni) or a *pinochet* of mixed clams and if you hear people saying *turista* they don't mean you, just another speciality – artichokes and anchovies. The drink to go with these is the draught red vermouth which flows by the gallon from the beer taps. Wonderful friendly atmosphere.

MODERATE

Amaya, Rambla Santa Monica, 24. Don't be put off by the window covered in flags, displaying menus in six different languages. The bar section next door has a local clientele and serves very enticing Basque *tapas*, The house wine is a pretty good Rioja.

Xarcuterie La Castellana, Rambla de Caputxins, 41 Typical old-fashioned Castilian charcuterie. One of the best places to come for a *tapa* of ham (*pernil* in Catalan) – they're all hanging from the ceiling. The *jamón serrano* and *jamón jabugo* are delicious.

Bodega Sepulveda, Carrer Sepulveda, 173. Just off Plaça Goya. Enormous variety of *tapas* in bodega setting with sawdust on the floor. Not cheap but the quality is excellent.

Hotel España, Carrer Sant Pau, 9–11, in the Barri Xinès. The restaurant of the hotel serves a surprisingly good tourist menu (excellent paella) and it's worth a visit just to see the marvellous *Modernista* dining room.

EXPENSIVE

Casa Leopoldo, Carrer Sant Rafael, 24, parallel to Sant Pau. Just yards from the pimps and pushers of the Barri Xinès is this respectable establishment which fills with bourgeois clientele at Sunday lunchtimes. Superb array of seafood dishes but the star of the show is the best *pan torrat amb tomaquet* (tomato bread) in Barcelona. Closed Sunday night, Monday and August.

Restaurante Elche, Carrer Vila i Vila, 71, beyond Avinguda Parallel. Smart, modern restaurant serving Valencian rice specialities such as paella and *arròs a banda*, where the seafood and rice are served separately. Their fish soup is wonderful.

Seafront

Barcelona's newly converted harbourfront – the Moll de la Fusta – has become an elegant tree-lined promenade with several fancy "snack bars", while the fishing quarter and beach district of Barceloneta is traditionally home to numerous seafood restaurants of every category.

CHEAP

Casa Paixano, Carrer Reina Cristina, 7, behind Passeig Isabel II. Hidden in a street of dodgy jewellers and spivvy electrical shops is Barcelona's cheapest and most incongruous champagne bar – prices start at 35 pesetas a glass! In warehouse surroundings with dangling hams and 15-foot-high tins of seafood, Barcelona's lowlife sips champagne from nine in the morning. The bar also does great *bocadillos* – big, fat bratwursts are its speciality. It's easy to miss it – make sure you don't. Closes at 22.30 and on Sundays.

El Vaso de Oro, Carrer Balboa, 6. One of the first roads perpendicular to the main Plaça Nacional in Barceloneta. A beerboy's heaven, this narrow *cerveceria* specializes in every beer imaginable – all the famous names are there but stocks change each month (except for the bar's unique brew) so there's always something new. If you become a privileged regular, you may get to drink from a *gerra* – the bar's own imported German beer pots. While you're there, sample the wide choice of cheap *tapas*.

Bar Jaica, Carrer Ginebra, 11. The next road along. Excellent seafood *tapas* bar full of locals and an impressive collection of pots.

MODERATE

Can Tipa, Passeig Nacional, 6. A favourite with locals and not that expensive in spite of credit-card stickers on the windows. Good solid dishes and a reasonably priced *menú del día* which includes tasty but very peppery mussels.

EXPENSIVE

Gambrinus, Moll de la Fusta, near Passeig de Colom. You can't miss this stylish seafood bar and restaurant – a giant, sculpted prawn sits on the roof, the work of the Olympic logo designer from Valencia, Javier Mariscal. The building looks like a breaking wave; inside, the bar is made out of an old cabin cruiser. Specializes in delicate seafood *tapas* and main courses.

Merendero de la Mari, Platja de San Miguel, 20. Another touch of sophistication and new-wave Barcelonian design, this time overlooking the beach. Eat outside on the seafront terrace or inside in the simple elegance of this excellent restaurant.

Set Portes (Siete Puertas), Passeig Isabel II, 14 (Tel: 319 30 46). This well-known favourite has been in the Perellada family for thirteen generations and owes its success and reputation to its consistently high standards. It is one of the best restaurants in Barcelona. Turn-of-the-century brasserie-style decor; the atmosphere is smart but not exclusive and the *zarzuela* and the seven different paellas are superb. Reservations recommended.

BARS AND NIGHTLIFE

Berimbau, Passeig del Borne, 17. Smoochy couples come here to snog with Brazilian passion. Others come to chat until dawn while listening to tropical music. Berimbau is a Brazilian cocktail. Specially recommended: Batida (made from *cachaca* – sugar-cane rum – and freshly squeezed lemon and lime). Not cheap.

El Paraigua, Plaça Sant Miquel. Well worth a visit for its wonderful Art Nouveau decor, despite the predictably high prices.

Els Quatre Gats, Carrer Montsió, 5. This is one of the most famous bars in the city, with Picasso its most famous customer. At one time he paid for his drinks here in sketches.

Las Torres de Avila, Avinguda Marqués de Comillas, Poble Espanyol, Montjuïc. Over-the-top designer bar; a late-night spot to see and to be seen in, Expensive.

La Eira, Carrer Provenca. Antique funfair theme bar.

Yabba Dabba Club, Avenir, 630, No, not Fred Flintstone, but wall-to-wall Goths with decor to match.

THE COSTA DORADA

Along the shores of Barcelona & Tarragona provinces, Spain's "golden coast" – the Costa Dorada – stretches down to the Ebro Delta. It's big camping and package-holiday country. French, Italians, and Scandinavians fill the campsites and Germans and Brits the hotels. There are no places of outstanding interest, but Sitges is one of the pleasantest seaside resorts, and an easy day trip from Barcelona, and Tarragona further south has some interesting Roman ruins.

SITGES

One of the first stops south, Sitges has been popular with Barcelonians ever since it briefly became an artists' colony in the 19th century. Today it's an international, trendy and very gay resort. There are big hotel blocks outside the centre but the narrow streets overhung with flowers retain the prettiness of the old town. This is at its best on Corpus Christi day when all the streets are carpeted with flowers.

The tourist office is at Passeig Villafranca.

Beaches

Sitges has some good beaches, although they get fairly packed in summer. Less crowded is the nudist beach about two kilometres outside the centre. Follow the shore round to the right, then cross the hill or go through the train tunnel and turn left.

The famous Playa del Muerto – "beach of death" – is two kilometres away at Villanova.

Things to See

Several museums remind visitors of Sitges' artistic past. The **Museu Cau Ferrat** on Carrer del Fonollar (behind the church) has works by Utrillo and El Greco. Next door, the **Museu Maricel del Mar** has some good medieval paintings and sculpture. The **Museu Romantic** on Carrer Sant Gaudenci contains a collection of antique artefacts including some 300-year-old dolls.

WHERE TO STAY
Cheap to moderate

Celimar. Paseo de la Ribera 18. Tel. 894 07 65
Parellades, Carrer Parellades, 11, has large rooms and is near the beach.

Lido, Carrer Bonaire, 26, Tel. 894 48 48 has clean rooms with telephone and is near the beach.
Internacional, San Francisco, 52. Tel. 894 26 90.
Mariángel HR*, Parelladas, 78. Tel. 894 08 01.

WHERE TO EAT

El Xalet, Illa de Cuba, 31, Tel: 894 55 79. This is a magical spot. You can sit out beneath the fruit trees and exotic palms of a grandiose garden. The food is inexpensive, and rather more straightforward than the location.
Calitia, Carrer Marques de Montroig, 5. Very popular and very cheap; good local cooking.
La Santa María, Passeig de la Ribera, 53. Sit out and look at the Med beyond rows of swaying palms while you enjoy the inexpensive seafood menu here.
Picnic, Passeig de la Ribera. Tel: 894 01 80. Perfect beachside bar-restaurant, farther away from town beyond La Santa María. Sit out on the terrace right on the beach for drinks or standard *platos*

combinados; a little overpriced because of the wonderful setting.

For good-value *menú del días*, try the restaurants of Carrer Sant Pere and Carrer Sant Pau which run up the hill from the seafront near the end of the beach overlooked by the old church.

Superpollo, Carrer Sant Josep, 8, does non-stop roast chickens on spits. Eat in or take away. The speciality is chicken and champagne.

NIGHTLIFE

Carrer Marques de Montroig and Carrer Primer de Maig, in the centre of town near the sea front, are busy with bars, pubs and discos.

Ricky's, Carrer de San Pau, 23, – widely publicized hetero disco.

Atlantida, 2 km out of town. Catch a bus from the seafront to this very popular disco.

SAN SALVADOR

One very pleasant surprise along the coast is San Salvador. It's a holiday town but very Spanish and still very charming. The beach is excellent with soft sand and it also has a pretty promenade.

The real treat, however, is the **Casals Museum**. This is in the former family home of the cellist and composer Pablo Casals (Pau Cassals in the Catalan spelling), whose fervent Catalanism and opposition to Franco prevented him from living in Spain after the Civil War. He died in 1973 in Puerto Rico but in 1979 his remains were brought back and buried in the cemetery of his nearby birthplace El Vendrells.

The Pau Cassals foundation converted the San Salvador house into the Casals Museum and the memorabilia it contains are quite touching – as well as Casals' first cello there are paintings, books, sheet music, photos and a lock of the German composer Felix Mendelssohn's hair. There's also a fascinating collection of personal letters from people as diverse as the playwright Arthur Miller, the Queen of Romania and the secretary of the Montreal Pipe Smokers' Club.

Open during the summer all week 11.00–14.00 and 17.00–20.00; winter Tuesday–Sunday. Entrance 150 pesetas.

TARRAGONA

Tarragona radiates its own sense of history. It is perfectly feasible to see Tarragona in a day but we spent a week here and could have quite happily spent more.

The Romans were pretty keen on Tarragona too. Tarraco was founded in 218 BC and in 45 BC Julius Caesar made it the capital of a huge province, Hispania Citerior, and renamed it Colonia Julia Triumphalis Tarraco. It became one of the most elegant cities in Roman Spain and by the 2nd century AD had over 30,000 inhabitants, Augustus and Hadrian both spent time here.

The evidence of Roman Tarragona remains impressive. Outside the city an aqueduct (El Pont del Diable – "Devil's bridge") is almost on a par with its more famous Segovian counterpart, and in the centre of town remains include those of two forums, a magnificent amphitheatre, a circus, a necropolis and a Roman wall supported by huge, and even more ancient, Iberian blocks. Walking round the old town you also come across remains, such as bits of pillar complete with Latin inscriptions, incorporated haphazardly into medieval houses.

The city has long Christian traditions. St Paul is alleged to have preached here and in Visigothic times it was an important bishopric. The cathedral is beautiful (an excellent example of the transitional style – Romanesque to Gothic) and to add to its attractions Tarragona has a great beach and a selection of good restaurants.

Tarragona is divided into two parts – the old medieval town, which is in the upper part (on a hill overlooking the sea), and the modern town, lower down. They are divided by the Rambla Nova (where you will find the tourist office at number 46), which begins at the Balcon del Mediterraneo overlooking the sea and the beach, a great place to sit out at a café during the evening. Two blocks west of the Rambla Nova runs the Rambla Vella, parallel with it.

Archaeology Museum
(Upper Tarragona. Tuesday–Saturday 10.00–13.30 and 16.30–20.00, Sunday 10.00–14.00.) 100 pesetas. Same ticket as for the Necropolis; free on Tuesdays.

Next to the Praetorium, the Archaeology Museum is packed with Roman artefacts – porcelain, amphorae, phallic charms and amulets. Downstairs friezes, columns and statues are so well

Roman Tarragona

If you approach Tarragona by car from Barcelona evidence of Roman occupation strikes before you even reach the city.

On the main road, 20 kilometres north of Tarragona, the Via Augusta (as it's still known) is the Arco de Bera, the triumphal arch erected in the 2nd century AD.

Eight kilometres north of the city, a monolith marks the centre of the former Roman stone quarry.

Six kilometres north of the city stands the Torre de los Escipiones, a funerary monument to General Publius Scipio and his brother General Gnaeus Scipio, who were killed in 212 BC fighting the Carthaginians.

The Aqueduct (Ponte del Diablo)

The aqueduct; which brought water to the city from the river Gaya, is Tarragona's most impressive Roman monument. About 120 metres tall, two storeys high and constructed from golden stone, it is spectacularly set among pine trees four kilometres outside the city walls. To see it, take bus number 5 for San Salvador and ask the driver to let you off at El Aqueducto. By car, take the main road to Valls and, just before San Salvador, turn off at the unmarked track (just before the Pont del Diablo restaurant) and bear right through the pine forest. Park the car and walk to the aqueduct a hundred metres through the trees.

Mausoleo Romano de Centcellas

The Mausoleo Romano de Centcellas is a former Roman villa, converted to a basilica in the 4th century AD. Dedicated to St Bartholomew, the basilica also served as a mortuary chapel. In 1877 mosaics of biblical scenes were discovered in one of its cupolas. It is situated 7 kilometres outside the city in the village of Constanti. Restoration work is going on in 1992.

set out you feel you're in a real Roman villa. The museum also contains some well-preserved mosaics, including a huge seafood scene and a perfect Medusa with eyes that look frighteningly real.

The Necropolis

(Lower Tarragona. 100 pesetas; same ticket as the Archaeology Museum; free Tuesday. Tuesday–Saturday 10.00–13.00 and 16.30–20.00.)

Used from the 3rd to 6th centuries AD, it contains the unusual combination of pagan and Christian Roman as well as Visigothic crypts. Some crypts are still in place but many funerary artefacts are in the museum next door.

Municipal Forum

(Lower Tarragona. Tuesday–Saturday 10.00–13.00 and 16.00–19.00.)

Although bisected by a main road (but joined by a footbridge), the smaller of the two forums is more completely preserved than its big sister. Among the ruins are the remains of a house, a sarchophagus and an elegant pair of reconstructed columns.

TARRAGONA FACTFILE

Tourist Office Rambla Nova, 46. Tel: 23 21 43 or 23 22 08. Open Monday–Saturday 10.00–20.00; Sunday 10.00–13.00.
Train Station Tel: 24 02 02 (6.00–22.00).
Bus Station Tel 22 91 26.
Plaça Imperial Tarraco, at the landward end of Rambla Nova.
Taxi Tel: 22 14 14.

WHERE TO STAY

Cheap to moderate

Noria HsR*, Plaça de la Font, 53. Tel: 23 87 17.
El Callejón HsR*, Vía Augusta, 221. Tel: 23 63 80.
Nuria H*, Vía Augusta, 217. Tel: 23 50 11.

Smarter Options

Urbis H***, Reding, 20. Tel: 21 01 16.
Lauria*, Rambla Nova, 20. Tel: 23 67 12.

WHERE TO EAT

Calle August, which runs between and parallel with Rambla Nova and Rambla Vella, has a handful of café-restaurants offering cheap tourist menus, and there are a few more in and around Plaça de la Font, just east of the Rambla Vella.
El Plata, Calle August, 20. Tel: 23 22 23. Excellent, meaty *tapas* and *raciones*.
El Caseron, Cos del Bou, 9 (just off Plaça de la Font). Tel: 23 93 28. Walls decked with scythes, ploughs and pitchforks give this traditional *mesón* a rustic flavour. Cheap and cheerful, it offers budget *menu del días*.

El Tiberi, Marti Ardenya, 5. Tel: 23 54 03. Typical Catalan buffet. This is one of the best places to sample lots of different local dishes in the course of one meal – just pay around 1,100 pesetas and help yourself.

La Cantonada Reding, 14 (parallel with, and a couple of blocks to the west of, Rambla Nova). Tel: 21 35 24. There's both a smart restaurant and a trendy young bar serving *raciones* here; either way it's good food.

Mistral, Plaça de la Font, 19. Tel: 23 72 22. Good pizzeria on a pleasant square in the old town, just east of the Rambla Vella.

Meson Fernando, Calle d'Armanya, 6. Tel: 23 81 44. Basque cuisine offering plenty of seafood dishes.

NIGHTLIFE

Most socializing in the city goes on along the Rambla Nova, where people sit out at the terrace café-bars for coffee, beer and ice cream. It's a fairly relaxed, provincial atmosphere, gently animated but rarely exciting. There are some interesting, less elegant places to drink around Plaça de la Font. For dancing and late-night drinking, head for the Rabassada beach.

Playa Rabassada

Take orange line bus number 3 from the town centre.

This beach is a few miles east of Tarragona and it's the place young people head for dancing through till 6.00; entrance to "pubs" (bars with dance floors) free.

It's a nice spot – a fair-sized beach with a handful of bars that look like they've just been washed ashore. Between dancing and drinking you can sit out beneath the stars and listen to the crashing waves. Playa Rabassada attracts a young crowd – late teens and early twenties.

FURTHER SOUTH . . .

The main road south of Tarragona is scarred by industrialization. Gas plants, oil refineries and factories make thoughts of swimming off the nearby coast very unappealing indeed.

Nevertheless, just down the road is the Costa Dorada's biggest resort: **Salou** – a sprawl of package-tour hotels.

There's not much to recommend it to the independent traveller – in summer it's crowded (or at least it used to be before the typhoid scare in 1989), expensive and very un-Spanish. However, **Cambrils,** the next resort south, feels more authentic and has a pretty harbour. It also has some good fish restaurants.

Carry on south and you arrive at a total change of scene

– the **Delta de l'Ebre Natural Park,** a must for ornithologists and geographers and a pleasant detour for anyone else. The whole area is a mass of peninsulas and islands and there are long deserted beaches and sand dunes. This is a result of the alluvium collected by the river Ebro on its way down to the sea. It's one of the most fertile regions in Spain and as well as producing many market-garden crops it is the centre of Spain's rice production (look out for the paddy fields). The area is also home to over 60 per cent of all bird species found in Europe – up to 100,000 birds altogether (depending on the time of year – winter and migration seasons are best).

It's difficult to get round the delta region on public transport but because it's so flat the best way is by bicycle. You can hire bikes on both sides of the river. On the north side: **Motos – Bicis Torne,** Goles de L'Ebre 184. Tel: 48 00 17. On the south side: **Tallers Lambrich,** Carren Unio 76, Sant Jaime d'Enveja. Tel: 46 81 90.

There are three main towns on the Delta. At Deltebre behind the tourist office there's an eco-museum in which acquariums display fish, frogs, lobsters, prawns and some extremely ugly toads – and on an allotment grow some of its crops (all kinds from tomatoes to sugar beet). Reed huts with spy holes give a close view of some of the birds.

There's a new youth hostel in Deltebre – the **Alberg Mossen Antoni Batlle** at Carreterra Venta Nova a far deBudz. Tel: 48 01 36.

From Deltebre you can either take an excursion up the river or the ferry to San Jaume de Veja on the south side. (You can take a car on this too – the cost is small.) Just down the road from San Jaume you can get to a huge windswept eucalyptus beach.

Boat trips: Venus Boat Excursions, Transbordador Olmos, La Cara, Deltebre. Tel: 48 04 73.

The biggest holiday town on the delta is **San Carlos de la Rapita.** Every restaurant proudly advertises its prawns (the delta is supposed to produce the best on the Mediterranean) but all the seafood here is unusually good.

COSTA BRAVA

Notoriously heavily developed, at its worst the Costa Brava delivers all that its image suggests: overcrowded hotels, miles of scratchy grey sand, bars awash with watery lager and more English breakfasts than you could eat in a lifetime. But there's far more to it than this, and this 130-km stretch of coast offers a varied range of sea and sand holidays, from the mass commercialism of Lloret de Mar to the smaller, more elegant resort of Cadaqués. Despite the tourist development there remain some intensely pretty stretches of coast, especially towards the north, with rocky, pine-clad hills tumbling to sandy coves of exquisite blue water. No matter where you choose to stay on the Costa Brava, there are a couple of places of interest inland you really should try and see: the wacky Salvador Dalí museum at Figueres, and the quiet, historic town of Gerona.

GERONA

The delightful walled town of Gerona nestles around a low hill beside the river Onyar. It's a small place, quietly picturesque, its streets breathing with the history of Roman, Arab, Jewish and Christian peoples. Aside from the charms of its cool lanes and alleyways, Gerona retains one of the largest medieval Jewish quarters in western Europe, Arab baths considered second only to those at Granada, and a handful of excellent museums and art galleries. There's more than enough to fill a day's exploration and you may well find yourself tempted to stop over and drink in the town's tranquil atmosphere by night.

GETTING YOUR BEARINGS

If you have arrived by train or bus (or by road from Barcelona), you will find yourself south of the river in the newer part of town. The old quarter is to the north of the river. If it's open when you arrive, pick up a map in the railway station tourist office. Walk up Carrer Santa Eugenia (round to the left you exit the train station) and straight up Carrer Nou and cross the river. Immediately to your left is the Rambla de la Llibertat, where you will find the main tourist office.

This is a good spot from which to get your bearings: the Rambla de la Llibertat runs alongside the river, heading west towards the oldest part of town. A lane off the far end of the Rambla takes you on to the Carrer de la Força which, like the Rambla, runs parallel with the river, below old Gerona. Off its (near) east end, a flight of broad steps climb up past the Agullana Palace, a hint of 18th-century grandeur. Follow Carreer de la Força along to its west end and off to the right you will find the narrow flight of steps of El Call, taking you through the heart of the old Jewish quarter. Alternatively, continue to the end of Carrer de la Força and you will eventually arrive at the cathedral. The Arab baths and monastery of Sant Pere de Galligants are beyond here, accessible through a stone gateway, out on the edge of town.

DON'T MISS . . .

El Call
(Off Carrer de la Força.)
Winding, shallow steps carve their way through the old Jewish quarter, dark and evocative of the medieval town. Midway up this narrow alleyway you can visit the **Centre Isaac El Cec** (open 10.00–19.00), where there is a small exhibition on the history of Jewish communities in Catalonia.

At the top of the narrow steps, follow the lane up the slope ahead to the Museu d'Art and the cathedral, or you can retrace your steps and head for the cathedral via Carrer de la Força.

Museu d'Art
(Palau Episcopal, Pujada de la Catedral, 12. Tel: (972) 20 38 34.)
Gerona's art museum has a wealth of paintings and carvings beautifully displayed, from the Romanesque period right up into the 20th century. It's housed in the Bishop's Palace,

Resorts

Port Bou

There's nothing special about Port Bou except that it's the start of Spain if you're coming by train (via Cerbère) and the start of the Costa Brava. If you're fed up with travelling it makes a pleasant enough stop. It has a pretty tree-lined Rambla, a small (pebbly) beach and a selection of seafront restaurants.

If you decide to make a night of it, there are plenty of *hostales* and you can get your first taste of Spanish nightlife in one of the several discos in town.

Inland: Monastery of Sant Pere de Rodes

Llança is the next town south of Port Bou, a small resort with quiet, clean beaches, but nothing exceptional to recommend it. Inland is this 10th-century monastery, one of the most picturesque sights in the area. Sitting on top of Mount Vedera (an early Pyrenean foothill) it offers great views of the surrounding countryside and coastline.

Cadaqués

Cadaqués is the chicest resort on the Costa Brava, attracting a highly discerning class of poser. Salvador Dalí set the trend in the sixties by building a house nearby, but there's a saner wave of fashionable rich young things who holiday here these days. Of course it's more expensive than other Costa Brava resorts, having the kind of social cachet more generally associated with the south of France. Rocky bays round about offer exquisite swimming in rippling turquoise waters.

Rosas

A busy resort, chock-full of people, Rosas is distinguished by a magnificent bay overlooked by the ruins of a 16th-century fort, and there's a fishing port here, too, guaranteeing excellent seafood in the town's restaurants.

Ampurias

Ampurias was a Greek trading station from around 550 BC; about 300 years later it was taken by the Romans who considerably developed the town. This extensive site will be of great interest to archaeologists: there are the ruins of temples, house foundations and water cisterns from the Greek settlement, and large areas of the Roman town have also been excavated — look out for the beautiful mosaics in a couple of the Roman villas. For a good overview of the whole site, take a look at the models in the museum here.

Calella, Llafranc and Tamariu
These are a handful of the prettiest spots along a rocky stretch of coast with idyllic — though crowded — sandy coves.

Palamós
Palamós has a thriving fishing harbour and nowadays attracts yachts to its marina, too. There are excellent beaches, easily accessible.

Playa de Aro
Playa de Aro is a wholly modern tourist development, popular with families renting self-catering accommodation.

Tossa de Mar
The busy, modern resort of Tossa de Mar still retains medieval walls and a charming old quarter worth exploring — which you will be able to do along with thousands of other holidaymakers. The town is backed by pine-covered slopes and the old quarter huddles on a hill offering great views over the ocean. If you enjoy the dreamlike paintings of Marc Chagall, call into the town's museum.

Lloret de Mar
Lloret de Mar beckons from just about every high-street travel shop in Britain — it's the most built up of all the package resorts along the Costa Brava, and the seafront bristles with high-rise hotels. Unless you have pre-booked accommodation, finding somewhere to stay is nightmarish.

The beach here has uncomfortably grainy sand and the water becomes deep very quickly, making it far from ideal for leisurely swimming. Lloret de Mar is the sort of resort to head for if all you want is guaranteed sunshine, a view of the sea and thousands of other Brits to enjoy it with. This said, if you do want to spice things up with a bit of cultural variety, Gerona and Barcelona are both easy (around 1–1.5 hours) bus rides away.

Blanes
Blanes marks the southernmost limit of the Costa Brava – a thriving fishing port and resort town.

Ferries
Ferries ply up and down this coast between the resorts and it is well worth taking the trip for the stunning views of the coastline this affords. Catch one at Blanes, Lloret de Mar, Tossa or Playa d'Aro.

a splendid Renaissance palace developed around an earlier building. Even if you are not a fan of contemporary art, it's well worth the climb to the top floor for the panoramic views over the town and countryside.

Cathedral

Although the door to the Cathedral is just across a small square from the art museum, for full effect approach it via the grandiose 17th-century stairway that reaches up to the towering Baroque façade.

The cavernous Gothic interior is light and lofty, its decorative highlight a 14th-century silver-gilt altarpiece, and there are some especially tranquil cloisters.

Museu Capitular: Chapter Museum

(Access via the Cathedral).

This is an excellent museum, housing the Cathedral treasures. There's a huge range of exhibits: look out for Beatus' *Book of the Apocalypse*, a fine 10th-century manuscript in Room 1; the exceptionally beautiful 14th-century processional cross in Room 2; and the "Tapestry of Creation" in Room 4. The tapestry is actually a massive embroidery. It dates from the 11th century and, for its era, is uniquely rich in colour and design. It shows Christ in majesty surrounded by creatures and seasonal scenes of medieval peasant life: digging, ploughing, fishing and, in winter, folk toasting their fingers and toes over a fire.

Baños Árabes: the Arab Baths

(Entrance 100 pesetas. Open Tuesday–Saturday 10.00–13.00 and 16.30–19.00; Sunday 10.00–13.00.)

The Arab Baths were built as a place both to bathe and to meet and talk, directly following Roman lines. Despite their name, they were in fact Christian civic baths and were built in the 11th century, and rebuilt in the 12th. There are hints of Moorish design here and there, and they were probably built by Mozarabic workers, but the overall style is Romanesque, with rounded arches and heavy, ornate carved capitals.

The baths are extremely well preserved: there's a tepidarium and two calderiums, but the most impressive room is the frigidarium (cool-bath room), with its central octagonal pool lit by a skylight above, and wall niches where bathers would leave their clothes.

Monastery Sant Pere de Galligants

Carrer de Santa Llúcia, 1. Tel 20 26 32.

This 11th–12th century Romanesque Benedictine monastery houses the city's archaelogical museum. Exhibits include local Greek and Roman finds and Jewish tombstones.

Las Casas del Onyar

The waterside houses that fringe the old town hang over the river just as the houses of medieval times did. Best viewed from the footbridge found through an alleyway off the westerly end of the Rambla.

Palacio de los Agullana

Steps from the east end of the Carrer de la Força lead up past one of Gerona's finest town palaces. It dates from the 14th–17th centuries and, along with the church of Sant Martí Sacosta, forms one of the most attractive Baroque areas of the town.

Town Walls

With so much of interest within Gerona, it's easy to forget that this is a walled town. There have been walls here for centuries, built by Iberians, Romans and again during medieval times. Once you have visited all the sights, take a walk along the walls. Several sections are accessible: perhaps the nicest is the stretch that runs from the top of the town down to its easterly end.

GERONA FACTFILE

Tourist Office, Rambla de la Llibertat, 1. Tel: 20 26 79.
Monday–Friday 8.00–20.00, Saturday 8.00–14.00 and 16.00–20.00.
There is also a tourist information centre at the train station.
Airport 13 kilometers from Gerona; there is no public transport to the airport.
Train Station Plaza de España. Tel: 20 70 93.
Bus Station Plaza de España. Tel: 21 16 54.
Phone code 972

WHERE TO STAY

Cheap to Moderate

Bellmirall HsR**, Carrer Bellmirall, 3. Tel: 20 40 09.
Reymar HsR**, Pujada del Rei Martí, 15. Tel: 20 02 28.
Europa HR**, Carrer Juli Garreta, 23. Tel: 20 27 50.

Smarter Option

Ultònia HR**, Avenida de Jaime 1, 22. Tel: 20 38 50.

EATING AND DRINKING

Gerona is not nearly as touristy as you might expect, but there are a handful of places where you can find a reasonably priced *menú del día*. The Rambla is a lively, pretty place to eat, with its café-restaurants spilling out on to the street, and nearby Carrer de la Força is similarly attractive. If you are looking for seafood, try one of the restaurants of the Plaça de Indepencia, just south of the river. It's quite a lively spot, with seating out under grandiose arcading, though a fair amount of traffic cuts through here and it can be noisy. Wonderfully laid-back **Le Bistrot**, lodged partway up the steps to the Agullana Palace, is something of a favourite haunt – a café-bar doing tasty pizzas and sweet and savoury crepes.

FIGUERES

Situated in the centre of the Empordanese plain, and capital of the High Emporda, Figueres is a friendly, bustling, commercial town. With good bus and train connections, it's a useful transport hub for the area.

Salvador Dalí is Figueres' most famous resident ever and the Salvador Dalí Museum is what tourists come to Figueres to see. Whatever your preconceptions about Dalí, this will convince you that he was a genius.

The town was also the birthplace of Narcis Monturiol – the not very famous alleged inventor of the submarine, who hardly gets a look-in. There are also an 18th-century castle with star-shaped walls, a museum of 4,500 toys and the **Museu de L'Empordan** containing Catalan art and archaelogical finds.

Figueres is a pleasant place to spend at least a night – accommodation is reasonably priced, cafés are lively and the Hotel **Duran** is an excellent and very famous local restaurant. There is also a variety of Chinese eateries.

Trains run to Port Bou and the bus station (just in front of the station) has connections to L'Escala and Cadaqués.

The tourist office is on the Plaza del Sol.

DON'T MISS . . .

The Salvador Dalí Museum
(Entrance 400 pesetas. Open Tuesday–Sunday 11.00–19.30.)

Even if you don't think you like Dalí's work, you'll love the Dalí museum. From the moment you see the bread on the red walls and the giant eggs on the roof of his house, you realize that Dalí was quite potty.

Inside the museum the alligators draped in Roman armour, the artificial leg dressed as a matador or the Cadillac full of passengers covered in ivy (that you can water by putting five pesetas in a slot) won't exactly change that opinion. But it will make you acknowledge that Dalí was a man whose imagination knew no bounds at all.

There's no guidebook to buy because Dalí insisted that visitors, too, should be led by their imagination. However, he didn't mind people putting questions to the museum attendants – most of them are so full of reverence for the man that they'll pour out their knowledge with passion.

Dalí started work on the museum in 1970 and it opened in 1974. The building is an old theatre that was badly damaged during the Civil War. After restoring it, Dalí put stumps of old beams into the auditorium walls to remind people of the earlier destruction. His obsession with bread – in addition to the loaves on his house, the devil and knight figures outside the museum carry baguettes on their heads – comes from his belief that bread is a symbol of life and normality after a period of devastation such as war.

In the theatre auditorium, gold dolls perched round the walls represent ghosts of the former theatre's ballet dancers. They stand there to welcome the public. Washbasins represent impure angels who suffer the wind and the rain in order to be cleansed of their sins. The Cadillac below them belonged to Dalí and was one of only seven similar models made. Al Capone owned another but for obvious reasons his was not a convertible.

In front of a Gala nude on the stage (which becomes Abraham Lincoln when viewed through the specially mounted lens), silver bottles of Ponche Caballero (a favourite Spanish liqueur) literally reflect Dalí's belief that ordinary objects can be art. See how they change the images they reflect – a face becomes a nude, a moon becomes a skull.

All the members of the band on the stage represent real people who played the *sardena* with a friend of Dalí's, Dr Angels. The doctor made the figures from bandages and plaster of Paris.

Dalí himself lies embalmed underneath the flat tomb on the stage. Most of the visitors seem to miss it and walk right over the man whose work they're admiring. Not that this would would bother him – he's apparently lying in eternal bliss on his back, with both his eyes open and focused on the glass cupola above him. Through this he can see the Ampurdan sky and the church where he was baptized.

ALSO WORTH SEEING

Castle of San Fernando
The massive 18th-century castle of San Fernando, overlooking the whole town, was named after Fernando VI who had it built. During the Civil War it served as the main transit centre for members of the International Brigade, and became the Republicans' final preserve after Barcelona was taken.

It's still occupied by the military so you can't go *into* it. But

---

Andorra

In 1278, 300 years after Charlemagne had driven out the Moors, a long-standing dispute over the ownership of a piece of Pyrenean heartland finally came to an end. The French Count of Foix and the Spanish Bishop of la Seu d'Urgell decided to grant it independence – with both of them as "co-princes" – and the Principality of Andorra was born.

For 650 years Andorra hardly changed (there wasn't a proper road to France until 1931) and Andorrans made a living from dairy farming and indulging in the national sport of smuggling. Then, in the 1940s, skiing developed as a sport, outsiders arrived in Andorra and the locals discovered that they didn't have to smuggle when they could sell tax-free goods on their doorstep.

Today the place is a giant duty-free shop in the mountains.

Six million people flood into Andorra each year to stock up on modern inessentials. (It's an area only a third of the size of the Isle of Wight, so parking is often a problem.) Cigarettes and booze are inevitably the favourites – and, along with petrol, also the best buys – but if you're tempted while you're in the Pyrenees you could buy a fur coat, a carpet or a video (although electrical goods aren't very cheap). There are also toy shops, perfumeries and shops selling nothing but dairy products, where you can buy two gallon buckets of skimmed-milk powder and cheeses the size of tractor wheels.

---

if you're feeling fit you can walk *round* the five kilometres of walls.

Museu Juguete

   (Rambla, 10. Open every day in summer 10.00–13.00 and 16.00–20.00; closed on Tuesday the rest of the year.)

This is one man's collection of 4,500 toys dating from 1860. The collection includes hundreds of dolls from all over the world (they stare out spookily from glass cases on the walls), dozens of Dinky toys, ancient rocking horses (and horses that don't rock but roll around on little wheels instead), drum-banging soldiers, an aeroplane bicycle and a huge model Eiffel Tower made from pieces of Meccano.

Museu de l'Empordan

(Free entrance. Open 11.00–13.00 and 15.30–19.00 and on Sunday 11.00–14.00).

This has some beautifully preserved amphorae from the Roman site in Ampurias, two floors of works by Catalan artists (including Dalí and Miró) and a selection of 18th-century dresses and fans.

WHERE TO STAY
Cheap

The **youth hostel** Calle Anicet Pages, 2. Tel: 972–501213. Behind the post office on Plaza del Sol.
Ronda H**, Ronda Barcelona, 104. Tel: 503911.
Europa H*, Ronda Firal, 18.

Smarter Options

Hotel Durán, Calle Lasauca, 5. Tel: 972–501250.
Ampurdán, Carretera General Madrid-Francia, 763 Tel: 972–500562.

WHERE TO EAT
Cheap

Chinese restaurants and an abundance of snack bars are found near the station; plenty of tourist restaurants crowd the streets near the museum, or you can sit out on the Ramblas.

Moderate.

Hotel de Paris on the Rambla. The café is a trendy meeting point for young locals and the restaurant next to it, as well as serving huge meals, has a wonderful selection of over twenty mouth-watering *tapas*.

Smarter Option

Hotel Durán Calle Lasauca, 5. Tel: 972–501 250. People come from miles around to sit in its giant, opulent dining room and sample its special brand of Catalan food, e.g. *zarzuela con angulas* (fish stew with eels). The dishes aren't cheap but its *menú del día* is wonderful value – three courses (all delicious and with copious portions) for the price of some of the starters, and rounded off with sweet wine from a *ganacha* that you pour down your throat.

VALENCIA AND MURCIA

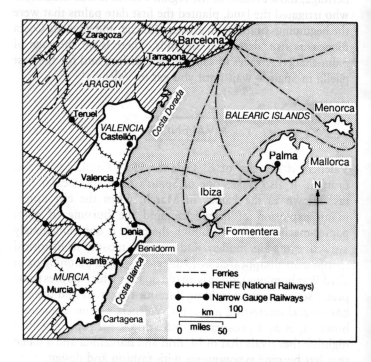

The huge sandy beaches of the Costa Blanca, and the riotous fiestas of Valencia and Alicante, are Valencia and Murcia's chief tourist attractions. Inland the region appears scantly picturesque: dry winds whisk around the whitewashed cubes of houses scratched in a dust-scoured countryside; empty villages dot arid hillsides, relieving seamless acres of sun-drenched orange groves. Valencian farms produce vast quantities of citrus fruit, but for most of the year they are not labour-intensive and a lack of development here and in Murcia has forced people to leave the land to find work in the cities and coastal resorts. Yet, despite this quiet rural emptiness, and despite the waves of tourist development that have engulfed the Costa Blanca, the whole area bears the lingering exotic aftertaste of far earlier cultures.

The Phoenicians, Greeks and, above all, the Moors who settled the area in pre-medieval times left a rich cultural heritage, most evident in the region's food. It was the Moors who irrigated the land, planted the first date palms that were the beginnings of the palm groves of Elche, and gave the Costa Blanca its rice, dates and almonds. There is no shortage of palm-shaded terraces to sample local dishes, and for the best paella in Spain – wait until you get to Valencia!

VALENCIA

Valencia is the city of El Cid, the Holy Grail, paella and oranges. It also stages one of Spain's most spectacular fiestas, known as the Fallas, in March, when the city erupts in an explosion of fireworks amid the burning of giant papier-mâché effigies. Although the place is not immediately attractive (it's big, modern and scruffy – most of its historical monuments disappeared in 19th-century town planning or in Civil War bombing), there is an old quarter which houses some pretty squares and crumbling Baroque mansions and the city has several interesting museums. Valencia's main attraction, however, is as a prosperous and vibrant metropolis with a nightlife that rivals that of Madrid and Barcelona and a name that has become synonomous with fashion and design.

GETTING YOUR BEARINGS

Most of the city consists of ugly, industrial scrawl. The former perimeters of the old city are marked by wide avenues on the site of the massive medieval city walls which were pulled down in 1868 and of which only two impressive gates remain. Inside this area, north of the train station, is the main square

A trading place established by the Greeks, it was under first the Romans and then the Moors that Valencia gained prominence as the centre of a rich and fertile plain, the Ruerta, irrigated by a system of canals and producing rice, oranges and almonds in abundance. The area was the scene of fierce confrontations between the Moors and the Christians (today mock re-enactments of these battles form part of popular fiestas) and Valencia fell to El Cid when he retook the city in 1054 in his last campaign. It was eventually conquered definitively by the joint Catalan-Aragon crown and the legacy of that lies in the local dialect of Valenciano, a derivative of Catalan. During the Civil War, Valencia was the last Republican stronghold to fall.

called both the Plaza del Pais Valenciano and the Plaza del Ayuntamiento – it is the central hub of the city. Between this and the river Turia to the north lie the market, the commercial sector, the Cathedral and the maze of dark, narrow streets of the old quarter – the Barrio del Carmen. Several bridges cross the dehydrated riverbed to the parks and university buildings on the other side.

DON'T MISS ...

Cathedral

The Cathedral is a cumbersome mixture of Gothic and Romanesque styles, well worth calling inside to view light filtering through the Flamboyant Gothic lantern, climb the tower for views over the city – and visit the Chapel of the Holy Grail (Monday–Saturday 13.00–14.00 and 16.00–18.00). The Holy Grail is believed to be the cup Christ drank from at the last supper, into which drops of his blood fell; several churches claim to house the original. Here the story goes that the cup first came to Spain in the 4th century, and was kept in the Monastery of San Juan de la Peña in Aragon. It was given to the cathedral in Valencia during the 15th century. Here it remains, a gold and agate chalice, set behind the altar, surrounded by alabaster carvings. There's also a small collection of paintings here by Zurbarán, Correggio and Goya.

Palacio de la Generalidad

This grand Gothic palace held the government offices of Valencia until the early 18th century. A series of stately chambers are hung with portraits, and look out for the golden ceilings in the two 17th-century tower rooms.

Lonja de la Seda: Silk Exchange

(Tuesday–Friday 10.00–14.00 and 16.00–18.00, Saturday and Sunday 10.00–13.00.)

The Flamboyant Gothic style of the Lonja immediately suggests the wealth and optimism of the medieval silk merchants for whom it was built. The spacious interior is exquisitely designed, with elegant, twisting pillars. Ask to see the 15th-century carved ceiling in the law court here.

Back outside, cross over to Valencia's new market – one of the biggest and most colourful displays of fruit and veg in Spain.

Museo Nacional de Cerámica: Ceramics Museum

(Tuesday–Saturday 10.00–14.00 and 16.00–18.00, Sunday 10.00–14.00.)

The extravagantly carved 18th-century alabaster doorway describes the name of the Marquess de Dos Aguas (who owned this palace) in an elaborate visual pun: two ancient vessels overflowing with water.

This is a vast collection of ceramics from the Iberian period up to the present day, and you can follow the changes in taste and the advances in technique over the centuries. Along with plenty of work from around Valencia there are displays of Majolica ware, medieval tiles, lustre ware, and even works by Picasso.

Colegio del Patriarca: Corpus Christi Collegiate Church

(Daily 11.00–13.00.)

The museum here displays Gothic and Renaissance sculpture and a varied collection of paintings. Works include paintings by Caravaggio, van der Weyden and El Greco, several pieces by Goya, and a Velázquez self-portrait.

El Salér

If you fancy a swim, catch a bus out to the beach at El Salér, 10 km away.

VALENCIA FACTFILE

Tourist Office Plaza dei Pais Valenciano, 1 (Tel: 351 04 17). Open Monday–Friday 9.00–13.30 and 16.30–19.00; Saturday mornings only. Other branches at airport and train station. Useful for maps.

Airport 10 km out of town at Manises on the N111 (Tel: 370 95 00 or 153 02 11). Bus number 15 every hour from the bus station. Iberia, Calle de la Paz, 14. Tel: 352 05 00. British Airways, Plaza Rodrigo Botet, 6. Tel: 351 22 84.

Trains RENFE (Termino Norte), Calle Játiva, 15 (Tel: 351 36 12). RENFE information and ticket office at Plaza Alfonoso el Magnanimo, 2. Frequent services to Barcelona, Madrid (via Cuenca or Albacete) and Malaga. Local towns are served by FEVE trains from station near the Museo de Bellas Artes opposite the Torres Serranos.

Buses main station Avenida de Menendez Pidal, 13 (Tel: 349 72 22) across the river – bus number 8 from Plaza del País Valenciano. Good connections to all cities and Eurolines to London via Barcelona. Buses to El Saler and beaches leave from the Puerta del Mar. Buy a Bono-Bus pass from a *tabaqueria* or the booth in the main square for bus travel in town.

Ferries to the Balearics: Trasmediterránea office Avenida Manuel Soto Ingeniero, 15 (Tel: 367 07 64). Tickets also from port office Estación Maritima (Tel: 367 39 72) before departure. Daily nine-hour crossings to Mallorca and twice a week to Ibiza. Buses number 3 and 4 go to the port from the main square.

Car hire Avis, Hertz and Atesa all have offices at the airport and in town. Cheaper option is Flycar, Calle San José de Calasanz, 3 (Tel: 326 71 55).

Telefonica, Plaza del País Valenciano, 27. Open Monday to Saturday 9.00–13.00 and 17.00–21.00. Code is 96.

Post Office also in main square.

Consulates No British consulate, USA, Calle Ribera, 3 (Tel: 351 69 73).

Police, Gran Vía de Ramón y Cajal, 40 (Tel: 351 08 62). Emergency dial 092.

WHERE TO STAY

Most *hostales* are in the streets off the Plaza del País Valenciano and in the old town. Finding a room shouldn't be a problem unless you arrive during Fallas week in March.

Cheap to Moderate

Hostal Alicante Calle Ribera, 8 (2nd floor). Tel: 352 74 99. Near the station and main square.
Hostal Venecia, Calle Llop, 5. Tel: 352 42 67. Near the main square.
Hostal del Rincon, Calle Carda, 11. Tel: 331 60 83. Near the market next to a garage.
America Residencia, Calle Saugre, 8. Tel: 352 24 42.
Hostal Universo, Calle Vilaragut, 5 (5th floor). Tel: 351 94 36. North of Calle Barcas, opposite the Hotel Astoria.
Hostal Residencia Universa, Calle Barcas, 5. Tel: 351 94 36. Just off the main square.
Kostal Granero, Calle Martinez Cubello, Tel: 351 25 84. Between the station and the main square.

Smarter Options

Hostal Bisbal, Plaza de la Cruz, 9. Tel: 331 70 84. Near the market. Very clean with nice owners. Good location.
Hotel Ingles, Calle Marques de Dos Aguas, 6. Tel: 351 64 26. Traditional old-fashioned style and charm. Expensive but you pay for luxury.

WHERE TO EAT

Valencia is home to paella, proper paella . . . As an alternative try *arros a banda*, where the rice and seafood are served separately; another popular dish using local produce is *anguilas all i pebre*, baby eels from the Albufera lagoon cooked in a spicy pepper sauce. *Horchata* a milky drink made from either almonds or tiger nuts, also originated here. Most restaurants are in the old part of town, especially in the Barrio del Carmen, e.g, on Calle Roteros.

Cheap to Moderate

Barrachina, Plaza del País Valenciano, 2. Vast mega-deli right on the main square. Pavement tables and upstairs terrace, counters serving everything from *tapas* to take-away.
Casa Cesareo, Calle Guillen de Castro, 15. On the main avenue near the station. Old-style *taberna* on three floors. Reasonable prices for good-quality food. Try their *mariscada cesareo*. Closed Mondays.
El Dintel, Calle/Murillo, 15, Near the market. Friendly and simple with interesting dishes and a wide menu.
Bar Glorieta, Plaza Alfonso el Magnanimo. Big old bar, Good for coffee or *tapas*.
Restaurante Salvas, Calle Salvas, 12, South of the cathedral near the university. Garden and good *menú del día*.

El Clot and **Bar Rotunda**, Plaza Rotunda. Two good places – terraces and nice food.

La Dehesa, Out of town on El Salér beach – the best *paella de langoustinas*.

La Carmela, Calle Isabell de Villena, 155. In the port district. Excellent paella done properly for two people.

Smarter Options

La Hacienda, Calle Navarro Reverter, 12 (Tel: 373 18 59), between the Puerta del Mar and the Plaza de America. Valencia's top restaurant with top prices to match.

Gargantus, Calle Navarro Reverter, 16 (Tel: 234 68 49). Almost next door to La Hacienda. *Nouvelle* Valencian cuisine with exquisite and imaginative dishes that change daily. Worth the splurge.

BARS AND NIGHTLIFE

There are lots of trendy pubs and bars in Valencia, some very designery. During termtime the atmosphere is lively to say the least but it quietens down in August. Areas of activity are dispersed but there is a good concentration of places in the Barro del Carmen (along Calle Caballeros and Calle Alta and Calle Baja, for example), which is the nicest and most convenient part of town. *Combinados* or cocktails, especially *agua de Valencia* – made from champagne, fresh orange juice, and sometimes vodka – are popular everyday drinks.

Café Claca, Calle San Martín, 8, Near the cathedral, below Plaza Zaragoza. Arty hang-out with good selection of exciting cocktails, often only for two people.

Cerveteria de Madrid, Calle San Martín, 10. Traditional bar with lots of pictures, live jazz and cocktails.

Café-Bar Juan Sebastian Bath, Calle Mar, 31. Near San Martin. Probably the most eccentric bar in town. Formerly part of the Palacio de valeriole, it's now been converted into a lot of Baroque decor, flowers and hundreds of candles.

Café-Bar, San Jaime, Plaza de Espartado. Does the best *aqua de Valencia*.

Café Malvarrosa, Calle Ruiz de Lihoro, off Calle de la Paz. Does its own version of the local cocktail – *agua de Malvarrosa*, made with lemon.

Cavallers de Neu, Calle Caballeros, 19, Trendy intellectuals' rendezvous.

Bar Barraca/Bolshoi, Calle Caballeros, 39, Stark. Postmodern.

Café Lisboa, Calle Caballeros, 35. Neo-Classical and Art Deco decor with Greek columns, piano and photographic exhibitions.

Evening, Calle Joaquim Costa, 3. South American music and Irish coffee.

Other Areas for Bars

• Around Plaza de Honduras (e.g. **Pipers, Bohemios, Chevalier**).

• Along the beachfront (bus number 1 or 2), especially Calle Eugenia Vines and Calle Isabel de Villena. The streets are lined with bars, pubs and discos and the area is particularly active in summer. Try **Genaro** or **Tropical**.

• Plaza Canoves del Castillo and along Calle Brabador Estave. Yuppie posers' bars.

• Around the university campus on the other side of the river. Very lively in term, especially Avenida Blasco Ibahez (e.g. **Publico** and **El Asesino**) and in Plaza Kulmer (e.g. **Café Maravillas** and **Pan de Azucar**).

• Also along Calle Ramón Gordillo (e.g. disco pubs **Mama Ya Lo Babe, Vao Veo** and **Delirio**).

Discotecas Worth Trying

Calcutta, Calle Reloj Viejo, in the centre near Plaza Zaragoza. Free.
Distrito 10, Calle General Ello S. Near the Puente del Real. Ultramodern disco.
Perha, Calle Emilo Baro, 71, Live concerts.
Spooke Factory and **Dreams Village**, Playa de Pinedo, out of town on the road to El Saler.

Jazz

Club Perdido, Calle Sueca, 17. Near the railway station.

PLUS . . .

• **Horchaterias** Santa Catalina and El Siglo in Plaza Santa Catalina near Plaza Zaragoza. Not to be missed.

• The **central market**, a huge construction of iron and glass. The biggest market in Spain and the prettiest building in Valencia after the *azulejo*-tiled railway station.

• **Street markets** Permanent flower market in the main square. Fleamarket in Plaza Rotunda on Sundays and stalls in Calle de la Paz and Plaza Alfonso Magnanimo every day.

• **Shopping** Lots of fashion and designer shops, e.g. Trafico de Modas for clothes in Calle Marino Albesa, 27. For ceramics, try Neri in Calle Poeta Querol and for embroidery Suay in Calle Bloseria, 31. The beautiful Plateria del Sol for silverware.

- **Modern architecture** Palau de la Musica by Ricardo Bofill in the Jardin Lineal in the middle of the Turia riverbed combines two celebrated Valentian ingredients – light and water. Especially pretty at night.

ALICANTE

A bustling port and resort town, Alicante is popular above all with Spanish holidaymakers. The airport may be one of the cheapest points of arrival for thousands of British tourists heading for the Costa Blanca, but the town itself is unmistakeably Spanish, and built on a grand scale. Here traditions can be enjoyed to the full. The Hogueras San Juan fiesta (20–24 June) celebrates the saint's day and the summer solstice with huge papier-mâché effigies set alight in the streets and fabulous firework displays fill the skies the last weekend in June. The evening *paseo* here is vibrant any time during the summer as everyone promenades along the Paseo Explanada, taking in the balmy Mediterranean air, and the town also has excellent *tapas* bars, many restaurants and a relentless nightlife.

The Castillo de Santa Bárbara careers high above the town, clinging to the craggy Mount Benacantil, Alicante's most dramatic sight. Below it the old historic quarter is rather small, a little shabby at the edges, and offers interesting explorations by day. Good beaches surge right up to the heart of the town and ferries to the Balearics and to small islands nearby operate from the harbour. If you want to combine a beach holiday with a distinctly Spanish scene, Alicante is a great place to head for.

GETTING YOUR BEARINGS

The Paseo Explanada de España is the key to getting your bearings in Alicante. A fine, broad walkway with an avenue of tall palms, it runs along the seafront beside a marina of yachts. It's the grandiose setting for the evening *paseo*; restaurants and café-bars provide terrace seating where you can watch the world parade by and an entertaining market keeps going till late in the evening. Towards the east end of the Paseo is the tourist office at Paseo de Explanada, 2; beyond this is Plaça

---

Benidorm

For all its reputation as hot, high-rise and hectic, the one thing the clichés about Benidorm omit is the town's fantastic beach. Six kilometres of spotless, silky-white sand rinsed clean every night ready for you to nestle your lotion-smeared shoulders in first thing the next morning. If all you want is a beach, sunshine and many, many discos, Benidorm is not a bad choice.

Benidorm actually does still have an old quarter – though you'd never guess from the mile upon mile of multistorey hotels that line the coast now. At its centre is a crumbling, whitewashed church topped with a glazed-tile roof that glints in the sunshine. It's set in a typical old-town scene of narrow stepped lanes, but expect them to be thronged with people.

Puerta del Mar, and just beyond this lies Playa del Postiguet, the city's beach.

Calle San Fernando and Calle de San Francisco (the latter pedestrianized) run immediately behind, and roughly parallel with, Paseo Explanada, offering some of the best of the city's bars and restaurants. Both head into the old quarter to the east, the heart of which is the Ayuntamiento and Plaça Santísima Faz right behind it.

Above Calle de San Francisco, the city extends on a grid pattern that quickly increases in scale: the farther away from the seafront you go, the bigger (and less attractive) the blocks of buildings become and the greater the distance between streets. Soon modern high-rise buildings take over. Plaça de San Cristobal is particularly impersonal, with characterless modern blocks all around; the only reasons to come here are the Vaya Vaya disco and the Chinatown restaurants above it. Cutting up through all this from roughly the centre of Paseo Explanada is Rambla de Méndez. It's a noisy, busy road as well as a bold, traditional, palm-lined *rambla*, and not at all the social focus the name suggests.

DON'T MISS

The Old Quarter

An hour or so spent strolling around the small old quarter offers a sense of the town's character beyond the cafés, clubs and beaches. It's best explored during the daytime; in the evening it can feel a little unwelcoming.

Start at the Plaça Ayuntamiento, a small colonnaded square with cafés to sit out at and a dignified 18th-century Baroque Ayuntamiento. The town hall is open on request (Monday– Friday 9.00–15.00), so call in and ask to see the elegant salons, the paintings and the chapel inside.

From here, follow Calle Jorge Juan and then take the steps off it up to Plaça Santa María, a shabby cobbled square, home to the quiet, dilapidated grandeur of Iglesia Santa María. An alarming crack runs through the church from top to bottom, but none the less it remains an attractive building: a joyous Baroque portal with tubular twisting columns and flamboyant statuary is flanked by two plain square belltowers. The rocky mass of Mount Benacantil and the castle overlooks the whole scene. The Museum of 20th-Century Art is also on this square: see below.

From here head down Calle Villavieja and then Calle Mayor to Plaça Santisima Faz, a pretty little square with tall palms, several restaurants and a good bodega. Continue straight along Calle Mayor (pedestrianized) and take the second right up Calle Muñoz to the Cathedral Church of San Nicolás de Bari. A severe façade is matched by a similarly cold, plain interior with a vast, vacant dome and silent walls. In the dour gloom shines a huge, gilt altarpiece, a vision lighting up the darkness. After a look inside, wander away from the front of the Cathedral down Calle San José until you hit the main road. Turn round and look at the Cathedral again for a good view of its distinctive azure glazed-tile roof glinting in the sunlight.

Paseo Explanada

The traditional *paseo* along this marine-side esplanade is a lively, colourful affair. Sit out at a café beneath the elegant tall palms in the early evening and soak up the scene; as light falls, wander beneath a canopy of lights and exotic palm fronds and explore the late-night market stalls; barter for anything from a snakeskin bumbag to a clockwork ostrich. Sample the scented ice creams and *gofres* – waffles covered in hot, gooey, melted chocolate, Grand Marnier or Cointreau.

Castillo de Santa Bárbara
(Take the lift from beside Playa del Postiguet, or drive up. Open October–March 9.00–20.00, April–September 10.00–20.00.) Entrance 200 pesetas.
Visit this castle for excellent views over Alicante. The first fort here was built by the Carthaginians in 3 BC; most of the complex that stands today dates from the 16th century. It includes battlements and embrasures, high parapeted walls and dungeons, stores and ovens, magazines and soldiers' quarters. The castle museum holds an intriguing collection of puppets and floats rescued from the flames of Alicante's annual fiestas.

La Asegurada: Museum of Contemporary Art
(Free. Open October–April Tuesday–Saturday 10.00–13.00 and 17.00–20.00, Sunday 10.00–13.00; May–September Tuesday–Saturday 10.30–13.30 and 18.00–21.00, Sunday 10.30–13.30.)
This extremely likeable gallery displays work by an impressive list of art names, on the whole represented in prints rather than paintings: Robert Rauschenberg, Dalí, Francis Bacon, Max Ernst, Giacometti, Braque, Chagall, Jean Arp, Picasso, Victor Pasmore, Jim Dine, Christo, Claes Oldenburg.

BEACHES

Playa del Postiguet
Alicante is an important Mediterranean resort and of course there's a big beach here. It's long, sandy, very busy and backed by high-rise hotels. A stone's throw from the town centre, there are plenty of places to buy as much seaside paraphernalia as anyone could desire. Great fun despite the crowds.

Playa San Juan
(This beach is 8 kilometres away; take a bus C1 from Plaça Puerta del Mar, or, if you are driving, take the coast road heading north.)
The sand here is not of such fine golden quality as that at Alicante and the busy resort is one of ugly hotels, but the

broader setting goes some way to make up for this: real waves, white foam, and panoramic views of the mountains that stretch around the bay, dwarfing the high-rise developments along the shoreline. It also has some of the best of Alicante's nightlife, and is very definitely the place to head for if you want to dance through till morning (see Nightlife below).

Isla Tabarca

(Accessible by boat from the port, more or less in front of the tourist office.)

The water here is crystal clear, perfect for swimming and snorkelling; Tabarca Island is protected as a natural aquatic reserve. Sample the shellfish and rice dishes of the region at one of the island's restaurants or cafés. All in all, a visit to Tabarca makes a very pleasant day trip.

ALSO WORTH SEEING . . .

Archaeological Museum

(Open Monday–Friday 9.00–13.30.)

Collection of Stone Age, Carthaginian and Roman finds from around the region – of specialist interest.

Boat Trips

Take a trip in a glass-bottomed boat to examine the fabulous marine life off this coast.

OUT OF TOWN . . .

Elche (Elx)

(21 km south of Alicante. Elche tourist office Tel: (96) 545 2747.)

The palm groves of Elx are unsurpassed in Europe, and a visit to this extraordinary village makes for a very exotic day trip from Alicante. Palm trees have grown here for over 2,000 years: planted by the Carthaginians, these groves were later developed by the Romans and then, most important of all, the Moors. The irrigation system introduced by Abderraman III in the 10th century remains highly efficient today – a living example of the level of agricultural sophistication that

Spain lost when the Moors were driven from the country. Palm fronds for Palm Sunday celebrations all over Spain are produced here, and there are pomegranate and orange trees and a huge cactus collection. **Alcázar de la Señoría,** an Arab fort, stands in the village centre, and nearby in the Plaza Raval the **Museu d'Art Contemporani** boasts works by Picasso, Miró, Braque and Juan Gris. There are a couple of archaeological museums, too; the most famous find in the area is **La Dama de Elche** Its origins are a mystery but this imperious figure wearing an elaborate headress certainly has presence. It is kept in the Prado in Madrid; only a replica can be seen here.

Not surprisingly, Elche has impressive Palm Sunday cel-ebrations, but the real highlight of the village's calendar is the Feast of the Assumption, 15 August. The fiesta starts at the beginning of the month, and its pageantry includes some of the best Moorish-Christian mock battles in Spain. The festivities come to a climax on the evenings of the 14th and 15th when the two-part medieval Elche mystery plays are performed in the Basilica of Santa María.

ALICANTE FACTFILE

Tourist Office Paseo Explanada de España, 2. Tel: 520 00 00. Open Monday–Saturday 10.00–14.00 and 16.00–20.00, Sunday 10.00–14.00.

Train Station RENFE (intercity services) Tel: 522 68 40. FGV (local network) Tel: 526 27 31.

Airport El Altet Airport Tel: 528 50 11. Iberia Airlines Tel: 520 60 00.

Bus Station Tel: 522 07 00.

Ferries Trasmediterránea for sailings to international destinations and Mediterranean islands. Tel: 520 60 11.

Taxis Tel: 510 16 11 and 525 25 11.

Moped Hire Turismoto, Tel: 516 05 27.

Telephone code: 96.

WHERE TO STAY

Cheap to Moderate

Habitaciones Mexico Calle Primo de Rivera, 10 (off the top of Rambla M. Núñez) Tel: 520 93 07.

Ventura HS** San Fernando 10–5, Tel: 520 83 37.

El Alamo HR* Calle San Fernando, 56, Tel: 521 83 55.

La Reforma HR** Reyes Católicos, 7, Tel: 522 21 47.

Goya H** Maestro Bretón, 19, Tel: 514 16 59.

Smarter Options

Hotel Palas H*** Cervantes, 5 – Plaza de Mar, 2, Tel: 520 93 10.

Palas HR*** Plaza del Ayuntamiento, 6, Tel: 520 66 90.

WHERE TO EAT

Being a decidedly Spanish resort town, Alicante has some very good tapas bars, and it can be more fun going from one to the next sampling a variety of dishes rather than stopping in one restaurant. Some of the tapas bars have a comedor to the rear, so when you find one you particularly like you can settle down for a full meal. Alternatively, if you want to relax and eat in peace there are plenty of restaurants to choose from.

Calle San Francisco is one of the best streets to look for typical Spanish menus at competitive prices. There are plenty of restaurants, plenty of people, and as the street is pedestrianised it's a particularly pleasant option to sit outside. **Calle Mayor** and **Calle de San Fernando** are similarly popular; food is generally served up until around midnight. The wonderful Explanada de España is the most stylish place to sit out, and you can expect to pay a little more for the atmosphere.

Bodega Las Garrafas, Calle Mayor and Placa Santissima Faz. Entertaining little bar with a great atmosphere serving a small range of delicious seafood *tapas*. The ceiling is hung with old shoes, bundles of keys and all sorts of dried fish – from piranah to crawfish – which the barman uses as props to demonstrate to visitors the ingredients of his *tapas*.

Cerveceria Rincón Huertano, Calle Bailén. Very busy, very popular tapas bar and restaurant serving good traditional food in a great atmosphere.

El Refugio, Canónigo Cilleros. This is a really pretty place to sit out in the heart of the old town, tucked down an alleyway beneath the arches of the Ayuntiamiento. Good seafood menu, reasonably priced.

Venta del Cordero Calle Jorge Juan. Popular, down-to-earth restaurant serving charcoal-grilled *cordero* (lamb) and *cordornices* (quails).

O'Pote Galego Plaça Santissima Faz, 6. Tel: 520 80 84. Prettily located restaurant in the old part of town serving Galician dishes.

Quo Venit, Plaça Santissima Faz, 3. Tel: 521 66 60. Situated in a quiet square with tall palms, this seafood restaurant has one of the prettiest terraces to sit out at in the old town. Expensive.

Rincón Gallego, Calle del Portico de Ansaldo (off Calle Rafael Altimira). Good restaurant serving Galician food; order anything from quick *tapas* to a full meal. If you are not going to make it to north-west Spain, this is a good place to savour the seafoods of the region; *empanada* (a tasty fish pie), and octopus are specialities.

La Taberna Restaurante, Calle Alberola Romero. Excellent seafood *tapas* and *raciones*.

Boutique del Jamón, Paseo Explanada (near the touriest office). Very good *tapas* and combined menus, speciality *jamón serrano*.

Mesón Labradores, Calle Labradores. Marble-topped tables, old crockery around the walls and tarnished copper pans; this worthy *tapas* bar has the atmosphere of a dingy, animated junk-shop. It's very busy and great fun.

BARS AND NIGHTLIFE

Calle de San Fernando, Calle Canalejas and around
Extremely popular for drinking and dancing, a late-teens/early twenties crowd overflows onto the pavements till around midnight; after that everybody heads for the beach (see below).

La Bocateria Calle de los Limones. Lively hole-in-the-wall bar that spills out into the street.

Selvas, Plaza Doctor Balmis. A Rousseau jungle of palms and creepers for crazed dancing.

470, Calle Canalejas. Loud disco-pub for sweaty dancing. Alternatively try the nameless disco on the corner of Calle de Valdés and Calle Rafael Terol for thumping indies sounds.

Litros, Calle Antonio Galdo Chapuli. Sweaty rock bar.

Donana, Calle de San Fernando, 57. Lively local bar; at fiesta time overbody dances flamenco here – great atmosphere.

Cha-Cha, Calle Canalejas. Lively bar for drinking and dancing to ska, rock, reggae. Open till 5.00 at weekends, 10.30 other days.

Plátano, Calle San Fernando, 58. *Plátano* is Spanish for banana. Really lively little local bar with plenty of dancing to rap, soul, 50's R&B

and lots of Spanish pop music. They keep serving as long as there's a crowd.

Asia, Paseo Explanada. A pale grey tiled, modern café-bar with a restrained, stylish atmosphere; sit out and view the *paseo* and the late-night market in this exotic setting of tall palms and soft sea breezes. The only bar in this area attracting a laid-back, slightly older crowd.

Around the Cathedral

Immediately around the Cathedral and in Calle San José and Calle Labradores you will find some of Alicante's most pretentious bars; you will also find some of the best, laid-back places to drink and sometimes dance. The whole area is popular with an older crowd – mid-twenties to early thirties.

Jamboree, Calle San José, 10. Late-night jazz-blues bar, often has live bands.

Café Epoca Calle San José. Muted, relaxed cafe with a vaguely *fin de siècle* feel. A pleasant choice for those in reflective mood wanting to drink Irish coffees, liqueurs, capuchinnos, fresh fruit juices or quiet beers.

Vanguard, Calle San José. Uncompromisingly modern bar for stylish soul and funk.

Status, Directly opposite the cathedral. Trendy mauve neon for would-be chic yuppie drinking. The name says it all.

La Naya, Calle Labradores (Cathedral end). Laid-back bar with decorative abstract paintings and swinging Spanish jazz. Great atmosphere – and you can hear yourself speak. Sit out on the pavement or lounge on comfy benches. Open till 3.00 or 4.00, not so late Sundays.

Labradores No. 11, Disco bar, popular drinking and dancing venue on Fridays and Saturdays. Open till 3.00 or 4.00.

Es Quinalo, at the very top of Calle Labradores. Pleasantly relaxed, laid-back watering-hole.

Discos: Playa San Juan

(5 miles from Alicante)

Alicante's night-creatures head out to the discos of San Juan where things only really get started at around 00.30-1.00. The last bus (number C 1 bus from Pl. Puerta del Mar) leaves Alicante at 22.30; if you want to return by the first bus in the morning, it leaves San Juan at 6.30. During high season trains shuttle back and forth throughout the night making things a lot easier; check with the tourist office for details. There are three major discos here:

Voy Voy and **Caligula** are both on the seafront, just beyond Calle Irlanda.

Copity is found away from the beach off Avda de la Condomina – take a taxi or follow the crowds.

They all have dance floors around a pool, so you dance out in the night air, and entrance is free.

Food

Locally produced rice forms the staple of many of the Costa Blanca's most popular meals – a legacy of the Moors who did so much to shape the land and the culture of the region. *Paella alicantina*, the town's variation of Spain's most famous dish, includes rabbit, mussels, red peppers and shrimp; *arroz a banda* is similarly popular – boiled saffron rice served with stewed angler fish and shellfish. Sweets are very important too – another leftover from the Moors. Try *turrón*, a very sweet nougat of honey and almonds, and *peladillas*, sugar-coated almonds.

PLUS
Flea Market

(Sunday Morning, Plaza Ayuntamiento)
Mounds of old clock faces, like the debris of a Dali workshop, books, kitsch Hollywood magazines from the 30s and 40s, old weight, scales, redundant technology from ancient gramophones to Bacolite radiograms; you name it, it's here.

Turrónes Try the Turrónes nougat they make here – painfully sweet, made of almonds and honey. Buy it at **Turrónes 1880** at Calle Mayor, 9.

THE BALEARIC ISLANDS
Baleares

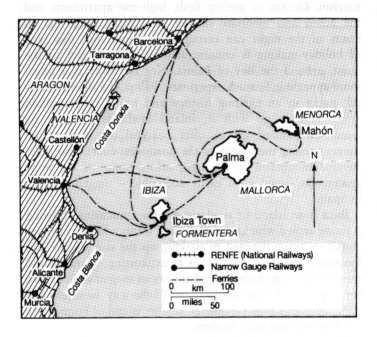

Mediterranean islands have an atmosphere all their own. While tourism can do its worst, remote and difficult terrain deters the progress of heavy industry and the islands retain an old, rural character. Intensely colourful plants glow vividly, strong scents fill the air and sun-blasted landscapes find relief in a limpid, blue sea glinting round rocky headlands, seeping into sandy bays. Bathed in a lambent evening light, soft ocean winds blow away the day's noise, fumes and congestion so that each morning delivers a new dose of rare natural beauty.

The Balearics, spattered over 95 km off Spain's south coast, all share these magical qualities, so it is not surprising that the four inhabited islands – Mallorca, Menorca Formentera and Ibiza – are among Spain's most popular holiday destinations. Their Mediterranean setting groups them together, yet each has such a distinct character that there is no reason to get them confused.

Mallorca defies its image of all that is worst in package tourism. Oceans of peeling flesh, high-rise apartments and the acned and inebriate singing the "Birdy Song" at all hours of the night can certainly be found, but this type of holiday-making is concentrated in a small part of the coast, around the Bay of Palma. Not far away is a much more appealing, Spanish experience. Palma, the island's capital, packs in an exciting history and has a cosmopolitan atmosphere to go with it; inland lowlands of quiet fig trees and almond groves offer peaceful day trips. High sierras surging the length of the northwest coast, and pine-covered mountains to the east, afford some of the most spectacular – and most easily accessible – rugged walking in Spain.

Ibiza is an island of similarly diverse attractions, drawing a young crowd who know what they want: a highly fashion-conscious scene devoted to soaking up the sun all day and frenzied partying all night. It can be exhausting; if you want to rest *before* you go home, the island has an ancient walled town for sequestered meanderings, out-of-the-way beaches, and regular ferries to the far quieter, smaller island of **Formentera** – a favourite for nude bathers.

Menorca has a distinctly conservative atmosphere compared to Mallorca, Ibiza and Formentera. Famous for its beaches – from minuscule coves to broad sweeps of sand – it is perfect if you just want to enjoy the sun and the sea in unruffled tranquillity.

Catalan is the language of the Balearic islands and you will find signposts in either Catalan or Castilian or both.

PALMA DE MALLORCA

Palma, Mallorca's largest town, has at its core a rich history embedded in fine ancient mansions and museums. Of course mass tourism plays a major role in the local economy, but despite the 3 million visitors who pass through its airport every year, Palma carries on with a traditional cultural life little disturbed by the smell of fast tans and the flow of cheap lager. The town remains very Spanish; somehow the annual onslaught seems to be a source of strength rather than a threat to cultural identity. An impressively progressive mood holds sway: small, modern art galleries thrive and among the great number of restaurants many display a refreshing independence and modernity of style. Everywhere a strong cultural identity is deeply rooted in a cosmopolitan Catalan history. All in all, there is a feeling that Palmans know who they are: proudly Spanish and determinedly modern.

GETTING YOUR BEARINGS

The Almudaina Palace and the cathedral, Palma's key historic sites, command a prime position high on a hill overlooking the waterfront. Below them lies the **Parc de la Mar**, the best spot from which to view this monumental part of town. The waterfront itself is not a beach, but a dull, modern seawall.

History

The Romans founded Palma in 1 BC, but little remains of their culture. The Moors, who inhabited Mallorca during the 10th–13th centuries, were the first people to make any lasting impression. They introduced the fruit trees and the almond groves that remain an important part of the local economy today. The Arab baths in Palma date from this period, too.

As on the mainland, the struggle for power on Mallorca was between the Moors and the Christians. In 1229 James I of Aragon took Mallorca in an extremely bloody battle, ensuring a lasting Spanish identity on the island. The communities that subsequently settled here were Catalan (the language remains) and included a significant Jewish sector. Trade flourished and Palma became a rich, cosmopolitan city, thriving on influences from way beyond the Spanish mainland. A wealth of artwork was commissioned here and 14th-century paintings show the influence of Sienese artists; the city adopted a Genoese banking system, and in architecture the superbly proportioned Italian styles became fashionable. The prosperity of merchants is most readily seen in their fine town mansions.

It was really only in the 16th century, when South America became the source of Spanish fortunes, that this period of prosperity began to wane. Mediterranean trading decreased as the Spanish economy was swamped by the great cargoes of precious metals the conquistadors brought back from the New World.

Streets from behind the cathedral head inland, via Palma's most interesting shopping area, towards the Plaza Mayor and its pavement cafés and street entertainers. Both the historic monuments and the plaza attract day-trippers, but there is more to the town that is just as accessible.

The Passeig del Born, with its promenade, is the town's central artery, running through a tunnel of greenery from the Plaça de la Reina, near the waterfront, up to the Plaça Rei Joan Carles I, where it forks into two large avenues. The arcaded Avenida Rey Jaime III is Palma's main commercial street and also home to the tourist office; Carrer de la Unió curls around below the high part of town, passing steps up to the Plaza Mayor.

To the west of Passeig del Born lies Palma's other old quarter – less spectacular, but still worth exploring. Here Carrer

Apuntadores is the gastronomic centre of town, a narrow lane crammed with busy, low-priced restaurants. Other lanes this side of Paseo del Born wind between quiet 18th-century town mansions of bold and grand proportions, whose plain, dusty exteriors conceal charming inner courtyards; try to catch a glimpse through any massive doorway left ajar.

DON'T MISS ...

La Sao, the Cathedral
(Open Monday–Saturday 8.15–9.30 and 18.30–19.30pm, Sunday and holidays 8.30–13.30 and 19.00–20.00.)

Palma Cathedral dominates the waterfront. It is a powerful Gothic structure dramatically lodged above the bay, with tremendous flying buttresses and decorative pinnacles. The Renaissance-style west doorway is quite at odds with the exterior and dates the completion of this medieval cathedral around 1601.

Way above any surrounding buildings, its height frees the cathedral from dull, urban shadows and inside is a riot of primary colours as strong sunlight bounces through modern stained-glass windows. The nave appears particularly vast and uplifting since there is no choir in the middle of it, as there is in most Spanish cathedrals, to obscure the sense of space.

The soaring columns seem impossibly spindly, and only the thought of the massive buttresses flanking the outside walls reassures you that the whole building is physically possible. Above the altar, the weird wrought-iron canopy is the work of Gaudí.

Almudaina Palace

(Entrance 350 pesetas, free on Wednesdays if you carry an EC passport. Open Monday–Friday 10.00–18.20, Saturday 10.00–13.20.)

Most impressive viewed from the Parc de la Mar below, the Almudaina Palace was built as an Islamic fort. The Mallorcan royal families of the 14th and 15th centuries transformed it into the palace we see today by adding elegant arches and a beautiful courtyard. Solid, lofty apartments are hung with 16th- and 17th-century Flemish tapestries and still-life paintings. The tour is led by an English-speaking guide.

Basílica de San Francisco

(Plaça Sat Francesc. Open Monday–Saturday 9.30–3.00 and 15.30–19.00.)

This basilica is stunning. The façade is of a pale salmon-coloured stone that seems to glow in the sunshine. Clearly influenced by the plateresque, its plain, smooth masonry is decorated by one central rose window, a whirl of intensity, delicately carved with the intricacy of lace. The portal below it is an effusion of baroque swirls and foliage.

Entrance to the basilica is via the adjacent building and takes you through cloisters of slender Gothic arches of Moorish influence. Inside the church, brilliant stained glass emphasizes the gracefulness of the Gothic structure, which has as a focal point a lavish gilt 18-century altarpiece.

Palau Solleric

(Calle Sant Gaietà, 10. Open Tuesday–Saturday 11.00–13.30 and 17.00–20.30.)

This modern art gallery is housed in an 18th-century mansion. Faint traces of its original decoration cover the façade overlooking the Passeig del Born, but it is the interior that really merits attention. Sculpted pillars of gently mottled marble support graceful Italianate arches around and above a cobbled courtyard. Exquisite proportions make this the most captivating of Palma's old mansions.

Castillo de Bellver
(Open 8.00–20.00; to 18.00 in winter).
Worth seeing not only for the municipal museum and the castle's perfectly circular 14th-century keep, but also for the postcard-perfect views across the bay.

ALSO WORTH SEEING . . .

Museo Diocesanó
(Near Almudaina Palace. Entrance 200 pesetas. Open Monday–Friday 10.00–20.00, Saturday 10.00am–19.00; these times are variable.)
This museum is a crammed and jumbled mixture of paintings, sculptures and other ecclesiastical treasures. Particularly fine is the 14th-century altarpiece by the Master of the Bishop of Galiana, and the vivid portrayals of purgatory, heaven and hell on 16th-century panels.

Museo de Mallorca
(Near Almudaina Palace. Entrance 200 pesetas. Open Monday–Saturday 10.00–14.00 and 16.00–19.00, Sunday and holidays 10.00–14.00.)
Along with archaelogical exhibits and a well-preserved Mudéjar ceiling, this museum has a collection of exceptionally fine religious paintings. Particularly worth catching is a 14th-century "Virgin and Child" by Maestro de Alaró, a triptych of "La Anunciacion y los Stos Juanes" and a taut and graphic portrayal of St George skewering a dragon by Franceschi Comes, a local artist.

Baños Árabes (Arab baths)
(Calle Serra, 7, near Almudaina Palace. Entrance 100 pesetas. Open 10.00–19.00 daily.)
The Arab baths are found in what in the 10th century was part of the old Majurka Medina. The Moors imitated the Romans in their construction and use of baths: bathhouses were as

much a place to meet as to enjoy the steam rooms and cold pools. The Palma Arab baths are quite small, grouped around a pretty garden. Through an Islamic horseshoe arch is a square room with a small brick dome – probably a caldarium, where the double-layered floor allowed hot air to circulate from the fireplace, so heating the room.

Plaça Mayor

The picturesque Plaza Mayor has rows of bold colonnading below burnt-peach walls, and terrace cafés cover the grey and pink marble pavings. It is a real magnet for tourists and comes alive during the summer with buskers, portrait artists and market stalls selling jewellery, clothes and souvenirs. Round about are the liveliest of Palma's shopping streets – particularly Calle Jaume II and Calle Sindicat.

The Lonja

The Lonja was the old commercial exchange, an elegant Spanish Gothic building built in the 15th century. Exhibitions are occasionally held here, offering a look inside.

Circulo de Bellas Artes

(Calle de la Unio, 3.)
Modern art gallery, worth seeing as much for the courtyard with its elegant palms as for the contemporary exhibitions. Mallorca has a great number of small, modern galleries; pick up a list from the tourist office for further information.

OUT OF TOWN . . .

Beaches

Mallorca is blessed with fabulous weather, so a trip to the beach must be high on anybody's agenda. Palma's beaches are some way from the centre. The extremely crowded beach of the Terreno suburb 2.5 km west of town can be visited on a trip to the Castillo de Bellver (see above); beyond this, Palma Bay reaches some of its worst commercial excesses in the notorious Magalluf and Palma Nova resorts.

To the east of town lie beaches popular with local Mallorcans – **Ca'n Pastilla** and **El Arenal** (10 km and 14 km away)

Art Nouveau

The part of town near Plaza Mayor is largely 19th century and a couple of fabulous Art Nouveau buildings are worth looking out for. **Joyeria José Miro**, Calle de Colo, is a weird, enamel-pocked building, clearly influenced by Anton Gaudí. Farther down, **Yoga Boutique** on Plaça del Marques del Palmer is a sugary fantasy piece with ribbon-twist wrought-iron balconies and decorated walls that rise to a frothy crest of ceramic floral collage. Similarly ornate but following more regular lines is the metal-framed building alongside it, **La Guila**, in 1991 undergoing restoration. There are yet more fanciful turn-of-the-century creations on and around the Plaça de Cort, while real enthusiasts should look out for less colourful examples of the era at Plaça del Mercat, 13 and 14.

---

are both popular, crowded and easily accessible by bus from Palma. Hire a car or moped and you can head farther afield for quiet, secluded shores.

Palma–Sóller Railway

A trip on the narrow-gauge Palma-Sóller train line makes a good day out, taking you through a varied countryside of quiet valleys filled with orange trees and almond groves and beneath rugged mountains, dry in the summer heat. An old tram connects the end of the line with the picturesque town of Sóller.

Valldemossa Cartuja

(Tel: 61 21 48. Open Monday–Saturday 9.30–13.00 and 15.00–18.30.)

The Valldemossa Cartuja monastery was originally a medieval palace, but the building was subsequently bequeathed to the Carthusians. In the 19th century it fell into private hands and became a popular retreat, and it is for the notoriety of its guests that it remains famous. Frédéric Chopin and the novelist George Sand spent the winter of 1838 together here; the great composer's manuscripts and his piano – which in fact arrived only three weeks before the pair left for Paris – are still here. There is also a small museum and an 18th-century pharmacy worth visiting.

PALMA DE MALLORCA FACTFILE

Tourist Office, Avenida Rey Jaime III, Tel: 71 22 16. Open Monday—
Friday 9.00–14.30 and 15.00–20.00. Saturday 10.00–13.30.
Airport Tel: 26 46 24 and 26 46 66. Iberia airline Tel: 26 26 00.
Train Station, Plaza España. Tel: 75 20 51.
Bus Station, Plaza España. Tel: 75 22 24.
Car Hire Bahia, Paseo Maritimo, 15. Tel: 23 30 07.
Ferries Trasmediterranea, Muelle Viejo, 5. Tel: 72 67 40.

WHERE TO STAY

Cheap to Moderate

Pons HsR*, General Barceló, 8. Tel: 72 26 58.
Palma HsR*, General Barceló, 8 II. Tel: 22 44 17.
Goya HsR*, Estanco, 7. Tel 72 69 86.
Florida HS*, Avenida Antonio Maura, 12. Tel: 21 59 13.
Esmeralda HS*, Ricardo Ankerman, 10. Tel: 46 27 06.
Borne HS*, Calle San Jaime, 3. Tel: 71 29 42.

Smarter Options

Sol Jaime III H***, Paseo Mallorca, 14 B. Tel: 72 59 43.
Saratoga H***, Paseo de Mallorca, 6. Tel: 72 72 40.
Palladium HR***, Paseo de Mallorca, 40. Tel: 71 39 45.
Almudaina HR***, Avenida Rey Jaime III, 9. Tel: 72 73 40.

WHERE TO EAT

The cheapest tourist menus are to be found in the restaurants on
Avenida Antonio Maura, where you can sit out at a pavement table
and look across to views of the Almudaina palace and the cathedral.
Try **Restaurante Moby Dick** or Restaurant **Almudaina** here for cheap
menú del días.

Calle Apuntadores and Around

Entrecote, Calle Apuntadores, 3. Tel: 72 59 05. Possibly the pokiest, and
definitely the daintiest, steakhouse in Spain. The owners are charming,
the food delightful, and it is very cheap.
La Zamorana, Calle Apuntadores. Plain Spanish food in cheerily
down-market cavernous restaurant. The gazpacho here is delicious.
Vecchio Giovanni, Calle de San Jaun, 4/6. Intimate, colourful restaurant
serving pizza, pasta and Mallorcan cuisine. Reasonably priced and very
popular.

Bon Lloc, Calle San Felió, 7. Tel: 71 12 63. Wholesome vegetarian restaurant with erratic opening hours.

La Lenteja, Calle San Felió, 7. Tel 71 20 38. Possibly the classiest place to eat in Palma; the restaurant is in an old stone barrel-vaulted room, with palatable classical music and crisp table linen. Castilian cuisine – plus exquisite shellfish.

Petit Rebost, Plaça Llotja de Mar. Tel: 71 02 14. Intimate restaurant serving imaginative menu: starters of herring mousse with beetroot sauce, for example, followed by trout with saffron sauce, or filet of pork with pinenuts, raisins and Rocquefort. Reasonably priced.

Restaurant Pazza, Plaça de Llotja de Mar. Extremely good pizzas in a lovely setting. Sit out beneath palm trees and admire the golden, Gothic Lonja across the square.

Caballito de Mar, Paseo Sagrera, 5. Tel: 72 10 74. Next to Pazza. Again the setting is excellent. This is a superior seafood restaurant, offering grilled shellfish, red bream, sea bass, marmite of lobster. Moderate to expensive.

Calle de la Concepción

Off Avenida Rey Jaime III.

Tierra Aranda, Calle de la Concepción, 4. Tel: 71 42 56. Smart restaurant in beautiful Mallorcan town mansion specializing in Castilian dishes.

Bodega Santurce, Calle de la Concepción, 34. Tel: 71 08 01. Traditional bodega restaurant full of well-seasoned barrels; serves Basque dishes.

O'Arco, Calle de la Concepción. Pleasant mid-range restaurant serving Galician food – lots of squid, octopus and shellfish.

Around Town

Tastevins, Plaça Merçat, 1. Fashionable bistro-style restaurant for pan-European chic eats.

Svarta Pannan, Calle Brondo. Off the top of Passeig del Born. Plaid seats, beamed ceilings, paintings on the walls and bags of atmosphere. This is a cosy little Swedish restaurant where you can sample delights from chillier climes: herrings in sour cream, bacon, pickles, red cabbage.

Raixa, Calle Zavellá, 8. Tel: 71 17 11. Whether you are vegetarian or not, this is one of the most endearing small restaurants in Palma. Vegetarian dishes both homely and adventurous are served in a charming atmosphere. It is also extremely good value. Open Monday 13.00–16.00 and on Friday evenings during June and July.

El Pinon, Calle Cifre, 1. Tel: 72 60 34. Excellent seafood restaurant and *tapas* bar serving just about everything you could want from the briny.

Ca'n Miguelet, Galería Jaime III, 4. Tel: 72 12 09. Off the avenue of the same name. Fairly smart and reasonably priced traditional bar and restaurant. Walls are lined with wine racks, hams swing from the ceiling and the restaurant serves traditional Mallorcan dishes, the bar excellent seafood *tapas*.

CAFÉS

La Croqueta, Calle San Felió, 6. Tiny, friendly, cheap and trendy café-bar with minimalist *tapas* menu. Sit out on the pavement listening to free-form jazz as you sip your morning coffee.
Café Lírico, Avenida Antonio Maura. Wonderfully battered, old-style Spanish café-bar with marble-topped tables and shelves of lethal liqueurs; popular with locals.
El Rey, Avenida Rey Jaime III. A regular café, good for breakfasts out under the arcading.

BARS AND NIGHTLIFE

Compared to the number of restaurants in Palma, there is a surprising shortage of bars.
Abaco, Calle San Jaun, 1,
(off Calle Apuntadores). An absolute must. Over-the-top cocktail bar housed in the courtyard of an ancient town mansion. The interior is an explosion of fruit and flowers accompanied by soul-wrenching classical music, the garden quiet and candle-lit. Expensive.
Harry's Palma Bar, Calle C'an Granada (off Plaça Rei Joan Carles I). Tel: 71 95 05.
Smart, fun cocktail bar playing raunchy 1940s jazz till around 1.00.
Café La Font, Calle de L'Aigua. (End of Calle Concepción.) Lively, trendy young bar that keeps going till 2.00.
C'an Angel, Calle San Jaime Down-to-earth, lively little cellar bar.
Bodega Bellver, Calle Cane Serinyer. Friendly bar full of well-seasoned barrels of cognac, vermouth, etc. Simple wooden tables and stools. You can sample the local wine, and this is also a handy place for early-evening snacks – try their delicious hot salami and tomato sandwiches.

Plaza Gomilla

Two km from the centre of town; buses run from Avenida Antonio Maura. This is the area to head for if you want to disco. Plaza Gomilla and Avenida Joan Miró are full of bars and clubs that serve holiday-makers from adjacent high-rise hotels. Things get going around 23.00 and keep going all night in high season; till around 2.00 at other times.
Thoroughly mainstream and unpretentious, you can have a lot of fun there. While the flashier discos are pretty pricey, bars with dance floors have no cover charge. As ever in Spain, the beauty is they are all close together; move from one to the next until you find what you want.
Tito's, Plaza Gomilla. This is the number-one mainstream disco in Palma – lots of mirrors and flashing lights. Cover charge.

La Bicoca, opposite Tito's. A bar with dance floor and thumping, grinding disco music. Open from 22.30 till everybody goes home; high season till 6.00. Free.

Café Carousel, Avenida Joan Miró, 53. Lively bar with a good atmosphere.

El Jardin, Avenida Joan Miró, 37. There are plenty of cheap eateries along this stretch, but this is the place if you want to sit out and eat pizzas in a grandiose, palm-filled garden. Open till 2.00 in season.

Dylan Avenida Joan Miró, 52. Relaxed bar for slowly, inevitably ageing devotees of Dylan, the Doors (first time round), Van Morrison, the Stones. Open till 4.00.

Big Bamboo, Avenida Joan Miró, heading towards town from Plaza Gomilla. Wonderful, larger-than-life underground world of pantomime palms and gushing streams, big bamboo chairs and exotic cocktails. If you've packed a Hawaiian shirt, wear it. Till 3.00.

PLUS

The most intriguing shopping streets in Palma run off the Plaza Mayor: Calle Colón, Calle Sindicat and the narrow, pedestrianized Calle Jaime II seem to have been designed for inspired dawdling. Here you can find whole windows full of fans, ancient brolly shops, flashy new boutiques and fabulous patisseries.

- The **Majolica ware** for which the island is famous is no longer as popular as it used to be. Nonetheless, if you want to take some home, it is available at Artesanias, Calle Unio, 45.

- Everything you could possibly want made of **wood** is at La Casa del Olivo, Calle Baratillo.

- **Ensaimadas** are light, sugar-dusted cakes, typically eaten for breakfast. They look rather like deflated buns and come in a range of sizes, from CD to bicycle wheel. Buy them at La Flor de Palma, Calle Jaume II, 27, or at Dalmau. Paseo Mallorca, 34. Also worth sampling are the *empanadas*, flans and pastries here; superb quality and inexpensive.

IBIZA TOWN

Ibiza (Elvissa) is an island of intense physical beauty. People come here for its notoriously laid-back atmosphere and to indulge in sensual pleasures. Fabulous beaches provide bathing in crystal-blue waters, nude or otherwise; inland are rugged mountains and gentle lowlands filled with orange and almond groves. Ibiza town clusters around massive walls on a great plug of rock commanding views over ocean and countryside, and everywhere is alive with the drenching heat. As evening falls, a soft, glowing light saturates the exotic Mediterranean landscape and brilliant flowers release their heady scents on to the balmy breeze. It is an atmosphere to relish in peace in Ibiza's Dalt Vila (high town) and forms the background to chic partying in the town's harbourside madness.

Liberal attitudes are a legacy of the hippie colonies that were sprinkled around the island during the 1960s, easily integrated with the relaxed and friendly ways of the islanders. Ibiza town is still very much at the heart of things. The children of the sixties came to enjoy a harmonious lifestyle and spawned, among other things, a free and fluid creativity still very much in evidence in the individuality and style of cafés, bars and restaurants, in artwork and boutiques.

Fashion is immensely important here and you can expect to find weirdly exotic clothes designed to enhance the human form: review the contents of your suitcase before booking in. The crowd is cosmopolitan and Ibiza is also where a lot of gay men and, less visibly, gay women choose to holiday.

Nothing so typifies the atmosphere here as the early-evening *paseo* around the Sa Peña area. It is a burlesque circus of activity: wildly dressed performance artists swoop on rollerskates, whooping and screeching like carnival beasts to advertise Ibiza's discos; human pyramids and madmen on stilts dance to draw the crowds. Discos are an essential part of Ibiza life. Each tries to be more outrageous than the next and yet, happily, they are not exclusive. This is the real strength of the place: even if you are not into wearing rabbit-trimmed skipants, have fewer than six studs in your ear, and do not have "lust" tattooed across your breast, you are still likely to have a really good time.

GETTING YOUR BEARINGS

The Avenida de España is a broad, straight, main road that leads into Ibiza town from the airport. It feeds directly into Paseo Vara de Rey, where you will find the tourist office. Most of the modern town lies parallel to these streets in a neat grid plan of low-rise apartments; it is all very small and easily manageable.

Dalt Vila is the oldest part of Ibiza, a walled hilltop citadel that has retained much of its old character. A walk round the walls affords excellent views of both the surrounding countryside and the ocean, while the narrow lanes within them remain very pretty. It is possible to drive up into the main streets of the Dalt Vila but steep, narrow lanes make the more interesting quarters extremely difficult for cars. There is a shortage of turning and parking space even in Dalt Vila's main squares; it makes sense to leave your car down below.

Immediately below the Dalt Vila, between its ancient walls and the new town network, is the old fishing quarter known as **Sa Peña**, a warren of dilapidated whitewashed houses long given over to Ibiza's weird and wild shock-me nightlife.

DON'T MISS ...

Dalt Vila

The cathedral-topped Dalt Vila forms the core of old Ibiza. Enter from the Plaça de la Constitución through a grand gateway flanked by headless Roman statues. Polished, cobbled stones take you up to the Plaça Mercat and the Plaça de Vila, a main street that cuts its way through the lower part of the Dalt Vila revealing a seam of restaurants and café-bars. Commercial tourist activity is largely confined to this strip, leaving the rest of the old town charmingly free for picturesque ramblings.

A walk around the battlements is a must if you want to appreciate the full effect of Ibiza's Mediterranean setting. The views are superb and you can see yachts and speedboats beetling about on the deep-blue water, surrounding hills cloaked in olive trees and almond groves, and immediately below is the bustling port. The air is full of the scent of frangipani blossom, honeysuckle and pine; lizards skittle from under shrubs and across walls; and everything reminds you that there is an exotic landscape worth further exploration inland.

Picking your way round the old town gets tricky. The crumbly orange and ochre tiled domes of the church of Santo Domingo crouch beside the town walls at the end of Calle Sa Carrossa. Follow the tarmac road from here past the cool, palm-lined Plaza de España up until it becomes Calle de Juan Ramón. At the end the road swings round to the left into Calle de San Ciriaco, a steep, slippery cobbled lane that eventually climbs to the cathedral square.

Visible from all around, the cathedral is a building of engaging simplicity, with a low, square tower, tall, unadorned buttresses and a plain Renaissance doorway. It stands in a quiet cobbled square.

Sa Peña

Shoved up between the waterfront and the massive walls of Dalt Vila, Sa Peña was the traditional fishing quarter. It is now the scene of the most outrageous and theatrical of Ibiza's nightlife. A honeycomb of crumbling, narrow, whitewashed streets, it is full of the most outlandish bars, restaurants and shops, all seething with people until late into the night. As darkness falls, the whole area takes on the character of an eastern souk or bazaar peopled by mythological creatures, a fantasy world full of possibilities.

People come here to people-watch, to shock and be shocked,

but it is oddly harmless and not at all as intimidating as the dress codes might suggest. After all, Ibiza is a small, friendly island and the town is first and foremost a holiday resort; people are here to enjoy themselves as well as to live out a fantasy image of who they would like to be.

Beaches

Playa d'en Bossa, Salinas and **Talamana** are Ibiza town's local beaches, all very popular and crowded, with fine sand and clear water. Buses run to these beaches roughly every 30 minutes from Avenida Isidoro Macábich, just by Plaza Enrique Fajamés y Tur. To get to the island's idyllic, empty, sandy coves you really need to hire a moped or a car and head away from the crowds.

ALSO WORTH SEEING . . .

Museo de Art Contemporáneo: Museum of Contemporary Art

(Open Monday–Friday 10.00–13.30 and 18.00–21.00, Saturday 10.00–13.30.) Entrance free.

This large exhibition space is housed in a finely renovated old building with steep, timbered ceilings and whitewashed walls. Exhibitions change regularly; while the art is primarily contemporary, paintings from the beginning of the 20th century are shown here, too.

Museo Dalt Vila: Archaeological Museum

(Plaça Catedral, 3. A 100-peseta ticket also buys access to the necropolis. Open Monday–Saturday 10.00–13.00.)

A large collection of Punic finds, including figures of goddesses, clay vessels and coins found in the necropolis nearby. Most of the exhibits date from 7 BC–AD 3.

Museu Puig des Molins: Necropolis of Puig des Molins

(Via Romana, 31. Tel: 30 17 71. Open Monday–Saturday 16.00–19.00.)

Phoenician necropolis, partially carved out of the rocky hillside, containing over 2,000 tombs.

IBIZA FACTFILE

Tourist Office, Calle Vara de Rey, 13. Tel: 30 19 00.
Airport Tel: 30 22 00.
Bus Station Avenida Isidoro Macábich, 42. Tel: 31 20 75.
Car Hire Avis Tel: 31 31 63.
Moped Hire Motos Valentin, Avenida Bartolomé Vicente Ramón, 19.
Speed-Boat Hire Tel: (908) 14 63 91 and 31 01 17.
Taxi Calle Vara de Rey, Tel: 30 17 94.
Ferries Trasmediteránea, Bartolomé Vicente Ramón. Tel: 30 16 50.
Services include ferries to Palma, Valencia, Barcelona, Menorca.
Transmapi ferries to Formentera. Tel: 30 01 00.
Maritima de Formentera ferries to Formentera. Tel: 32 22 10.
Hydrofoil to Palma and Denia Tel: 72 67 40.
Flebasa, Calle de Bartolomé Vicente Ramón. Tel: 34 28 71. Services
from Puerto San Antonio (on Ibiza's west coast) to Denia (connections
with Alicante).
Telephone code: 971.

WHERE TO STAY
Cheap to Moderate

Sol y Brisa HsR*, Avenida Bartolomé Vicente Ramón, 15. Tel:
31 08 18.
Ripoll HsR*, Vicente Cuervo, 14. Tel: 31 42 75.
Las Nieves HsR*, Juan de Austria, 18. Tel: 31 58 22.
Juanito HsR, Juan de Austria, 17. Tel: 31 58 22.
España Hs*, Avenida Bartolomé Vicente Ramón, 1. Tel: 31 13
17.
Corsario HsR**, Poniente, 5, Dalt Vila. Tel: 30 12 48.

Smarter Options

All Ibiza's smarter hotels are away from the town centre.
Argos H***, Playa de Talamanca. Tel: 31 21 62.
Algarb-Fiesta H***, Playa D'en Bossa. Tel: 30 17 16.
Los Molinos H****, Ramón Muntaner, 60. Tel: 30 22 50.

WHERE TO EAT

There are plenty of places to eat in Ibiza, and you will have no trouble
finding somewhere to suit your tastes and your pocket. The areas of La
Marina and Sa Peña are hectic from early evening till around midnight,
while in the Dalt Vila Calle Sa Carrossa and Plaça de Vila are similarly
thick with restaurants and cafés.

Cheap to Moderate

Several cheap, basic café-restaurants in the low town offer a range of simple meals in plain surroundings: grilled fish, chops, salads, soups and omelettes are typical fare. They are excellent value, particularly around midday when most have a *menú del día* available.

C'an Costa, Calle Cruz, 19. Tel: 31 08 65. Very popular cheap restaurant serving typical Ibiçian menu.

Victoria, Calle Riambau, 1.
This traditional *comidas* has just one whitewashed room with bright, checked tablecloths; it is clean, spruce and simple. The typical Spanish menu is homely and welcoming: try their *flaó*, an Ibiçian cheesecake with a mild, creamy flavour, slighly crumbly and concealing fragrant explosions of caraway seeds.

San Juan, Calle de Guillem de Montgrf, 8. A pleasant haven of old-style simplicity in a town of wild exhibitionists. It has a quaint little bar, marble-topped tables and a friendly atmosphere. A cheap menu offers typical Spanish fare: pork, chicken, hake, chips, omelettes many styles, and excellent local soups. It is very popular so go early if you want to get a seat around midday.

Fonda Sport, Avenida Bartolomé Ramón y Tur (opposite the marina). You can eat well at this cheap, down-to-earth café. Extremely popular with locals, it serves a good standard menu including omelettes, chops and salads – all very tasty.

Pizzeria de Franco er Romano, Avenida Bartolomé Vicente Ramón. Good pizzas, pastas and meat dishes in family-style Italian restaurant.

Café Cantina, Teatro Pereira, Calle Conde Rosellon. This stylish bar serves delicious, filling Mexican snacks: *tostado, burritos, natches*: their Texas tacos are particularly tasty. Excellent food and atmosphere.

Sagova, Calle de Santa Llucia, 5. Tricky to find – follow the steep narrow lane off Calle Alfonso XII, beside El Brasserie. This place looks like a rough-and-ready hole-in-the-wall café, but the food is exquisite. The French cook serves just a handful of dishes a day – ask to have a look at what's on the stove before you order. Try the *ninos revueltos* if it's on the menu – parcels of beef filled with minced pork and plums. Sensational.

Formentera, Calle Eugenio Molina, 4. Tel: 31 10 24. Sit out and look across to the marina or take a seat under the awning in the bustling heart of town to enjoy typical Ibiçian food. The menu includes prawns in garlic, skate with almond sauce, *greixonera* – an Ibiçian pudding. Moderately priced, good food.

Formentera

The island of Formentera has no ancient monuments, no great sights, just plenty of mopeds to hire and mile upon mile of white, sandy beaches. It is *the* place to head for if you fancy a bit of naked sun-worship, with plenty of nudist beaches. The water is clear, the sun guaranteed and among the dunes lie occasional beach bars where you can get a bite to eat.

If you come on a day trip — about an hour by boat from Ibiza — it makes sense to decide how you want to spend your day before you arrive. A bus to the main "town" of San Francisco meets the ferry, but once there you have no easy way of getting to the beaches. If you want to spend your day exploring the beautiful sand-fringed coast, it is best to hire a moped or a bicycle as soon as you get off the ferry. The tourist information booth on the quays has details of accommodation, windsurf-hire and horse-riding. San Francisco itself is really just a little inland village with a cluster of fairly new, low-rise holiday apartments, a light sprinkling of café-bars and restaurants, a post office, supermarket and a bank.

Do check the return times of the ferries before you buy your ticket in Ibiza — two different companies ply this route and you can't switch company for the return journey.

Smarter Options

In the seamy depths of **Sa Peña** are many weird and wonderful places to eat. The more expensive of these are exotic rather than "smart", and the atmosphere is unmistakably Ibiçian. Plaça de sa Riba, at the end of the marina, is one of the prettiest places to eat in Sa Peña; a square filled with green palms, huge blood-orange Mediterranean flowers and frangipani blossom.

El Rubio, Plaça de sa Riba, 7 and 8. Sit out on the terrace overlooking the harbour, magically lit at night. The restaurant serves good seafood dishes: you pay as much for the setting as for the food, but it is worth it.

Sausalito, Plaça de sa Riba, 6. This pricey restaurant is good for people-watching, and also has a view of the harbour. The walls are covered in prints of 1940s film stars; fans whir slowly overhead and the atmosphere is both relaxed and suave. A popular choice for excellent seafood.

El Brasserie, Calle Alfonso XII. French restaurant for hip, image-conscious nihilists: black-and-white tables, walls, clothes and chairs, along with deathly white lilies, all reflected in fabulous mirror collages. You pay for style.

Chez Françoise, Calle de Abel Matutes. Bijou restaurant offering superior French cuisine in chic atmosphere. Inexpensive considering the excellent quality.

Sa Caldera, Calle Obispo Padre Huix, 19. Tel: 30 64 16. A little more expensive than average, but good-quality traditional restaurant in Sa Peña.

If you fancy a break from the theatrical exoticism of Sa Peña, several good-quality restaurants in the **Dalt Vila** are worth trying. The less smart places up here, ranged along Plaça Mercat and Plaça De Vila, tend not to be particularly good value. The prettiest places to sit out and eat are along Calle Sa Carrossa beneath the palms, looking over to ancient walls hung with vivid purple tapestries of flowering bougainvillea.

C'an De'n Parra, Calle San Rafael, 3. Tucked away up a cobbled lane off Plaça de Vila, this French restaurant has a charming little terrace hung with lights and vines. Somewhat expensive, the menu offers delights such as salmon marinated in lemon and mint, and *conflit* of duck with garlic potatoes; desserts include profiteroles dripping with delicious runny chocolate, and refreshing sorbets.

El Olivo, Plaça de Vila. Moderately expensive, the menu is rather more adventurous than in typical Spanish resort restaurants: try the chicken breasts in honey and thyme – sweet and succulent.

El Jardin, Calle Mayor

This is a beautiful whitewashed balcony bar tucked away in the heart of the old city, a magical place to sit in the evening. El Jardin only serves very basic meals, but it is worth eking one out to sit beneath the vines and clambering bougainvillea.

NIGHTLIFE
La Marina

Bars and cafés stretch from Avenida Ramón y Tur right along the harbourfront and you can sit out on wicker chairs beneath the palms and look out across the port – an extremely pleasant way to spend your evening from 20.00 till around 2.00. Of the bars here, **Mariana's** serves good early-evening cocktails, **Mar y Sol** offers delicious ice creams, while **Zurito** has tasty *tapas* throughout the day till late.

Head a little way from the crowds down Avenida Ramón y Tur and **La Cantina** at Teatro Pereyra is a great bar for live music (jazz, blues, soul, funk) from 23.00 to 3.00. They also serve Mexican snacks.

Calle Barcelona and Plaça Marino Riquer

Parallel with the waterfront, these streets forge their way through a seething mass of people drinking, eating and perusing the souvenir and jewellery stalls. Be wary of bars and restaurants that appear to offer tourist "bargains" here – some of the drinks can be extremely expensive, and the hectic atmosphere makes it only too easy to be duped.

Sa Peña

Sa Penya is the nerve centre of Ibiza's lively, offbeat scene, full of wacky, antwacky, hippy and gay bars and restaurants, and yet more late-night boutiques. These streets are busy till around 2.00.

Dalt Vila

The oldest part of Ibiza town, this is a good option if you want to soak in the balmy Mediterranean air, smell the scent of bougainvillea, pines and honeysuckle in the evening breeze, and altogether take things easy. With the views of the sea and the surrounding mountains, and with twisting vines tumbling over whitewashed walls and cobbled lanes, it offers great spots to sit with a beer and reflect on the magical qualities of the island. Wander away from the crowds and admire the views from the ramparts, or find the secluded bar **El Jardin** in Calle Mayor.

Discos

Discos are hugely important here. Performance artists at the evening *paseo* draw the crowds, and it is worth picking up any leaflets they throw around in their mad street acts because there are sometimes discounts on entrance charges. **Pacha** and **Amnesia** are both notorious for attracting outlandish crowds, but neither is exclusive; there is a good mix of people and age groups. **Pacha,** found behind the casino on the other side of the port, open from midnight to around 3.00 or 4.00, costs around 3,000 pesetas. **Amnesia,** about 3 km out of Ibiza on the San Antonio road, keeps going till morning; costs around 2,500 pesetas.

Two more really popular discos are at Playa d'en Bossa. Each attracts a younger crowd (from teenagers to mid-twenties). **Space** costs around 2,000 pesetas and winds down at 3.00 or 4.00. **Kiss** costs around 1,500 pesetas, though it is often free for women, and keeps going till around 2.00.

Finally, check at the tourist office to see if **Ku** has reopened; it was the ultimate in Ibiçian nightlife for years and may reopen soon.

MAHÓN, MENORCA

Menorca's capital Mahón – popularly known as Maó – has something of an old colonial flavour. Confident, up-market and conservative, it sits around a perfect harbour scene: across the bay lies a marine station of low, white walls and red roofs, all spic and span like model-railway accessories.

Tucked beneath the old town is the marina, busy with yachts and lined with bars and restaurants; stout palm trees are dotted along the shore. The town centre lies some way above all this, a collection of small plazas linked by quiet roads. None of them is particularly special, but they are worth wandering through even so to get a measure of the place and absorb its character. The tastes of the colonial British are evident throughout the town in a restrained domestic architecture of sash windows and clean masonry, tasteful and understated.

Unless you have booked into a resort hotel, Maó makes a good base from which to explore the island's fabulous beaches. These range from tiny coves of white sand and crystal-clear water to busy resorts with bars, cafés and plenty of opportunities for water sports. To get to the really exquisite, secret beaches on the island you need a car (or, better still, a boat) – and even then access can be down very difficult, bumpy roads. Persevere; it is well worth it.

DON'T MISS . . .

The Harbour
The harbour is undoubtedly the prettiest part of Maó. Descend to it from the high town via the curving road from Plaça d'España; once at the quays, follow them round to the right. The scene becomes almost too perfect. The bay has the character of a wooded inlet: low hills amble tree-covered to the water's edge sprinkled with little pink and white villas, while yachts drift silently across the placid water. It is all very choice, very select; activity centres on the bustling marina, which has some good restaurants and bars, largely catering for the cruising crowd. For a view from the water, take one of the harbour boat trips that leave from beside the gin factory.

ALSO WORTH SEEING . . .

The High Town
The most interesting area of the town is that immediately above the port, around the Plaça de la Constitució. The

plaza is more of a road than a square, pleasantly sheltered by the 18th-century Iglesia Santa María, a restrained building of clean stonework with an octagonal tower visible from the port below. From here lanes lead up to Plaça Bastió and Plaza Reiál, both of which have quiet terrace cafés. Calle Isabelle II cuts between narrow whitewashed walls past an old military headquarters, which looks more like an iced cake than an army base, to the church of San Francisco and the museum. The church is beautiful in its simplicity and dates from 1717; the museum may be closed for renovation – ask at the tourist office for details. Further inland, the Plaça de S'Esplanada has less character, though it serves as Maó's central square. It is a wide open space with a handful of terrace cafés and is used for the local market.

The Gin Factory
(Anden de Poniente, 91 – on the quays.)
Gin is one of Menorca's major exports: they have been making it here in one form or another since the Middle Ages. The arrival of the Brits in 1708 greatly increased demand – one needs refreshment while watching the sun go down. *Xoriguer* is the gin made here and you can visit the factory any time during the working week. Rather more absorbing is the shop alongside it where you can sample different varieties of mother's ruin.

OUT OF TOWN . . .

Cuitadella
Narrow, arcaded streets form the centre of this town, a throw-back to the days when Menorca was a Moorish island and Cuitadella was the capital. A fortified cathedral and massive town walls remain from the days of the Christian Reconquest; both are best viewed from the harbour. Cuitadella is far less English in feel than Maó, a popular alternative base for exploring the island.

Archaeology: Talayots, Navetas, Taulas and Caves

Menorca has an outstanding number of archaeological sites: over 1,000 have been identified so far. They are very easy to spot and you are bound to see them as you travel about the island. The most impressive types of structure are *talayots, navetas* and *taulas,* dating from around 1400–300 BC.

Talayots are large, circular towers – often 10 metres high – that may have been used as look-out posts. **Navetas** are stone buildings that look like upturned boats (which is how they got their name). It is thought that they were originally dwellings, but came to be used as communal burial chambers. Most enigmatic of all are **taulas**, formed by two rectangular stone slabs, one wedged vertically deep into the ground, the other placed on top forming a gigantic T-shape. Whether they were temples, sacrificial tables, or just part of workaday buildings is not known. Whatever their function, they are certainly impressive: twice the height of a man and perfectly balanced. Look out for them.

Aside from these signs of prehistoric humans, there are underground dwellings and burial caves carved into the faces of the rocky cliffs along the island's coast.

Around Maó

Trepucó This remarkable village has a *taula* enclosure, a *talayot* and other ancient buildings. Find it 2 km out of Maó off the San Luis road.

Torelló The *talayot* here is one of the best examples on the island and has an entrance door to its upper section. Some 300 m north of here is part of the floor of a Palaeochristian basilica. To find the site, take the San Clement road from Maó, pass the turning for the airport and then take a road to the right.

Talatí de Dalt There are remains of various dwellings here, along with a *talayot* and a *taula*. Find it 4 km from Maó along the Cuitadella road signposted after the turning for the airport.

Cales Coves Over 40 caves are carved from the rocks in this Iron Age necropolis. This delightful cove is one of the prettiest spots on the island. Find it by taking the road from Maó to Cala'n Porter.

Torralba d'en Salord A very fine *taula*, a *talayot*, a prehistoric well and various other remains can be found here, off to the left on the main road from Alayor to Cala'n Porter.

Rafal Rubi Two excellent *navetes*. Find them 7 km from Maó along the main Maó–Cuitadella road.

Torre d'en Gaumes An extensive site with three *talayots*, a *taula*, an antechamber, caves and remains of dwellings. There is also a reservoir and tank system with wells. Find it clearly signposted to the left off the road to Son Bou beach.

Son Bou The precinct of a Palaeochristian basilica from the 5th century AD, with a monolithic baptismal font from 6 AD. Burial caves are visible in the cliff face nearby. Find it on the eastern side of Son Bou beach.

Around Ferreries

Son Mercer de Baix An interesting settlement of *navetas*. Tricky to find; take the first right turning off the Ferreries to Migjorn road.

Around Cuitadella

El Tudons Very impressive *naveta* with an unusual two-storey interior. Find it 4 km from Cuitadella off the main road to Maó.

Cala Morell An Iron Age necropolis carved out of the rocks at Cala Morell beach.

Mount Toro

Church-capped Mount Toro is the highest point on the island, rising to 358 m. The walk affords excellent views.

Beaches

All beaches are easily accessible by bus from Maó.

Es Grau is a very popular beach, particularly good for windsurfing. Headland walks from here lead to quieter coves, or you can take a boat to the Illa de Colón. The island has two big beaches but no facilities, so take a picnic; arrange with the boatman when you want to return.

S'Alga has no sand; you swim straight off the rocks or in the pool right out by the waterfront. There is a diving school here or you can ride the "sausage" – the latest water-sport craze. This involves being strapped to a giant sausage and pulled through the waves by a speedboat.

Fiestas

Fiestas of San Juan, Cuitadella, 23 and 24 June. St John's or Midsummer Eve is celebrated in towns throughout Spain with huge bonfires symbolizing the triumph of light over darkness. It falls on the shortest night of the year, the start of the summer solstice, a festival of pagan origins. The Cuitadella festival is perhaps the most important in Spain and certainly among the most spectacular, with flamboyant *caixers* riding through the streets on galloping horses. It is a great festival to catch if you can, packed with music, colour and riotous celebration.

The **Fiestas de Gracia** in Maó on 7 and 8 September is a festival of puppet giants and dwarfs parading through the streets.

Punta Prima Shallow water here makes this an excellent beach for windsurfing.

Binibeca The pleasant little sandy cove with sheltered, clear water can get crowded in high season, largely because the modern harbour village is so pretty: a jumble of whitewashed houses climb the slopes like clusters of sugarcubes just tossed there. Binibeca is also popular for excellent (and expensive) seafood restaurants.

Cala en Porter is something of a mini-Benidorm, with bars, discos and lots of people.

Son Bou is a 1.5-km-long beach that easily absorbs even the busiest of crowds; the far end is popular for nude bathing. This beach also offers rides on the "sausage".

Between here and Es Canutells to the east is a series of secluded, sandy coves, many difficult to get to.

Cala Galdana, a long, gently curved, sandy beach, is very popular with crowds from the nearby hotels and apartments.

Arenal d'en Castell is a beautiful beach, though very crowded because of the hotels and apartments here.

Fornells Low, whitewashed buildings line this old fishing harbour set in gently hilly countryside. Fornells is extremely popular for day trips; it is also *the* place to eat the island's speciality, *caldereta de langoste* – if you can afford it. If you can't there is still a lovely beach to enjoy.

MAHÓN FACTFILE

Tourist Office, Plaça Esplanada, 40. Tel: 36 37 90.
Open Monday – Friday 9.00–14.00 and 17.00–19.00, Saturday 9.30–13.00.
Airport Tel: 36 01 50.
Bus Station TMSA, Avenida J. M. Quardrado, 7. Tel: 36 03 61.
Ferry Trasmediterránea, Nuevo Muelle Commercial. Tel: 36 29 50.
Car Hire Town and Country Car Hire, Tel: 35 11 93 and 35 12 99.
Ibercars, Tel: 36 42 08.
Taxi Tel: 36 71 11.
Telephone Code: 971

WHERE TO STAY
Cheap to Moderate

Sheila HS*, Santa Cecilia, 41. Tel: 36 48 55.
SA Roqueta HsR*, Calle Carmen, 122. Tel: 36 43 35.
Roca HsR*, Calle Carmen, 37. Tel: 35 08 39.
Orsi HsR*, Calle Infanta, 19. Tel: 36 47 51.
Noa HsR**, Cos de Gracia, 157. Tel: 36 12 00.

Smarter Options

Capri HR***, San Esteban, 8. Tel: 36 14 00.
Port Mahón H****, Avenida Fort de L'Eau. Tel: 36 26 00.

WHERE TO EAT
Around Town

CHEAP TO MODERATE
Sa Placeta, Plaça Bastió. A pleasant spot to sit out on the square and eat paella. Around midday the *menú del día* is very good value.
La Bombilla, Plaça Bastió. Good for plain Spanish food, kebabs and fish; this restaurant and café also has a terrace.
La Dolce Vita, San Roque, 25. Tel: 36 48 24. Good pizzeria in the upper part of town.
Buscas, Canil d'es Castell, 203. English-run restaurant serving a variety of styles – curries, Chinese – and definitely the place to head for if you long for a Sunday roast. Wednesdays and Fridays live music accompanies your meal.
La Tropical, Calle La Luna, 36. Tel: 36 05 56. Reasonably priced, good Spanish food; they offer a cheap *menú del día* around lunchtime.

SMARTER OPTIONS
Pilar, Calle des Forn Cardona Orfila. Typical Menorcan cuisine.

Around The Harbour

CHEAP TO MODERATE
Roma, Moll de Llevant, 295. Tel: 35 37 77. Extremely popular Italian restaurant serving excellent pizzas and pasta. Sit out on the terrace and admire the clutter of yachts alongside.
Alba, Moll de Llevant, 302. Tel: 35 06 06. Lots of seafood and good *tapas*; a good option for a light meal.

SMARTER OPTIONS
Gregal, Moll de Llevant, 306. Tel: 36 66 06. Menorcan and Greek cuisine. This is a very popular up-market restaurant. The menu includes traditional Greek dishes along with excellent salads, steaks, rabbit, duck, and *caldereta de langoste* – very expensive and needs to be ordered in advance.
C'an Pau, Anden de Levante, 200. Tel: 35 07 40. French-owned restaurant serving French and Spanish cuisine. Plenty of couscous and paella served in a convivial atmosphere.

BARS AND NIGHTLIFE
The Harbour

Small though it may be, Mahón has a thriving, trendy night scene down by the waterfront. Bars squeezed between the restaurants around the curve of Moll de Llevant offer picturesque early-evening drinking, but the best of the young bars are along Moll de Ponent, busy till around midnight during the week and 3.30 at weekends.
Icaro and **Akelarre**, Moll de Ponent. Found down towards the gin factory, these are two of the liveliest bars in town; they are not discos, but don't be surprised to find them packed with people dancing.
Café Baixamar, Anden de Pontiente, 17. Marble-topped tables, elegant mirrors and Art Nouveau bar stools set the tone for far less boisterous goings-on. It is popular, trendy and, beer aside, serves what are probably the best French-omelette sandwiches in Spain.
Acuarium Menorca, Moll de Poniente, 73. Play a game of pool or drink like a fish in this cavernous converted aquarium.

High Town

The upper part of town has lost most of what nightlife it once had to the newly developed harbourside. Few café-bars remain and these are only (mildly) busy till about 22.30.
El Café Charcutería, corner of Calle Rosario and Calle Isabel II. Extremely elegant old-world café with Edwardian lamps and fine polished bar.
Nou, Plaça de la Constitució. Pleasantly worn old-style café-bar.
Café Mirador, off Plaza España, just behind the market. A good place to sit with a beer and watch the white villas across the bay turn pink in the fading sunlight.

Food Specialities

Caldereta de langoste is Menorca's greatest speciality: a delicious lobster stew. It is expensive, so try it at one of the smarter restaurants by the marina in Maó, or make a trip out to a little fishing village like Binibeca or Fornells. It is usually a good idea to order your *caldereta* a day ahead.

Menorcan **gin** is a very clean spirit with a smooth juniper-berry scent. It is quite distinct from other gins because the alcohol is produced from wine and not the more usual cereals. It has been popular with the colonial British since they first arrived here in the early 18th century, and with the local Menorcans for far longer. Diluted with soda and given a slice of lemon, it is known as *pellofa*, and is highly refreshing. Buy it to take home from the Xoriguer distillery at Anden de Poniente, 91, Maó.

Coinga is the most popular of Menorcan **cheeses**. It is made from cow's milk, with a touch of sheep's milk added, and is a sharp, highly palatable, smooth-textured cheese. The cheapest place to buy it is in Alayor, where it is made, but it is also readily available around the island. Look out too for *caserio*, a soft cheese flavoured with pieces of salmon, ham or peppers.

Discos

Si, Calle de Gracia. Around 800–1,000 pesetas cover, including a drink. Open from midnight. At weekends things get going at 2.00 and keep going until everybody drops or leaves at 6.30–7.00.

Factory, on the road out to Es Castell, open till 6.00 or 7.00 weekends.

Cova d'en Xoroi, out of town ner Cala'n Porter. These fabulous cliffside caves conceal a bar which becomes a disco from midnight until 7.00 at weekends, till around 1.00 during the week. Part of the club is in the open air and this can prove a very romantic place to spend an evening. Cover charge.

GLOSSARY

Alcazabar Fortified area within a walled town.

Alcázar Moorish fortress or fortified palace.

Art Nouveau Artistic and architectural style of the late 19th and early 20th centuries.

Ayuntamiento Town Hall.

Baroque Bold, ornamental style of architecture of the 17th and 18th centuries.

Bodega Wine cellar or warehouse.

Catholic Kings, Catholic Monarchs, *Los Reyes Católicos* – all of these names refer to Ferdinand of Aragon and Isabella of Castile.

Churrisgueresque Form of Baroque architecture.

Coro Part of church for the choir.

Crossing The part of a church or cathedral where the nave, transepts and chancel meet.

Lonja A financial exchange building.

Iglesia Church.

Meseta Plateau.

Morisco Moor living as a Christian after the Reconquest.

Mozarabe Christian living in Spain under Muslim rule; Mozarabic – Mozarabe style of art and architecture.

Mudéjar Term used to describe a style of architecture produced by Muslims working under Christian rule.

Parador State-run luxury hotel, often housed in impressive historic buildings.

Paseo Evening stroll or promenade, an important part of Spanish social life enjoyed by all ages; also the name of the place where this happens.

Plateresque Spanish architectural style of the late 15th and 16th centuries.

Plaza Square.

Reredos Altarpiece.

Retablo Altarpiece.

Reconquest The name given to the gradual Christian takeover of the Iberian Peninsula from Muslim control. The Reconquest began in 727 AD and was only finally completed in 1492, the 11th and 13th centuries being particularly important periods.

Romanesque Architectural style of the 9th-12th centuries characterised by bold, simple arches and heavily cut decoration.

Sierra Range of Mountains.

Telefónica Company operating phone booths with a facility to pay after your call using cash or credit cards.

Turismo Tourist office.

INDEX